VOICES ON WAR AND GENOCIDE

War and Genocide

General Editors: Omer Bartov, Brown University; A. Dirk Moses, University of Sydney

In recent years there has been a growing interest in the study of war and genocide, not from a traditional military history perspective, but within the framework of social and cultural history. This series offers a forum for scholarly works that reflect these new approaches.

The Berghahn series Studies on War and Genocide has immeasurably enriched the English-language scholarship available to scholars and students of genocide and, in particular, the Holocaust. —**Totalitarian Movements and Political Religions**

Recent volumes:

For a full volume listing, please see the series page on our website:
http://berghahnbooks.com/series/war-and-genocide

VOICES ON WAR AND GENOCIDE

Three Accounts of the World Wars in a Galician Town

Edited and with an Introduction by Omer Bartov

berghahn
NEW YORK · OXFORD
www.berghahnbooks.com

First published in 2020 by
Berghahn Books
www.berghahnbooks.com

© 2020, 2023 Omer Bartov
First paperback edition published in 2023

Library of Congress Cataloging-in-Publication Data
Names: Bartov, Omer, editor, writer of introduction.
Title: Voices on war and genocide : three accounts of the World Wars in a
  Galician town / edited and with an introduction by Omer Bartov.
Other titles: Three accounts of the World Wars in a Galician town
Description: New York : Berghahn, 2020. | Series: War and genocide ; volume
  30 | Includes bibliographical references and index.
Identifiers: LCCN 2020009352 (print) | LCCN 2020009353 (ebook) | ISBN
  9781789207187 (hardback) | ISBN 9781789207194 (ebook)
Subjects: LCSH: World War, 1914-1918--Ukraine--Buchach. | World War,
  1914-1918--Personal narratives. | Siewiński, Antoni, 1858-1939? |
  Petrykevych, Viktor, 1883-1956. | Wizinger, Moshe, 1920- | World War,
  1939-1945--Ukraine--Buchach. | World War, 1939-1945--Personal
  narratives. | Polish people--Ukraine--Buchach--Biography. |
  Jews--Ukraine--Buchach--Biography.
Classification: LCC D557.B88 V63 2020 (print) | LCC D557.B88 (ebook) |
  DDC 940.53/4779--dc23
LC record available at https://lccn.loc.gov/2020009352
LC ebook record available at https://lccn.loc.gov/2020009353

British Library Cataloguing in Publication Data
A catalog record for this book is available from the British Library.

ISBN 978-1-78920-718-7 hardback
ISBN 978-1-80073-639-9 paperback
ISBN 978-1-78920-719-4 ebook

https://doi.org/10.3167/9781789207187

CONTENTS

ILLUSTRATIONS

⁓

Figures

Maps

ABBREVIATIONS

⚬§§⚬

BDO	League of German Officers (*Bund Deutscher Offiziere*)
CPSU	Communist Party of the Soviet Union
Gestapo	Secret State Police (*Geheime Staatspolizei*)
GPU	State Political Directorate (*Gosudarstvennoe Politicheskoe Upravlenie*), renamed in 1923 OGPU, Joint State Political Directorate (*Obedinyonnoe Gosudarstvennoe Politicheskoe Upravlenie*), 1922–34.
KGB	Committee for State Security (*Komitet Gosudarstvennoy Bezopasnosti*), 1954-1991
Komsomol	Communist Youth Union (*Kommunisticheskiy Soyuz Molodyozhi*)
Kripo	Criminal Police (*Kriminalpolizei*)
OD	Jewish police (*Ordnungsdienst*)
OUN	Organization of Ukrainian Nationalists (*Orhanizatsiya Ukrayinskykh Natsionalistiv*)
OZN	Camp of National Unity (*Obóz Zjednoczenia Narodowego*, aka Ozon)
Sipo	Security Police (*Sicherheitzpolizei*)
SS	Protection Squadron (*Schutzstaffel*)
SSR	Soviet Socialist Republic
NKFD	National Committee for a Free Germany (*Nationalkomitee Freies Deutschland*)
NKGB	People's Commissariat for State Security (*Narodny Komissariat Gosudarstvennoi Bezopasnosti*), 1941–46
NKVD	People's Commissariat for Internal Affairs (*Narodny Komissariat Vnutrennikh Del*), 1922–46

UCC	Ukrainian Central Committee
UNDO	Ukrainian National Democratic Alliance (*Ukrayinske Natsionalno-Demokratichne Obyednannia*)
UPA	Ukrainian Insurgent Army (*Ukrainska Povstanska Armiya*)
UPRA	Ukrainian Insurgent Revolutionary Army (*Ukrainska Povstanska Narodno-Revolutsiyna Armiya*)
USSR	Union of Soviet Socialist Republics
ZUNR	West Ukrainian People's Republic (*Zakhidnoukrayinska Narodna Respublika*)

NOTES ON LANGUAGE, PLACE, AND PERSONAL NAMES

⊶§§⊷

Because the accounts by Antoni Siewiński and Moshe Wizinger were originally written in Polish, I have retained the Polish spelling of most place names, except those for which there is a conventional English spelling. Thus, I have used the Polish spelling of Buczacz, but have preferred Warsaw to the Polish Warszawa. All personal names appear in their Polish spelling, except Moshe Wizinger, whose name would have been spelled Mosze at the time but who subsequently used the more common English version. In some documents, Wizinger appears in its German version as Weisinger, but I have not adopted this version. Conversely, because Viktor Petrykevych's diary was originally written in Ukrainian, I have transliterated the Ukrainian spelling of most place names, except those for which there is a conventional English spelling. Thus, Buchach rather than Buczacz, and Stanyslaviv rather than Stanisławów. I have also transliterated all Ukrainian personal names as they appear in the diary.

INTRODUCTION

Omer Bartov

The importance of Eastern Europe as the site of genocide in World War II has only come into focus in the last few decades, especially following the collapse of the communist system.[1] In the intervening years many scholarly works have appeared on various aspects of violence in what has been described as "the lands between," "the bloodlands," or the "shatterzone of empires."[2] Some studies took the long view, examining the formation of states, nations, and ideologies in a region that had been ruled for extensive periods by vast, multiethnic and multi-religious empires, which then splintered into often belligerent and unstable nation states with significant ethnic and religious minorities.[3] Other scholars concentrated on national histories, whether of majority or minority nations, and national struggles for self-assertion or survival in a century marked by unprecedented violence.[4] Still other scholars chose to undertake local studies, examining coexistence and violence in specific regions or towns, and highlighting the extraordinary demographic, cultural, social, and political transformations that occurred there, invariably to the detriment of their previous rich diversity.[5] Looking at the more recent past and our own time, a number of studies have examined the politics of memory in a region whose heavy reliance on history as an anchor of identity was matched by a remarkable facility to erase vast chunks of the past from its practices of education, commemoration, and political discourse.[6] Finally, and at times reaching into their own personal recollections and family traumas, some authors have delved into the lost and, at times, regained memories of a vanished world.[7]

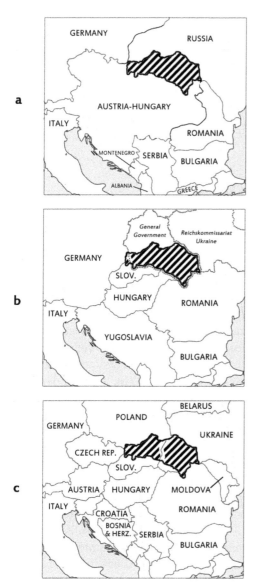

Map 0.1 Galicia in a changing Europe: a. as part of Austria-Hungary, 1914; b. under German occupation, as part of the General Government, 1942; c. divided between Poland and Ukraine, present-day.

My own recent contributions to this rich scholarship have been in two areas. In 2007, while conducting research for a monograph on the town of Buczacz, now located in West Ukraine and previously part of interwar Poland and pre-1914 Austria-Hungary, I published a study on the politics of memory in the region. Surveying the history of several cities and towns in what was known before World War I as Eastern Galicia, I briefly described their thriving, if increasingly fraught, interethnic communities prior to 1939; the violence, both external and internal, that eradicated these towns' Jewish populations and subjected their Polish inhabitants to ethnic cleansing during World War II; the silence over that rich past and its violent termination that descended on the region, whose population had become by then almost exclusively Ukrainian, following its absorption into the Soviet Union; and, finally, the post-Soviet politics of memory in independent Ukraine's western regions, which both glorified the freedom fighters previously vilified by the Soviet authorities, and denied or ignored these same resurrected national heroes' collaboration with the Nazis in the mass murder of the Jews and, following their own agenda, their concerted effort to expel the Polish population from what they hoped to remake into an independent, Jew- and Pole-free Ukraine.[8]

As I traveled in West Ukraine/Eastern Galicia in the 2000s, I was struck by the abandonment and neglect of the remnants of a Jewish civilization that had existed and thrived in the region for four centuries. Ruined synagogues, some of them empty shells in which little forests had grown or local garbage was dumped; Jewish cemeteries, many of whose more useable tombstones had been carted off and where cows and goats led by local children were grazing; unmarked mass graves that surrounded each of these towns, where vast numbers of their previous Jewish inhabitants had been dumped during the German occupation; and an almost total absence of commemoration or any kind of local memory of these communities and their destruction, let alone of their neighbors' participation in the genocide, compounded by newly erected local memorials, at times built directly on or near Jewish cemeteries and sites of mass shootings, to the martyrs of the Ukrainian struggle for liberation.[9]

Erased: Vanishing Traces of Jewish Galicia in Present-Day Ukraine, the book I wrote on the region's politics of memory, was largely about a void: it spoke of emptied spaces, forgetting of the past, and covering up misdeeds; in other words, it was literally about Galicia's depopulation and West Ukraine's amnesia. But as noted above, *Erased* was conceived while I was researching a very different study, whose very goal was in fact to repopulate one Galician site, the town of Buczacz, in order to understand the dynamics of relations in a single interethnic community.[10] The case of Buczacz, I argued, was representative not only of the reality of life in Galicia as a whole, but also in many ways of hundreds of towns throughout the vast swath of Europe's eastern borderlands, stretching from the Baltic to the Balkans. Specifically, the recently published *Anatomy of a Genocide: The Life and Death of a Town Called Buczacz,* was an attempt to reconstruct, on the local level, how a community of Poles, Ukrainians, and Jews, who had lived side-by-side since the 1500s, ended up turning against its own members, whereby neighbors, colleagues, and friends took part in denouncing, rounding up, deporting, and massacring each other, in actions both orchestrated by foreign invaders and locally initiated.

Several insights I gained from researching the monograph on Buczacz are especially pertinent to the present volume. First, it quickly became clear to me that one cannot grasp the dynamic of interethnic relations by beginning at the end, that is, when the killing actually starts. Rather, one has to go back in time in order to find when interethnic relations began to deteriorate and living together, which had been seen for centuries as the only possible way of life, appeared to increasing numbers of people as unbearable and unacceptable, thereby facilitating, first rhetorically and then through violent action, the transformation of a community of coexistence into a community of genocide. As I argue, this process began with the rise of nationalism in Galicia in the latter part of the nineteenth century, whereby Polish nationalists presented themselves as carrying out a civilizing mission geared to transform Ruthenians (as they preferred to call Galician Ukrainians in order to differentiate them from their brethren in Russian-ruled Ukraine) into Poles; Ukrainians presented themselves as the indigenous population colonized, enserfed, exploited, and brutalized by the Poles and their Jewish lackeys, and both groups agreed that in the distinct, future nation states they aspired to create there would be no room for Jews.

This increasingly violent rhetoric did not translate into physical violence until the outbreak of World War I. But as the second relevant insight of *Anatomy of a Genocide* demonstrates, the extraordinary violence of the war, both in terms of remarkably bloody battles between multiethnic armies, and as expressed in widespread brutality against civilian populations, and especially against Jews by the invading Russian armies, transformed people's perceptions of each other and of what they perceived as the boundaries of ethics, morality, and law. Moreover, the Great War in this region did not end in 1918 but transmuted into a brutal civil war between Poles and Ukrainians over control of Eastern Galicia, accompanied by many massacres of local Christian civilians as well as anti-Jewish pogroms by both sides. Hence the central point to be made here is that we cannot comprehend events two decades later under Soviet and German rule without taking into account that the license for internecine bloodshed and brutality had already been given in World War I and its aftermath and that the experience of living through those years of mayhem had a profound impact on the youngsters of the time, those who became the activists of the 1930s and 1940s.

Perhaps the most important and pertinent insight I gained from researching *Anatomy of a Genocide* was that in trying to understand the changing dynamics of an interethnic local community, one must literally listen to voices of its members and strive to see and present reality through their own eyes. What these eyes saw was in large part ethnically determined, in that Galician Poles, Ukrainians, and Jews perceived the same reality very differently (and have continued to do so many decades after the demise of that world); at the same time, each individual also had his and her own unique perception of events and twist on reality. In writing the book, I tried to eschew imposing my understanding of the logic of events and then merely illustrate it through selective citations from personal accounts; instead, I wanted to let those first-person accounts, especially in the latter parts of the period, speak for themselves, even if admittedly I could not avoid ultimately orchestrating them in order to fit this cacophony of voices into the framework of a readable text of reasonable proportions.

To some extent, as I wrote elsewhere,[11] this methodology rejected the convention practiced in particular by many historians of the Holocaust, namely, that eyewitness testimonies and other personal accounts had to be treated with great circumspection because of their alleged "subjective" nature; and that consequently, archival documents, albeit usually produced by the perpetrators, must be preferred thanks to their supposed greater "objectivity" and accuracy, certainly as far as dates and geographical locations were concerned.[12] My own view, which has been further strengthened since writing the book, was that in reconstructing events in a small community or region, especially at times of crisis, it was essential to listen to all protagonists, both because that enables us to gain a richer, three-dimensional picture of events that are seen radically differently by particular groups and individuals, and because so much of what actually occurs, as well as how such occurrences are experienced, was entirely missing from the official documentation favored in conventional historiography.

And yet, as I hinted above, it remained very difficult to give personal accounts their due place in a monograph that encompassed a long historical period and relied on hundreds of first-person accounts, be they letters, diaries, postwar testimonies, courtroom depositions, interviews, or memoirs. Indeed, I was torn between wanting to let these witnesses tell the reader more about their experience as a whole, thereby making them into complete individuals rather that illustrative and often disembodied voices, on the one hand; and, on the other hand, the need to produce an accessible text that would respond especially to the Jewish witnesses' demand that we historians tell their often chaotic

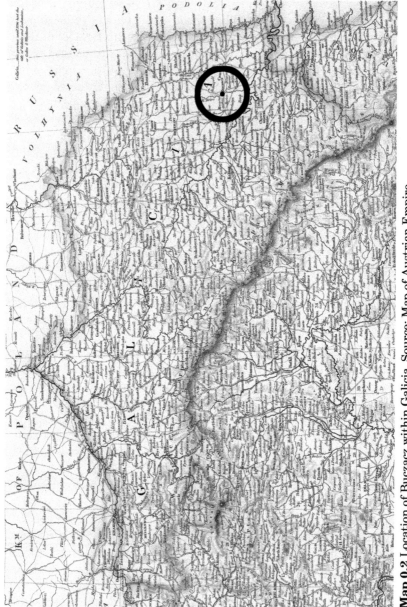

Map 0.2 Location of Buczacz within Galicia. Source: Map of Austrian Empire by J. Arrowsmith, 1842, via Wikimedia Commons.

and seemingly unbelievable stories, juxtaposed with their neighbors' no less traumatized and at times contradictory accounts, rather than choose the orderly, bureaucratic, and essentially deceptive accounts of the organizers of genocide.

It is for this reason that I was glad to have the opportunity to publish three extensive and previously unknown accounts from Buczacz covering events there in both world wars. It should be emphasized that these are particularly rare and therefore highly valuable accounts that give us a personal glimpse into the daily life of a Galician town at times of crisis from three very distinct perspectives. While I have somewhat abridged them, mostly taking out sections that would be of lesser interest to the reader, they remain substantial, detailed, and insightful accounts. Each account provides us with a very personal narrative of the events experienced, including sufficient information for us to familiarize ourselves with the writer's character and personal circumstances. As we get to know these writers, we therefore not only follow the events they describe but also empathize with their fate and acquire an intimate knowledge of their opinions, prejudices, hopes, and disillusionments. In other words, the three authors allow us to observe a world far removed and very different from our own through a unique personal prism, thereby enabling us to understand how people not much unlike ourselves responded to mass violence and destruction.

A few lines from these accounts are cited in *Anatomy of a Genocide*; but as will become clear from reading this volume, there is a vast difference between limited selections from such narratives and reading them in full. All three writers intended their accounts to be read by others, and took care to compose them as records of what they had seen, as articulate ruminations on their personal experiences, emotions, and views, and as accusations of those they perceived as the makers, facilitators, and beneficiaries of the catastrophes that befell their town. These three voices, therefore, are both manifestly personal and representative of larger communities of fate and experience; they tell us much that we would otherwise not know and provide us with very different views and perspectives of those events we thought we knew. The authors wanted us to read their accounts, yet for many decades their meticulously written narratives remained unknown and unread. To my mind they remain valuable today not only because they shed light on a murky past but also because they highlight the importance of first-person history and enlighten us as to the experience of individual human beings in times of crisis.

The first account is by the teacher and school principal Antoni Siewiński. Born in 1858, Siewiński was a Polish patriot and nationalist, a dedicated teacher, a keen observer, proud and loving father to his four sons, a faithful Roman Catholic, and an antisemite. As he explains in the opening of his diary, he began writing it when World War I broke out, by which time he was fifty-six years old. Both the original manuscript and the one that followed it were lost or destroyed, but Siewiński did not give up, and the final manuscript, parts of which were reconstructions of the original and other parts written in real time, provides an unparalleled picture of a Galician town under the Russian occupation of 1914–15 and under Ukrainian rule in 1918–19. Deposited in a Polish manuscript collection, presumably by Siewiński's sons following his death on the eve of World War II, the account remained unread, collecting dust for many decades. If we know far less about events on the eastern front than on the western front of the Great War, we similarly know much less about what happened in these parts of Eastern Europe in World War I than during World War II. Most especially, what we lack are detailed accounts of how things transpired on the local level, of the kind offered by Siewiński.

Possibly the only competitor, which has only recently been translated into English, albeit in a much-abridged version, is the extensive account of the fate of the Jews in Poland, Galicia, and Bukovina (a province just south of Galicia) under the Russian occupation by the author, playwright, and ethnographer S. An-sky. Remembered today mostly for his play "The Dybbuk," An-sky recorded his experiences as he followed the Russian armies occupying these regions and tried to help the devastated Jewish communities there in a Russian-language diary. After the war he rewrote and expanded the diary into a multivolume account in Yiddish, which was soon thereafter translated into Hebrew. But while his account remains of great value, it provides largely a bird's-eye view by an outsider coming from Russia, rather than an insider's account of events as they unfolded in a single town, which is precisely what Siewiński gives us.[13] Indeed, reading Siewiński's account of events in Buczacz, we conclude that the manner in which World War I and the Polish-Ukrainian War that followed were experienced by the local population constituted a crucial precondition to people's subsequent conduct in Buczacz, as in many other towns in the region, in the decades that followed, not least under the Soviet and German occupations of 1939–41 and 1941–44, and most specifically during the genocide of the Jews and the ethnic cleansing of the Poles.

Siewiński had very clear opinions about his Buczacz, the role that Poles, Jews, and Ukrainians played in it, as well as its place in Polish history and its necessary and inevitable future. For him, the Jews were always a malign influence. Although he repeatedly asserts that there were some highly admirable individuals among them, he just as often stresses that the exception only proves the rule. And while he similarly believes that the Jews could and would be transformed, were they to take up the Roman Catholic faith and become part of the Polish nation, he does not expect that to happen. As for the Ruthenians, or pseudo-Ukrainians, as he calls them especially during the civil war of 1918–19, Siewiński firmly believes that they are a sister nation that belongs by ethnicity, religion, and history to the greater Poland of which he dreams, a sort of reenactment of the Polish-Lithuanian Commonwealth that had ceased to exist at the end of the eighteenth century.[14] For Siewiński, as for many other nationalist Poles of his generation as well as their sons, World War I was not at all about preserving the Austro-Hungarian Empire, to which he bitterly referred as one of the "ignominious partition powers." Rather, it was about reestablishing Poland. For this reason, too, he detested the Jews, since they were in fact the only group in Galicia that hoped to preserve the empire, rightly fearing that the nation states that might inherit its territories would be much less tolerant of them as a stateless national minority.[15]

Siewiński lived to see the success of Polish nationalism in resurrecting the Polish state and taking over Eastern Galicia despite the fact that its majority Ukrainian population vehemently opposed Polish rule. But he was also aware that the six years of mayhem in the region had brutalized people, not least the youth, and looked to the future with a fair amount of trepidation. Perhaps fortunately for him, he did not live to see the end of Polish rule in Buczacz and the destruction of Polish presence in Galicia in World War II.

One of the men who fought for his own national cause rather than the survival of the empire in World War I, and then served in the ranks of the Ukrainian Galician Army that fought against the Poles, was Viktor Petrykevych, the author of the second account. Born in Drohobycz (Ukrainian: Drohobych, 170 km west of Buczacz), in 1883, Petrykevych spent most of his life as a teacher of Latin, German, and Ukrainian. After the war and a period of internment in Czechoslovakia, he served for a few years as the principal of a private Ukrainian gymnasium in Czortków (Ukrainian: Chortkiv), where he also married and had two children. In the late 1920s Petrykevych took up a teaching position in the state gymnasium of Buczacz (Ukrainian: Buchach, 36 km west of Czortków). He bought a house and intended to spend the rest of his life there, but in 1938 the Polish authorities transferred him to a teaching position in the bigger city of Stanisławów (Ukrainian: Stanyslaviv, now

Ivano-Frankivsk). It was there that he experienced the outbreak of
World War II and decided to write a diary. Just like Siewiński, he was
fifty-six years old at the time.

Similarly to his Polish counterpart, Petrykevych was a patriot and a
nationalist; he perceived Poland as a colonizer of Ukrainian lands and
had a poor opinion of Jews, whom he saw as enthusiastic facilitators of
Bolshevik rule. Yet he too was a keen and critical observer of the events
he experienced during the war and in its aftermath. His diary, which,
following his death in 1956, remained in his son Bohdan's possession, is
an especially valuable document, since such extensive accounts of Soviet
and German rule in Galicia by members of the local Ukrainian intelligentsia are exceedingly rare. Petrykevych describes in detail the entry
of the Red Army and the establishment of Soviet rule in Stanisławów
in September 1939, as Poland was divided between the USSR and Nazi
Germany according to the Molotov-Ribbentrop Pact. Delighted about
the end of Polish rule, Petrykevych, over time, grew increasingly critical of the new Bolshevik masters, both for pedagogical-ideological and
material reasons, as is reflected in his entries on the organization of
fake elections meant to legitimize Soviet rule as well as his frequent
references to the growing impoverishment of the population.

Petrykevych's presumably more critical comments on Soviet power
were deemed too dangerous by his son when he came into possession
of the diary and were torn out. Similarly, the entries covering the first
months of German rule in the region were also seen as too compromising,
likely because of Petrykevych's enthusiasm about the end of Soviet rule
as well as his initial participation in the local Ukrainian administration.
Hence, we are missing the parts of the diary describing events between
early July 1940 and late June 1941, as well as between 5 July and the
end of 1941. As Viktor's son Bohdan recalled in 2006, Petrykevych was
dismissed from his teaching position in Stanisławów in the second half
of 1940. He then moved back with his family to their house in Buczacz
but was unable to secure a position in the town and had to earn his
living teaching in the nearby town of Jazłowiec (Ukrainian: Yazlovets,
17 km south of Buczacz). In early July 1941 Buczacz was taken over by
the invading German forces, and Petrykevych was appointed director of
the district education department by the short-lived Ukrainian nationalist administration in Buczacz. By October this self-rule apparatus
was dissolved by the Germans and Petrykevych was relegated to the
position of an ordinary schoolteacher in Buczacz without any further
engagement in local politics.[16]

The bulk of Petrykevych's diary is devoted to the entire period of
German rule in Buczacz, while the latter parts depict his rather wretched

postwar life under the reinstalled Soviet administration in the town of Kołomyja (Ukrainian: Kolomyya, 75 km southwest of Buczacz)—to which his family evacuated in mid-March 1944—until his death at the age of seventy-three. What is remarkable about this diary is that it provides an almost day-by-day account of an older Ukrainian nationalist's view of the extermination of the Jews, the lives of the Christian population of the town, and the Polish-Ukrainian conflict toward the end of German rule. Although Petrykevych does not devote a great deal of space to the mass murder of his Jewish neighbors, and does not express particular glee about their fate, he appears remarkably detached and hardly empathic. He is also quite worried about the continued presence of Jews in the town and its vicinity even after it is declared "Judenrein" (clean of Jews) and wryly notes that the inhabitants expect "Jewish revenge" once the Soviets return, thereby reflecting the notion that Jews and communists are synonymous. Conversely, Petrykevych both increasingly bemoans the material circumstances of such civil servants as himself and the general privations entailed in living ever closer to the front, and, at the same time, harshly criticizes those who profit from the suffering of others, not least from the property of the Jews and the job and business opportunities created by their murder. Finally, as a veteran nationalist fighter, Petrykevych is loath to criticize the massacres of Polish civilians in the ethnic cleansing operations conducted by Ukrainian militias in 1944, but eventually concedes that both sides have descended to barbarism.

Just as Petrykevych is ambivalent about the first period of Soviet rule from 1939 to 1941, because it liberated Ukrainians from Polish rule and united them with their brethren in Soviet Ukraine, on the one hand, but on the other hand imposed an ideologically rigid and economically inefficient system on the population, he remains similarly ambivalent about the benefits and failures of postwar Soviet rule. What his diary lacks entirely is any sense of regret, remorse, or grief about the murder of the Jews and the "removal" of the Poles from West Ukraine. Like many other Ukrainians of his generation, who recalled the injustices of Polish rule in the interwar period and the suppression of Ukrainian national aspirations, and who had internalized strong antisemitic sentiments, Petrykevych was glad to be finally living in an ethnically homogeneous land, even if his own postwar daily existence was quite miserable in this devastated region. He suffered from the severe lack of even the most elementary food items and was troubled by the imposition of the Russian language to the detriment of Ukrainian. Yet he could also look forward with some hope to the eventual recovery of Ukrainian culture and identity. From this perspective, while this diary is unique, the sentiments it expresses during and after the war can be said to reflect those of a significant proportion of Petrykevych's generation, as well as younger cohorts of Ukrainian patriots.

The third account is similarly singular, even as it provides an entirely different picture of events in Buczacz under German rule. Its author, the radio technician Moshe Wizinger, was twenty-one years old when the Germans marched into his hometown of Buczacz in 1941. At the time he was living with his mother and younger brother in a small house on the outskirts of the town, near the Christian cemetery on the slopes of Fedor Hill, which eventually became a main killing site of Jews. Wizinger's older brother and sister had already immigrated to Palestine, and he too was inclined toward Zionism. A tough and resourceful young man, obviously also with some literary aspirations but lacking the higher education of Siewiński and Petrykevych, Wizinger gives us a vivid and colorful description of Jewish life under German rule in Buczacz until the city was declared "Judenrein" in June 1943, following the mass murder of most of its Jewish inhabitants.

In the second, fascinating part of his account, Wizinger depicts a world that we rarely hear about in Jewish testimonies and memoirs from this region. After his mother and brother are murdered, Wizinger, along with a few other surviving young Jews, joins a local Polish resistance group, which fights both the Germans and Ukrainian collaborators and militias, and subsequently joins forces with a Soviet partisan formation operating in the area. Eventually the leader of the Polish resistance group is killed (by a local ethnic German), and only Wizinger and a few other Jews survive to see the first liberation of Buczacz in March 1944. Buczacz was in fact reoccupied by the Germans a couple of weeks later, and only taken over again by the Red Army in July, by which time most of the original eight hundred survivors were murdered, but Wizinger apparently retreated with the Soviets in April and later fought in a Polish formation during the last phases of the war. He sought to immigrate to Palestine in 1947, but the ship on which he was traveling was intercepted by the British and he found himself incarcerated in an internment camp in Cyprus for several months before finally reaching his destination. It was during that period of enforced detention that he wrote his account, based on notes he had written and preserved during the war.

Several aspects of this account stand out. First, even as he is hunted down as a Jew, Wizinger always relies on various Christian friends and helpers, both Polish and Ukrainian, whom he not only trusts but who, on a number of occasions, literally save him. He appears to interact with local non-Jews freely, both in Polish and in Ukrainian;

he has no dietary restrictions and often mentions eating pork; and he never shies away from a fight and other types of violence, be it against the Jewish police, which he despises (even as he is obviously connected to the Jewish council), local Christians, Ukrainian police, or, when the occasion presents itself, Germans. Second, from the very beginning of the German occupation, Wizinger is engaged in various forms of resistance, together with his band of friends, most of whom are Zionists, and along with non-Jewish locals. Most importantly in this early phase, he builds a radio with which they can listen to news from the outside, which they then disseminate among the population to boost their morale.

Third, Wizinger consistently distinguishes between both Jews and Christians that can be trusted and are behaving as decently as they can under the circumstances, and those who collaborate with the Germans or act brutally and greedily of their own accord. In many ways then, Wizinger represents a local community of young working-class Jews (including both Zionists and communists), not all completely secular (he celebrates the Sabbath with his mother and brother) but able to easily overcome religious restrictions for reasons of survival, who respond to the calamity of German occupation with energy and determination, and repeatedly find men and women, Jewish and Christian, who help and at times participate in small acts of resistance and desperate attempts at survival.

This is not to say that Wizinger shies away from condemning the general indifference of the Christian population and the collaboration of some, especially Ukrainian policemen, in the mass murder of the Jews. He also eventually almost succumbs to despair when one of his Christian friends refuses to offer him shelter, just after his brother is murdered in the last roundup. But in what is perhaps the most remarkable part of this account, once Wizinger joins the Polish resistance group, the relations he depicts there between Jews and non-Jews, at the height of the Holocaust, in their forest hideout, and during perilous partisan operations, are not merely utilitarian or comradely but nothing short of deep mutual compassion and love. In this small band of brothers and sisters, they are all dedicated to the cause of revenge, retribution, and liberation from German rule, and most of all, to each other. And in the process, not least thanks to the encouragement of his admired Polish leader, Wizinger is transformed from a desperate young man hunted down as one of the last survivors of his community into a fierce, long-bearded, merciless partisan. And yet, after all the power and the glory of the resistance, Wizinger ends his account by acknowledging, just before the Soviet tanks roll in, that he and the few other starving

Jewish comrades hiding in a cave next to their murdered town are the "last of a dying nation."

It is my hope that these three extended accounts of the violent events in one Eastern European town during the first half of the twentieth century, will provide readers with a greater understanding of the complexity and nuances of communal relations at times of war and genocide. First-person narratives suffer from the limitations of subjectivity: they tell us how specific individuals saw and experienced the tiny segment of a historical event in which they played a role. But this is also their strength, since they draw us in and help us empathize with the historical actors in a manner that historical studies often fail to accomplish. These three men saw the same world and each other through different eyes, and readers may well have more sympathy with one view than with another. But the study of history is not simply an undertaking in establishing what happened, or in taking sides as to who was right and who was wrong, who tells the truth and who lies. It is, ultimately, about understanding human motivation: why people acted as they did at other times and under different circumstances. Such understanding also helps us decipher the world in which we live and may dispel the fog of prejudice, opinion, media representations, and political bias that cloud our vision. Just as we might have all found ourselves in a little town like Buczacz had we been born at another time and place, so too our own neighborhoods, towns, cities, and countries may at some point, perhaps not so far from today, be transformed into sites of violence and social disintegration. Reading the accounts of Siewiński, Petrykevych, and Wizinger about their own struggles with chaos and mayhem should help prepare us for what may be in store for our own communities sooner than we would like to believe.

Acknowledgments

In finding, transcribing, and translating these accounts I was immensely helped by several research assistants, friends, and colleagues. Frank Grelka, who helped me beyond measure in researching *Anatomy of a Genocide*, found Siewiński's diary in the recesses of the Jagiellonian Library in Krakow, where it had lain untouched for decades. He then expertly transcribed the handwritten notes and provided me with an initial translation. Sofia Grachova, who traveled with me throughout West Ukraine and provided endless help and advice during the years of working on both *Erased* and *Anatomy of a Genocide*, found Petrykevych's diary in the possession of his son Bohdan, transcribed the handwritten manuscript, and provided an initial translation. In the latter stages of editing the translation and translating some extra passages, I was also greatly helped by Elena Medvedev, who read through the entire manuscript and made important corrections and suggestions. Moshe Wizinger's account, which I found at Yad Vashem Archives in Jerusalem, was initially translated exceedingly well by Eva Lutkiewicz. In the latter stages of editing it, I was given some valuable suggestions and corrections by Adam Musiał, who has now also beautifully translated *Anatomy of a Genocide* into Polish.

Notes

1. Omer Bartov, "Eastern Europe as the Site of Genocide," *The Journal of Modern History* 80, no. 3 (September 2008): 557–93.
2. Alexander Victor Prusin, *The Lands Between: Conflict in the East European Borderlands, 1870–1992* (Oxford: Oxford University Press, 2010); Timothy Snyder, *Bloodlands: Europe Between Hitler and Stalin* (New York: Basic Books, 2010); Omer Bartov and Eric D. Weitz, eds, *Shatterzone of Empires: Coexistence and Violence in the German, Habsburg, Russian, and Ottoman Borderlands* (Bloomington: Indiana University Press, 2013).
3. See Timothy Snyder, *The Reconstruction of Nations: Poland, Ukraine, Lithuania, Belarus, 1569-1999* (New Haven: Yale University Press, 2003).
4. See Pieter M. Judson and Marsha L. Rozenblit, eds., *Constructing Nationalities in East Central Europe* (New York: Berghahn Books, 2006); Keely Stauter-Halsted, *The Nation in the Village: The Genesis of Peasant National Identity in Austrian Poland, 1848–1914* (Ithaca: Cornell University Press, 2001); Brian A. Porter, *When Nationalism Began to Hate: Imagining Modern Politics in Nineteenth Century Poland* (New York: Oxford University Press, 2000); John-Paul Himka, *Galician Villagers and the Ukrainian National Movement in the Nineteenth Century* (New York: St. Martin's Press, 1988); Paul Robert Magocsi, *The Roots of Ukrainian Nationalism: Galicia as Ukraine's Piedmont* (Toronto: University of Toronto Press, 2002); Joshua Shanes, *Diaspora Nationalism and Jewish Identity in Habsburg Galicia* (New York: Cambridge University Press, 2012); Joshua M. Karlip, *The Tragedy of a Generation: The Rise and Fall of Jewish Nationalism in Eastern Europe* (Cambridge, MA: Harvard University Press, 2013).
5. For example, Eva Hoffman, *Shtetl: The Life and Death of a Small Town and the World of Polish Jews* (Boston: Houghton Mifflin, 1997); Shimon Redlich, *Together and Apart in Brzeżany: Poles, Jews, and Ukrainians, 1919–1945* (Bloomington: Indiana University Press, 2002); Natan Meir, *Kiev, Jewish Metropolis: A History, 1859-1914* (Bloomington: Indiana University Press, 2010); Charles King, *Odessa: Genius and Death in a City of Dreams* (New York: W.W. Norton, 2011); Theodore R. Weeks, *Vilnius Between Nations, 1795–2000* (DeKalb: Northern Illinois University Press, 2015); Christoph Mick, *Lemberg, Lwów, L'viv, 1914–1947: Violence and Ethnicity in a Contested City* (West Lafayette: Purdue University Press, 2016); Omer Bartov, *Anatomy of a Genocide: The Life and Death of a Town Called Buczacz* (New York: Simon and Schuster, 2018).

6. For example, David R. Marples, *Heroes and Villains: Creating National History in Contemporary Ukraine* (Budapest: Central European University Press, 2007); Omer Bartov, *Erased: Vanishing Traces of Jewish Galicia in Present-Day Ukraine* (Princeton: Princeton University Press, 2007); John-Paul Himka and Joanna Beata Michlic, eds, *Bringing the Dark Past to Light: The Reception of the Holocaust in Postcommunist Europe* (Lincoln: University of Nebraska Press, 2013); Tarik Cyril Amar, *The Paradox of Ukrainian Lviv: A Borderland City Between Stalinists, Nazis, and Nationalists* (Ithaca: Cornell University Press, 2015).

7. For example, Daniel Mendelsohn, *The Lost: A Search for Six of Six Million* (New York: HarperCollins, 2006); Marianne Hirsch and Leo Spitzer, *Ghosts of Home: The Afterlife of Czernowitz in Jewish Memory* (Berkeley: University of California Press, 2010).

8. Bartov, *Erased*.

9. Since the publication of *Erased* there have been some efforts, both by Jewish and other groups from outside Ukraine, and by some local activists, to change this situation, preserve or even restore some Jewish edifices and cemeteries, identify sites of mass murder, and erect local memorials. Such attempts have often been hampered by the local authorities' indifference or even hostility to such efforts, as well as by the persistent poverty of the communities in question. Local populations are also generally indifferent to or resentful of outsiders' intervention in their lives, and local schools provide children with little knowledge of their own towns' multiethnic past; there are also very few Jews in the region who might have otherwise promoted preservation or rekindled Jewish life there. Foreign Jewish visitors, mostly from the United States and Israel, tend to travel in their own buses, insulated from the population, and are focused on recalling the Jewish past and local anti-Jewish violence rather than seeking to establish a dialogue over dignified restoration and commemoration. For two major exceptions, see the work of Jewish Heritage Europe director Ruth Gruber at: https://jewish-heritage-europe.eu/2018/12/26/listen-to-or-read-an-interview-with-jhe-director-ruth-ellen-gruber/ and the work of Father Patrick Debois's Yahad in Unum at: https://www.yahadinunum.org/patrick-desbois/ (last accessed 24 January 2020). For recent commemoration and preservation work in Buczacz, see http://jgaliciabukovina.net/183010/cemetery/buczacz; https://jewish-heritage-europe.eu/2017/08/22/ukraine-ancient-buchach-jewish-cemetery-documented/; https://www.esjf-cemeteries.org/fencing-completed-at-historic-buchach-jewish-cemetery-in-ukraine/; https://ukrainianjewishencounter.org/en/category/sponsored-projects/other-programs/agnon_literary_centre/ (all last accessed 24 January 2020).

10. I was animated by the great author Shmuel Yosef Agnon, who once described writing his vast, unfinished biography of his extinguished hometown of Buczacz with the words: "I am building a city." See Alan Mintz, *Ancestral Tales: Reading the Buczacz Stories of S. Y. Agnon* (Stanford: Stanford University Press, 2017), 1.

11. Omer Bartov, "Wartime Lies and Other Testimonies: Jewish-Christian Relationships in Buczacz, 1939–44," *East European Politics and Societies* 25, no. 3 (August 2011): 486–511.

12. Perhaps the most outstanding example of this perpetrator-centered scholarship is Raul Hilberg, *The Destruction of the European Jews*, 3rd ed., 3 vols. (New Haven: Yale University Press, 2003). But see also Martin Broszat and Saul Friedländer, "A Controversy about the Historicization of National Socialism," in *Reworking the Past: Hitler, the Holocaust, and the Historians' Debate*, edited by Peter Baldwin, 77–134, (Boston: Beacon Press, 1990).

13. S. An-sky, *The Enemy at His Pleasure: A Journey through the Jewish Pale of Settlement During World War I*, translated and edited by Joachim Neugroschel

(New York: Metropolitan Books, 2003); S. An-sky, *The Destruction of the Jews in Poland, Galicia, and Bukovina*, 4 vols., translated by Samuel Leib Zitron (Tel Aviv: Shtibel, 1929); S. An-sky, *1915 Diary of S. An-sky: A Russian Jewish Writer at the Eastern Front*, translated and edited by Polly Zavadivker (Bloomington: Indiana University Press, 2016); S. An-sky, *The Dybbuk and the Yiddish Imagination: A Haunted Reader*, translated and edited by Joachim Neugroschel (Syracuse: Syracuse University Press, 2000); Gabriella Safran, *Wandering Soul:* The Dybbuk*'s Creator, S. An-sky,* (Cambridge, MA: Harvard University Press, 2010). For the most recent research on the national struggle that followed the end of World War I, see Jochen Böhler, *Civil War in Central Europe, 1918–1921: The Reconstruction of Poland* (Oxford: Oxford University Press, 2019).

14. In this he shared Polish leader Józef Piłsudki's vision. See, e.g., Timothy Snyder, *Sketches from a Secret War: A Polish Artist's Mission to Liberate Soviet Ukraine* (New Haven: Yale University Press, 2005).

15. See, e.g., Marsha L. Rozenblit, *Reconstructing a National Identity: The Jews of Habsburg Austria during World War I* (New York: Oxford University Press, 2001).

16. Sofia Grachova's interview with Bohdan Petrykevych in Ivano-Frankivsk, May 2006, in Sofia Grachova, "The Diary of Viktor Petrykevych: A Gymnasium Teacher's View of the Soviet and German Occupation of Eastern Galicia (1939–1944)," unpublished paper, Herder Institute, University of Marburg, 2007.

THE ACCOUNTS

Antoni Siewiński. Source: "Pamiętniki
buczacko-jazłowieckie z czasów wojny wszechświatowej od roku 1914 do roku 1920: pamiętnik
rodzinny," Biblioteka Jagiellońska, Kraków, BJ
Rkp. 7367 II. Published with permission.

Antoni Siewiński

Memories of Buczacz and Jazłowiec during the Great War, 1914–20

Part I

As soon as the world war broke out, I began writing and taking note of everything that occurred in the city of Buczacz and its environs. These notes were written very tightly on about forty sheets of paper. When the Muscovites[1] combed through all the houses [before they withdrew from Buczacz] in May 1915, seeking to grab all valuables and precious metals they could lay their hands on, I regrettably threw these notes into the oven and burned them, fearful that if they were found I would suffer the consequences. Since these entries clearly indicated the abuses carried out by the Russian army, and especially by Muscovite civil servants, had they fallen into their hands they would have surely hanged me.

And so, I rewrote these notes and sent them in 1915 to the editor of the newspaper *Słowo Polskie* ["The Polish Word," a newspaper published in Lwów (German: Lemberg; Ukrainian: Lviv), 155 km northwest of Buczacz], yet as I later found out, they never reached their destination but were confiscated by the Austrian authorities in Stanisławów [70 km southwest of Buczacz]. Rather than being forwarded they were lost in the officers' casino. Again, I was not deterred and wrote these memoirs for a third time, taking them all the way to the end of the world war and further to the peace treaty [of Poland] with the Russians in 1920.

I wrote these memoirs for my sons in remembrance of the city in which they had spent their youth and school years, as well as for friends and acquaintances from Jazłowiec [17 km south of Buczacz]. Now that the war is over, I have already forgotten many events; my imagination and memory have weakened, and like many other Poles a great deal has changed for me. I still regret having lost my earlier notes. All four of my sons took part in the war; if they wish, they can expand these notes and presumably write a hundred-fold more than I have written in these memoirs and perhaps also correct this or that point.

Buczacz is a little town whose prewar population numbered fourteen thousand people. It stretches along the Strypa River, which descends into a little waterfall below the church. The city was founded in the fourteenth century by the Turowski clan, who later took up the name Buczacki, since there were many beech forests in the area.[2] Unfortunately these forests no longer exist today. In the valleys all the trees were felled. [... And now] the city is surrounded by forests, in which birch, oak, and other trees grow, all apart from beeches. Three kilometers away are the ruins of a so-called cloister. In the past there was a church and some kind of monastery there. And right next to these ruins flows a stream that eventually runs to a waterfall. When the sun shines the drops form a rainbow. In Buczacz people relate that at the time of the Tatars the monastery was plundered and burned down, and all of its forty inhabitants were murdered.

The Potocki clan inherited Buczacz [in 1612] and remained there ever since .... The cities of Buczacz, Jazłowiec, Trembowla, and Kamieniec Podolski [17 km southeast, 48 km northeast, and 115 km southeast of Buczacz, respectively] were once border posts that protected Poland. They were held by knights who watched over the entire region with eagle eyes, so that no enemy could come close to these cities; and if the Tatars or other enemies approached, the knights would repel them and take booty. By the Strypa, overlooking a huge gorge, a vast castle once stood, of which only ruins are left. The walls of this castle withstood the Turkish and Tatar hordes.

After Kamieniec Podolski was captured by the Turks, the Sultan Mehmet IV came to Buczacz [in 1672] and signed the peace of shame with Poland next to the linden tree that still stands there today, in which Poland conceded Podolia and Ukraine to the Turks and agreed to pay a penalty of 22,000 ducats.[3] But God sent the courageous hero [King Jan III] Sobieski to the Poles, who refused to implement this treaty and dealt such a defeat to the Turks, that they abandoned the region and kept only Kamieniec Podolski. In Kolejowa [Railroad] Street, also known as Potocki Street, there is a fountain that was named after Jan Sobieski. Legend tells that King Sobieski drank from this fountain.

During the partition of Poland in 1772 [Austrian Empress] Maria Theresa, fearing an uprising by the Poles, ordered all castles destroyed in Lesser Poland [the annexed southeastern lands renamed Galicia by Austria], with the exception of the castles of Żółkiew, Olesko, and Podhorcy [125 to 185 km northwest of Buczacz], in remembrance of the fact that these castles had belonged to King Sobieski—which, to my mind, is a beautiful gesture of gratitude! For had the Poles not helped out at the time of the siege of Vienna [by the Ottomans] in 1683, there would have been no Austria. Yet ninety-one [should be eighty-nine] years later the greedy clan of Habsburg, instead of helping Poland, exposed its claws and annexed the entire southern part of Poland. At that time the castle of Buczacz was also demolished ....

The city jewel is the town hall, whose construction was funded by [Polish magnate and city owner] Mikołaj Potocki [1712–82]. He also built the monastery of the Basilian [Greek Catholic order] monks, large churches, the [Roman Catholic] parish church and the synagogue.[4]

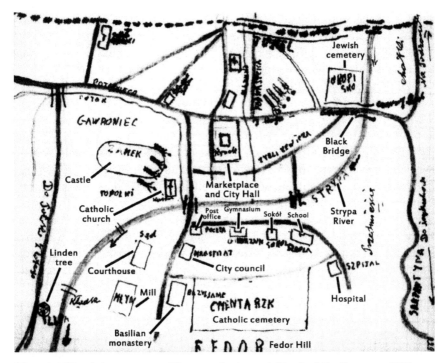

Map 1.1 Hand-drawn map of Buczacz in Antoni Siewinski's diary, ca. 1922.

Additionally, Mikołaj Potocki was appointed administrator of Kamieniec, and people say that he was also a jolly man and a bon vivant. Many of these stories were invented by bad and foolish people without honor; the churches and cloisters that Potocki built not only in Buczacz but throughout Eastern Lesser Poland demonstrate that Potocki was a great patriot and man of honor.[5]

In the city there are two schools, which were built in 1904. Each of these school buildings has over twenty classrooms and accommodations for the principals. There is also a large building, the gymnasium, from which brave men and good patriots graduate. Before the war the city had 8,000 Jews, 3,000 Poles, and 3,000 Ruthenians. The girls' school was attended by 750 Jews and 350 Catholics.[6] In my [boys'] school [where Siewiński was the principal] there were 180 Jews and 120 Catholics. Now, in the immediate aftermath of the war, this relationship has changed somewhat, so that in 1922 there were 154 Catholics and only 70 Jews in my school.

Having been rebuilt after a fire [in 1865], the city had beautiful houses and stone buildings filled with wares; it had the largest warehouses in all of Podolia. In these stores there were vast supplies of fabrics, linens, clothing, ironware, furniture, food items, and so forth. All of this was Jewish property. The Poles and Ruthenians also owned houses, but they were in the outskirts; the Catholic population was engaged in craftsmanship, such as locksmiths, forgers, builders, tailors, furriers, and in the more distant outskirts they worked on the land. The women planted maize and other vegetables in the gardens.

The town had always had a Jewish mayor. For thirty-six years Mayor Bernard Stern ruled the city.[7] He was an interesting man, keen on eating, even more so on drinking, but he never became a drunk; he liked playing cards, although he almost always lost. The city officials were all Jews, except for the Catholic Zatarnowski. In the gymnasium too there were Jewish teachers, as well as in the general-education schools. Now everyone makes mistakes, but whenever a Jew did something wrong, and a Catholic pointed this out to him, the Catholic would immediately be accused of antisemitism and come into many difficulties. That is to say that the Jews, even the most honest among them, could always take revenge, and then hide behind the claim that the Catholic was at fault and say, "we are innocent," although anyone could see that the Jews were behind it. Well, nothing could be done about that, since Jewish religion postulates: "An eye for an eye, a tooth for a tooth."

While I do know some honest and honorable Jews, the exception only proves the rule. The Jews care a great deal about schooling, they educate their children, send them to elementary school, middle school, and to the gymnasium, and as an old and experienced teacher I can say that the Jews are good students. The [Christian] citizens care much less about education. Before the war there were many watering holes here, in which people drank in the evenings and on holidays, so that eventually the Catholics drank away the entire inner city, while the Jews became the owners of the most beautiful houses in town: who is to be blamed for that?

But enough with this description of what is now a completely dilapidated and ruined city; let me get down to the main issue at hand ....

The opening of hostilities came sooner than expected. On 28 June 1914 the Serb Gavrilo Princip[8] shot the Austrian heir presumptive and his wife. When the news reached Buczacz, the first thing I said was: "This murder will result in great bloodshed." And that is precisely what happened .... But I do not want to speak about politics, because there are others who can express themselves on this topic at greater length and depth. What concerns me primarily is to write my memoirs for my three [living] sons, as well as for my friends, who may read them at some point.[9]

At the beginning of the war I had four sons. The two older ones [Józef and Zygmunt] had already gone to university; the third, Marian, was seventeen years old and a student in the 7th grade; the youngest [Roman] was only fourteen and had just graduated from the local gymnasium.[10] Living with us was also a cousin, fourteen-year-old Stefania Gruszyńska, a very good and lovely young woman, whom we raised. The eldest son, Józef, had been called up for military service and would have volunteered in the fall. He was riding his bicycle in the direction of Hungary when the news arrived that Austria had declared war on Serbia. Having been enlisted, he had to return right away in order to report to the army. In-between we received increasingly bad news, namely, that war had broken out with Russia, France, and Belgium. The Prussians[11] invaded and without paying attention to international law occupied Belgium and were marching on French soil.

In Buczacz mobilization was announced. Thousands of older and younger men were called to arms. Whole trainloads of recruits passed through Buczacz on the way to the West. One could detect no signs of worry on these people's faces: "On to the Muscovites!" they all called out. Everyone thought that in three months the entire Muscovite state would be vanquished, and the war would be over.

Then we received some remarkable news. A certain formerly unknown Józef Piłsudski[12] had put together a military formation called the Polish Legion and had crossed the border into Congress Poland,[13] where it defeated the Muscovites and occupied the city of Kielce. News of this spread like wildfire and inspired the souls of Polish youth. Józef had already presented himself to the Austrian army in Stanisławów; the younger two, Zygmunt and Marian, prepared to join the Polish Legion along with another two hundred youths from Buczacz and its environs. These included students, craftsmen, and peasants from the villages.

Some of the adults wanted to hold the youth back, since they thought the mobilization was an error. The members of the local [nationalist gymnastics] Sokół [Falcon] Association had a similar attitude. During calmer times, they had all sung patriotic songs, but now, when the moment had come to take up arms, none of them was seen and no one showed up to lead the youth. Nowadays [1922] they want to have their say in politics, but at the time, when the Fatherland had to be defended, they could not be found.

At the lead of the Buczacz formation stood Władek Winiarski (now a lieutenant), a student of the 7th grade in the gymnasium, a courageous youth who knew his way in the world. All the others obeyed his orders—students, craftsmen, peasants, everyone, including academics, Riflemen and members of other associations.[14] The members of the Sokół Gymnastics Association had called the youths of the Riflemen's Association cowards, but now the latter were about to demonstrate who had greater love for the Fatherland.

News came that the Austrians had already taken Kamieniec Podolski and were pushing further into Muscovite areas, and that Belgrade had been taken; it was also reported that the Prussians had crushed Belgium and were now advancing on to Paris, and that the Russians in Congress Poland had been defeated. In one word—only victories! There were also skeptics who did not believe any of this news. There were rumors about how many men from Lwów had fallen in Belgrade, that the entire 30th Lwów Brigade had been wiped out there; and, that the Muscovites had amassed powerful formations and were advancing toward Galicia with an army of five million men.

It was also said that the Austrians did not want to share the fate of Napoleon I and Charles XII,[15] and instead would lure the Muscovites into Galicia in order to encircle them there. The greatest battle was expected in Niżniów on the Dniester [40 km southwest of Buczacz], where the Russian army was to be defeated. After all, as early as 1912 the supreme commander of the Austrian army, [Field Marshal Franz Conrad von] Hötzendorf, had come to Buczacz with his entire staff and remained here for several days, in order to explore the area and to forge war plans. Hötzendorf was considered a brave soldier and seen as equal to Napoleon I.

Winiarski ordered his formation to undertake military training in the Buczacz district. The formation included also several older people, especially schoolteachers, who did the right thing by joining. But they believed it would be easy to participate in long, strenuous marches; they hurt their feet and had to recognize that while the spirit was strong, the flesh was weak. After five days only those youngsters remained who had a strong will and stamina.

On 18 August 1914, Emperor Franz Josef I's [84th] birthday, Mayor Stern invited a Jewish choir to sing imperial hymns on the streets of Buczacz. As is usual on such occasions, mostly Jews assembled on the street and made tremendous noise, with the music alternating between "Kołomyja" and "Krakowiaczek."[16] They held up a portrait of the emperor and the mayor made a speech to the crowd: "What was the Serb thinking? We will show him, what a real emperor is! Today we give Belgrade to our emperor! Long live our illustrious master!" "Long live, hurrah!" yelled the crowd. Then someone suddenly called out: "Long live linoleum! Long live, hurrah!" "Who called out linoleum?" the mayor shouted back. But although they looked for the joker, he could not be found in the crowd.

Thereafter they marched down May Third Street[17] to the Kachkovsky reading room.[18] This was a Muscophile [i.e., Russophile] reading room, where a woman and her three children were living. Suddenly stones were thrown from all sides and fragments flew everywhere, almost striking the children and their mother, who were entirely innocent and had nothing to do with politics. Thereafter the crowd wanted to march on to the Black Bridge,[19] where a Muscophile boarding school was situated ... but Police Inspector Stefanus sent the noisy crowd back to the marketplace. Just a year later nothing was to remain of that boarding school, a beautiful brick building, since the followers of Piłsudski took it apart to make use of the building materials.

That evening the city was wonderfully lit up. The Jews put lights in all their windows and hoisted the black-and-yellow Austrian flag. They put up posters on the walls, announcing that a meeting concerning the Jewish question would be taking place in the city council, to which all residents of the city were invited. The most distinguished representatives of the Poles and the Ukrainians received a special invitation. I was also sent such an invitation and chose to attend.

The hall was full of Jews and a few members of the Catholic intelligentsia. At the podium one kike[20] was speaking. He began by reading out several phrases in Aramaic [likely Hebrew] from a book, and then went on to make a speech in this language. He was followed by some attorney, called Eisenberg, who spoke in Polish, and addressed the Poles and the Ruthenians, asking them to help the Jews achieve equal status, so that they too would be able to establish their own [paramilitary] legions and fight the Russians alongside the Polish legions and the Ruthenians in order to defend the Fatherland together. This speech betrayed the speaker's fear of the Muscovite hordes, since he spoke about that many times.

He was answered by Mr. [Józef] Chlebek, a gymnasium teacher, who remarked that the Jews had never had it badly in Poland, as can best be seen from the fact that when they fled persecution [in the Middle Ages] throughout Europe the Jews found refuge, protection, and a living in Poland, so that today the Jews are the richest group in Poland. Since they are in Poland, they should also think like Poles and feel like Poles despite their Mosaic faith. The Ukrainian postal official Siyak then also spoke in a similar vein.

But the Jews wanted to prove that they could also do something. "Why can't we establish legions?" they asked. And so, the attorney Alter assembled the entire Jewish youth and took them to the outskirts of the city, where he arranged them in columns of four rows and marched with them back to the city. I was just on my way to the district administration when I heard the sound of a trumpet coming from the [soccer] field on the Fedor [hill on the outskirts of Buczacz]: "Tratata! Tratata!" At first, I thought that these were our Polish legionnaires returning from their exercises, since they had already been away from Buczacz for five days. In the city all the inhabitants were trembling with fear that perhaps they had been snatched by the Cossacks, who had already captured Husiatyn [75 km east of Buczacz], and the Austrian troops were already on the retreat. Masses of people were fleeing from the city, on carts, carriages, and on foot with their belongings on their backs, and the dull roar of the cannons in the east could already be heard in the city. While all this was going on, I watched the kikes marching. Each and every one of them was as fat as a well-nourished ox, their snouts lit up like lacquered lamps. They were marching in four rows, and in order to give themselves courage as well as to stay in step, they were yelling, "ans, zwa, ans, zwa!"[21] with Doctor Alter in the lead ....

The stupid Jews thought that they could accomplish in one day what Polish youth had worked its heart out to achieve for many years. The courage of these fat, pigheaded Jewish cowards was demonstrated already the following day. As the Jews heard the first shots from the direction of Dżuryn [17 km east of Buczacz], the entire crew fled in all directions of the wind and further to the west all the way to Vienna, where they finally stopped to take a breath. Others hid in cellars inside the city, from which they later emerged like rats and made up a legion of black-marketeers, traitors, and informers, who always stood on the side of the most powerful. It is true that I have also seen truly noble and honest Jews willing to sacrifice themselves, but no more than a small handful, so that the term "Jew" must stand as a profanity for any honest person.

At first Austrian troops streamed ceaselessly through Buczacz to the East, especially Hungarian Hussars with red pants and hats, infantry in light blue uniforms, artillery, and ammunition supplies. It initially appeared to us like a powerful army. First and foremost, the Magyars, a jolly people, were making merry with our girls who brought them sweets and sour milk from their homes, along with pickled cucumbers, bread rolls, and cigarettes, which the Magyars eagerly accepted. Reserve units also marched through, composed entirely of Poles and Ruthenians, and the city made lunch for them. Everyone was convinced that the troops had been ordered to draw the Russians deep into Galicia and that this was the only reason they later retreated.

The young legionnaires, who had gone off to train for battle, had not returned to Buczacz and no one knew where they were. Among them was my younger son Marian who carried the alarm trumpet, because he played the horn well. Having heard several times that Cossack guard units had conducted raids in the Czortków district [the town is 36 km east of Buczacz], numerous reservists were sent on bicycles from Buczacz with instructions to find the youngsters and order them to return immediately to Buczacz. They were found near Potok Złoty [20 km south of Buczacz] and on the very same evening they returned home. The youngsters were completely exhausted.

A few days later a huge herd of children, women, and elderly people came from the area of Czortków to Buczacz. They were mostly Jews, yelling and panicking. All of them fled to the train station and climbed on the roofs of the railcars, trying to escape by any means. But they could find no room in the trains, and so they fled on foot further to Monasterzyska [18 km west of Buczacz]. Anxiety is infectious, and the panic was such that even the most respectable people fled, including many Catholics, who packed their belongings and abandoned the city.

Soon news arrived that the Austrians were bringing Russian prisoners of war to the city. Already from afar one could see them coming down the road that people called the "serpentines to Trybuchowce" [7 km southeast of Buczacz]. Anyone who could walk crowded into the marketplace and the city streets, because they all wanted to see what the Muscovites looked like. What did we see? In reality several people arrived dressed in ordinary civilian clothes along with several Jews and a soldier in a green Russian uniform. They were guarded by Austrian soldiers with bayonets and a police constable, so that they marched uniformly in six rows. "What have they done? they are not even soldiers," everyone said. They responded: "These people have gouged the eyes of wounded Hungarian soldiers, they rubbed salt into their wounds, and they burned down Husiatyn." No one knew if this was true. Only later did we find out that this was a lie. They were held temporarily in the buildings of Count Potocki, located in a park overlooking the Strypa, and were later driven further back.

The elders of the Sokół Association were standing on the bridge and discussing what should be done with the youths, who had just returned from their excursion. People talked about the atrocities perpetrated by the Muscovites and warned that they would capture and hang all the youngsters. They therefore advised the youths to leave the city as quickly as possible; but none of these so-called elders, who before the war had presented themselves as great politicians and patriots, accompanied the youngsters. Once again those who shouted the loudest did the least.

The Buczacz legion soon returned and posted a guard over the building of the Sokół. They also put out an order that as soon as rifle shots or an alarm trumpet were heard, all citizens of Buczacz should gather in front of the Sokół.

All rooms in the Sokół building were converted into workshops. As the population of the district found out that the youth would be going to war, but had no shoes, underwear, or clothes, they began a donation campaign, in which many women from the villages brought underwear for the youngsters. The local shoemakers, apprentices as well as their masters, selflessly made proper boots day and night for the young legionnaires. A Jewish tailor sewed uniforms out of cloth for the legionnaires, but because he was a poor man, he was paid for this labor. In the main hall of the Sokół building bails of straw were placed so that the youths from outside the city could sleep there. Most of the youths were recruited from the villages of Petlikowce Stare and Puźniki [11 km north and 18 km southwest of Buczacz, respectively]. Only the inhabitants of the villages of Podzameczek und Podlesie [5 km northeast and 4 km east of Buczacz, respectively] did not provide a single youth to the legions and would not help in any other way. The people there are very greedy.

In the evening Marian returned and was so tired that he did not even want to eat but went to bed right away and slept like a log. Meanwhile my older son Zygmunt packed their things in a backpack, only the most necessary items for him and his brother, so as to be ready at any moment to march off. Then his mother asked him: "Son, do you want to leave me—your mother?" "My dear Mother," responded Zygmunt, "I must leave and defend another mother, who is the mother of us all, Mother Poland; she has come back from the dead and we must support her. For what other reason have you raised us as Poles?" After these words we spoke no more.

At around 11 p.m. a young legionnaire stormed in and said: "Marian must wake up right away and sound the alarm, since we are marching off in half an hour." We had much difficulty waking him up, but as soon as he came to his senses he got dressed and wanted to leave, when Mother said to him: "Have you eaten? Wait, I'll give you some bread for the way." "I have bread," said Marian, and when we looked, we saw that he had a small piece of bread, hard as stone, which one would have to break with a hammer in order to eat. And so, we packed bread and a few other things for him to eat in his backpack, along with a little money.

Soon one could hear the sorrowful sound of the alarm trumpet in the city. The whole town trembled with fear. The sound of the trumpet rang out in the middle of the night's rest and much farther to Heaven and bade God for help. The youths dashed out of their houses to the Sokół building. There were about sixty youngsters, each equipped with a backpack. Some of them were armed. My son Zygmunt had a pistol, with which he could shoot very well. A few other youths had little knowledge of firearms. Now they stood in the Sokół in formation, and the student Wladzio Winiarski made a speech—to be sure not a very good one but whose tone touched the heart. After that he gave the order to march out to the street.

They marched in four rows through the city, past the marketplace and along Kolejowa Street. As they marched, they sang "God Save Poland" and then the Dąbrowski-March.[22] The city filled with great sorrow and grief, since not a few of these youths would never return to their families. In the train station they were informed that they would have to wait until 5 a.m., after which they went back home and had a bite, but the Austrian army would still not let them into the train, and therefore they had to go on foot to Barysz [13 km southwest of Buczacz], where they stayed at Prince Świdrygiełło's manor house. This good man welcomed the young legionnaires, shared everything he had with them, and when he discovered that the youngsters had no warm clothes, brought out his own garments and said, "Take these, boys, whatever you want, since if you don't take them, the Muscovites will loot them." They all took what they needed, and my Marian found a pair of solid officer pants, which served him well all over the Carpathian range. From that point on we received no more news about the legionnaires.

Sunday, 23 August 1914, was a memorable day for the city of Buczacz. After the legionnaires left the city, there was great sorrow and a solemn silence. The Austrian troops retreated in the direction of Monasterzyska and were replaced by an infantry formation of eight hundred soldiers. This was a reserve unit, all of them from the regions of Buczacz and Czortków. They stood in two rows on the marketplace and along the Grunwaldzka Street and waited. The field kitchens had not arrived, and therefore the inhabitants of the city made lunch for the troops in their homes, and all the civilians who were at the marketplace gave the soldiers cigarettes, a piece of bread, and so forth.

At the marketplace a Jewish woman was selling melon seeds. One of the soldiers came by, leaned down, and took a handful of seeds. At that very moment the Jewish woman sprang up and slapped the soldier on his face. The soldier did not stir, threw down the seeds, and stood still. What discipline there was at the time! But the following day things went differently for the Jews. At 10 a.m. the soldiers were ordered to retreat from Pyszkowce [5.5 km east of Buczacz]. In the city there was dead silence, everyone was now waiting for something dreadful to happen. My wife, after all she had been through, having seen three of our sons going to war within the space of a single week, lay down for a moment in bed and slept like a log after that previous sleepless night, whereas I walked over to the schoolyard.

Suddenly there was thunder over the forest, four loud cannon shots from the direction of Trybuchowce. I pulled out my watch—it was 12:55 p.m. After a while there were another four cannon shots. It went on like this with one-minute intervals. In the city suddenly everyone began to move, and the remaining inhabitants fled from town. I did not think of fleeing; why should I?

My youngest son Roman and his cousin Stefcia [diminutive for Stefania] woke up from the cannon shots and awakened Mother: "Mama, mama, get up!" Still half asleep my wife said to them: "Don't slam the doors so loudly!" "Mama, this is cannon fire, should we flee?" Our house was at the time not in the school building but in Zyblikiewicz Street. Mother said: "Go to Father and ask him what we should do." I told them to come to the schoolyard. At the schoolyard some fifteen people had assembled and were listening to the artillery fire. At the same time Austrian officers were having lunch at the officers' mess, and the restaurant owner asked them, "Will the Muscovites strike here?" "Oh no," one of the officers answered: "We will defend ourselves until half-past-five in the afternoon and then retreat." "How is that possible, what will happen to us?" "Well, when the Russians come, they won't eat you up, and we have prepared for them such a cauldron that they will never get out of it." Yet the battle became ever more bitter, the artillery fire drew ever nearer, and clearly the Austrians were not retreating.

To us the bombardment sounded like a single huge uproar; one could no longer distinguish between individual shell shots, nor tell whether the fire was near or far, and our thoughts filled with the death and destruction that was occurring nearby.

Around 4 p.m. everything suddenly went quiet. Only a few shots indicated that no one was fooling around. Then we heard a loud order: "Forward!" and a moment later came the roar from thousands of throats: "Hurrraaah!" This was the battle cry of the Muscovites. Then we heard again the sound of machine guns, a demonic noise, and once more silence, from one moment to the next. We could see the Hungarian cavalry fleeing at great speed, emerging from the forest and climbing up the serpentine road, riding over the Black Bridge and passing through the Jewish quarter, then heading up the street toward the village of Nagórzanka. The cavalry was followed by automobiles, in which Hungarian officers were sitting, and as they drove through the city they called out: "Victory! Victory! Hail the Emperor!" Seeing this, I was reminded of the Jew who oppresses the peasant (with his demands to pay him back) and calls out: "Take him away from me, otherwise I'll chop him up!"

Then about a hundred horsemen emerged from the forest, chasing the [Hungarian] cavalry along the same route …. At some point one of the Magyars fell off his horse; the horse remained standing, the Magyar remounted and rode on. Another horse that lost its rider turned around against the general flight and trotted all the way back to the Black Bridge but was stopped there by a salvo of machine gun fire; it then turned again and galloped back to the Magyars. Horses are very prudent animals.

Along the serpentine road approximately eight hundred reserve soldiers were standing in trenches. Obviously, their role was to cover the retreat of the Austrians. I saw them standing one next to the other, holding their weapons and shooting in the direction of the forest at the attacking Muscovites. Suddenly all these soldiers rose up, crossed the Strypa, and headed directly to my school. The Muscovites shot thousands of rounds at them, but did not hit a single soldier; instead, they hit my school, and one could see one hole next to the other as the plaster peeled off the walls. These were tracer bullets; the people who had assembled in the schoolyard were watching this battle; I ordered them to get into the school building and to sit quietly in the classrooms, but here too they looked out of the windows and thought that the bullets could not harm them since they were not soldiers. One of the bullets killed a chicken in our yard, another struck a birch tree, which suddenly began to tremble. Although I was not a soldier, I could tell that the Muscovites were bad shots. A peasant from Podzameczek called Prorok had just harnessed his horse on a rather remote farm when a bullet struck him in the shoulder.

The Austrian soldiers stood in front of the school building, led by a student in a boy scouts' uniform; at the front were also two gendarmes and in the back were three treasury guards; officers were nowhere to be seen. Were they killed? Between the school building and the cemetery lay the road leading to the Basilian monastery, but the soldiers did not know which way to go, because they wanted to go around the city. Then my youngest son Roman ran up to them and showed them the right way. The Russians began shooting again and singing their song; they fired a hail of cannon fire that struck the school building, but fortunately my boy managed to get back home.

At about 8 p.m. four artillery shells were fired from the Buczacz castle in the direction of the attacking Russians. The shells flew over the city and fell far away in the forest near Trybuchowce.

The battle was over and evening set in. Many displaced women and girls from different social classes sought refuge in the school. Among them was Mrs. Kolankowski with her daughters, the young women Sobolewska and Simonówna, the couple Czyżewski and their daughters, and others. All were very tired and terrified and lay down to sleep on the school benches. People were still not used to the fighting, and death appeared to them as something shocking; but not long thereafter everyone would sleep very peacefully under the thunder of artillery and rifle fire. Because no one could be certain what the next day would bring, we prayed the Rosary aloud and lay down in the classrooms, wherever we could, but most importantly all together. At about 10 p.m. that night Mr. Czyszewski, a tax official, knocked on the window of the school and called out: "They have brought the wounded, but there is no more place for them; there are some thirty of them with the Basilian monks, twenty with me, and the rest need to be taken to the nurses in the hospital."

I rushed to the hospital right away; it was located behind the school building, but the door had been locked by the terrified nuns and priests. I knocked on the door so as to let in the wounded. There were approximately forty people. The local intelligentsia came to help, including the Zychowiec, Czyżewski, and Nowak families, several female teachers and my own family. Mrs. Markowska, the council chairman's wife, took over the yard in the Basilian monastery, and Mrs. Rogozińska and her daughters took control of the hospital in the school next to the barracks. We also thought about the fact that right after the outbreak of war first aid courses for women had been offered in the building of the Sokół gymnastics society, in which they were taught how to care for wounded soldiers. Numerous women attended this course and were given a Red Cross armband when they completed it. Clearly this became a hobby, and they made noise in the halls and paraded on the streets with white kerchiefs; but when it came to the actual work with the wounded, not a single one of them showed up. A cow that moos loudly gives little milk.

We took the uniforms off the wounded and gave them the hospital garb and laid them in the beds. Hospital director Zych brought a few bottles of good red wine, but the wounded did not want to drink because they had fever. Around midnight a doctor arrived, who dressed their wounds with the help of the nurses. The soldiers' injuries were horrific. One Hungarian soldier had already been attended to by a Russian doctor on the battlefield, who then had to leave him so as to take care of others. Then some monster came and stabbed the Hungarian with his bayonet once more. It is great barbarism to wound a defenseless, wounded soldier.

In the hospital there was no light, so I went with my wife to the school to bring lamps. The night was dark and so still that one could hear the leaves crackling. We returned to the hospital with lit lamps. At that very moment the Muscovites opened fire on us from the direction of Trybuchowce Forest. The bullets hissed by our heads. As we came to the hospital, everyone became terrified and wanted to extinguish the light. But we did not let that happen, and when we came closer to the window with the light, the Muscovites stopped shooting, since they recognized that this was a house. Obviously, the Muscovites are not as barbarous as we had previously thought.

The following day we wanted to hoist the flag of the Red Cross over the hospital. I therefore went to Grunwaldzka Street across the market to the town hall. In the city there was an eerie silence, and not a soul on the streets; the city felt dead. I then went to the fire brigade, picked up a long rod and brought it back to the hospital. We immediately made it into a flagpole and secured it to the roof.

Just before sunrise I went to the school in order to get some brine, and as I was about to turn back, standing on the stairs right next to the school, I found myself eye-to-eye ... with a Cossack.

This was the first time in my life that I came face-to-face with a real Cossack; up to now I knew them only from descriptions or woodcuts. Along the side road that wound down from the hill known as Fedor approximately fifty Cossacks were lined up, one behind the other, facing the city. This Cossack was a large man who wore a huge hat over his head and was holding a rifle in his hands. But his eyes were small, his hair just as smooth as mine, his expression friendly, but sorrowful. I could tell right away that this was no monster but simply an honest man. Behind him came others, just like this first Cossack. One of them, an older fellow, likely a doctor, even had a Red Cross on his uniform; he greeted me, and I greeted him in return.

This scene was observed by everyone from the porch of the hospital, where the wounded soldiers were being treated, and Miecio Krzyżanowski, a customs official, who was trembling from fear, said to my wife: "Oy! Oy! The Cossacks are slaying the headmaster." The others were silent in expectation of what was about to happen.

By evening, out of the eight hundred members of the Austrian infantry formation, only three men had stayed behind, since they had hurt their feet and had set up for themselves a place to sleep at the city administration. In the morning the policeman Świstek alerted the Austrian soldiers: "What are you doing here? The Cossacks are already all over the city. Get out of here!" One of these soldiers was a Jew. He instantly took off his shirt, pulled an old piece of cloth from the wall, wrapped it around himself and walked out. Only two remained, a Pole and a Ruthenian from Czortków. They picked up their rifles, walked in the direction of the mill, and sat down under the famous linden tree named after Sultan Mehmet IV. After a while a squad of Cossacks rode by. The soldiers began firing at them with their rifles and wounded a number of Cossacks and horses. As the Cossacks saw that there were only two of them, they seized them, took them prisoner, and tortured them frightfully. They then brought their bodies to Buczacz and dumped them on the street near the church, after which they were buried in a common grave on the Fedor next to the hospital on the banks of the Strypa. They were the first two warriors buried in this field. Unfortunately, thousands more were subsequently buried there.

Then the Russian troops came to Buczacz from the direction of Czortków. The soldiers marched in clusters, but not in the manner of the Austrians. The mounted troops came together, followed by the infantry. They all stank already from a distance and they polluted the entire city. The soldiers themselves related that they were wearing new uniforms made of oilskins, which was why they smelled so badly. Later the soldiers told us that many of them fell ill because of these uniforms. We watched these troops in amazement. Their clothes were simple, their color similar to dry hay; on their heads they wore not a cap but a sort of hat, and they carried long rifles with long and heavy bayonets; they held the riles over their shoulders. There was nothing impressive about these troops except for their numbers. Conversely, the horses were remarkably beautiful, all dark with huge breasts and long tails. The infantry column and mounted troops marched for about three hours through the city. The Muscovites said they numbered about seventy thousand men.

Watching these troops, I felt no fear at all, but rather remembered a color pictured in [an edition of the ancient Greek historian] Herodotus, depicting the Persian troops of Xerxes. And so, while I was not very impressed, it was still somewhat strange that at the beginning of the war everyone [among the Poles] was hoping not for Austria's but rather for Poland's victory.

The Muscovites did not march only through Buczacz but along other paths in the district. One formation attacked the village of Zielona [8 km north of Buczacz], where the teacher Longin Kornaszewski, who was a well-known beekeeper, had 105 beehives in his garden. When the Cossacks saw this, they smashed the beehives, took out the honey, and within a few hours destroyed almost the entire beehive complex, and thus put an end to the bees. Furthermore, they plundered the houses in that locality and set fire to them. They broke into the home of the teacher, went through his cabinets and drawers and looted everything that came into their hands: silverware, underclothes, linens, clothing. They carried the books from the library to one of the rooms and poured filth over them, so that no one would be able to use them any longer. Kornaszewski himself fled through a window. A Cossack noticed him and started chasing the teacher, but as he could not catch up with him, he shot at him. The bullet struck a twelve-year-old girl from the village in the stomach and she died half an hour later.

The Cossacks then set the village on fire and shot at the villagers who tried to save their houses. They killed four peasants and others were wounded. A twenty-three-year-old pregnant woman was hit in the womb. She was taken to her father in Dźwinogród [7 km northeast of Buczacz] where she died after three hours of torment. The Cossacks blamed the villagers for the fire, especially Kornaszewski. They dragged the inhabitants of the village to a large square in front of the school building and one of the Cossacks yelled: "Whoever is standing now, should stand, whoever is sitting, should sit, whoever moves, will be shot." They all waited, filled with terror, for what would happen next. Then a Cossack officer arrived, and another Cossack pointed at Kornaszewski and said: "He set fire to the village." "Who witnessed this?" asked the officer. "She saw it," said the Cossack, pointing at one of the women. "Did you see how this man set fire to the village?" asked the officer. "I have not seen this, and he is my husband." The officer burst out laughing and ordered all present to return to their homes and to protect them, so that the Cossacks won't loot them, since they had already begun plundering and burning everything.

In the village of Dżuryn a Cossack ordered the inhabitants to bring him four eggs each. When they brought him the eggs, he put them in a large basket and rode off. The Cossacks caused much damage in the other villages as well.

The following day (25 August 1914) there was a firefight west of Buczacz all night long. Between the train station in Gaje Buczackie and Jezierzany [8 km northwest of Buczacz] one could hear all night the clatter of machine guns. Only in the morning did the shooting die down and it was reported that the Russians had reached Gaje Wielkie and had been under fire from the station in Jezierzany. The Muscovites were said to have suffered great losses; some eight hundred of the wounded were cared for at the train station of Buczacz. Other train stations in the district also took in wounded soldiers. Soon thereafter the Russians pushed on, past Jezierzany and on to Monasterzyska. But there the Austrian troops were positioned on the hills and held the Russian troops in check. The Russian mounted troops attacked. Behind them were the medics with bandages and the doctors.

The battle was witnessed by my brother-in-law Adam Gruszczyński, a representative of the city council in Dżuryn. When the Muscovites entered Dżuryn, they immediately set fire to the distillery and plundered all houses with great thoroughness, taking along with them all the horses and carts. One Russian ordered my brother-in-law to harness the horses and follow the troops. When they approached Monasterzyska, the Russians removed their bayonets and left them in the field, since the Austrians were firing with artillery. Suddenly they came under a mortar attack, and my brother-in-law, as he related himself, jumped up in the air from fright. He then lay down on the ground without moving for many hours and watched the battle.

The four-hundred-man cavalry unit attacked the city and right away the Austrians fired back with artillery. In a few minutes all of the cavalry and their horses had been hit. Then came a second Russian formation, a much larger one, with men as strong as oaks, led by a handsome officer wearing a Polish cape. He drew his sword, waved his cloak in the air and yelled: "Those sons-of-bitches, forward!" and charged ahead. He was struck by a bullet in the face and fell from his horse; the Cossacks rode past him and fell in turn, not one of them survived.

Then the Russian infantry and cavalry reassembled for the third time and entered the city in the evening without encountering any resistance; they stood in the marketplace of Monasterzyska, which the Austrians had meanwhile abandoned. That was at 6 p.m. The Russians set up camp in the marketplace, lit a fire and cooked dinner. The Jews came out of the surrounding houses and began to trade with the Russians right away. Suddenly the Austrians began firing with machine guns and rifles from all sides. The Russians fell into utter chaos and fled en masse. Many of them were killed, along with ninety Jews who had mixed in with the Russians previously on the marketplace. As if from nowhere the Hungarian cavalry rode in and the Cossacks fled ....

In Buczacz we soon understood that for the Russians things were not going as smoothly and easily as had initially appeared. After only three days the great and proud Russian mounted troops had to withdraw to Buczacz. Altogether the Russian column stretched all the way from Buczacz to Trybuchowce. As I walked with Mrs. Chymiakowska from the hospital to the city, it was impossible to cross the road because of the Muscovite retreat. Finally, there was a space between two columns; at the head of the second column a handsome officer wearing a Polish cape was riding. I asked him: "May we cross?" And he answered in excellent Polish: "Ladies and Gentlemen, you may cross," and greeted us with his sabre. We greeted him back and were amazed by the politeness of these people.

Everyone in the city was afraid to utter a word, we communicated with our eyes, in the hope that the Russians would soon leave. When we suddenly heard the order "Attention!" and the cavalry cry, "Forward!" our hoped were dashed.

Wounded Muscovites and Austrians were brought into the city. There was no longer enough space in the schools and the public buildings, and the wounded had to be brought into private homes. The city was full of Russians and Cossacks. The most unpleasant among them, however, were the Kuban Cossacks, who were simply referred to as Kubans. Whenever these Cossacks encountered anyone on the street, especially a Jew, or a well-dressed Jewish woman, they would loot them right there and then, laughing merrily as they robbed, especially watches, necklaces, brooches, rings, and money. One Cossack robbed a certain rich Jewish woman of her beautiful fur, mounted his horse, and rode away.

I observed such a scene myself. On Zyblikiewicz Street, right next to Świstek's house, two soldiers noticed Anderman, a house-owner.[23] One of the Muscovites immediately fixed his bayonet and yelled: "Stop!" As Anderman stood there, the other soldiers took from him his golden watch, a necklace, and a briefcase with 4,000 crowns, which at the time was a huge amount of money; and as they saw that Anderman was wearing beautiful new shoes, they yelled at him: "Take your shoes off!" Anderman removed his shoes and gave them to the soldiers. One of them put the shoes on right away and threw his old ones over Świstek's house's fence, then turned around to Anderman, finally kicked him, and called out: "Let's go." Anderman went home without watch, necklace, or money. No one was safe or protected from such looting.

In one case a Cossack attacked the court official Małachowski, a not particularly well-off man with many children. The Cossack took away his watch and his last 12 crowns. The incensed Małachowski said to him: "I hope that you will never see your own children again for what you did to me." The moment the Cossack heard that, he turned around, gave him back his watch and his money, and said: "Take back your curse." He also begged Małachowski to give him something. The latter gave him a crown, and the Cossack thanked him and went off. This was, I think, a devout and honest man.

The Muscovites were most thorough in plundering Jewish homes along Podhajecki Street. There they drove all the Jews out of their houses and left for themselves only the young and beautiful Jewish women, who offered no resistance whatsoever, since that would have not helped them in any way. The revelries on this street were most joyous, since as one group of soldiers left, another group arrived.

The Fire in the City

The defeat of the Muscovites in Monasterzyska caused the torching of Buczacz. The Russians thought they would be forced into a rapid retreat, and quickly gave the order to burn down Buczacz. For this task they had a special unit, the so-called igniters. They carried some kind of rags drenched with petrol in their hands. They went from house to house in the inner city and informed the inhabitants that they had half an hour to vacate their house, and to take with them whatever they could carry. An officer called Majer stood there with a watch and after half an hour would give the order to throw a lit torch into each of the houses through the window. Another soldier shot at the gasoline, which exploded instantly, so that the old stone houses in the city center were all burned down from the roof to the ground. Most of all the soldiers wanted to know whether the houses belonged to "yevreyi" [Jews]. If the owner was a Jew, the house was burned down right away. First the alcohol refinery and Binder's liquor factory on Kolejowa Street were burned down, then the private apartment of city councilor Aptykiewicz. They drenched wooden boards with schnapps and petrol and put them in the houses. Someone then lit them with matches and subsequently the whole street went up in flames. The brewery, the distillery, and Count Potocki's steam mill were also set on fire and the heat was so great that even at a great distance one could not pass by.

The real fire in the city center and the looting began on 24 August. But the Muscovites had to come up with a reason to perpetrate something so terrible. This happened as follows. A Kuban Cossack went to the central kiosk in the marketplace, and instead of paying demanded 10 crowns from the owner. But the owner refused to give away his money. The Cossack and his comrades then immediately began to throw all the goods out to the street, and whoever passed by took whatever they wanted. Thereafter an entire squad of soldiers arrived and began breaking into other businesses as well and threw whatever they could put their hands on out to the street. The Jews locked up their businesses, but the Cossacks broke open the doors with their bayonets.

In this manner all sorts of goods were thrown out to the street, such as cloth, shoes, bicycles, books, linen, musical instruments, irons. From Wrzesiński's pharmacy all medicines were plundered and thrown out to the marketplace; it did not even occur to them that they might need these medicines themselves. Ukrainians drove or walked from the outskirts and the nearby villages of Soroki, Żyznomierz, Nagórzanka, Podzameczek, and Podlesie and looted alongside the Cossacks, and our Jews also came with carts so that everyone grabbed what came into their hands.

War awakens the basest instincts in people. It was calculated that the goods plundered that day were valued at 46 million crowns in prewar currency.

We went to sleep, but in our clothes. Yet just as we shut our eyes the carpenter Tiszler, a very poor but honest Jew, knocked on our door, saying: "Please get up, the city is burning!"

We stepped out of the house and saw a vast sea of flames over the marketplace. All the mansions in the square, in which the wealthiest residents lived, had been torched without exception; here were also the most beautiful and finest businesses, such as that of Seligdowicz, or Prusak's drugstore. Right next to them the peasant cooperative store was on fire, as were Rogozinski and Müller's stores, Halberg's bookstore, and others. When the merchant Szwarcberg tried to save his property, they stabbed him in the stomach with bayonets. The fire spread out to the May Third Street and there burned down stores with clothing, furniture, ironware, bicycles, kosher food, the pharmacy, the watchmaker, in short, millions of crowns in prewar currency were burned down. The Cossacks, soldiers, peasants, Jews, city folk, threw all the goods, household appliances, and bed linen out to the street and everyone took what they wanted. The Muscovites took the more valuable things for themselves and transported them to Russia.

This fire continued for no less than two weeks.

Lieutenant Majer systematically inspected all the houses, and when anyone tried to save anything, the Muscovites fired their weapons; to be sure, no one was killed, but everyone was anxious. The Muscovites had dismantled and shipped to Russia all storage casks, barrels, and firefighting equipment right at the beginning of the occupation. The fire gradually came nearer to Zyblikiewicz Street, where the residents lived in smaller houses with thatched roofs. The residents took their belongings out to the gardens and waited, since soon their houses too would burn down, because huge sparks were raining down on us.

Because we had not eaten for three days, and the children were hungry, my wife went to the bakery on the marketplace to buy three loaves of bread from a baker we knew. The Muscovites had also not received any bread supplies at that time. Suddenly Lieutenant Majer was standing in front of us and asking: "Do you have bread?" "I have some," answered my wife. "Hand it over, please." The children handed him the bread reluctantly, and Majer ordered the Cossacks to put the bread in a basket; but when he saw the children's sad expressions he asked: "Do you have any bread at home?" "No, this is all we have." Majer then pulled a loaf out of the basket and gave it to the children while my wife asked: "Will you burn down our houses too?" To which Majer said: "Drench your roofs with water so they don't catch fire."

Right away I climbed with my son and Świstek's younger son on the roof. The others brought water from the Strypa and drenched the endangered spots. As the neighbors saw this, they thought the Muscovites would shoot me. But then a Cossack came riding by and called out: "Yes, save your houses, pour water on them, we burn down only the Jews."

Then the neighbors and even the Jews flocked in to help. For days and nights, we sat on the roofs of the houses and in this manner the houses on our street were saved. Five days long we had almost nothing to eat; only on Friday did we receive some flour and had a meal, which tasted better than the food served by Lucullus.[24] On that day we moved from the apartment to the school building and took with us only the most essential household items.

More and more wounded Austrians and Muscovites were being brought into the city, and I gave instructions to collect the mattresses that were scattered in the streets and to bring them into the school building, so that we could take into the great hall of the school thirteen Muscovites and one Austrian soldier—a certain Tarfikowski from Czortków with a rifle shot in the face.

Mrs. Markowska brought rice, tea, and sugar and my wife prepared from that meals to fortify the sick and the wounded, who were very thankful for this help. Among the wounded was also a Kuban Cossack, who had broken into a jewelry store, stolen many watches and attached a golden brooch to his shirt. He had a head wound and fever, but every once in a while, he checked his loot, fearful that it might be taken from him. The Muscovites made fun of him and said: "The idiot doesn't even know whether he will be alive tomorrow. There are no doctors; but he is happy with this treasure."

Another Kuban Cossack was lying under the oven, and when my wife brought him a cup of tea, he looked at her suspiciously and said: "Drink that yourself." He was clearly certain that we wanted to poison him. My wife tried the tea in his presence with a smile, and only then did he drink it. The Muscovites were having great fun over this and said: "This woman takes you in here with all her heart and you don't trust her." The man had a gunshot wound in his leg, over the knee. As he got better, he took my walking stick in order to go to the market, and the Muscovites asked him, "Where are you going?" to which he answered, "to loot." He came back after a couple of hours with a backpack full of sweets, chocolate and other treats. He distributed everything to the soldiers. They ate them, because they were hungry, but they still chided him: "For sure the candy is yummy, but you are a thief," and they all laughed together with the Cossack.

That same evening three "igniters" with petrol showed up intending to burn down the school, but when they saw the wounded soldiers they said: "This is a hospital," and left. This is how the good Lord rewards good deeds, since, had I not taken in the wounded, the school would have most definitely been burned down.

Among the wounded there was also a Jew from Wilno, but he was not wounded, only a malingerer, who drank tea and ate barley soup, and once he had rested, he took his rifle and fled to the Jews of Buczacz. He hid among them for several weeks and sold matches on the marketplace. It was there that my own son recognized him, and that kike became so scared that he was never seen again in the city. Yet no one denounced him, neither the Catholics nor the Jews.

The fighting in the district went on, and the Muscovites kept advancing, all the way to Niżniów [40 km southwest of Buczacz]. After the battle of Bertniki [on the eastern approaches of Monasterzyska], the fallen warriors were buried in such shallow graves, that dogs and foxes pulled out the corpses and ate them, and the sky filled with flocks of ravens and crows. We heard that the Russians had been held back by the Austrians near Niżniów, where the latter had built a massive network of trenches and barbed wire obstacles. Had the Dniester crested, the Russians could have been halted here, but the cunning General Hötzendorf had not taken into account that the level of water in the

Dniester at that time would be so low, since there had been a drought,
and that the river could be crossed on foot in several locations, where
the water reached only one's chin, something that happened only once
every thirty years. Several Tyrolean[25] peasants showed the Muscovites
where to go, and thus they crossed to the right bank of the Dniester
by the heights of the village of Ostrów [northwest of Niżniów] and
then advanced on to Stanisławów, Halicz, Kalusz, and Kołomyja in the
Carpathians.

A week later the Muscovites told us that Lwów had also been captured, as well as Gródek Jagielloński [some 30 km west of Lwów], and
that now their troops were already at the gates of Przemyśl [on the San
river and the current Polish-Ukrainian border]. It must have been a
huge battle, because we could hear the weeks-long roar of the artillery,
day and night. I would often stand on the Fedor with a map in my hands
and could locate more or less precisely where the battle was taking place
by the thunder of the artillery shells. I could identify where the fighting
was occurring by listening to the cannon fire. The sound of the fighting
came from the southwest, from which we assumed that the Muscovites
were in the Carpathians but had not yet crossed over; nor did the
Muscovite newspapers report anything to that effect.

From the direction of Przemyśl one could also hear shell fire, although
Przemyśl and Buczacz are 210 km from each other [in reality 240 km].
We received news of bloody battles. The Cossacks and the Muscovites
who returned from the battlefields related that to us. There were also
Austrian prisoners of war, as well as many women and girls who returned
to the city. All of them told us about the fighting in the West. Newspapers
were also being sold, but they were very expensive; for instance, the
"Neue Presse," a newspaper published in Vienna, cost as much as 50
crowns per issue, so that whoever wanted to read the newspaper, paid a
crown per hour. Often one could read that Hötzendorf was not much of
a hero; he was cited as saying that the war would last only a few weeks
and that soon we would think about it only as a bad dream.

But we waited in vain.

Buczacz was burning for the third week. The houses by the St.
Pokrova [Greek Catholic] Church now also began to burn. But there we
saw the Muscovites themselves put out the fire. What happened? The
houses in Buczacz straddle the main road, along which the Muscovites
were transporting their munitions to the battlefields. This road had
become so hot because of the fire, that it became impossible to travel
on it, until finally even the Muscovites recognized that it was senseless
to let the city burn down, since they were thereby causing damage to
themselves. By my calculation, by that time 125 of the most beautiful

and largest mansions had burned down, not counting the commercial buildings and smaller homes, nor the large steam mills, in whose stores thousands of flour and grain sacks were stored, nor the distilleries, the breweries, and the liquor refinery. Only the outskirts had been spared, along with the school building, the [Roman Catholic] church, two Greek Catholic churches, the court building, the district council, and Kolejowa Street. All businesses were plundered, but also the houses and apartments of those people who had fled.

After the capture of Monasterzyska the Muscovites wanted to loot the famous tobacco factory there. They found the gate locked and ordered the two guards to open it. Since these two refused to do so, they stabbed them with their bayonets, took their keys from them, and entered the factory. In the main offices they ordered one of the clerks to show them around the factory, the machines and the stocks. This clerk went with them from one room to the other. At that point the soldiers rushed into the factory and began to throw the inventory out of the windows; they took for themselves the most expensive cigars and cigarettes and sold them cheaply in Buczacz and other towns. A pack of cigarettes made by the firm Regalitas could be purchased for 10 talers, or just a few kopeks. Even schoolchildren and those in the first grade, Catholics as well as Jews, smoked thick cigars on the street and on the marketplace and laughed straight in the faces of their old teachers, because they knew that they could not tell them anything in that environment. The youth had no shame and became unrestrained, stealing what they could, whereas others did not even have to steal, since one could find objects on the street, and there was no one there to admonish them. Had anyone dared to berate the youth, he would receive such an impolite response that would make even an oven blush from shame. The Jews with their foresight sold tobacco and cigarettes for knockdown prices and thereby made brilliant business.

The city residents flocked to the fields to collect potatoes, without asking themselves who owned these fields, because ultimately the potatoes would have all frozen as the distilleries [normally using them to make vodka] had been entirely burned own. The stores of the landowners and merchants in the train station were destroyed, and the Muscovites sold the grain, flour, and barley as well as other wares for close to nothing. Moreover, every Muscovite had a woman in the city and the outskirts, whose husband was at the front. Young women from Nagórzanka threw themselves so eagerly at the Muscovites that the latter came to despise them. For half a ruble one could buy a sack full of unbaked barley. The entire main street from the railroad station to the other side of the city was partially covered with flour and grains. Entire pieces of equipment and machines were being dismantled in the tobacco factory, the steam mills, the breweries, and the mansions and carried off on carts.

The city looked terrible; everywhere there were blankets and pillows scattered on the streets and in the ditches, and anyone could pick up whatever they liked. Fumes were still rising from several houses, and a thick, black cloud of smoke hung over the entire city for several more weeks, so that one's eyes would fill with tears; human jackals were wandering the streets in search of loot.

Nevertheless, we had a governing authority; several days after the Muscovites marched in, a commandant came to the city. It was reported that he forbade looting, so that we had to worry more about looting by our own citizens than by the Cossacks and the Muscovites. Gradually the looting ceased, a Russian gendarmerie was established, and when looting did happen it was considered more or less legal. As I was coming out of the school building, a large, handsome, and well-dressed officer came up to me. He turned out to be the city commandant. He asked me: "Which way are you going, principal?" He stretched out his hand, introduced himself and said in perfect Polish: "Lieutenant Savitsky."[26] "Siewiński," I answered. "Our family names are very similar, but unfortunately we belong to opposing camps." "That is true," I responded. "Perhaps we are also mistaken in our politics." He agreed and went off to inspect the school building. Within a few moments he had looked through the entire building, all classrooms and floors.

Shortly after he left the building a soldier came to ask whether he could take the map of the district the lieutenant had seen hanging on the wall. I wondered how Savitsky had noticed that map during such a brief visit. Several more Russian officers who had visited together the building of the Sokół gymnastics association were standing on the street. They were impressed by the large gymnastics' hall, as well as by the portraits of famous Polish statesmen that were hanging there. The Russian Lieutenant removed his cap in view of these paintings, as if he were in a church or a sitting room. He might have asked himself whether these were Poles. A few days later Savitsky marched on with the army and was killed near Bertniki, perhaps struck by a Polish bullet, since the troops fighting there were Austrian reservists who came from this region.

A few days after the capture of Buczacz a Russian hospital was put up here, but I will say more about it later. Lieutenant Savitsky was replaced by a new [district] administrator, who came to Buczacz with an entire staff of clerks, gendarmes, and armed soldiers. The head of this office was called Sheptelich.[27] This was a man of considerable height, very slim, with a most agreeable and sympathetic face, always smoothly shaven. In his interactions with people, especially the intelligentsia, he was very pleasant; he also spoke outstanding Polish, Russian, French, and German and also knew the Ukrainian dialect typically spoken in the region of Białystok. He was said to have come from the Romanov clan ....

The following other people were members of the city administration: Dziewanowski, a Pole ..., an honest peasant, but also a regular drinker, who was always drunk. Antoniewicz, formerly a teacher at the Buczacz gymnasium and leader of the Polish youth in the Sokół Association. Although this defector never hurt anyone, no one wanted to shake his hand, neither the Poles nor the Muscovites, since they all saw him as a traitor and would have nothing to do with him .... Rudenko, who was a real Ukrainian, a Haidamak,[28] and was always neatly dressed ....

The best among the Muscovites was Tomychek. A true Don Juan. To be sure, he had a very nice and attractive wife, but he sent her back to Russia, and found himself many other Julias in Buczacz. He constantly slept with them. One of these Julias became pregnant by him, but the child died in childbirth. Tomychek was so depressed by this that he shot himself in the head. One of the least pleasant among [the Russian administrators] was a certain Pawlot, a former Austrian officer, who had deserted, and was previously the director of the railwaymen's home in Buczacz. He came from Sambor [200 km northwest of Buczacz] and was the son of a peasant. He did not provide for his father, who lived with him in Buczacz, and so the poor old man suffered hunger. I'll have more to say about this Pawlot.

The commander of the gendarmerie was Medinsky,[29] a Russified Pole, whose wife was a pretty, clever, and agreeable Pole. Despite that, Medinsky had another mistress in Buczacz and did not even try to conceal this. I will not give the family name of this mistress here on account of her children, and so she will die forgotten. She was a very handsome woman whose husband was serving at the front. Medinsky looked just like Kuklinowski from Sienkiewicz's novel, *The Deluge*,[30] a tall, stooped man. The Jews were very scared of him, because he always walked around with a whip and not a day would go by without him punishing a couple of Jews with it on account of their impertinence. But at times he also struck Catholics.

The Muscovites ordered the butchers to at least cover the pork meat sold at the market with paper. This instruction was completely correct, since during the war thousands of people, carts, and animals went through the city, and the dust from the main street covered all roofs, the air being so full of dust that one could hardly breathe.

The district governor Sheptelich and his underlings made brilliant business in Buczacz. They ordered all the inhabitants of the district to pay the war taxes in crowns. The official rate for the ruble was at the time 3 crowns and 33 hellers.[31] The Jews sold the ruble for 2 crowns. Sheptelich bought the ruble for 2 crowns and paid the taxes to the government in rubles at the official rate. He kept the profit for himself.

Various decrees were issued [by the city administration], for instance: people were not allowed to have more vodka at home than needed for personal consumption, but that amount was not determined. The gendarmes would therefore go to the homes of the rich Jews and search for vodka, and if they could find none, one of them would hide a liter of vodka under the bed. Immediately thereafter another gendarmerie squad would arrive, find the vodka, and order the Jews to pay a fine of 3,000 rubles or spend three months in jail. This would usually set off negotiations that normally ended with the payment of 500 rubles. One Jew refused to pay the 500 rubles and was immediately imprisoned and treated so badly that he paid the fine within a couple of days.

The apartment of postal director Getter was looted to the ground and destroyed. He wanted to marry his daughter and had prepared everything for the event. It was all plundered, however, and the loot was brought to the district offices, to Mrs. Sheptelich and her daughters Mica, Kica, and Marina.

Instructions were disseminated throughout the district that villagers and estate leasers may not leave their places of residence. It thus happened that when an estate owner or leaser had to travel to the forest or a fair on business, this was reported right away to the district office. Immediately thereafter a district commission would make its way to the property, eject the wife and children, including their nanny, from the house, and seal the door. No one dared touch the seal! The owner would then have to travel to Buczacz and only after he paid his way out of this business would the seal be removed.

In several stores there was still some cloth .... The Russian ladies would visit such stores and demand to be shown everything; they would then have the material cut and adjusted and sent to their homes. And woe to a merchant who failed to deliver or asked for payment! The Muscovites led a merry life in Buczacz and, generally speaking, they were not even bad people.

The poorest of all were the elementary school teachers, whereas the civil servants and tax officials could still borrow money from the Jews and groceries were not expensive .... The teachers were independent civil servants, whom no one wanted to help; that is, those who worked most closely with the people were left with no bread to eat. As winter rapidly approached, there were no stocks of coal in Buczacz or in all of Podolia. One might have saved oneself with wood from the surrounding forests, but among the teachers no one had enough money to buy even one cubic meter of wood.

I therefore went to [District Governor] Sheptelich and reported to him on the dire state of the teachers in the city. He instructed me to prepare a list of those teachers and on that basis, I was assigned 120 cubic meters of timber from the manorial estate of Mr. Hortyński, so that each [teacher] would receive 3 cubic meters.

As regards money things looked even worse. Thanks to the efforts by Mr. Seligdowicz, the merchants in the city collected 2,000 crowns for us teachers and gave the money to the mayor to keep. But the latter had nothing better to do than to report this to [Gendarmerie Chief] Medinsky, who claimed that he should distribute the money to the teachers himself. When my colleague Keffermüller heard about this he went to Sheptelich and asked for the money to be handed over. Medinsky also arrived and the two of them whispered to each other in a foreign language, precisely in the manner that the Jews speak with each other when they want to cheat someone. Then Sheptelich turned back to Keffermüller and asserted that in this matter his hands were tied. And so, the money was lost like a dog in a country fair.

The Soup Kitchen

The Muscovites wanted to appear humane and established a soup kitchen for the city poor in the Sokół building. They installed there an oven and sent written requests to the estate owners for wood, potatoes, flour, meat, bacon, beets, semolina, beans, money, and so forth. This friendly request was accompanied by an order. Woe to anyone who dares not to donate! They would destroy the entire estate. Mrs. Sheptelich invited the city's intelligentsia to a symposium. I too received an invitation. This was the first time that I saw her at close quarters. She was an unusually beautiful woman; next to her sat Mr. Medinsky, as well as Sheptelich's three daughters, Mica, Kica, and Marina, who were also just as beautiful, but were made up. It has come this far, that the Muscovite women put on make-up!

On the right sat the women of Buczacz, and next to them the Russian administrators as well as our gentlemen of the intelligentsia. Medinsky made a short speech in Russian; he claimed that he could not speak Polish, which was in fact untrue. Mrs. Sheptelich made a very long and beautiful speech, also in Russian. This was the first time that I heard Russian spoken by an educated woman. The speech changed my view of the Russian language. We had become used to hearing only curses from the Muscovites, such as "son of a bitch" or "son of a whore," and we thought that if we could say these words, we would know Russian. In fact, the Russian language is very melodic and charming. Although I now know Czech and Croatian and a few other Slavic languages, I would rank Russian in second place after Polish. Mrs. Sheptelich said that because of the war the city population was suffering from hunger and want, and that in order to help it the Russian government would obtain food, and all those present were asked to cooperate. No one refused.

The soup kitchen was ceremoniously opened. The building of the Sokół had been festively decorated, the stairs and the hallways were furnished with branches of spruce, and on the roof of the Sokół building, where in the past the Polish flag had been hoisted, a huge red-blue-and-white [Russian] flag was hung, which caused pain in our hearts.

Long tables were also put up, bedecked with red tablecloths seized from the stores [in town]. On the wall a simple portrait of Tsar Nicholas II was put up, and to its right and left hung the artistically painted and beautiful portraits of [Tadeusz] Kościuszko and [Adam] Mickiewicz.[32] I don't know what Tadeusz and Adam would have said about this, had they seen it. The Greek Catholic priest Nastayko conducted Mass and made a short speech. The hall of the Sokół was full, and everyone behaved as if they were in a festive mood, although many were about to burst out laughing. Finally, the plates were handed out and a Russian dish was served, a pot with some cabbage, potatoes, beans, beef, pork, and bacon. Everything was doused with borscht and boiled; at the time the population of Buczacz was still picky, whereas a year later one would have queued up for such a nourishing meal.

Later the nuns cooked in the soup kitchen and better met the city residents' taste. The following morning the previously mentioned Pawlot came to the hall of the Sokół, pointed at the portraits of Kościuszko und Mickiewicz, and said: "Where do the paintings of these agitators come from?" He ordered the paintings removed, and the only remaining portrait was that of Tsar Nicholas II. A few days later, as Mrs. Medinsky was sitting at one of the tables, a peasant from one of the nearby villages bowed to her, pointed at the portrait of Nicholas II, and asked: "Is it true that this is our best beloved Tsar?" Mrs. Medinsky made it appear as if she did not understand (she is Polish). The peasant asked again. Mrs. Medinsky indignantly turned away from him. But the stubborn peasant persisted and asked for a third time. Then she answered with an angry voice: "That is true! That is true!" Could she have responded in any other way in this situation and under these circumstances?

This kitchen remained open until the end of 1915. The establishment of such a kitchen proved that the Muscovites were not bad people. During the severe frosts in winter the Russians positioned a large samovar in the marketplace, where hot tea was offered to the Jews day and night, along with a slice of bread.

In November 1914, when the Muscovites were still at the height of their power, all the officers stationed in Buczacz met in my school and one of them said: "What have we gained from having occupied almost all of Galicia if we have already lost our campaign? We should have begun it like Peter the Great, Charles XII, or Alexander I against Napoleon, we should have delivered the deadly strike against the Germans, but now our entire élan is already lost." None of the officers present there contradicted him.

How Did We Live?

In my house there was great poverty; we had run out of money and we did not have a single potato for winter, nor flour, although there were four of us. Things were the same for all civil servants and teachers, who had been subjected to the Muscovite invasion. But the good Lord does not forsake anyone, as long as one appeals to His help. Right at the beginning of the war I decided to go to church every day. There I appealed to the Lord, the Holy Mother of God, and the Guardian Angel for the good fortune of my sons at the front, and I was certain that God would hear me, as the Lord Jesus Christ had said: "Knock, and it shall be opened unto you; ask, and it shall be given you."[33] And so the Lord sent me a strange dream, in which my deceased father came to me in the cellar, and pointed at the barrel with cabbage and the [stored] potatoes and said: "Have no worries, you do not have to starve in war." [In the dream] I was also walking through the city, where there were no Russians, only legionnaires, among them my sons, and the book trader Halber offered me a map, in which I saw the Polish borders extended far to the north and far east from Równe and Dubno [220 and 180 km north of Buczacz, respectively].[34]

On the very same day my colleague Chymiakowski sent me a sack of potatoes and then my colleague Czeżanowski sent me another four sacks of potatoes. In the afternoon we were visited by my wife's brother, Adam, and received five sacks from him, along with cabbage and bacon; he also loaned us some money. Finally, school inspector Zenon Zaklika also sent me four sacks of potatoes. Here I must recall one person who deserves it. This is the Greek Catholic priest Lapinsky, the provost of Bobulińce [15 km north of Buczacz]. When he heard about the poverty in Buczacz, he appealed to his congregation, and the honest villagers, all Ruthenians, donated eight carts full of potatoes, beans, and beets. Of those, seven were donated to the residents of the city and one for me. The venerable Father Lapinsky asked me to take the potatoes, and if I did not need them, then to distribute them to my acquaintances. Naturally this was a great help to the acquaintances during these difficult times. Honor to these people and the worthy residents of Bobulińce.

Unexplained, Strange Apparitions

I had a habit of going every day to the cemetery on the Fedor [Hill]. This site was located next to the river above the school building and a steep ravine. There I would pray to the Lord's angel and for the souls of the dead, while hearing the distant thunder of the artillery firing ceaselessly near Przemyśl. The event I wish to recall happened on 24 October 1914. Standing there with a map in my hands, I could estimate where the battles were taking place at that moment. Suddenly I heard the heavy breathing of my two legionnaire sons coming from the south and could hear the clear sound of shots from their rifles. I then turned to the west and could feel my eldest son Józef's breath. At first, I thought I was hallucinating, yet I clearly heard my sons' breathing and gunfire.

After that I went to the cemetery every day, and after a prayer for the souls of the dead I would go further on the Fedor and would hear in the silence where my sons were and always knew on which battlefield they were fighting. Sometimes my wife and I would see in a dream that the boys were sick. When our sons returned home, they told us that they had indeed been sick at that time, and that when I heard their shots and breathing for the first time on the Fedor, the Legions were fighting next to Mołotków [100 km southwest of Buczacz]. Later Zygmunt wrote me that at the outskirts of Mołotków on 24 October 1914 his rifle became so hot from constant firing, that he could no longer hold it in his hands and had to let the rifle cool off in the snow. Next to him two hundred brothers fell, while he was protected by a guardian angel. Our eldest son [Józef] was wounded near Użok [250 km west of Buczacz] in the Carpathians. At the time we had an odd foreboding and ended up being proven right. The was the work of the guardian angel ....

The Tsar's Name Day

The tsar's name day arrived on 14 December 1914. Orders went out to hoist Russian flags throughout the city and to position candles in the windows in the evening. The Jews especially outdid themselves in decorating the town; the larger the building, the larger the flag that was hoisted from it. In the evening the building of the district administration, where the Russian administration was located at the time, was lit up with paper lanterns; instructions were also given to celebrate the victory of the Muscovites that very day in Przemyśl, which was presented to Tsar Nicholas II as a gift.

This was precisely what had happened four months earlier, when city Mayor Stern offered the city of Belgrade as a gift to Emperor Franz Josef. During the day Medinsky and Stern searched the cellars in town for wine and found some at the home of the Roman Catholic priest. This was the sacramental wine for Mass kept by Father Stanisław Gromnicki. The elated Medinsky requisitioned the entire stock and brought it to the district administration office.

The Jewish musicians booked for the event had been standing on the street next to the administration office since early evening. Apart from them some two hundred soldiers were there, arrayed in two rows. All of a sudden Medinsky emerged from the building and called upon the soldiers to salute, upon which the two hundred soldiers called out, "Hail our great emperor!" Thereafter the musicians began to play, and everyone sang, "God save our Tsar." Many Jews wearing hats were also standing around, and they did not notice that they were surrounded from all sides by gendarmes carrying leather whips. Suddenly Medinsky called out: "Caps off!" and the Jews, whether because they did not understand the order [given in Russian] or did not hear it because of all the noise, did not remove their hats. At that very moment they were attacked with whips. The Jews tried to flee, but that was not allowed, and they were compelled to stand there in the cold without hats on their heads. One of the Jews was struck so hard on the head that he passed out and had to be carried home.

As the celebrations were going on in the administration office, one of the Jews came by and said softly: "Here you are having a ball, while over there in Przemyśl seventy thousand Russians were killed today!"

That news spread like wildfire in the city as well as among the celebrating Muscovites. An hour later, precisely at 9 p.m., a Cossack came galloping with a dispatch. He stopped the horse on the street and ran directly to Sheptelich. Crowds of guests were assembled there, among them also Father Nestayko and Mayor Stern. Suddenly all the lamps and lanterns were snuffed out and the crowd was sent home. The musicians were also sent home, and when they asked for their fee, Medinsky threatened them with a leather whip. On the same day an order had been issued in Stanisławów that lanterns should be lit in the marketplace and the center city, a meter apart from each other, but already at

5 p.m. instructions went to remove the lanterns and put out the lights. Curiously, the Jews already knew about the defeat of the Muscovites an hour before the Russian rulers did. Thereupon the Russian governor [of Galicia Georgiy] Bobrinsky issued a new order: whereas Jews had already been forbidden to leave their places of residence, now they were not even allowed to go to another village. Any Jew who wished to travel had to acquire a travel permit, for which the officials charged money. But what happened? When the Jews showed the permit to the soldiers, the soldier would tear it up and demand money from them.

The local female residents often fell in love with the Russians. In the house under the castle a company of Muscovites was quartered for several months; they were sent to the front only in January [1915], and the women cried and lamented their departure. One of these women even hung a necklace around the neck of a Russian soldier, and as the Russian took it, he said: "I take it, who knows what good it is, but woe to you, if they beat us, we'll be back." Our priests were troubled by this, especially Father Wracha, who accused the woman of adultery, but this was of very little use.

In Podlesie [just across the Strypa east of Buczacz] lived a beautiful young lady called Fipałkowska. The Muscovite who was quartered in her house fell in love with her and wanted to marry her, claiming that at home he had forty hectares of land. Fijałkowska consulted a priest, who told her to decline, which she did. The Muscovite took it so much to heart that he went out to the street with a gun and shot himself and died right there and then. He was placed in an open coffin. Miss Fijałkowska followed the deceased in the funeral procession and wept, but she was innocent of his death. The conduct of this Muscovite made a great impression on us, and we recognized that Muscovites, too, had feelings.

On one occasion a senior officer showed up in our school, a slim and tall man, clearly intelligent, and said in Russian: "Please show me the classrooms." My colleague Pfeffermülle came over and we chatted with the officer. Strangely, this Pole [Pfeffermülle] suggested that when he spoke Ruthenian with the Russian, the Muscovite understood him. But the Muscovites cannot stand this language, and I have seen Muscovites throwing books written in Ruthenian to the ground with great disgust.

And so, I began speaking Ruthenian with this officer, but he responded by saying: "Speak Polish with me, since I don't understand this Khokhol-language." The Muscovites called the Ruthenians Khokhols [a pejorative term]. We acceded to his wish and understood each other perfectly. The corridors and halls [of the school] were decorated with beautiful paintings and ornaments. There were portraits of Polish kings by [Jan] Matejko, and [Artur] Grottger's paintings inspired by [Henryk] Sienkiewicz's novel *With Fire and Sword*.[35] The officer looked carefully at all the paintings and suddenly said: "[Jan] Skrzetuski [the fictional hero of *With Fire and Sword*] was a bandit!" "So you've read the Trilogy?" we asked. "Oh yes, I know Polish literature..." ... We returned to Grottger's cycle, titled "War," and the officer said: "This is a real painter, poet, and artist." I responded: "The Russians have a soul mate of Grottger's—[Vasily] Vereshchagin."[36] "Oh, yes, Vereshchagin is old Russia." I responded to this: "Such masters as Vereshchagin, Grottger, Rubens, Raphael, give honor not only to their own nations, but honor humanity as a whole." He liked this statement very much, after which he took a pamphlet out of his briefcase and gave it to me to read.

This was an appeal by the Grand Duke Nicholas to the Poles, printed in Polish and Russian. He then said to us: "You Poles already have your Poland." He bid farewell with a military gesture and left. Already on the following day a rumor went around Buczacz that the Grand Duke Nicholas was in the city.[37] On the same day that he was with us, he also went incognito to the officers' quarters, where he encountered a drunk officer, became enraged and tore the officer's epaulets off his uniform. When I later described to the officers the appearance of the refined officer who had visited our school, they confirmed that it was the Grand Duke Nicholas....

In the girls' school there had been a cooking course before the war, where young women learned to cook; and what they cooked, they also had to eat. There was a large kitchen there, with copper ovens, three large cabinets, and in them beautiful porcelain plates, new cutlery, spoons, forks, and knives. This had cost 8,000 crowns before the war. One of the teachers, who was very talkative, was incautious and told Mrs. Sheptelich about this kitchen. She came to the kitchen with gendarmes right after lunch and ordered to open the cabinets and took the entire tableware, plates, and cutlery, as war booty; in this manner, it was all lost.

With the Jews things were always taken care of quickly. When one of them was caught black marketeering, he would be brought to the administration office right away and given fifteen strokes with a cane, not over the pants but on the naked flesh, so that blood was running. Israel was seized with great fear and they tried at least to be a little more honest, and thereby to diminish this furious zeal of the goyim. The Jews gave the entire city a Russian look. They hung huge signs and notice boards in Russian script from the storefronts such as "tobacco store" and so forth ....

At one point when Sheptelich and his clique needed money they ordered [Mayor] Stern to produce a list of rich Jews. They were then taken as prisoners of war in the direction of Tarnopol, and it was announced that they would be liberated in return for payment. These approximately twenty Jews went on foot to Chodaczków [80 km northeast of Buczacz]. There the Jews collected some 10,000 rubles and handed them to the escorting gendarme. He then turned back to Buczacz along with the soldiers assigned to him but left the Jews on the way. These Jews complained about Stern: "Haman was hanged from a fifty-foot high gallows, but the gallows for Stern should be even higher." ...

In Potok Złoty, the painter Bergstof together with some other Jews got hold of a whole cartload of matches. They brought them to Buczacz, but then the six of them began to fight with each other. A gendarme came along and ordered to bring the matches to the administration office, where they were confiscated. Bergstof and his partners were each given ten strokes on the naked flesh and then thrown out of the door. The nurse Dudiowa, for long a wealthy businesswoman, also sold sweets on the marketplace. A youth came along and stole the sweets. The Jewish woman began to scream. A gendarme heard her and brought both the youth and the Jewish woman to the office. No one asked them anything, the Jewish woman and the youth were both put on the bench and she was given fifteen strokes with a leather whip on the naked flesh; the youth was only threatened with the whip and thrown out.

This is what justice looked like!

The Retreat of the Muscovites from the Carpathians

Things continued this way until 22 February 1915. That night there was a great commotion among the Muscovites in the administration office. A formation of Muscovites, who called themselves Samarians[38] had come from the area of Niżniów. These were large fellows with gentle faces, but all rather downcast and traumatized. Many of them had no leather jackets, no weapons, and their legs were wrapped in all kinds of rags. One of these units was led by a Pole named Pendykowski. He came on horseback directly to our school. I had to show him all the classrooms and hallways in the school. As he observed the good facilities in the school, he said: "I pity this beautiful building, the soldiers will destroy everything."

As he had warned, the soldiers, who marched into the city in rows of four, quickly occupied the entire building. Only now did I begin to feel the occupation in my own school. The whole building shook from their hobnailed boots and weapons; day and night it was as loud as a beehive, and the yells and noise could be heard throughout the neighborhood.

Within a few short days the beautiful school could no longer be recognized. The soldiers destroyed everything, plundered the cabinets and the bookshelves and burned the school papers in the oven; they met the call of nature directly out of the windows. Six officers set themselves up in my school offices, right next to my study. They were actually honorable men, though without much education .... In one of the classrooms stood a samovar for thirty cups (sixty glasses). This samovar was constantly in use, from morning at 4 a.m. to evening at 10 p.m., each of them drank at least thirty cups per day of so-called chai .... Along with that they ate bread, meat, butter, bacon, and let us too try everything. We would have offended them had we not eaten their food.

We asked them where they came from; initially they did not respond, but then they were seized by sorrow and rage and told us: "We have been fighting in the Carpathians for half a year, and many of us have fallen there, which no one counts, but the worst were the legionnaires. These little devils would sneak in from everywhere, hiding behind schools, firing again and again with their rifles, but never visible. Finally, we retreated from the mountains all the way to Kołomyja [75 km southwest of Buczacz] and were ambushed there .... Then a huge artillery shell fell on our unit of three hundred men, but we ... kept going without any supplies to Buczacz. We once numbered sixty thousand. Today there is only a handful of us left."

Another one related that before the war he was a gymnasium teacher: "Is it not a disgrace for our civilization in the twentieth century that human beings are slaughtering each other like beasts, and for what reason? So that this dynasty and its lackeys can live in comfort, while you wretches drop dead for that? What have we got against the Austrians, the Germans, the Poles that we need to fight them? Still the stupid people, instead of destroying the whole power clique, go over there and murder the innocent, who would like to live just as much as we do."

That was the first time I heard the Russians cursing the Tsar. They turned out to be honest people, unlike the way our people described them. Every Muscovite, even those from the remotest province, was able to write and read extremely well, since the Russian government made sure that each Muscovite could attend a good school, whereas Poles [in Russian-ruled Poland] were not allowed to study unless it was in Russian ....

It was repeatedly said that soldiers in Russia were flogged. On the third day after the arrival of the Samarians in Buczacz I noticed a row of soldiers in the marketplace. People said that someone was about to be shot. But then a bench was brought out, a soldier lay on it and received fifty strokes. The bloodied soldier was then taken to the hospital.

The soldiers related that this punishment was worse than execution, since in the latter case one died right away, whereas after receiving fifty lashes the internal organs were damaged, and one would die within a year. "What was this man's offense that he was so terribly punished?" "He stole five pounds from the store and distributed that among his comrades." "It is a sin to punish someone so terribly for such a minor offense." "It serves as a deterrence," [responded one of the Russian NCOs]. "Had he stolen from a Jew, or from a wealthy person, nothing would have happened to him, he would have even been praised, had he done so cunningly and elegantly, but one may not steal from an army store." ...

I locked my house and brought the most important private items to the school building. In between I found out that the soldiers had taken over my private apartment. When I came there, the door had been taken out, the cabinets were smashed, and the drawers with all my own and my wife's things had been ransacked. The Muscovites had looted them and walked over our things. There must have been forty people there, some were sleeping, and others were sitting around drinking vodka, others still were cooking something on the pans and in the chamber pots. I possessed about two thousand books, which were scattered everywhere, some of them in the oven, serving as fuel. Even my glasses were intentionally trodden under and left by the window. I recalled the German proverb "make the best of a bad situation"[39] and said politely to the soldiers: "Zdrast" ["Hello" in Russian]. I was answered impolitely, and one of the senior men asked me: "Who are you?" "I am the owner of this house, and everything here belongs to me." "Then you're not a Jew?" he asked me. "No, I'm a Christian, a Catholic." The soldier responded: "Oh, that's too bad, we thought that everything here belonged to a Jew, that's why we caused so much damage; forgive us."

They had not eaten anything, since their field kitchen had not arrived yet, and thus one of them asked: "Host, do you have potatoes?" "I have some, come with me, I'll give you some." One of them took a sack and went with me to the school, where I gave him half a sackful, ignoring the fact that I was dealing with enemies, who possibly had only recently been fighting against my sons. When I came to them for the second time, they behaved politely with me, and caused no more damage, and one of them opined: "Host, you are good; we caused you so much suffering, and in return you gave us potatoes." ...

Overall all soldiers were very frustrated by the war, and one of them said: "What business do we have here, don't we have food at home? My plot and property at home is worth a million rubles, and I am dying of hunger here and must be happy that the gentleman offers me potatoes. Do we need this Galicia? Do we put chunks of it in our pockets? The Tsar wants to be a great ruler, but not us." "Yeah, yeah!" said another one of the soldiers. Even then we sensed that an overthrow was being prepared in Russia, because the Muscovites were railing against the Tsar.

The Chechens

Since the retreat of the Muscovites from the Carpathians Buczacz was once more on the move; some came, others left, just like in an anthill. Finally, the Chechens arrived.

Right at the beginning of the war, even before the Muscovites marched into the city, the Christians strove to distinguish themselves from the Jews and hung images of saints in their houses. Every woman regularly wore a cross on her neck, not for reasons of faith, not at all, but in order to protect herself from looting by Cossacks .... Yet this did not last very long, because soon people became convinced that the devil was not as terrible as they had thought.

Before the Chechens arrived—replacing the Cossack troops in Buczacz—Medinsky ordered all residents, who had previously hung images of saints in their homes, to remove them, since the Chechens were heathens, and Christian faith would only provoke them. Some listened to him, others did not, but for the Chechens themselves the entire affair was completely meaningless. There was also a terrifying rumor that the Chechens eat children.

When Chechens and new Cossack troops did arrive from the East, they set up camp in Nagórzanka and in the nearby villages surrounding Buczacz, because they needed stalls for their horses. In each tent in their camps between four and six men were housed, and they conducted themselves very properly, that is they stole less than the Muscovites, if stealing food items and bread can be described as theft in the first place.

Five thousand of them, along with their leaders, who were called "sheikhs," struck their camp in Count Potocki's palace .... The Chechens often rode together in groups of five hundred into the city. They were young men with small black eyes; some of them had broad boney faces and slit eyes, but they all maintained an elegant posture. There were also among them men with noble, white facial features, and one could have sworn they were Poles. Clearly the term Caucasian race came from them. On their heads they wore lamb's wool hats, but not as tall as those of the Cossacks. Under their belts they carried a dagger, which they could also hold between their teeth, and they carried a rifle on their backs ....

On Easter Sunday 1915 we were sitting at the table and sharing an Easter egg sent to us by a priest. Suddenly a Chechen with noble facial features appeared at the door. We were as astonished as he was. After a long silence the Chechen's eyes filled with tears and he said in pure Polish: "Christ, the Lord, is risen!" "Truly risen," we responded. "Are you Polish?" "Yes, I am a Pole, but I have not heard Polish for five years." He presented himself as Wojciechowski from Warsaw and we invited him to share the Easter breakfast with us. He remained with us for several hours, and later came back repeatedly, telling us a number of interesting things about the Chechens. He belonged to the Sheikh's escort, and was doing well, but he missed Warsaw and the Polish language ....

The Chechens could also plunder houses for food, where they would loot eggs, chickens, and geese, but when they saw bacon or pork, they would leave the house and not touch anything. Since the price of milk had greatly risen in Buczacz, the Chechens would milk the cows themselves and drink their milk. Women and girls were also not safe from them, but they were especially interested in Jewish women. Once four Chechens came to Przewłoka [8 km north of Buczacz], walked into a house and wanted to have their way with the housewife. But the peasant, a man of dignity and courage, called the neighbors and began to fight the Chechens; two Chechens were killed, another wounded, and the others fled to Buczacz and reported to their unit.

Right away an entire squad of Chechens was sent there and arrested six peasants. Everyone thought they would be hanged, because under the Austrians this would have happened summarily and without trial. The Sheikh himself led the investigation, assisted by a Polish interpreter. Once the trial was over, the Sheikh asked one of the Chechens what he would have done had someone tried to seize his wife, and the Chechen answered: "I would have killed him, because he would have destroyed my property." Then the Sheikh took three swords and ordered to hand them to the peasants as compensation for the woman and let the peasants go home. According to the customs of the Chechens this was a just verdict ....

At the beginning of the war seventy thousand Chechens came to Galicia, and the Muscovites sent them regularly to the frontline. At Przemyśl many of them were killed, but especially in Bochnia [50 km southeast of Kraków] as a result of landmines. Only five thousand were left. They were incited to go into battle by being told that the Austrians had particularly beautiful revolvers which were worth a lot of money.

But later they became more cunning, stopped fighting and even in Buczacz they began to rebel: "What are we actually fighting for here? At home we have our wives, and now the Turks are taking them. Let us go back home."

The Muscovites did not like that at all, since this was an open strike, and they sought to make that clear to the Chechens. In the spring there was a Muslim holiday, which as far as I can remember was called "Bayram."[40] ... On the seventh day of the full moon a feast was organized for the Chechens in the Potocki palace .... After this great feast the Chechens were ordered to move out .... The residents of Buczacz and Nagórzanka were very glad about this. The Chechens prepared their horses and rode away .... But that same evening we looked over to the serpentine road and saw a column of cavalry, which grew ever longer. Who were they? The Chechens were coming back .... The Chechens had been promised that they would be able to go back east to their homeland, but the Muscovites ... decided to send them first toward the Dniester .... Realizing they had been deceived, they all stopped, each and every one of them, and decided to turn around on the spot and return to Buczacz. At another time this would have been insubordination, but the Muscovites preferred to keep the Chechens as a fighting force on hand, ... divided them into units of one or two hundred soldiers and sent them off at intervals, no longer to the Dniester but rather further north to Congress Poland and Lithuania. The Chechens might have refused that too, but they no longer felt secure in Buczacz, either, because by then Austrian and Polish troops were already on the right bank of the Dniester in the proximity of Niżniów.

Airplanes

On the second day after the return of the Chechens we heard an unusual, loud noise in the sky above Buczacz. Everyone looked up to see what that was and saw an airplane, which circled over the city like a giant eagle. No one in the city had ever seen anything like it before, although everyone knew that such things existed. All the Muscovites and Chechens ran out to the streets and squares with their weapons. No one knew whose airplane this was, was it Russian, Austrian, or Prussian? We could not determine. The Russian general also came out of Markov's apartment. Old and tall, with thin legs, he had just finished eating his substantial breakfast, since he was still licking his mouth with his tongue. He looked up and ordered: "Bring me binoculars!" ... He looked through the binoculars for a long time; next to him stood thirty Muscovites with weapons pointing to the sky. Then the general jumped like a stork on one leg, lifted the other leg up, as if he wanted to climb up to the airplane, and yelled: "Fire!"

The soldiers who were standing by him began to shoot. Upon this signal all the Muscovites, of whom there were about seven thousand, opened fire with their rifles. This made so much noise, that women and children, but especially all the Jews, began to cry: "gevalt!"[41] The noise was so great that the city appeared to be breaking into pieces. This went on for a while. But the airplane was indifferent to all this and kept flying above back and forth. At one point there were two powerful explosions. Then the airplane turned to the southeast. There, on the serpentine road leading to Trybuchowce a company of soldiers was marching. They also began shooting, and two large bombs dropped from the airplane, right in the midst of the unit, and a whole lot of them were hit. Twelve were brought to my school. I asked the medics where the others were: "They are already with the dear Lord," they responded.

The airplane then swung over the forest in the direction of the village of Podlesie. Next to the school building there is a little garden. Five Russian officers had taken up quarters in the school building. They had ordered the soldiers to bring out a table, chairs, and breakfast to the garden. This was also around the time of Easter. On the table they had vodka, wine, sausage, ham, rolls, and tea. The village dogs were attracted by the smell and knew that they would get something, because the Russians happily share not only with humans but also with animals. Suddenly the airplane emerged over the forest in the sky, and the terrified officers forgot all about their breakfast and hid in the barn or lay under the fence. The airplane had only contempt for them, as an eagle would for sparrows, and flew further south to where it had come from. The officers came out of their hiding places, but there was no sign left of the ham and the sausage, because the dogs had eaten everything up, and the bottle of vodka had fallen down. This, then, was the first visit by an airplane.

The next day at about 8 a.m. an airplane arrived again but did not drop any bombs; yet the city shook once more from gunfire, and it was dangerous to come out to the streets because bullets were flying overhead. At one point the Chechens were standing on a hill where the horse market was situated and shooting at a reconnaissance plane. Two medics walked over to Mrs. Tycholisowa's house; they were standing no more than ten steps from me. Suddenly one of them was hit by a bullet in the head and collapsed on the spot, and then the second one was struck by a bullet in the lungs and died half an hour later. The Russians' bullets had made a great deal of noise, but as they came down again, they struck two of their own men. These medics were buried in a common grave with a three-armed [Russian Orthodox] cross, on which it was inscribed that they had been killed by Austrian bullets, although that was not at all the truth. There was much mourning, because these were honest men who were always on the side of the wounded and who cared not only for the Muscovites but also for the Austrians and Germans. The commander of the hospital, General Dr. Voronov, issued an order that no one should try again to shoot at airplanes, and warned that airplanes would drop bombs only where they were being shot at.

Whereas up to then the Russian staff had set up camp outdoors, after the two bombs the officers fled into the city and lived in simple houses. These daily visits by Austrian airplanes were not at all to the liking of the Chechens, and they were glad to leave Buczacz unit after unit; within two weeks, there were no more Chechens in Buczacz ....

In mid-April we began hearing the first rumors about the return of the Polish Legions. The very first news that reached us was that the Legions had been disbanded and that the large estate owners had divided the young soldiers among themselves so that they could work on the fields.

Suddenly the Polish Legions appeared in the Carpathians and did real wonders in Rafajłówa, Zielona [125 and 115 km southwest of Buczacz, respectively] and on the Prut [River, 90 km south of Buczacz]. The Muscovites sometimes captured prisoners, but never legionnaires ..., because none would be caught alive. We also heard about a Russian train that was attacked in Stanisławów. The legionnaires stormed the railcars and threw all the luggage out of the train. Even Russian soldiers participated in the looting. This attack frightened the Russians, because it occurred in their rear ....

Another piece of news informed us that the Legions had united in the Hutsul Mountains [in the Carpathian range] and were fighting victoriously against the Muscovites. I asked wounded soldiers arriving from the front whether they had seen Polish legions, and they confirmed that there were constant clashes in the mountains with smaller groups .... One of the Muscovites related that when fighting them in Nadwórna [100 km southwest of Buczacz] he saw how a legionnaire stabbed a Muscovite with a bayonet in the trenches, but the latter fought back until both of them were impaled on bayonets.

And at the beginning of April my former student Kokoł, a seventeen-year-old lad, came back to Buczacz and brought us news from our sons Zygmunt and Marian. One can imagine our relief. We asked where he had seen them and Kokoł answered: "Zygmunt and Marian are alive, I saw them in Kołomyja." "How did it happen?" "I went for private lessons with a landowner in the village of Łuka [36 km south of

Buczacz] by the Dniester .... Forty Muscovites were sitting there in a
pub and drinking until midnight. Meanwhile ten legionnaires crossed
the Dniester, entered the pub and ordered the Muscovites to drop their
weapons, which they did right away. The legionnaires drank the remaining vodka and took the Russians with them to the other bank of the
Dniester. The Muscovites came along gladly, they even carried their
own weapons, and I also went along with them all the way to Kołomyja.
There were many legionnaires there and among them acquaintances
from Buczacz. I asked about Siewiński and Marian was very glad when
he saw me. Then Zygmunt also came and could hardly believe it when
he saw me. Both asked about their parents and requested to send them
greetings. But I was not long with them, because I had to go back."

This news spread around town like wildfire, but there were also skeptics, who would not believe it. But we had not the slightest doubt that
Kokoł had told the truth. About two weeks later a poor but honest Jew
came to us and brought us news from our sons, who were near Niżniów.
So close, and yet they could not reach Buczacz. As proof of his mission
he showed us a jacket and said: "I was cold, so one of your sons took off
this jacket and gave it to me. May God reward him for this."

We still had no news from our eldest son Józef. From the beginning
of the war to 22 February 1915, Russian troops and trains were advancing ceaselessly to the West, until the catastrophe in the Carpathians
took place and they began to withdraw. We knew nothing about the
Muscovite defeats in Limanowa and at the Masurian Lakes.[42] No one
withdraws as skillfully and systematically as the Muscovites. Initially
they had wanted to take over all of Galicia, and now they had been
withdrawing for half a year and were still in Galicia. A major connecting
road runs through Buczacz to Russia, and, daily, thousands of motor
cars drove through, as well as so many pieces of furniture and other articles of daily use, such as machines, ovens, blankets, and belts, that we
asked ourselves whether all this could have actually come from Galicia.
No wonder that things are so bad here now [1922], after the Muscovites
plundered so much, that we will not be able to return to the prewar level
of property even in fifty years, not to mention the burnt down towns,
farms, distilleries, mills, and stores.

We were also told that the Prussians in Congress Poland were even
greater looters, even though the Prussians at the time were actually still
our allies.

In March 1915 the entire [district] office was on the move and
we could see what was going on. This was because the guards in the
Muscovite office, who worked alongside the Russian clerks, were ours,
Poles and Ruthenians from our city, simple but honest men who loved

the soil of their homeland. They pretended not to know Russian, and the clerks paid them no heed. From these guards we received all kinds of news, sometimes also very interesting information, such as the bad news about Przemyśl.[43] We thought that after the capture of that great fortress the Russians would order us to celebrate, to light up and decorate the city, but somehow that order never came.

Only the Jews hoisted red-and-blue [Russian] flags instead of black-and-yellow [Austrian] ones of their own accord to express their joy. Szwarc hoisted such a large a flag from the roof of his house that it was bigger than the house itself. The flag hung from his house for a whole month. At one point I met Szwarc on the street and asked him: "Aren't you afraid to hang such a large flag?" "Why should I be?" he asked me rather sharply, and I answered quietly and sincerely: "Look here, Austrian airplanes fly over us every day, and if they see such a large flag from above, they might think that a general with his staff has taken up quarters in your house and drop a bomb on it, and then what?" "Oy, vey!" screamed Szwarc, "You are saying the truth, you're right." The kike was so scared, that he immediately rolled up the flag. Half an hour later there was not a single Russian flag in the city. The Jews' loyalty and patriotism are merely a result of their fear of those in power.

The squad of Samarians stayed at my house for three weeks. I had already seen a great sobering process among them, as they cursed the tsar and the king; not only among the simple troops but also the ranked soldiers. In the room over my study the soldiers were cleaning their rifles, and they struck the floor so hard with the butts of their weapons that it felt as though the ceiling would collapse. Sergeant Tomishev heard this and ran up and forbade the soldiers to strike the floor in order to spare the house.

A few days later Cossack infantry units arrived and took over the space in the first floor, where there were large bookcases. The books belonged to the district education council and I served as the librarian. The collection included very rare and costly books such as a dictionary of basswood paper, Polish and German classics, as well as volumes of literature, philosophy, pedagogy, and atlases. The Muscovites destroyed the bookshelves and scattered the books everywhere. I saw with my own eyes how soldiers used the books as pillows. That would not have been so bad. I greeted the soldiers and requested that they do not tear up the books, upon which one of the soldiers responded in perfect Polish: "We will spare these books, they are of no use to us, and we will certainly not destroy them." Surprised by this, I asked him: "Are you Polish?" "Yes, I am Polish from Volhynia."

While there I discovered a filthy bundle in the corner and asked: "What is that?" Immediately one of the soldiers pointed a bayonet at my chest and exclaimed, "Don't say a word about this! Get out!" I could not defend myself against that and left the room. An hour later the same soldier came to me and asked me for a cup of hot tea. I gave him the tea and asked: "Did you really want to stab me?" He said: "This is our unit's flag. It is always guarded by someone, and if a stranger wants to touch it, he must die. You did well to leave right away." By the time these soldiers departed, the books were so badly damaged that they could no longer be used.

Military Hospitals

Then there were the military hospitals. The first military hospital belonged to a formation of soldiers from Kazan, all Tatars; only the doctors were Russians, Poles, or Germans. Every Tatar is a born thief. The Muscovite or Cossack, if he is in a bad mood or enraged, will destroy things, but when his heart is captured, his soul will be revealed. But the Tatar can only steal. Within half an hour the school had been stripped bare of all maps, pictures, clocks, and so on. One of the soldiers stole a large mirror out of the school office, took a diamond out of his pocket, and cut the mirror into pieces which he then gave to each soldier. Whatever was not secured with screws and nails was carried out to the schoolyard, including the oven, on top of which a huge pot made of iron was put. But they placed this oven so close to the school building, that it almost burned down, along with the sick and wounded soldiers; fortunately, they managed to put out the fire in the last minute ....

The chief physician in the military hospital was Dr. Körber, the others were the Muscovite Uspensky, a very intelligent man, and the Pole Krzyżanowski. There were also nurses; the oldest was Mrs. Gordonova, a very earnest woman whom the younger nurses shunned as best they could. One of the nurses was called Chervonogradzka and spoke excellent Polish, German, and Russian. At one point she sat on a bench and spoke with Dr. Krzyżanowski, and when Mrs. Gordonova saw this, she ordered her to return to her room right away. Even the doctors were afraid of Mrs. Gordonova, because she came from a famous family and had a great deal of influence.

The Trip to Lwów

The poverty of civil servants and teachers was terrible, and no one could help us. In other districts the local administration was instructed to pay the teachers and civil servants for three months in advance. But the district administrator in Buczacz did not pay us until the last moment, and then fled, taking the treasury with him. Only the treasurer of Potok Złoty behaved decently and paid two months in advance.

The school inspector at the time, Kasper Molnanowski (who died in 1938), traveled to Lwów and with the support of the Polish Teachers' Association managed to receive a few rubles for each of us. He did all this at his own cost and traveled by cart rather than by train. This was very brave on his part, because the whole land was on fire and in enemy hands. Everywhere there were soldiers, and especially Cossacks, who robbed every traveler of their gold, watches, rings, furs—especially Jewish women. This was a funny sight—a Cossack on horseback wearing women's clothes; but I have not heard of the Cossacks murdering anyone.

A certain soldier called Konvalov once told me how they robbed the Jews. Two or three soldiers come into a room, one of them rests his bayonet on the Jewish man or woman's chest and begins to jump, so that the terrified Jew immediately tells him where the gold and valuables are. The soldiers collect everything and leave the house.

Nevertheless, Molnanowski managed to make it to Lwów, where he received 12 rubles for each teacher and fortunately managed to bring the money back to Buczacz. This was a great help but not for long.

The school inspector Zenon Zaklika suggested that I travel with him and the estate manager Dancewicz to Lwów, where we might be given a little more. But this time the trip was even more dangerous, because unlike the way things had been even at the beginning of the war, the tremendous chaos meant that anything was allowed, and the law was arbitrary. The Russian administrative leaders gave us free travel permits—only Jews had to pay for those permits—which at the time had great value.

On the day of our trip the Muscovites took eight hundred prisoners of war and brought them to Buczacz. These were Austrian soldiers at whose head was a Prussian with an arrogant expression, since this was when the Prussians had won a great victory over the Muscovites. Among them was also a certain Austrian official who associated with the prisoners of war and changed Austrian money into rubles for them. He changed money according to the official rate of 1 ruble for 3.33 crowns, but from Jews he bought rubles for 2 crowns and thereby made a profit over each ruble of 1.33 crowns. When he proposed this to the Prussian officer, the latter said to him: "I will have nothing to do with a traitor." This was a legal but dishonorable action, because [the Austrian official] made a significant profit from the prisoners of war.

Next to the Muscovites the Austrians also had their own police, who reported everything right away to Lwów, and shortly thereafter a senior Austrian officer arrived and asked us: "Who is this person who makes money off the prisoners of war in such an inhuman manner?" We pretended not to know, upon which he said: "The name of this gentleman is very well known."

On 15 May we traveled with Mr. Dancewicz in a horse-drawn carriage to Lwów in order to carry out our task. The marketplace and Kolejowa Street in Buczacz were jammed with Russian automobiles and it took much skill to weave our way through the traffic. It was noticeable that despite all this jostling the Muscovites did not harm anyone, whereas the Austrians would have carelessly driven their vehicles over their own soldiers, as well as dogs and horses. Once we got out of the city, we saw the damage cause by the war in Galicia ....

Just out of the city we could see postal carriages whose horses were being fed with grains side-by-side with the cows. In Podolia thousands of cattle, cows, horses, goats, and even camels were being fed on the fields no matter who the land belonged to. The cattle came from our farms and peasants. They were requisitioned without asking permission, and in return their owners were given receipts. This was also what the Germans and Austrians did. On the way I saw the destroyed farms and distilleries and the burned down mills; the churches had no bells, since the Muscovites had melted them into artillery shells. As the bells of the Roman and Greek Catholic churches were removed, the Cossack in charge of this work said: "How can God help us, if our government orders us to do such unholy things. The bells are there to call people to Mass in the churches, and the government orders us to make them into tools of death." ...

We drove through the village of Złotnik [31 km north of Buczacz], which was part of Lord Serwatowski's property. Everything was in ruins there, including the distillery and the farm; the windowpanes were smashed, the columns of the manor house demolished. Unfortunately, this was not the work of the Muscovites, but of Piłsudski's beloved followers.

From Złotnik we traveled further to Chodaszków, a large village, beautiful and entirely Polish, and then through the village of Nastasów [59 km north of Buczacz]. Everywhere the farms were wrecked and burnt down. Oh, what the Muscovite government had perpetrated was such a disgrace! In his appeal to the Poles, [Grand Duke] Nicholas Nikolaevich had called on us to fight with united forces against the Crusaders, by which he meant the current Prussians, but instead [the Russians] destroyed our Polish farms.

It should therefore come as no surprise that a Russian nation taught such immorality, a nation that attacked its own friends, that did not recognize the value of foreign land and property, and that inflicted vast destruction, would generate Bolshevism and the loss of religion. Such crimes never bring the criminal any good fortune, for sooner or later they will be punished by a higher justice.

At the train station of Tarnopol there was great commotion, with Muscovites everywhere; Russian was spoken on every street corner. The train officials and the stationmaster officiated with Russian hats on their heads. The restaurants were full of generals, officers and super-intendents, nurses and soldiers, all shouting as if they were masters of the universe. We went to Hotel Panczer, where we had trouble finding a small room, since the Muscovites had already occupied everything.

The next morning, I saw Austrian prisoners of war walking through the street in four columns, about 300 in each, so altogether 1,200 POWs, all Czechs. A Jew standing next to me said, these were 12,000 prisoners of war. I answered that they were only 1,200, since I counted them myself. That is how it went with figures during the war, one added a zero or two, since it would make no difference one way or the other, and in this manner rumors and falsehoods were generated ....

In the morning we boarded the train, but because of the great press of military troops in the train station we had to wait for a long time. The previous evening an unusually long train with casualties from Limanowa, Sieniawa,[44] and other battlefields had apparently arrived. There were also wonderful hospital trains, painted with red and white crosses, all filled with Muscovites, and only rarely would one also find there an Austrian or a Prussian soldier.

Finally, we arrived in Lwów. The train station was unrecognizable. Previously this building was a showpiece, the pride and jewel of the city. Now the entire platform was full of luggage, everywhere filthy soldiers were sitting or lying, not a single joyful face, all filled with horror and despair, all downcast; and not only the simple soldiers but also the officers and the nurses and civilians. These are no longer the faces of a victorious military but of a defeated army, which has no strength for a counterattack. Even the sparrows were not as before, but black like tiny chunks of tar, you could tell what they were only by hearing their song.

In Lwów we stayed at Hotel Stadtmüller, now [1922] Hotel Ludwig. This had been one of the best and most honest hotels in the city; it had since been destroyed. Everywhere one could see the work of the looters—there were no bathroom sinks, no tiles or glasses, the beds were broken, the varnish scraped. In the neighboring rooms there were puddles. Everywhere there were Muscovites, who drank the whole night and went with the crassest prostitutes. The streets of the city were filthy, everywhere there was waste, and yet this was the city of heroes, the nest of the Polish eagle, this was my city of birth, the jewel and splendor of the entire land.

We went straight away to the board of the teachers' association. My colleagues came with me directly to the department of land affairs, and on the recommendation of Mrs. Napatiewicz we received 4,000 rubles and were reimbursed for our travel costs, which were horrendous at the time, and after only two days we were able to return. In the meantime, we observed what was happening in the city. The military were everywhere, officers, generals with golden uniforms. They paraded in the streets of Lwów full of pride, together with their wives, and what with their high hats and wraps they looked to us like Syrian kings ....

The unrest among the Muscovites was visibly growing. Next to St. Antony's Church one could already hear the explosions of shells from the direction of Krzywoczyce [a district in Lwów], and thousands of soldiers with dejected expressions were marching out of town [to the front] along Łyzakowska Street. They were some sort of Turkish troops, all of them looking rather terrified. One could only see a bit of black hair on their heads, and the glitter of their black eyes and their pointed beards no longer evoked any fear. They went like lambs to the slaughter.

The troops marching down Legion Street in the direction of Gródek Jagielloński offered another impression, albeit also a sad one. These twenty-five thousand men marched in large formations, through the center of the city, singing Russian songs. They were young, handsome, healthy youths, who were looking forward to their experience. Clearly, they had not spent much time in the trenches. They sang with all their might. One of them would sing out and then the entire unit would repeat after him. I felt sorry that so many people were going to the slaughter, or perhaps would themselves murder others, because on the other side stood Austrians and Poles, among them also my sons! ...

For the sake of security, we divided the money we received in three parts between ourselves. Mr. Zaklika took one part, Mr. Dancewicz the second, I took the third, and we hid the money in our clothes. We bought tickets in first class in order not to sit together with the Cossacks, or with the soldiers, since we feared they would rob us. Russian passenger trains were wonderful, they had folding chairs and one could convert them into four bunks. There was even a samovar in the cars, in which water was constantly boiling, so that one could make a cup of tea at any time.

Next to us were two generals, an engineer and a man wearing simple shoes and simple clothes; it soon turned out he was a magnate and a nobleman. After we introduced ourselves, we chatted quite happily, both in Polish and in Russian, and we understood each other splendidly. I impressed them with my detailed knowledge of the history of the Russian state .... The Russians pulled out of their pockets good vodka, ham, sausages, and confectionary, that is sweets. They ate and offered us some, insisting that we do not reject their offer, and we regretted that we could not reciprocate.

On the way five trains passed by, full of Russian troops, heading toward the front. Their eyes were full of terror, because like us they had seen trains full of casualties going back. What can a poor soldier do, when he observes so much misfortune and those total cripples coming back while he must go and fight foreigners for a cause he does not understand? One of the generals, who clearly had had enough of the war, watched these soldiers and said: "Cannon fodder." ... After a nine-hour journey we arrived in Tarnopol. One could say we were lucky, because this was the last train in which civilians were allowed to travel.

The defeat of the Muscovites at Przemyśl was already known in Tarnopol. Again, there were eight thousand Austrian prisoners of war in the city. They were all Czech. As they came into the city, they were singing cheerfully, marching not in formation but in any way they wished. On several wagons sat officers, all joyful and happy. At the time we did not understand that a soldier could be happy as a war prisoner. Only later did we learn that they had given themselves up without fighting and went over to the Russian side voluntarily.

We were picked up by Mr. Dancewicz's carriage coming from Złotniki [32 km north of Buczacz] and we continued our journey. Directly in the hinterland of Tarnopol ... one could see entire formations of unarmed soldiers, numbering in the thousands. They appeared downcast and hungry and looked at us with mistrust. This was a dangerous journey in the carriage, because hungry people were coming out of their houses and begging for bread or something to eat, and those traveling were searched for food items as they passed through. Could one wonder about that?

West of Tarnopol ... we saw the trenches that had been dug in the fields in the form of large arches, protected by barbed wire, in preparation for the battle in the areas surrounding Tarnopol. There were many such trenches and they formed a so-called defensive ring. Fortunately, we then arrived in Złotniki, where we were welcomed by Dancewicz as guests and were provided with another carriage to take us to Buczacz.

Our colleagues heard about our return and came to visit us. They were not only anxious about the money that we brought but especially for the news that could not be found in the Muscovite newspapers published in Lwów under Russian censorship.

The Kazan military hospital was gone from my school, having moved further east to Czortków. Instead a military hospital arrived from Kharkov. When I came to the school, a soldier would not let me in, but two older acquaintances called out: "This is our boss, the principal!" Immediately they let me in and apologized. I got to know the administrator of the hospital, called Salyukov, a real Muscovite, an intelligent, humane, and honest man. To be sure he could not speak Polish, but honest people have something about them that makes them attractive. I would not have known in advance that while my sons were fighting against Moscow—a battle I would have gladly joined, but only as a soldier—I would find Muscovites worthy of being respected, among them even some one could love as good friends.

There were eleven military hospitals in Buczacz. And because the Muscovites had burned down the town already in the fall [of 1914], the wounded soldiers could not be treated in buildings but rather had to be put up in tents that were pitched in the open squares and burned down buildings. And again, the military hospital troops changed, as the soldiers from Kharkov moved to the east and a Ukrainian military hospital arrived in Buczacz. A real Ukrainian military hospital. These were honest and worthy people, starting off with the senior physician, a real Muscovite called Voronich. Among the doctors was also Abraham Schwarzman, a Jew, the most noble man that I have ever known; had all Jews been like this Schwarzman, the word "Jew" would not have been a derogatory term and a synonym for thieves and usurers. The second doctor was a tall Muscovite, whose name I have forgotten, since he did not distinguish himself in anything and was generally quite mediocre. Then there was also Edward Friedman, the son of a Protestant priest from Wilno. He was born German but loved Poles as his own brothers. He could recite [German poet Friedrich Schiller's 1798 poem] "The Song of the Bell" beautifully, as well as several ballads by Mickiewicz in Polish.

At the time there were fierce battles to the west [of Buczacz], and the front stretched from Riga all the way to Bessarabia. Every day we read news about these battles in the Russian newspapers, but one had to know how to read them, because often what was described as a great victory was actually a defeat on the battlefield .... The Muscovites railed ever louder against the war and criticized the camarilla in their command staffs ever more openly. Russian troops had pulled back up to the Złota Lipa River, which flows along the western edge of the Buczacz district [30 km west of Buczacz], and in the south runs into the Dniester, and Russian troops were positioned only as far as its heights. Even when standing among the peddlers in the marketplace one could already hear the ceaseless artillery fire.

Every day at least five hundred soldiers were brought to my school and precisely as many were sent daily back deep into Russia. Many of them died not only in my school but also in other buildings, where military hospitals were located. Austrians and Prussians were also brought there. The latter were treated with special respect. On one occasion they brought two wounded Prussian brothers called Matuszak. A Polish family name, is it not? Both were senior officers and had been robbed by Cossacks, who looted their money and watches. They were wealthy men and said they were counts. They claimed not to understand Polish. The Jews immediately brought them money for the onward journey. They did not want to take anything from the Muscovites and looked at them with disdain ... as if they were their subjects. They took bread and ham from my wife as food for the journey. It clearly never occurred to them that this war might go badly for the Prussians—but perhaps they were Poles after all? ...

One day a twenty-year-old man came into the kitchen with a Muscovite flag; this was Zainkim, the son of the stationmaster in Rostov. The moment he saw my wife he began to weep loudly, and we asked him why: "Because you look so much like my mother," he answered. He was in a military hospital because of an illness of the nerves, because he had almost drowned in the Dniester. We invited him for lunch with us, and he liked rice with sugar and cream very much, because his mother also often made that for him at home. He told us about his war experiences, crossing the Dniester, where many soldiers were killed: "Mnogo, mnogo!" ["many" in Russian], and how they pulled him out [of the water] and he was saved.

A military hospital was put up in the schoolyard, in which thirty-eight Muscovites were being treated for syphilis; no one was allowed to feed them. At about that same time one hundred wounded Magyars were brought from the front. This was a good example of what national chauvinism can cause. The Magyars, as we know, consider their language to be world language number one, and at their schools they also learned German but cannot speak a single Slavic language .... These Magyars ... could have asked for bread, wine, tobacco, and anyone would have given a little to these poor POWs, but no one understood these wretches or knew what they wanted. Thus, the Magyars went to the Muscovites who were ill with syphilis and communicated with them by way of gestures.

When General Voronov found out about this, he flew into a rage [...
and] he asked me to explain to them that no one should come close to
those infected with syphilis. Fortunately, one of those soldiers knew
German and he translated this into Hungarian for his colleagues. The
Hungarians moved away immediately and said: "This is a good man,"
about which Dr. Voronov was very pleased ....

Each Muscovite hospital had its own priest. Some of them were very
pious and God-fearing, others were greedy and immoral, and it was
shameful that some of them also drank. On Saturdays and Sundays
these priests held Masses at the schoolyard, where there was a primitive
altar with a painting of the Mother of God. The Muscovites sang very
beautifully .... The choir sang in four-part harmony.

Because more wounded constantly arrived, and there were not enough
Muscovite medics on hand, our female teachers and Jewish female
teachers selflessly helped the wounded, which made the Muscovites very
happy, because the women were very devoted to the wounded and con-
scientiously cared for them. Many women from Podzameczek, Podlesie,
Dżuryn, and Nagórzanka brought milk to my wife for the wounded in
the hospital and asked for no payment. In handing out these donations
my wife made no distinction between the Austrians and the Muscovites,
which was appreciated by all.

A certain great princess from a Russian noble family sent the hospital
a large barrel of Caucasian wine, which the medics poured into small
buckets. On this occasion Dr. Friedman sent us two half buckets of this
wine and we immediately served it to the Magyars in cups, since they like
wine very much. They were very grateful for that and thanked my wife,
Voronov, and Friedman, who in their modesty denied any knowledge of
this. Friedman also gave us several pieces of bacon and a few loaves of
bread to distribute to the Magyars, because they could not adapt to the
Russian cuisine. [... The] Muscovites served their sick two pots full of
semolina daily [... and then] gave us the leftovers that we distributed to
the poor in the city. Things were different with the Austrian kitchens,
which did not share the remains of the soup, but instead feasted on it
and dumped the remains in the drain.

My youngest son Roman wanted to help the medics in the sickrooms,
especially because he spoke German. It turned out that three wounded
men were lying next to each other: a Muscovite, an Austrian, and a
Prussian. The first two were Poles, and he served them tea and bread,
but he did not even look at the Prussian. But it turned out that this
Prussian could speak excellent Polish, since he said: "Dear Sir, may
I please have a cup of coffee?" He was a Pole from the area of Posen.
Naturally he immediately received his coffee. And so here were three

Poles, sons of the same [national] Polish mother, divided by the three partitions, sent out to commit murder by their supposed allies. It is already a great enough crime for sons of the same God to fight each other. But it is an even greater crime when brothers are incited to kill each other ....

Three Magyar officers were brought in. One of the lightly wounded men came to us in the kitchen and said to my wife in a commanding tone in German: "Please bring us two cups of coffee and four cooked eggs at 6 p.m." At 6 p.m. precisely the coffee was brought in, along with eggs and bread. Then the third officer said: "Bring me the same." He was served in the same manner. As Romcio [diminutive for Roman] was about to leave, the officer asked: "How much is that?" "Nothing," said the boy. "How so?" asked the officer again. "Because we don't take money from anyone, my father is this school's principal," answered Romcio. They were astonished and the healthiest among them came to apologize and offer his thanks right away. These officers' clothes were as hard as leather because of the blood. We took them to our house, washed and returned them. All three were lawyers from Budapest. We befriended them and promised to stay in contact by mail after the war. Unfortunately, in war one does not remember surnames.

Once, during the night of 3–4 August 1915, the soldiers on the southern slope of the Fedor heard a great cheer come up from the Austrian trenches on the right bank of the Dniester. The Muscovites wondered what the cause of this cheer was, as it could be heard all the way to the city, a distance of several kilometers. One could hear the shouts "Warsaw, Warsaw," celebrating the capture of Warsaw by the Central Powers.

The Muscovites were asking themselves: "What is this war for? Now we must retreat in shame; wouldn't it have been better had we given the Poles right away what belongs to them, and had won their friendship? And how do we go on now?" ... The Muscovite newspapers reported on the Prussian capture of Warsaw only two weeks later. The Prussians and Austrians did the same [delaying news of setbacks], because no one wanted to report a defeat, so as not to demoralize their army.

Cholera and Typhus

The Muscovites had expelled the Jews from their houses already in November 1914, and the latter fled to the Jewish cemetery and spent a day and a night there. This cemetery is located on a hill between a gorge and the Strypa in the valley below. The water flows here in a wide stream, to be sure, but is very shallow, so that you can cross it with the water reaching up to your neck. The Cossacks came to the cemetery on horseback with their leather whips and ordered the Jews to leave the cemetery and cross the Strypa to the other bank ....

One can imagine the uproar when four thousand men, and especially women and children, climbed down into the cold water, with the Cossacks yelling behind them on horseback with leather whips in their hands. They just crossed the river when a Russian officer on the left bank ordered them to go back to where they came from. The people could not take off their clothes and were wet and cold, and since they could not get warm, they became sick and many of them died. After that many more Jews were expelled to Buczacz, not only from the Buczacz district but also from other regions. These people were pressed like sardines in a can into filthy houses on the Podhajecki and Batory Streets.

Jews were expelled to Buczacz also from Potok Złoty, and since they had no clothes to change, many of them went back to Potok Złoty and stayed there. The Muscovites clearly did not want to have so many Jews near the front. And so, they waited until a sufficient number of Jews had returned to Potok Złoty. Then they launched a sudden roundup and caught fifty-three Jews who had fled and gave each of them fifty-nine lashes right away. Six Jews died on the spot during this flogging, the rest were expelled once more to Buczacz.

The following spring a cholera and typhus epidemic broke out. In my school [serving as a military hospital] many soldiers died, not to mention the Jews, who were living in great filth and congestion. Every day numerous corpses were carried to the Jewish cemetery and buried there. All the doctors, and especially the above-mentioned Schwarzman, worked not only for the army, but also for the state, saving human lives, no matter whether they were Catholic, Jewish, rich or poor. This was Sisyphean work, but some could still be saved. Schwarzman always said that typhus was in large part the consequence of hunger and poverty, and consequently whenever he was paid by the rich, he gave the money back to the poor.

During the years 1883–85 I had known similar people in Lwów. There was doctor there called Mojżesz Beizer, who was one of the best doctors and made a lot of money, but always lived in poverty, because whatever he earned, he gave to the poor. He helped needy students without any concern for their religion. One time he was called to a lady who was pregnant, and whose life was threatened because of the loss of blood. In the house there was not a single piece of cloth, and the doctor took off his apron and bandaged the woman with it. One hundred thousand Catholics and Jews attended his funeral and accompanied his coffin to the Jewish cemetery.

The Jews fought the cholera epidemic as follows: they chose a very poor bachelor and a very young girl who did not know each other and instructed them to marry. They went from house to house and collected money for the couple. Even Sheptelich donated 50 rubles. The two were dressed in black cloth and escorted to the cemetery with music, song, and much noise. There they were married, and only then were they allowed to remove their veils. The freshly married couple looked at each other and were very happy. Then they went back home full of joy. But the cholera epidemic did not ebb.

Later on, yet another marriage was celebrated in the same manner, but this too did not help. I spoke with a very sincere Jew and remarked that this measure did not help with the cholera, to which he replied: "What makes people happy at a time of misfortune? To be sure, we cannot stop the cholera epidemic, but we did accomplish a good deed in helping poor families."

In order to stop these epidemics, the Muscovites put a guard at the Strypa. It was forbidden to bathe in the Strypa or to do washing there. A certain type of powdered soap was handed out, and the clothing of all wounded soldiers and the straw on which they had been lying were burned. In the yard between the school and the Sokół building several stacks of hay were put up, over which the pieces of clothing were laid out and everything was set on fire. This made a huge fire and the windows began to crack. Several soldiers tried to put out the fire but then there was an explosion and objects flew in all directions. All the Muscovites there who survived ran off, and soon the window frames appeared to catch fire, when one brave soldier called Rubal managed to get the fire under control. From that time on the clothing of the dead were only burned by the Strypa River.

Between the Strypa and the building of the district administration, where the Russian administration office was located, there is a large marketplace. This site was now full of dirt and filth, because the first Austrian and later Muscovite barracks had been built there. And so Sheptelich pronounced: "I must be remembered well by the inhabitants." He sent his gendarmes to the surrounding villages and brought a hundred villagers into the city, whom he ordered to clean the marketplace and the ditches. He then ordered to plant trees in these trenches from the forest of Count Potocki, which he had arbitrarily uprooted from the forest. The trees grew and would have made a nice park, but in the fall of the same year the Austrians arrived, and the inhabitants uprooted the trees out of hatred for Sheptelich and Medinsky, so that not a trace would be left of them and of the manner they had ruled Buczacz as if it were their foreign garden.

Sheptelich also brought villagers to build a road to the horse market, all the way to the railroad bridge over the Strypa. There a solid wooden bridge was build, which remained there, because when the Muscovites fled from Buczacz they neglected to destroy it. One of the most beautiful streets in Buczacz, Mickiewicz Street, was renamed Sheptelich, and he behaved as if no one surpassed him in importance, but pride precedes the fall. One of the Muscovites complained [to the governor in Tarnopol] about his various abuses of office and the latter suspended Sheptelich and ordered him to leave Buczacz; Sheptelich could not bear this humiliation and died suddenly. Yet he was not a bad person.

His place was taken by Baron Kronenberg, about whom I can report nothing, because a few days after his arrival he was infected with typhus and died. Then the Muscovite Markov was made city and district administrator alongside the chief of the gendarmerie Medinsky.

At that time death visited our home as well. Our cousin Stefcia Gruszyńska was visiting us at the time. She was a very quiet and nice young woman, who had completed two years at the junior high school before the war. She lived at our home, was fourteen years old, and was growing so fast and becoming so attractive that people already thought she was a young woman. The doctors and the Russian officers appreciated her because she behaved well. And General Voronov liked her, because she looked like his daughter, who had stayed back at home. One day she complained about headaches and lay down in bed; Dr. Schwarzman came to see her. What he heard was that the child had gone down to the cellar and sucked ice [stored there] that had been brought from the Strypa. In the hospital the doctors never left her bedside. Voronov and Schwarzman brought her lemons, which at the time were extremely hard to come by. After examining her Voronov wept and said: "The girl's heart will not hold out." My wife would not move from her bedside and the child died in her arms. Everyone wept, the entire hospital was in mourning, Voronov and Schwarzman cried like children.

The funeral was modest, because how could one imagine something special at that time. One of the Muscovites made a coffin and a cross and would not take any payment for his work. The funeral procession was led by Father Chorodnik, who has since died; he too would accept no money. All the Russian officers, doctors, soldiers and the intelligentsia of Buczacz came to the burial.

Ever more wounded Muscovites and Austrians were being brought to Buczacz, since near the Złota Lipa River and by the Dniester [30 and 40 km west of Buczacz, respectively] there was increasingly fiercer

fighting. Every day thousands of automobiles and vehicles with munitions traveled through Buczacz, all in the direction of Czortków and
further east. Every day thousands of heads of cattle, horses, sheep,
and swine were led through the city. Entire caravans of wagons full of
furniture and various wares went through the city. It appeared like a
migration of nations from the west to the east.

At one point eight hundred wounded soldiers were brought to my
school. There was not enough space, and so they were placed in the
school hallways, one next to the other. As they were dying, they called
out "Mama! Mama!"—clearly they were hallucinating—it was a terrible
sight. Every day I asked myself, how many people had died, I even made
note of the names of the dead, but all these notes have been unfortunately lost. I can only remember the number of the dead between 28
August 1914 and 2 September 1915, during which time 1,002 men died
in my school. Among them there were 900 Muscovites and 95 Austrians,
all young men, in the prime of their lives, of which they were robbed by
the war . . . .

Did they fall for the Fatherland? No—a sort of divine punishment
hung over humanity. During this war the basest instincts were awoken
among some people, which had slumbered deep in their hearts; but
there were also virtuous people, who did not stray off the path. Perhaps
humanity will return to the right path of faith after this terrible war,
and things will improve with the coming generations.

Austrian aircraft were flying daily over the city, but no one shot at
them and they did not drop any bombs; they flew so low that from below
we could see the pilots leaning out of the plane.

The Return of the Austrians and the Battle

A rumor spread through the city that the Russians would drill holes in
the granite supports of the railroad bridge. The glorious railroad bridge
over the Strypa, twenty-five meters high, was supported by these granite columns. It was also said: "The Muscovites have laid mines in the
tunnel." This railroad tunnel was quite long, it took ten minutes to walk
through it. "The trains are no longer running." We understood from this
news that the Muscovites would be withdrawing. In the Russian administration all paperwork was being packed into crates, which were loaded
onto carts along with furniture that had been plundered by the staff the
day before. Orders went out to conduct inspections of all houses and
remove from them everything made of metal, and so samovars, ovens
and copperware, massive door handles and so forth were looted. They
also searched for silver and gold, since they too are metals.

My wife, having observed this looting, became frightened and threw my scrupulously written diaries into the oven, where they were burned. In fact, the Muscovites did not come into my house at all. All three bridges over the Strypa, excluding the iron bridge, were mined, and next to the bridges they placed barrels with tar and oil, which were heavily guarded. On 24 August 1915, at 10 p.m., I was lying in bed and reading poems by [Gotthold Ephraim] Lessing,[45] while my wife and my son were sitting outside on the garden bench, where Dr. Schwarzman was telling them about the famous bacteriologist [Ilya Ilyich] Mechnikov, whom the Muscovites had not appreciated and whose importance was first recognized by the French.[46] At that time twenty-five automobiles and a large number of horse-drawn wagons were passing by. The automobiles and wagons were empty; an officer jumped out from one of them and walked directly to Voronov, followed by the doctors. A moment later one of them came out and as he passed by, he whispered to us: "We are getting out!"

My wife was so shocked that she could not speak. Then Schwarzman came and said: "The Austrians are two kilometers from Monasterzyska; we have to transfer all the wounded within an hour and by 5 a.m. our entire hospital must already be on the road." With this news my wife came into the room and repeated the words of the doctor. At that moment I did not know what was happening to me, whether it was because of the unexpected news, or the joy, in any case my heart began beating like crazy, like a hammer; I wanted to appear calm and looked again at my book, but the letters began to swim. I have never experienced anything like that since, although I have found myself again in dangerous situations. After a while I stood up, got dressed, and my nervous state dissipated. No one was sleeping any more in the entire building. In the hospital and the city everything was in indescribable motion. The wounded were being taken away, belongings were being packed, but in such an orderly fashion, as if it was the simplest thing in the world. My wife asked the doctor when would the Austrians arrive: "Oh, not right away, today is Sunday, tomorrow the battle will begin, and it will last until Thursday."

At 2 a.m. Schwarzman showed up again and said: "The Austrians have left Monasterzyska and are two kilometers from Jezierzany [8 km west of Buczacz]; they are advancing rapidly."

Even before 5 a.m. no one was left in the hospital. Next to the eastern gate, an automobile was waiting, into which the doctors climbed. They bid farewell from us not as enemies but as the dearest friends. They were very honest people, and although I would never again see them in my life, my good memories of them remain, and [I hope] that they returned happily to their families, which they dearly missed. At 6 a.m.

we heard Russian artillery fire. The guns were just over the city, on the side of Żyznomierz [5 km south of Buczacz], under the forest of Załanowski. The battery had six guns, which were firing without pause, and the noise traveled so loudly through the many turns of the Strypa valley that the entire city shook, and several windows cracked. The Muscovites rode out of town at full gallop, taking along their munitions and equipment. The sky seemed to grow dark over all the wounded, the clouds took on human shapes, the shapes of the wounded and dead Cossacks along with their horses, all hurrying to the East. The air and the sky took on a yellow hue, and the Muscovites looked up to heaven, at these strange clouds, bid farewell, and said: "These are not clouds, but the ghosts of the soldiers and Cossacks who fell in battle, who are flying over the earth toward the East, in order to return to their families."

On Tuesday morning Sergeant Mizanov, our good acquaintance, rode up to us on his horse, since he was searching for yet another field kitchen, but as he was standing in the schoolyard he found himself in the midst of an artillery barrage, turned white as a sheet, stopped searching, and fled as quickly as he could. The Austrian shells were falling on the city, but did not hurt anyone, only the windows of the post office building were shattered.

On Wednesday afternoon we heard such a horrible screaming and screeching, that it sounded as if a huge, terrifying, demonic child was flying over Buczacz, yelling with a shrill voice at the highest pitch: "Ay! Ay! Ay!" This was a huge artillery shell that was called Bertusiz.[47] Right after this shot, numerous Muscovite units moved through the city and went up the serpentine road toward Trybuchowce. The Muscovite guns stopped firing. The following morning the first soldiers rode in, among them a mounted officer who loudly asked: "Are there enough artillery shells?" "No, there are not." The officer nodded and rode on to the guns. On this memorable day no one could sleep all night, but we were also not afraid, because people had already become used to the fighting. In the city no one could be seen, because marauding gangs were roaming about, certain that they could plunder with impunity.

In the evening I went to the cemetery, located just above the school, thinking that perhaps I would be able to see something. I walked carefully through the overgrowth among the tombstones and observed that a guard had been established above the valley, firing at anything that approached it. Returning home, I met the undertaker's daughter, who said: "If the doctor has good eyes, he should look in the direction of Jezierzany; there below, the forest is completely blue from our troops." (At the time Austrian troops were called "ours.")[48] I looked in that direction but since I was shortsighted, I could see only a blur.

It was a dark night with good weather. Suddenly the city was shaken by such a powerful blast that people almost fell to the ground. After that there was a muffled explosion, a strange noise, as if it had come from underground. The granite supports of the railroad bridge as well as the tunnel had been blown up with dynamite. Over the city bright flames flickered and then disappeared. This was presumably the second bridge over the Strypa, the so-called Palace Bridge. The bridge had been soaked in oil and began to burn, and when the fire reached the mine it exploded and brought down the bridge. Guns were being towed quietly through the city, because their wheels had been wrapped with straw and cloth. They had just crossed the Black Bridge when that bridge too was ignited and blown up. At the end of the column the Muscovites were marching on foot; they would run into the houses on either side of the street, break the windows with stones, and then run as fast as they could. Occasionally the sorrowful cry of a Jewish woman could be heard, but they did not kill anyone. A moment later we could hear the rattle of machine gun fire over the city, the shots coming in such rapid bursts, that we could not distinguish the sound of individual bullets. It was akin to the sound of a huge organ. Then it became still again.

One bridge still remained, very close to my school; it too was ignited right at the end. The last four soldiers set it on fire, lighting up the straw and tar that they had previously poured over the bridge. The fire broke out in large flames. My colleague Keffermüller, his son, and another citizen were standing in the schoolyard, some 100 meters from the bridge. Suddenly there was a huge bang; the blast of the explosion was so great that all three were blown up in the air. They fell about fifteen steps away from where they had been standing, but they were not injured. Only a part of the bridge was destroyed, because then the fire went out. The Muscovites threw their weapons on the ground and lay down in Leszczyński's cornfield, calling out: "We did as we were ordered and now, we give ourselves up." And that's what they did.

At midnight the shooting resumed, right next to us, and by the manner of their shooting we already knew that it had to be Austrian troops. After waiting for another couple of days, I went out to the street, looked around and saw in front of me several Austrian soldiers. "You are ours," I greeted them. "That's right, it's us," they responded. This was the 13th Infantry Company from Kraków. The cunning Austrians had deployed Poles against the Russians in the frontline, because they knew that that Poles and Muscovites lived in strife with each other on account of Poland's partition. We immediately made tea in the samovar for the heroes. The residents of other houses began coming out, and all served the soldiers with whatever they had. The joy in the city was indescribably great. After 372 days of Russian occupation we were liberated by our own soldiers. This can only be understood by those who know what it means to be invaded, especially by one who for an extended period of time had no idea of what was happening in the rest of the world nor the fate of his sons. The Strypa Bridge, also called the Palace Bridge, was only partially damaged, and could be repaired sufficiently to made it usable. About a hundred young, strong Jews were standing there. The tax official Erazm Czyszewski asked these Jews to help him save this bridge, but none of them would budge.

These Jews are a strange people. During the Russian invasion they had hidden in various holes, from which they then emerged like rats, in order to do good business with the Muscovites. That despite this they were frequently flogged with a leather whip does not seem to have disturbed them. Most importantly during the Muscovite invasion they gave the city a Muscovite face, since they hoisted huge Russian flags from their houses and put up signs in Russian over their stores. Now, from one moment to the next, the city took on a black-and-yellow face, as the Russian flags were rolled up, and the signs over the stores were once again written in German. Even as the war was still going on, these Jews must have prepared those flags and signs! While Poles and Ukrainians were taken to the war and not a few of them returned from it as cripples, or never saw the soil of the homeland again at all, these fat Jews were laughing about the stupid "goyim," having never gotten around to serving in the army themselves.[49] Yesterday the Jews were still Muscovites; today they threw away their portraits of the Tsar, tied the Russian flag to the tail of a pig and drove it through the town with music and great [cries of] "Ay, Ay."

Several Russian POWs were marched through the city, and the Jews came out of their houses to spit at them; one Jewish woman asked a prisoner: "Did they perhaps pay you?" Even the Austrian sergeant escorting the POWs through the city was enraged that the Jews had no respect for soldierly honor. He therefore ordered his squad to beat the Jews with their rifle butts for any abuse of the Muscovites. This helped.

In the afternoon I went into town in order to examine the damage caused by the fighting. The previously beautiful railroad bridge had been blown up into two parts and was hanging in the air, while the mighty granite supports were spread out in innumerable fragments underneath. What extraordinary power this dynamite has! The railroad tunnel was similarly damaged, but it was repaired within three days. An engineer and his people were already on the spot. Next to the railroad bridge the Muscovites had built a practical wooden bridge which they

had neglected to demolish before their retreat. Now the work of remov-
ing the mines began, and a guard was posted there, which was good for
the safety of the Austrian army.

In the village of Nagórzanka I encountered a unit of Kraków troops
from the 13th Regiment, led by Major Rylski. I greeted him, he greeted
me, and because there were many winding paths in the village, he asked
me to show him the way to that bridge. I chatted on the way with the
major and the soldiers. They were jolly fellows and the major was to
them like a father. They were joking that the Muscovites had left that
[wooden] bridge undamaged not for themselves but for the sake of those
who were chasing after them.

Upon seeing this huge army fleeing and the Austrians on their heels I
wondered whether the Muscovites had not perhaps prepared an ambush,
since they were several times more numerous, and who knew how many
of them were still waiting in the East. My fears proved groundless, since
the flight continued all the way to Wygnanka just next to Czortków [35
km east of Buczacz]. [But] there the Muscovites had built a fortified
line over several months and were prepared for a large-scale defense.
About four thousand Austrians had crossed the Strypa. Of those four
thousand about nine hundred returned to Buczacz the following day.
The rest were either killed, taken prisoner, or vanished in the region.
After precise counting it was determined that one thousand had been
killed. Major Rylski had fallen.

In Buczacz there was indescribable panic. Austrian trains were
coming from the direction of Czortków, and the Jews cried "gevalt!"
and quickly pulled down the black-and-yellow flags, recalling that only
yesterday they had rolled up the Muscovite colors and taken off the portraits of the Tsar; they knew what to expect, because the Muscovites had
their spies and informers. They therefore took all their belongings and
fled with much lamentation to the train station, where the Magyars,
however, beat them on their heads with canes, forcing them to make
their way to Monasterzyska on foot. He who has the heart of a coward
should stay away from lions and bears.

Fortunately, the situation improved, as fresh troops drove into the
city in automobiles. But the Muscovites were no longer being chased,
since they refused to flee, and the Austrians settled into digging trenches
on their side between Trybuchowce, Dżuryn, and Czortków, as well as
other sites. With these troops came also an Austrian military hospital.
But they were not as well equipped as the Russians. In my school,
military hospital Nr. 36 was quartered. As the defeat of the Austrians
near Wygnanka became known, [the hospital staff] began packing their
things with great haste, loading the wagons with provisions, and putting

the medicines back in their containers, so that by 11 p.m. they were
ready to leave just as the order to remain in place was issued. Only the
following morning, after the Muscovites had been halted, did they once
again take over the school building.

The following day a happy surprise waited for us. My wife met an
acquaintance of ours on the street, the railroad man Korzyński, who
gave her a letter from the honorable Adam Hełczyński, at the time
a doctor with the Polish troops and an acquaintance of our sons. He
wrote that our sons were alive and gave us their addresses. The eldest
son Jozio [diminutive for Józef] was standard bearer in a Bosnian unit,
while the two younger sons were fighting in the Polish Legions. One
can imagine how happy we were; my wife cried from joy, and I did not
know what to do with myself. I looked for some paper right away and
wrote letters to all three sons as well as to Adam Hełczyński. After three
weeks we received replies from all three sons at almost the same time ....
All of them had fought in the Carpathians against Moscow ....

With the arrival of the Austrians the prices of all goods rose fivefold.
Price gouging now became quite wild, and the Jews could now get
away with anything .... Additionally, there were now denunciations on
a previously unknown scale .... Certainly, [under Russian occupation]
there were some arrests, and people complained about their neighbors
for revenge .... Now, since the reconquest by the Austrians, the Jews
denounced both Poles and Ukrainians. The Jews had traveled as far
as Russia in order to buy goods, and woe to any Catholic who dared to
stand in their way. But now [... those they denounced as having worked
for the] Muscovites ... were deported .... At one point I had to go all the
way to Stanisławów with my colleague Keffermüller, in order to defend
them. Many of them were sent to Tellerhofen in Tirol and imprisoned
there.

Already at the time of the Russian occupation a certain Russian
officer described the character of the Jews. At that time he used his
leather whip against a Jew, and when I asked him why he behaved that
way with the Jews, he answered: "The Jews are guilty of everything
and they deserve nothing more than to be despised. The reason for
this is the Talmud, and other related writings, which have transformed
the Jews into an unworthy people. The Jew will never be a Pole, nor a
German nor a Muscovite as long as he does not believe in Jesus Christ
and does not adopt the Christian faith. There are always some upright
and honest Jews, but we speak too much about them. Why? Judaism
is a sheet of black paper, on which one can find a white spot. Whoever
looks at such a sheet of paper says: 'There is a white spot here,' and will
speak more about this spot. Those few Jews are therefore akin to the

white spot on the black paper. That spot has no influence on the black paper, because we need to paint the entire paper white. The Jews are the misfortune of any state in which they live. This was already the case in Egypt, from which the wise Pharaohs expelled them. The Jews destroyed the Philistine people, they destroyed Spain and Germany. Now they are destroying Russia, Poland, and Austria, and I promise you that Europe too will sooner or later go to the dogs. History repeats itself; the Jews amass treasures, and the other nations observe them with growing contempt. The origin for this hate is Jewish greed. Finally, it was they who called out, when Pilate did not want to deliver Jesus to them: 'His blood be on us, and on our children.'"

According to this Russian officer this Jewish greed developed through trade. I personally have also seen Catholic, Christian merchants, who enriched themselves from the war, and were not one iota better than the Jews.

After the defeat in Wygnanka, the Austrians erected a new trench system east of Buczacz. These trenches spread over the fields of the villages of Medwedowce, Pilawa, Petlikowce, Dobropole [between 8 and 18 km north and northeast of Buczacz], and further north. Not a single night passed without a fire; it was astounding how many houses there were, since every day many of them were in flames. Each night the sky was lit by searchlights pointing in different directions. Behind the searchlights there were guns, and one heard the sound of rifles as well as the rattle of machine guns. This went on for months. Among the soldiers it was said that the Austrian positions could not be taken and that they would remain there until the Muscovite front was penetrated somewhere and the advance to the east resumed. We believed it. Every day new equipment and new guns were brought in. Every day Austrian and Muscovite wounded were brought to the hospital

But this hospital was not as large as the Russian one, and one had to save not only on food items but also on hygienic supplies. The doctor was a hulking Jew; when he stood in the sickroom or next to the patients, he would scream at them like a dog that should be pulled away. While Schwarzman was a man of sensibility, intelligence, and possibly a more honorable man than anyone who had ever existed under the sun, this new doctor was not worthy of polishing Schwarzman's shoes.

The medical staff was made up of different nationalities. There were Germans, Czechs, Dalmatians, Italians from Tirol, Hungarians, and Poles. The Sergeant was a Hungarian of the Mosaic religion. He … could not bear Galician Jews; he often said: "What does faith have to do with nationality? Ultimately you can be French, German, or Polish and at the same time be of the Mosaic confession; only the Galician Jew cannot

understand that, and he causes shame to all others of the Jewish faith."
I said to him that there were also Poles and Lithuanians of Jewish faith,
who were great patriots ....

In addition to the music of the artillery and rifle fire we now also had
the sound of the airplanes. Fresh snow had fallen. By moonlight three
Russian aircraft appeared, circled the city in various directions, and
began dropping bombs. A poor Jew was running across the marketplace
carrying water. He had nothing to do with the war; he worked, because
he wanted to live. Suddenly a bomb fell in front of him, exploded, and
ripped the poor man in two.

From that moment on everyone hid in their houses as soon as an
aircraft appeared in the sky. But this did not always help. Behind
the Black Bridge a bomb went through the roof of a house and killed
a Jewish woman, who was sleeping with her three children in bed.
Nothing happened to the children, apart from the fact that they became
orphans. At the house of Mrs. Rusińska, who lived right next to the
train station, three telephone technicians were sleeping; a bomb fell
through the roof and killed all three. A very beautiful young woman
was standing by the window, when a bomb suddenly fell right behind
the wall. As a result of the impact the window was shattered, and the
glass shards cut the Jewish woman's face. Another time, six horses
were killed by a bomb.

Perhaps ten paces from the school, on the path to the Fedor, the
Austrians positioned two anti-aircraft guns, which were meant to shoot
down airplanes. This made for a real battle, with the guns shooting at
the airplanes from below. In the sky the shell would burst, and the explosion would create a little cloud. Sometimes there were many dozens of
such clouds, but the airplanes were not hit. On one occasion during this
fighting a sergeant came by and said: "You can't shoot!" The resigned
officer replied: "Try it yourself." The sergeant ... fired, God directed
the bullet toward the aircraft, and the aircraft began to shake and lose
altitude; it made it to Pilawa [11 km northeast of Buczacz] and then
crashed between the Austrian and Muscovite lines. Both sides wanted to
reach the airplane and fought each other over it until it was completely
destroyed. The sergeant for his part had to flee, because the humiliated
artillerymen would have otherwise shot him.

Because of the school's proximity to the anti-aircraft guns, Russian
planes occasionally dropped up to thirty bombs on it, but none of them
struck it. They fell on the schoolyard or in the neighbors' gardens,
creating huge craters in the ground; sometimes they also fell into the
river. The court official Szebesta, a very aged man, was so terrified by
the torrent of bombs that he went mad and died.

Sometimes airplanes from both sides encountered each other over the city and we could observe the aerial battles from below. These airplanes flew in the air like magical, huge mushrooms, they flew in circles and each of them tried to rise higher than the other, they shot at each other, but finally they each returned behind their own lines without result. But on one occasion Russian aircraft caused great damage. That was in May 1916. Six Russian airplanes were flying over Buczacz, and then continued further toward Monasterzyska. There was an Austrian camp there on the marketplace. The mayor, who was a Jew, had organized a celebration in the hall of the city council and invited the officers, but they turned him down, saying: "This is not the time to celebrate," and did not attend. The airplanes arrived and bombed the camp and the city. In the camp a dozen horses and a couple of soldiers were killed; a bomb struck the municipal building and fell through the roof directly into the ballroom and killed many women. Other bombs fell on the house of the restaurateur Sziter and killed his mother. The airplanes then turned back to Buczacz and returned home in perfect tranquility.

Although Austrian soldiers claimed that their positions could not be seized, many military personnel and civilians did not believe this, because neither the railroad bridge nor the tunnel were rebuilt, and the wagon bridge was protected by a strong guard and was rigged with mines.

In winter 1916 I dreamt that my son Marian was looking into my room with a smile.

My school was always full of soldiers, who would come to the kitchen with various requests; one would ask for a pot, another wanted to sew something on the machine, and we no longer paid attention.

One day someone came through the door and remained standing next to us. We turned around and who do we see in front of us? A smiling Marian. One cannot imagine our joy when we saw him, since he had not been home for a year-and-a-half. He was the first legionnaire to have shown up in the city for all that time. The entire hospital found out about this instantaneously and right away there was great interest, because everyone wanted to see him. He was now already a big young man, with smooth skin like a young woman, a head taller than me, strong and good looking. He told us about his adventures, experiences, lucky escapes, and misfortunes, and about the battles in which he took part during the Carpathian campaign .... Together with his older brother Zygmunt, Marian was with the most advanced units right at the front and, upon orders from [Lieutenant-Colonel and commander of the 3rd Polish Legion's 13th brigade Józef] Haller,[50] he fired the first shot on Polish land in the direction of the Muscovites. Later both of them were sick with typhus for a long time. Strangely we always felt in Buczacz when one of our sons was ill.

But at that time soldiers on leave were in fact not allowed into Buczacz because of its proximity to the Russian line. Yet this order made no difference to the legionnaires. They had fought like lions and could not be rattled. Behind their backs there were informers, but when they found that this had to do with my son, they left him in peace. He stayed with us for two weeks, but time flew like the wind. He was at the time an NCO.

A few days after Marian's departure we received a telegram from our eldest son Józef in Stanisławów; he was at the time an NCO with a Bosnian unit and asked that we visit him. We went there right away. In the meantime, he had become a real man, had been awarded a silver medal for bravery in the battles against the Muscovites, and although he was smaller than Marian, he was more mature, since he was several years older. We had several friends in Stanisławów, … and consequently had a very entertaining time there and were amazed how quickly it passed until the sad day of departure.

Only those who send their son to war can grasp the sorrow and pain of the parents. This is impossible to describe. When a daughter marries and leaves home with her chosen one, her mother will shed a few tears, but this is a joyous event compared to what it means to send a son to war, since no one knows whether he will come back. Could this be the last time we see each other?

No one had dared dream that we would be as fortunate as to have a free and independent Poland. Presumably not even [Roman] Dmowski[51] and Piłsudski had dreamt of this at the time. We reckoned that we might perhaps gain autonomy. Thinkers and analysts argued then that neither the Germans nor the Russians would make concessions, since these were barbarous nations, plunderers, robbers of possessions and property, bloodsuckers akin to vampires. We kept quiet and fearful. No one had any inkling of God's plans.

Only my son Zygmunt, who was serving as a sergeant and commander of two machine guns in the second Lancers Brigade …, could not come home because he was at the front in Stochód [300 km north of Buczacz]. Instead he wrote long and detailed letters, describing the battles in which he took part ….

And so, the days passed, week after week, without hope that the war would end. The newspapers wrote about great offensives and battles on the Italian front, always victorious for the Austrians, yet such reports were akin to the shrieks of a Jew, who pushes a peasant to the wall and screams: "Take him away from me or I'll tear him apart!" We also observed that the hospital staff had packed their belongings and harnessed the horses, and while the Austrian soldiers would not tell us anything, we could guess on our own that the positions of the Austrians at the front were not as secure as they claimed.

In Easter 1916 the Muscovites along the front line in Dżuryn sent a soldier with a white flag to the Austrians and proposed a twenty-four-hour armistice, to which the Austrians agreed. Thereafter the Muscovites gave the Austrians various gifts, such as tea, sugar, and tobacco. The Austrians reciprocated with wine, vodka, and rum. That was not all; they also went over to the Muscovites, where they were hosted and then allowed to go back. Following that a couple of Muscovites came over to the Austrian line, and were taken all the way to Przewłoka, where the Austrian command was located at the time; there everyone celebrated joyfully until the end of the armistice. But when the Muscovites wanted to go back, they were not allowed to leave, and were told: "We did not keep any secrets from you, you came willingly to us as we had proposed, without covering your eyes, and not a few of our men might have betrayed secrets to you. We do not know who you are, perhaps there is among you also an excellent observer, and therefore please forgive us, but we cannot let you go."

This was sensible caution on the part of the Austrians, although it was immoral and dishonorable.

On this first Easter Friday it was quiet for the first time in a year and a half, not a single shot was heard. All the inhabitants, without distinction of religion and confession, celebrated this day. Suddenly, precisely at noon, an Austrian observation officer fired a shot in the direction of the Muscovites; later it was said to have been a mistake. At that very same moment the Muscovites responded; but their fire was so powerful and accurate, that the shells exploded on the Fedor and the entire city shook; in the school building all the wounded woke up, because the shells struck not far from us. After that the fire ceased again.

During the Christmas holiday of 1915 there had also been a three-week ceasefire; the reason that time was not a truce but because of the odd circumstances. As a result of the heavy snow, all the roads were snowed over, and the soldiers on both sides had nothing to eat, since no one could receive supplies. Both sides agreed unanimously that under these circumstances, had an enemy come over, they would not have fired a single shot.

The district administrator of Buczacz was Councilor Dniestrzański, and his office had a great deal of work. Since all twenty teachers in Buczacz were unemployed, they were called in for office work, and I was charged with supervising them. I was therefore to some extent back in "the army" as in days gone by. The district administration office was located in the building of the Basilian monastery. The Muscovites found out somehow that the office was there and sent their airplanes to bomb it. Everyone fled to the hallways, but I sat at my desk not far from the window. At some point a bomb exploded directly next to the window, the glass shattered, and the shards fell over me, but I kept on writing. The employees asked me whether I was not afraid, and I answered: "Previously I had no fear, because I could not know whether any bomb would fall next to me, and now, since they have already fallen, there is no point to being afraid." That's what I said at the time, but it was not advisable to trust one's luck a second time.

On one occasion the Governor Count [Hermann von] Colard[52] came to Buczacz and spent the night in Count Potocki's palace in Gawroniec [on the outskirts of Buczacz], where at the time also General [Adolf Baron von] Remen[53] and his staff were accommodated. Colard wanted to observe the front line and drove together with his adjutant Kuźmiński in an automobile to the village of Medwedowce [8 km northeast of Buczacz]. The Muscovites recognized the car already from afar and began firing at the car with their guns. The first shells struck forty paces from the car, they next came even closer, and the rest fell behind it, striking a restaurant; the shrapnel struck Kuźmiński and tore his coat. Colard then gave the order to return to Buczacz.

The governor then met representatives of various institutions in the district council office. City commissar Keffermüller asked for more provisions for the city, since the inhabitants were threatened by famine. When Colard heard this, he pointed with his finger to his bald head and said: "Do you see the few hairs on this head? Because of my vexation these last hairs will also fall out! At this moment I cannot do anything about this situation, but if I only get out of here, I will remember Buczacz." But these were empty promises. The count declined to meet the deputies, although he finally spent a moment with them. He would absolutely not meet the teachers, because where Mars rules, the muses are silent.

In early 1916 the district office gathered all its documents and transferred them to Niżniów; the city residents were told that the officials needed additional rooms for their work. In the remaining rooms I was expected to establish a school for boys and girls and for this purpose I was assigned ten female teachers. I set up the enrollment, and 614 boys and 546 girls registered. We looked for school benches and desks in various homes and put together a primitive classroom. General Remen instructed the district administrator to collect the necessary number of school benches, including those that had been previously used by soldiers.

I dressed neatly and made my way to Remen. At the gate of the palace garden a guard was posted made up of eight wounded Magyar soldiers. The sergeant asked me in Hungarian what I wanted. "I'm going to the general." Since he understood the word "general," he ordered the soldiers to lead me into the garden. There another NCO was posted, one who could speak German. Again, I had to explain the reason for my presence. He then led me part of the way and pointed with his hand toward an elderly officer, who was sitting on the park bench. This was Remen himself. At his side was a pile of German newspapers that he was reading. Right next to him stood a long table, covered with a white tablecloth, on which plates, bottles of wine, glasses of schnapps, knives, forks, and spoons were set for about twenty people. And next to the table a cook dressed in a snow-white apron and a white cap on his head was making himself useful. Clearly, they were getting ready for lunch.

The general saw me, and as I presented myself, calling him "your excellency," he asked me to sit next to him and to tell him what I wanted. He then inquired about my ancestry, which I answered. After he heard my response he motioned to the officer on duty and suggested that he call Major Kuźmiński. Then he asked me about my family. I reported to him that I had four sons, that the eldest was an officer in the Austrian army, and that the two younger boys had gone to the legions, while the fourth was in school. Upon hearing this Remen opined: "Polish legionnaires are brave and courageous heroes; I can only praise you for having such sons." The major arrived and Remen said in German: "Please take care of all the principal's requests." Major Kuźmiński promised to provide a larger number of benches and desks, as well as four carpenters and a couple of workers, in order to construct a so-called "foxhole" next to the monastery, that is, a kind of trench where one could shelter in case of a Muscovite air raid.

The following day I indeed received sixteen broken benches, but none of the carpenters and workers who were supposed to dig the "foxhole" arrived. It immediately occurred to me that things must be going badly at the front, since such an earnest general would not promise something he could not keep. The fire at the front was becoming ever more intense, and Muscovite airplanes were dropping ever more bombs, which blasted deep craters in the earth and spread an unpleasant smell in the area, as well as covering everything with yellow dust. On one occasion thirty bombs were dropped at the same time on our school, but not a single one struck it or exploded. People said that these were Japanese bombs, which the Muscovites were given by the Japanese, but I cannot say whether this was true. The Austrians buried them in the ground, but very cautiously.

The Cemetery

The number of the dead in the field hospitals was rising; every day there were more burials. This reminds me that at the beginning the Muscovites either did not bury the dead at all, or did not hold any funerals, presumably out of a sense of insecurity, whereas the Austrians, as soon as they arrived, cleared the cemetery, laid down wide paths, arranged the graves symmetrically, and enclosed the entire cemetery with a wooden fence; in the center of the cemetery a large cross was erected with the German inscription: "The Heroes who died while defending the Fatherland." The three-armed Muscovite crosses [of which the lower arm is slanted] were straightened and their inscriptions were covered up with paint, so that there was no difference between the fallen soldiers, in the sense that "in Heaven with God there are no enemies." On All Saints Day, 1 November 1915, a service was held at the cemetery. All the graves were lit with small lights. The general was present with his staff, the soldiers stood in ranks. The priests, a Czech, a Cossack, a Hungarian, and a German each made a little sermon. The music played for a prayer that began with the words, "Father, I call thee."

During this service the artillery was roaring from the East and from the West, so powerfully that the earth was shaking. This was no farewell salute, but shells bringing death, while nearby one could also hear ceaseless gunfire, ranging from rifle shots to machine gun rounds. But in the cemetery, there was a festive and tranquil air, as if one was afraid of waking up the dead, who were lying here in the cemetery. This service has remained etched in my memory.

Following the withdrawal of the Austrians, Piłsudski's followers damaged the cemetery layout so thoroughly that it was necessary to build a new one; they even stole wooden crosses from the graves, which had once been put up by the Muscovites. In Buczacz stone crosses and stonewalls are easier to come by than wooden planks.

During the Kerensky offensive[54] the Muscovites expanded the cemetery once more and surrounded it with stone posts and barbed wire. But they could not complete the work. And so, there are some stone military graves, on one of which Saint George slaying the dragon is chiseled. There are also several Muslim graves as well as Jewish ones. The Muslim graves are made of bricks in the shape of an obelisk, on which a half-crescent is chiseled; Jewish graves are made of a simple plaque with a Star of David. The ignominious partition powers sitting on their golden thrones set in motion entire peoples for their outlandish goals, and perpetrated murder under foreign skies and on foreign lands far from home and family. How many similar graveyards are there throughout Poland? ...

After the Lord granted them eternal peace I returned to my school. Possibly no school existed in all of Poland, indeed, in the whole world, as the one in which I taught the fourth grade. In the school there were no benches, only sixty barrels filled with vodka. I sat on a large barrel full of spirits, like Mephistopheles, and my students [sitting on smaller barrels] were like little demons. The stench of the spirits was bearable only when all the windows were open, but outdoors the artillery and gunfire were becoming ever louder, even as Russian aircraft flew over-head daily, dropping bombs nearby. By now large trumpets, so-called sirens, had been installed to protect cities, and as soon as a soldier observed an incoming airplane, the sirens howled and people hid in their houses, while we fled with our students into the church of the Basilian monastery.

One Sunday we brought the children into the church. There were about six hundred of us. We marched in pairs and in orderly columns, each teacher walking next to her class. Suddenly a Russian plane appeared in the sky and began shooting, since it took our large group for a military unit. The bullets flew around the whole city and landed on the roofs, but we marched in great calm into the church. Clearly it was not so easy to hit targets with submachine guns from an airplane.

The Second Muscovite Invasion

It happened on 1 June 1916, as bitter battles were raging between Uścieczko [45 km southeast of Buczacz] and Jazłowiec. Almost the entire city of Jazłowiec burned down, and the Muscovite bullets struck as far as Potok Złoty. All Austrian reserve formations were moved to Uścieczko. Additionally, on 3–6 June the weather was very misty and cloudy. Only on 7 June, as the clouds dispersed and the weather cleared up, could Austrian aircraft take off and evaluate the situation at the front. As always, we were clueless. The aircraft returned swiftly, having determined that in the region of Dżuryń a vast army was making its way toward Buczacz. In order to gain a clearer picture, the airplane in Buczacz took off for a second time.

While this was going on district administrator Dniestrzański and school inspector Zenon Zaklika arrived in Buczacz with the best inten-tions. They lauded me for the exemplary establishment of the school (on barrels of spirits)! Mr. Dniestrzański pronounced: "You are awarded the

golden cross for having kept up the morale of the people in this city."
I laughed over that, because we Polish teachers did not make much of
Austrian service medals. At 5 p.m. we let the children out of the school.
But the city was no longer protected, since the soldiers had left it in
haste, having rapidly moved their bivouacs to Monasterzyska.

I went home. The entire building was in turmoil and chaos, as is
common during a sudden retreat. The streets were jammed with carts
and automobiles, all fully packed with equipment from the field hospitals and ready to go. My wife was already waiting impatiently for
me, because she did not know what to do. We did not want to stay
with the Muscovites under any circumstances, since three of our sons
were fighting against them, and the fourth had gone to gymnasium
in Stanisławów. We did not think about it much, and within ten minutes we put on our best clothes and our coats, put the most important
documents and two loaves of bread in a bag, and went off with the
assumption that our entire thirty-year lifework and property would now
be lost. These feelings lasted only a few minutes, however. Regret over a
lost watch is the same as over one's entire property. One waves goodbye
and tries not to think about it.

The officers and doctors were quite astounded when they saw that
we had left our entire property behind and said: "We did not believe you
and thought that you were waiting for the Muscovites." At the train station there was total chaos: fleeing and whining Jews were pushing into
the railcars. The Germans beat them with rods and canes and shouted:
"Go away, you damned Jews!" The Jews responded: "We love our master
the emperor so much, and you won't let us in." "To the devil with you
and your love!" And from this moment on they would not let anyone in.

The railroad officials Mr. Kroczyński and Mr. Rasiewicz noticed us
and took us to one of the railcars, where the entire railroad personnel
was sitting next to the telegraph equipment. The friendly railroaders
offered us tea and at 11 p.m. the train set off. We went very slowly
toward Jezierzany. From the window we already saw the light of the
fires over Jazłowiec and the surrounding villages. Even during the railroad journey, we could hear the thunder of the artillery. The following
day, as we went through the Podolian heights we saw far in the east the
smoke and dust, and occasionally we could see the sparks of the fires
and guns ....

Return to Buczacz

In early April 1918 my superiors instructed me to return to my old
position in Buczacz. I was given the position of administrative head of

the junior high school for girls in the so-called barracks, since my own school on the Strypa served as an Austrian military hospital.

I found the building housing my school wrecked by the war; the windows and window frames were smashed, the doors broken, everywhere there was filth and disorder, and there were only a few broken school benches. It is better not to describe how under such condition one could conduct classes. It was unbelievable how demoralized the youth were by the war. Girls are usually distinguished by their shyness and politeness. This was not the case here. First and foremost, they had no respect for the property of others, they stole whatever came into their hands, even those broken benches were not safe from them. But I will not write about this, because it causes me much pain ....

On 12 November 1918, Poland rose from the dead, just as our national poet had predicted. Here I should break my quill and end my memoirs. And yet so many unexpected things occurred, as well as a civil war, that I cannot simply ignore these terrible events, not least because I and my family were deeply involved in them.[55]

Part II

The Civil War in 1918

... At 10 a.m. on All Souls Day (2 November 1918), the attorney [Ilarion] Bochurkiv, the merchant Klimicho Rohoshynsky (scion of the old Polish nobility), the engineer Viktor Luchkiv, and Siyak, a post office official, came to the local district administration, and demanded that district administrator Dniestrzański hand over to them the administrative papers (both Bochurkiv and Luchkiv's wives are Polish). The latter saw no alternative, and did as he was ordered, not least because he could see from the window many men with clubs and guns and was convinced that resistance would be senseless.

All other officials followed his example. Similarly, all the files were stolen from the district court as well as from the post office. Only Józef Wagner, a school inspector and a hard-boiled man, responded to the demand for the school records with the following words: "No, you have taken over my office, and there is no reason for me to hand over documents to you, or to justify myself to you, and if I were to hand over materials, that would be only on orders from the authorities." Having said that he left his office.

The businessman Klimicho Rohoshynsky was appointed city mayor. That morning the trains were no longer running, because the railroad

officials and workers had been dismissed after being told that they would
have to sign a loyalty declaration to West Ukraine. The railroad men
would not sign this declaration and stated that they would only accept
instructions from the legitimate authorities and in any case would not
support the uprising. They were removed from their offices and replaced
by people without any higher education who had little knowledge about
the work of railroad men.

The handover of offices proceeded relatively calmly; only in the gendarmerie was there a scuffle, when a crowd of people converged on the
gendarmerie station and demanded a handover of the weapons, which
the gendarmes did right away. Only one of them resisted and was consequently beaten up badly. In the city there was a great deal of traffic,
because the Ukrainians brought the population from the nearby villages
and armed them. The peasants and farm laborers were equipped with
clubs, and it was said they would loot Jewish businesses and Polish
citizens. These people came from Żyznomierz, Soroki, Trybuchowce and
Medwedowce, as well as Nagórzanka and the outskirts of Buczacz. The
majority of them spent the night at the home of Father Natayko.

I was just heading to church when I saw a dozen carts filled with
armed men drive by. They were led by the town clerk Luchiv of
Żyznomierz, who saw me and greeted me. My impression was that he
had a calming effect on these people. In the afternoon a train arrived in
Buczacz with three railcars full of soldiers with two machine guns ....
The soldiers disembarked from the railcars and, displaying heroic courage, positioned both guns right next to the rails and began shooting at
the defenseless, calm city, targeting also the gendarmerie building, in
which there were only women and children. The bullets smashed the
windows [of the gendarmerie building], tore up the roof, and flew all
over the city, which was enveloped in a thick fog.

Suddenly a woman holding a broom popped out of one of the nearby
huts and when she saw these stupid gangs, she threatened them with
her broom and yelled at them: "May the devil take you and your shooting spree, who are shooting at? My children are terrified, you better
watch out, or I will chase you down with my broom right away and
scratch out your eye." The heroes, humiliated and frightened by the
woman's threats, formed into four rows and marched to the marketplace, so as to conquer the city, as was reported in their new newspaper,
"Nove Zhyttia" [New Life]. They were led by the hero Kardan, who had
once been a student at the local gymnasium and a former classmate of
my sons.

At night the "heroes" walked through the city, and just like the
Chechens before them, shot up street after street, until they were

ordered to stop shooting on account of the ammunition shortage. Still they would not stop, especially in the evenings and at night, for instance when one of the residents had to go out to the street. Sometimes the soldiers would shoot at the washing hung up to dry when it appeared to them too long and they would keep shooting until it fell down. They took weapons and uniforms from the gendarmerie supplies and equipped the soldiers with them.

This new gendarmerie distinguished itself by arresting passersby in the evening and at night and beating them up as badly as criminals used to be beaten in the old days. Among them there were also Ruthenian peasants, the so-called volunteers, who had, however, not known that they would be attached to these criminal gangs. Every evening we could hear the screams and cries of people being beaten. All of this occurred with the knowledge and in accordance with the will of the Ukrainian Ataman [chief] Luchkiv, the commandant of our district. Only later was an order issued in Stanisławów which forbade corporal punishment.

The new rulers introduced the Ukrainian language right away in all offices. This was still not so bad, since in Podolia all Poles spoke that language very well, but this new pseudo-Ukrainian power completely forbade the use of Polish in offices and schools. As a cultivated people, the Poles were never against the Ukrainian language, since already in earlier times everyone could speak and write whatever they wished. Polish had always been the language of instruction in the local gymnasium, but now Ukrainian was made into the language of instruction, forgetting that in the past both languages had been taught there. Now the Polish language was completely removed, all Poles were kicked out of the gymnasium, and only Ukrainians and Jews remained.

All former civil servants, tax officials, post office clerks, railroad workers, teachers in elementary schools, in the boys' and girls' schools, and in the gymnasium, had to sign a declaration. This declaration stated that the undersigned was sworn to unconditional obedience, loyalty, and honesty to the "West Ukrainian Republic." Naturally, the Poles did not sign this declaration. First the railroad men refused in solidarity with each other, although they were immediately driven out of their homes to the street. Among other officials, the judges did sign the declaration, since they feared to lose their work permits, and there were a few others, who were afraid of falling into oblivion.

When Professor Niebieszczański was asked to sign, he refused so emphatically, that he almost had to be carried away. The Jews all signed with the exception of Professor Izaak Patterko, who actually stated that while he adhered to the Mosaic religion, he was a Pole. Conversely, the declaration was signed by a man who was at the head of the Poles before the war and had always been at the forefront of all patriotic festivities. And then there was a member of the Sokół Association, who actually requested to be allowed to sign, but the Haidamaks ridiculed him and refused his signature. Ataman Luchkiv himself made fun of these [signatures] and said: "They look like Poles to me. At best you could fill holes in the fireplace with them!" …

News was arriving that the Haidamaks were looting homes and stealing horses, cattle, swine, agricultural implements, furniture, clothes, shoes, and underclothes, in other words, that they were behaving even worse than the Muscovites, or later the Austrian or Prussian armies. All grain stocks were looted from the district offices and the post office, as well as sugar, clothes, and money. At the district offices alone cash money valued at 3 million crowns was stolen—a very considerable sum at the time.

Only two months before the outbreak of this uprising the central clothing department in Lwów had sent dozens of suits for sale to the officials and teachers of the city. Because we were afraid of storing these suits in the district offices, the sale took place in my apartment. From this fabric 250 meters were left with me. Bochurkiv knew about the fabric that remained with me and sent a squad of soldiers to confiscate it. But I demanded proof from the soldiers. One of the soldiers went off and returned with a signed order stating that this fabric was to be confiscated. The order carried Bochurkiv's signature. I put away the card and the soldiers carried off the fabric. I do not know what they did with it.

The position of School Inspector Wagner in the school directorate was now taken over by the gymnasium professor Vasyl Vynar, who was well liked by both Polish and Ruthenian students. Whenever one of the boys made no progress in their Latin class, he would beat and punish him, but would never give him a bad grade. But generally, he had no idea about elementary school issues and merely did what Bochurkiv demanded. In his first official action he instructed all school principals to provide lists of teachers clearly indicating their nationality. One could already see that Bochurkiv had something up his sleeve.

Next the school inspector convened a teachers' conference, which took place in my school. Here the curriculum for the district schools was to be determined. But this was in fact a side matter, since the main goal was to compel us to sign the declaration …. Finally, Vynar informed us that only teachers who signed the loyalty declaration to the West Ukrainian Republic would receive their salary and teaching credentials. Since none of the Poles were ready to sign the declaration, and the

Ruthenians and the Jews had already signed it before and received their salaries and teachers' authorization, the farce came to an end ....

A month before the outbreak of this civil war our eldest son Józef, who was by then a lieutenant, came home. He arrived sick, since he had contracted typhus. He had been hospitalized for a long time, and after his condition improved somewhat, he was allowed to stay home for convalescence. Our younger son Zygmunt, a legionnaire and Polish lancer, later transferred to the 20th Czortków Rifle Regiment, and had served on the Tirol Front. He too received leave and the two of them were together with me at home ....

Right at the beginning of this Haidamak rule both my sons had to hand over their officers' sabers and were ordered to remove the officer insignia from their collars. On 13 November 1918, one pseudo-Ukrainian,[56] our neighbor [Antoni] Dembytskyi (who was a teacher at my school) came to Józef and said to him: "Mr. Józef, I request that you sell us your officer's uniform, we have no uniforms for officers." "And what should I wear?" asked Józef. "We'll give you fabric from the store of the same kind that we already confiscated from your father, so that you'll have something to wear; if you don't agree to this you will be compelled in any case to give up your army clothes." "Ha, well in that case, I will absolutely not give up my clothes, and you will have to loot them from me."

That same day, the first case of plunder occurred in the city: At half-past-midnight, someone knocked loudly with a heavy object on our door. We all woke up right away, and I went to the window to see what was going on, and what did I see? A large fellow holding a lantern in his hand and next to him some twelve to fourteen men armed with rifles and bayonets. "Open the door," called the fellow, and I opened the door. That fellow walked in through the door and spotted the flour that had been prepared for the teachers of the district, for which they had already paid. The fellow asked: "What's this flour?"

"This flour is the property of the teachers, tomorrow it will be distributed," I said. "Who allowed this?" "Luchkiv" (I was actually convinced of this). "You are lying, since I have given no such permission." It was only then I realized that I was speaking with Luchkiv himself who, without drawing special attention to his dignity as Ataman, was walking around like a regular soldier and looting other people's property instead of sending some police constable to do this. And so, since he admitted that it was actually him in person, I said to him: "If it was not Luchkiv, then it was Bochurkiv." But the Ataman insisted that he be addressed as Mr. Luchkiv, because he wanted to save face in front of his soldiers. He walked over to the first room and called out: "Hand over your arms!"

Our weapons were well hidden, and so I declared that we had no arms. But he turned to Zygmunt and said: "If I find any weapons, I will order to execute you on the spot, understood?" "Now I know," Zygmunt responded but stayed in bed and did not get up. Meanwhile Luchkiv began looting, ordering the soldiers to open all the cabinets and drawers; the soldiers pulled out underclothes, handkerchiefs, items of clothing, and linen, while Luchkiv kept yelling, "Take that, take that!" In the corner there were twelve sacks that belonged to Inspector Wagner. Everything Luchkiv looted from us was packed into these sacks, and all that remained were the clothes on our backs. One of the soldiers also wanted to take Zygmunt's pants, but when Zygmunt saw this he got out of bed quickly and put them on, otherwise he would have remained in his underpants only. My sons' officers' overcoats were hanging in the cabinets. The soldiers took them right away and put them on. Luchkiv also took part in the looting, and when he found my son's army binoculars in one of the boxes, his eyes flashed like a cat's and he stashed them in his pocket.

We had twenty-four kinds of yarn, which he tore up with his nails, as well as a sewing machine. I also had a stock of cigarettes, ink, quills, and envelopes for the teachers' association. Luchkiv ordered his men to pack all this into the sacks and took for himself also the entire family correspondence. When my son Józef asked him to return the letters, he responded: "We are now enemies, which is why I will not give you back these letters." On the oven there were 1,400 crowns, ... set aside for the purchase of shoes for poor students. When I said that to Luchkiv, he did not touch the money. On the table Luchkiv noticed my wristwatch, but he did not touch it. He took a school broom from the cellar, and then went to the attic, where the Brownings [pistols] were hidden, but he did not find them. Under Józef's mattress were boxes with rifles. One of the soldiers, who came from Trybuchowce, found them, but did not pull them out, and instead pushed them further under, so that no one would see them. The soldiers were ashamed and said: "We have fought on many fronts but have never seen anything like this anywhere." The looting of my house went on until 3:30 a.m. All they left behind was a pile of broken objects.

This was the first requisition and looting of the [Polish-Ukrainian] war in Buczacz. Later there were several more requisitions in my home, and each time something was discovered and looted.

This [first] case of plunder quickly became known throughout Buczacz. Everyone was enraged, since Luchkiv was actually considered to be a cultivated person, yet now he had shown his real face. Ruthenian women, who had not expected their Ataman Luchkiv to act like a looter, spoke out especially: "We feel ashamed of him." Luchkiv himself felt that he had caused great damage, but by now it was too late. My wife went to Bochurkiv, in order to retrieve a few items, and he summoned Luchkiv, ordered him to return the plundered items, and said to him: "Why did you make such a mess, you idiot?" But we got back only two blankets and a shirt, because by the time the soldiers had reached the storeroom, they had already stolen half of the things, and in the storeroom, everyone traded as they pleased.

Our courageous colleagues Keffermüller and Czyżewski helped us out with a couple of shirts once they found out that we had been plundered. The two of them had hearts of gold. We were given ration cards that allowed us to buy a liter of crude oil for 3 crowns, whereas those who had no cards had to pay 16 crowns.

As I write this, something keeps happening on the street all the time, here some looting, there another shootout, and meanwhile the quill freezes in my hand from the cold, and I have so many worries that I cannot gather my thoughts, but perhaps one day these notes will become real memoirs.[57]

About a week before Christmas we were called again to the hall in the gymnasium, in order to agree on a finalized teaching plan for the schools, but our Ruthenian colleagues told us in confidence that this had nothing to do with the plan but was rather aimed at forcing us to sign a "declaration." Now that we knew what was going on in Bochurkiv's office, we passed this information on to the village teachers, since we were acting here [in Buczacz] a little like a [military] staff. On one occasion the teacher Żeromski came to me and asked whether we had signed the declaration, and I asked in return: "Would a Żeromski attach his good name to something like this?" "I understand" he replied and turned away, since it was dangerous to speak with each other for long. News of our conduct spread throughout the district, but it was transmitted only in confidence, because we wanted to prevent anyone from being betrayed; but this did not help, because walls have ears.

The meeting was attended by teachers opposed to signing the declaration of loyalty to the Ukrainian government from all over the district, Poles and Ukrainians. Our friends (?) the Jews also came. Everyone was in a very somber mood, since we all knew the stakes were very high. After a long wait Bochurkiv arrived and called us [presumably only the principals] into his office, where he proceeded to berate us like a dictator with the voice of a rooster, since he was, after all, the "commissar of commissars." ... Bochurkiv first spoke in Ruthenian. He used the intonation of a teacher, spoke about our poverty, our meager income, but stated that now things would be better, and urged us to sign the declaration. Since he had come to the meeting, he said, "I will sort things out with the elementary school teachers, even if I have to jail the lot of them."

We requested to think this over for five minutes and went out the hallway. There we then chose the colleague Keffermüller, who was to declare in all our names that none of us would sign the declaration. When Keffermüller began speaking, Bochurkiv interrupted him and asked whether he was speaking for himself or on everyone's behalf. Keffermüller responded: "In everyone's name. The Commissar has of course the best intentions, but we must decline to sign until there is a general European peace, because we Poles do not recognize a West Ukrainian republic, and no one is a prophet, or can predict what will happen."

Bochurkiv turned red with rage and answered angrily: "Ha, if that's the way things are, you will not receive permits to work as teachers, and I will eject all school principals from their homes." At that point Father Władysław Olbrycht asked permission to speak and said: "How can we trust you, if you use every opportunity to harm Poles? You have removed the Polish language from the gymnasium and the elementary schools, and instead force us to do things that a Polish tongue will not dare utter. You have thrown out the students from the dormitories, which were funded by Polish money, and your soldiers have taken over all the beds. When a child says in school 'praised be Christ,' then he is struck in the face by his teacher." "That is not true!" interrupted him Bochurkiv. "Who did that?"

"Viniarska, the teacher from Dźwinogród [7 km northeast of Buczacz]." "We will discipline her," said Bochurkiv .... This teacher's father was a Pole, and her brother had served as a volunteer in the Polish legions [presumably her mother was Ukrainian]. This is how mixed up people's thinking was. Other teachers also wanted to speak, but they were no longer allowed to and thus all Poles left the room with much commotion, and only the so-called Ukrainians and Jews stayed behind. Father Olbrycht was accused of defaming Viniarska. Testifying before the court in his defense was a girl who had also been beaten, along with her mother, and Olbrycht was acquitted. But despite these developments, Viniarska remained school principal, whereas the previous principal, a deserving teacher, was removed from the school and was then sent to Jazłowiec, where she was imprisoned with us [see the next section, "Jazłowiec"].

Lukash Danylov [former teacher of foreign languages] was appointed principal of the [Buczacz] middle school, although he had not taught for four years .... He immediately abolished the use of Polish in the school.

In response all Polish children left the institution .... In the schools nothing sensible was taught, everything was politicized, and as a result there were frequent brawls between the students. In our home we hosted a boy called Marcinkowski, who attended second grade in the middle school and was a good student. When his teacher, Chekanovskyi, wanted to motivate the Ruthenian students to study, he always said: "Aren't you ashamed that a Pole knows more than you do? He alone is worth more than ten of you Ukrainians." When Danylov and later Bochurkiv heard about this they launched a disciplinary process against Chekanovskyi, who came within a hair's breadth of losing his job. Marcinkowski was similarly hounded in an attempt to make him give up his Polishness, provoking the enraged boy into uttering all kinds of stupidities about pseudo-Ukraine. Having heard about this, Danylov ... pronounced: "We can say whatever we like about the Poles, but the Poles are forbidden from speaking about us!" Consequently, he expelled the boy from the school. That's the kind of educator he was!

The teachers in this school were: [the Ukrainians] Chekanovskyi and Kizimovych, as well as the Jews, Nacht, Seifer, Niemand and Bauer, since the Jews had signed the declaration [of loyalty], and curiously, all suddenly forgot how to speak Polish ....

On Saint Nicholas Day [19 December 1918], a big celebration was held in the Buczacz marketplace. An altar was erected next to the city hall and the entire marketplace was surrounded by soldiers so that Poles could not get through. The Jews were allowed to be present at this service. A large number of people came from the surroundings; all village elders, who were grandly designated commissars—whether they could read and write or not—were invited. A Basilian priest led the Mass, and gave a rather good sermon, in which he said: "You want to have Ukraine, but you forget God the Father and the love of your neighbor. Many of you have participated in lootings, have caused pain to your neighbors, and you still want the Lord to help you?!" ...

After him Bochurkiv made a speech. At first everyone was irritated that he dared to speak from the pulpit that had been placed next to the altar and from which only priests should speak—an act of disrespect toward the clergy—but such were the times, that even the Basilians could not prevent this. Bochurkiv positioned himself with his back to the altar and spoke in a completely different tone from the Catholic monk:

"In the past, if your cow grazed in the pasture of a landowner, his agents would show up right away and fine you. We are now done with that! And when you had nothing to cook your food with and your shack was cold, and you went to the edge of the forest and cut off few branches, the forester would catch you right away and confiscate your ax, the whole affair would go to court, and you'd end up in prison because of these sticks of wood. This will not happen again."

When the peasants heard this nonsense, one of them said to another [in Ukrainian]: "Did you hear this? That means we can steal!" And the other responded: "Just try to steal anything from me and see if you can keep your teeth."

Following the celebration Bochurkiv ordered all the "commissars" to swear an oath to the "West Ukrainian People's Republic." When the peasants heard that they said [in Ukrainian]: "Did you see that? This Bochurkiv swore an oath wearing gloves, he is a wise man, because this means that the oath is not valid and because of that we too can swear an oath."

That's the kind of circus that Bochurkiv organized ....

Jazłowiec

The war taught people to label crimes and other rights violations with fancy Latin terms. Thus, simple robbery was called requisition, and the expulsion of entire families from their homes, whereby they died somewhere from hunger and poverty, was called evacuation. The imprisonment of completely innocent people and their incarceration in various cells was called internment. When they were not kept in prison cells, they were expelled to other towns, where the enemy and poverty awaited them. Such pompous terms were employed in order to cover up the crimes.

On 13 December 1918, at 11 p.m.—since evil men are afraid of the light—someone knocked on my front door. I rose and saw through the window four soldiers armed with bayonets and carrying lanterns. "Perhaps another search," I thought to myself and let them in. The NCO, nowadays a polite fellow, handed me a piece of paper from Bochurkiv, which said: "Mr. Siewiński and his two sons are hereby summoned to an interrogation." This interrogation in the middle of the night appeared very peculiar, and so I figured that it had to be some kind of trap. The soldiers lingered while we got dressed, and I took a little money with me just in case. We went out to the street and our four companions guarded us from all sides; we paraded in this manner across town. The city was entirely dark and there was light only in the homes of the engineer Ostrowski and at Pożycki's. We gathered that this involved the arrest of the city's Polish elites.

We were led to the school building by the Strypa. It would have never occurred to me that I would find myself in these rooms, where I had taught and conducted examinations ..., as a prisoner guarded by soldiers. There were already several dozen people there and more and more were being brought in. There were priests, officials, teachers, respected craftsmen, school principals, villagers, and among them was also—miraculously!—an Israelite, the attorney Ausschnitt, who was as much use there as a dog in a church. We certainly did not feel like laughing, but at the sight of the attorney's desperate face and terrified eyes we burst out laughing.

"Woof! Woof! Woof! [Ausschnitt barked]. What have I done to deserve coming here? I haven't done anything, what has this got to do with me? Why am I being held here? ... For this I should thank Bochurkiv, with whom I have an appointment on Tuesday and who is in competition with me. Woof! Woof! Woof!" And so Ausschnitt went around the room, lamenting his fate and constantly puffing on his cigar. And indeed, three days after that appointment, Ausschnitt signed the declaration and was released. Now that he was a truly loyal Ruthenian he was instructed to write his nameplate in Ukrainian with Cyrillic letters painted yellow ....

The Jews were real chameleons, always changing the signs over their stores and flying flags of different colors, one time the Austrian, then the Prussian, the Hungarian, the Russian, the pseudo-Ukrainian, the Polish, and, had the Chinese shown up, they would have hoisted the Chinese flag as well; yet in their hearts their only shield of arms is money. There are only a few among them who love this land with all their heart, who would sacrifice their lives for it. Their politics is very strange, as well as shortsighted. They have no inkling of what catastrophe may befall them (read the book *Caesar's Column*).[58] Their only hope is conversion to the Catholic faith, whereby they will become true sons of the soil on which they dwell. Indeed, we have many Polish families of Jewish origin, who nowadays are the honor of Poland and have become exemplary Catholics.

We were taken individually to interrogation in the school office, where we were questioned by our good acquaintance Yavorskyi, who had once been a law clerk in Buczacz. The questionnaires, printed on a typewriter, had been prepared in advance. We were asked about our ancestry, place of birth, denomination, nationality, and profession. We all had to sign these forms, after which each of us was informed that we would be interned in Jazłowiec.

Before the interrogation we were taken to another room; by the door stood two armed soldiers, and each of us was searched for weapons. We waited in the room until 5:30 a.m. Then we were led to the schoolyard. Twenty sleds were already waiting there, prepared by the inhabitants of Nagórzanka, who were, of course, compelled to do this. The older people were seated in fours on the sleds, the younger and stronger ones were seated in groups of six next to the soldiers and the coachmen. We drove quickly through the city, because the Haidamaks were ashamed of the Ruthenian and Polish inhabitants of the town seeing them interning us. Past the Black Bridge and going up the serpentine road, the horses slowed down, and dawn began breaking. In the town the lights in some houses were being lit, but no one went out to the street, because everyone had a bad feeling and was afraid. We could already recognize some of the houses emerging from the darkness in Pyszkowce, as well as the forest, which stood out clearly against the white background. Here in the midst of fields and woods we stopped to wait for the other transports.

It was very cold, but bearable, since we Podolians are a tough people. We stepped off the sleds and began singing; we were at that time sixty-seven people from Buczacz; later some additional internees arrived. We first sang [Polish] Christmas carols ...; then we sang Polish patriotic songs with such joy, that even the trees in the forest were astonished, having never before heard such beautiful songs. The peasants and the soldiers looked on with gaping mouths, wondering why we were so joyous. Then we sang songs of the legionnaires, Polish and Ruthenian songs. In the silence our singing could be heard for miles around. The soldiers' stern faces brightened up and along with the coachmen they joined in the singing and made fun of Bochurkiv, Luchkiv, and all the other idiots who had ordered them to intern us ....

After a few hours in the cold the passion to sing clearly weakened; nobody had brought anything to eat, since none of us had expected that they would play such a trick on us and let us wait for so long, and thus we were all hungry. Some had brought tobacco and so everyone smoked to make the time pass. At some point in the morning a train arrived from Monasterzyska and added more internees to our group. There were not enough sleds for everyone, and so the older people were seated in the sleds and the younger ones marched in four rows, which gave this the semblance of an outing full of song and good cheer; even the accompanying soldiers sang along: "Poland is not yet lost," as well as other Polish songs, and had they not been afraid, they would have thrown away their bayonets and run off. In this manner we marched through the villages of Rzepińce, Cwitowa, Pomorze, and Zaleszczyki Małe [10–14 km southeast of Buczacz]. Everywhere people came out of their houses and bid farewell to us, since we were all well known to them, but we were now accompanied by guardian angles with bayonets ....

We went on to Jazłowiec. The town was in a frightful condition. Buczacz was of course also burned down and lay in ruins, but at least its suburbs as well as several buildings had remained standing; in Jazłowiec, however, everything was in ruins, people were living in cellars, and the church had been burned to the ground. All that remained was the convent of the Sisters of the Immaculate Conception, one church, and a few houses. Everywhere there were ruined walls and collapsed chimneys, as if they were weeping over the fate of their former residents. Whereas Buczacz had been intentionally burned down by the occupiers, Jazłowiec was destroyed by the extended battles between the Austrians and the Muscovites .... The convent itself was built on a hill over the Olechów, a tributary of the Strypa ....

We came into the front court of the convent. Here we were received by other soldiers with bayonets and were then taken individually to the offices of the dungeon boss, that is, the commandant of the convent, [Sergeant Zakhar] Bylo. [... Then] we were taken up the narrow stairs to the first hall, where we were ordered to hand in all our papers, notes, pencils, watches and money .... After they took our personal belongings from us, we were led to yet another hall. Another group of soldiers was standing by the door, under the command of a certain Mr. Zagraychuck of Zubrzec, not far from Koropiec [13 and 23 km southwest of Buczacz, respectively]. He confiscated our suspenders and even our belts and we had to hold our pants with our hands so that they would not fall down. Items of any worth were immediately stolen by the soldiers ....

About two weeks after we arrived additional internees were brought in ..., altogether eighty-five people. Also seventeen prisoners of war were interned there. The treatment of Polish soldiers was very rough. They sat in isolated cells, by the doors there were guards, and whenever they had to take care of their needs, they were accompanied by an armed Haidamak .... All of them were captured in the vicinity of Jaworów [200 km northwest of Buczacz], and many of their comrades were murdered right on the spot; in Krasne [130 km northwest of Buczacz] their uniforms were torn off their bodies and each of them was given fifty lashes .... In this manner the Haidamaks demonstrated that they were uncivilized and unworthy of being called soldiers, since even wild Africans do not beat prisoners of war ....

As I have already said, upon our arrival they took away our suspenders, so that we had to hold up our pants with our hands. It was only on the third day that we were told that an Ataman from Buczacz would be coming to visit; this was not Luchkiv but someone else, a young, attractive man, called Sokolovskyi, and certainly a Pole; he greeted us and asked whether we needed anything. Niebieszcański stood up and requested that we be given back our suspenders, our shoelaces, our watches, and our money, and that we be allowed to walk around the yard every day, so that we would be able to breathe some fresh air and visit the chapel for holy Mass. Sokolovskyi did not respond but stood up and walked out …. The following day an order arrived from Buczacz to hand us back all our belongings, as well as allowing us to buy tobacco …. Additionally, we were allowed to go to the chapel for half an hour but under heavy guard ….

Around 10 January 1919, a new transport arrived with internees from Jaworów, Sokal, and Żółkiew [250 to 175 km northwest of Buczacz], altogether about eighty people. They included mostly lawyers, teachers, craftsmen, peasants, nobility, and priests. These people were in such a bad state, filthy and disheveled, that they made a pitiful sight …. They could not get over the injustices perpetrated upon them. Father Samborski related that a very small unit of the Polish army had come to Jaworów, [… where] they were attacked by Haidamaks from all sides. Some were killed on the spot, twenty-three others were wounded, and could not keep moving, and the rest fled. Then the residents of Jaworów came from the suburbs, carrying axes, and killed the wounded, splitting their heads with axes and hatchets …. Those interned in Jaworów were driven to Żółkiew, where the county administrator, the priests, and six women were taken prisoner, including one Ruthenian woman, whose brother had served in the Polish legions …. They were driven further to Krasne, where … a Haidamak sergeant with more of his ilk simply tore off their clothes, as well as their hats and money and even their underclothes. Then some people took pity on them and gave them something to wear, so that they would not freeze to death ….

[In] the convent, the supplies were running out …. Along with the nuns and the children, we were altogether about five hundred people, apart from the guards, who were receiving supplies, naturally. For breakfast, lunch, and dinner we received only a little saltwater with potatoes, or red beans, which we called "our chocolate soup"; we were given one slice of bread of a few grams per day, and the children also received sometimes the same amount of bread ….

Around mid-January we heard distant shots and artillery fire from the west, and since we had already developed an ear for this, we assumed that these battle sounds were coming from the direction of Lwów ….

The Return to Buczacz

On 21 January 1919, a pleasant man wearing a uniform with two stars on his collar arrived from Czortków. Later I learned that this was the attorney Vydrak who was supposed to be a decent person. He announced that the internees could go home, but only those who lived in Buczacz;

we merely had to sign a declaration that we would not get mixed up in any political affairs, and that we would report daily to the commissariat, as proof that we had not fled. Everyone was happy to agree to that …. The following day several eager helpers arrived from Nagórzanka and took us on their sleds free of charge to Buczacz …. Only someone who comes out to the fresh air after a long illness, or a prisoner, who has at least won back some of his freedom, can appreciate how beautiful the world is, even when it is covered in snow. We drove cheerfully over the Strypa River, through the valley of the Buczacz forest, over the Fedor and past the Basilian monastery into the city.

It was market day. When people saw us, everyone began running toward us with happy faces, townspeople and villagers, Poles and Ruthenians, all were endlessly happy. Finally, we drove with Father Olbrycht to the front of the rectory. Here our arrival was already awaited, and lunch had been prepared, indeed a very luxurious meal for those times. Although there was only chicken soup with semolina, it tasted better than ever …. Then came Father Dziurzycki, who had not been interned, [… and he] told us about the impression our imprisonment had made on the city. For one thing, the townspeople of both religions as well as the peasants of Podzameczek had threatened to tear down the commissariat, and as a result the number of guards in the city was doubled. At the end of the year the church had filled up with villagers, and on the following day, New Year's, the priest announced in his sermon that he would hold Mass in honor of the internees. Upon this the entire congregation began weeping, demonstrating the patriotism of the village population, whose empathy for our suffering was such that it experienced it as its own pain ….

25 January 1919

I was ordered to move out of the school building right away. The order was signed by Bochurkiv. Perhaps that was the best way to simply throw me out to the street. Fortunately, one of my oldest colleagues still had a free apartment, … and we moved there. The window opened to the street and we could not find any curtains. Every pedestrian could see precisely what was going on inside, and from that time on no one ever looted our home again.

Another funny thing—what did we actually live on? None of the civil servants and teachers had any money, no one received a salary, and the Haidamaks provided no sort of pay. On the initiative of the engineer Władysław Ostrowski a committee was established, … which borrowed money from the bank in Czortków—which was given on credit against our future income .... With this money many other Poles from Eastern Galicia, who were under house arrest in Buczacz, were provided with food. The Haidamaks brought ever more people there but had no way of feeding them and naturally looked out for their own benefit and profit. Somehow the Haidamaks found out that we had an endowment, on which we could support ourselves, and subjected Ostrowski's home to frequent inspections ....

Here it is also necessary to say something about the Jews. This is a peculiar people. Among them one can find individuals with a noble soul, but they can be counted on the fingers of one hand, whereas in general one can say that it is impossible to rely on Jews. After all, they have been living for centuries together with us, they came here and acquired possessions, of which their ancestors would have never dared dream. Yet their politics is shortsighted, since they do not love this soil, upon which they live and work, nor the people with whom they have lived together for centuries. At a time of misfortune, a Jew will abandon even his best friend, indeed, he can betray his friend even for the slightest opportunity to make a profit; and as for Jewish gratitude to the nation with which they have grown together, don't even dream of it. How many times have they changed their sympathies and support during this seven-year war!

No people can rely on the Jews; they work with the powerful only for the sake of business, and once the powerful have been deflated, they treat them like a donkey gasping for air that nonetheless gets kicked again .... They demoralize nations. Why are there no thieves in Norway? Well, because there are no Jews there. The Jew does not have the courage to plunder on his own, but he buys everything from the thief; and who trades in living goods? On account of this dishonorable attitude, they are loathed by all peoples. The Jews feel this, and occasionally one noble person among them converts to the Christian faith and those who do so become true sons of the soil on which they live.

At the beginning of this frightful civil war I spoke with serious Jews, who viewed me as a forward-looking politician, and they asked me how they should conduct themselves during this war. "A curious question," I responded. "The Poles took you in when you were poor, in Poland you have come into your possessions, and everything that you are today is thanks to the Poles." "That is all true," said the Jews, "But we are afraid." "If you are afraid, at least don't get mixed up in this business." "We want to do that, but who among us can put his hand in the fire for those fools who are ready to take bribes, for which we will all end up paying." And that's what happened. Under the rule of the Haidamaks there was an event in the Polish Sokół building, in which almost only

Jews took part, and they screamed at the end of the performance, "Long live Ukraine, down with Poland!"

Those shouting were students, who owed their entire education to the Poles. The Jewish farmers allowed themselves to be recruited as spies, watching us through the windows at night and observing what we were doing. Once my son Zygmunt walked past the Sokół building. On the street some ten soldiers were standing. Suddenly a Jew aged about seventeen appeared and pointed his finger at my son, shouting: "This one is a Polish legionnaire!" The soldiers blocked Zygmunt's path and called out: "Wait, legionnaire, hand over your shoes." ... The Haidamak regime preferred the Jews, since they needed them, but the simple soldiers beat the Jews over the head or whipped them with canes on their backsides and plundered Jewish stores wherever there was something to loot. For example, because Mr. Eisenberger spoke Polish, all his underclothes were removed from his home ....

There was at the time a trade association for oil sales made up of three Jews from the oil industry and three Catholics, one of whom was a priest, the other a post office official, and the third a teacher. The business was doing so well, that instead of selling a liter of oil for 3 crowns they could sell it for 16, and when anyone wanted oil for 3 crowns, they had to procure a certificate from the commissariat .... Initially even Bochurkiv ... belonged to this association, but people whispered that this was not a particularly clean business, and because [Bochurkiv] wanted to be considered honest, [he] left the association .... The scandal with the oil reached such dimensions that ... all six men were jailed. Bochurkiv was dismissed from the commissariat, but I don't know in what context ....

He was replaced by Kryzhanovskiy, scion of an old noble Polish family. The lion's share of the current Haidamaks stemmed from Polish noble clans, as can be seen from their family names, but for long no one cared about that, and it made no difference to which confession one belonged. You would bring your child to a Ruthenian baptism, and by the time he went to church he was a Pole; yet since every village had a Greek Catholic church, whereas there were only a few Roman Catholic churches, millions of Poles became Ruthenians willy-nilly, and the Ruthenian priests registered their children in the Ruthenian baptismal records .... Poles and Ruthenians are the same flesh and blood—members of the same family ....

Yet when I spoke with Jews about this [oil corruption] affair, they said: "The [three imprisoned] Jews will not be harmed by this, and when they return every one of us will be eager to establish a trade association with them, since they already have experience. The worst is to have a trade association with Catholics, because when a Catholic finally does good business, he immediately begins to live above his means, and behaves as if he were some big lord; whereas when a Jew makes profits, he puts the money in his pocket, and no one can tell from his old clothes that he is already well endowed. And when the Jew slips up and gets into prison, he does not lose his pride, the exact opposite of the Catholics, who will immediately speak about 'great injustice!'"

Meanwhile the Poles were getting closer to Stanisławów, and the entire affair was terminated, which was in fact the best solution.

Principal Zych established a private pedagogical institution for gymnasium youths and children aspiring to become teachers in the Polish students' dormitory. When Bochurkiv heard about this, he sent soldiers immediately to close down the school and chase out the students. The soldiers carried out their task in a brutal fashion. They struck the girls with their rifle butts, so that they had blue marks on their backsides, and one of the rifles actually fired, the bullet flying just over one of the girls. It is unknown whether this shot was fired intentionally or by mistake. Mr. Issak Palek was also not allowed to establish a school for girls of the mosaic faith, because he would not sign the declaration.[59]

13 April 1919

Ataman Sokolovskyi, who replaced Luchkiv, was incapable of plundering his neighbors, and therefore he too was replaced. His place was taken by Ataman Oleksyn of Bukovina, but he too was not a supporter of the looters and was no Haidamak, but rather a righteous and honest Ruthenian.

Some two hundred people from various regions were under house arrest in Buczacz at the time. They therefore established a committee under the secret chairmanship of Władysław Ostrowski. No internee or anyone under house arrest was allowed to be at the head of the committee because ... they were all political prisoners. The documents of this committee were hidden with me. This committee of men and women dealt with food and accommodation for all prisoners. Kryzhanovskiy allowed us to organize one day of donations, during which clothes, food items, and money were collected for the prisoners. The city and the neighboring villages were destitute, and yet each gave what they could .... During this long war, whenever any side took POWs or hostages, they also took care of feeding them, but the Haidamaks did not recognize this need, and so the unfortunates would have died of hunger, without anyone being bothered by it, and had it not been for our committee and the good residents of the city, half of the imprisoned would not have returned home ....

23 April 1919

For several days now strange rumors had been circulating in Buczacz. This had to do with the freight trains rolling through Buczacz. These were simple railcars, on which various types of military equipment were loaded. Through the open railcar doors, one could see rifles, artillery batteries, munitions, uniforms, and field beds, all chaotically piled up. It had become clear that this had to do with flight from the front. The unsecured munitions raised the risk of an explosion, but no one seemed to mind. It was said that Podwołoczyska [95 km northeast of Buczacz] had been taken by some Bolshevik forces. Who were these Bolsheviks? No one knew. The Haidamaks were afraid of them. They said that when the Bolsheviks arrive, they would plunder everything, and then would divide the plunder into equal parts. They said that the Bolsheviks' artillery shells were already reaching Tarnopol. They had already occupied Husiatyn.

The Jews were anxious and did not know whether they should be happy or fearful. We could not tell them either; all we knew was that the Bolsheviks had overthrown the Tsar and were now in power. The military commander had ordered that all [Jewish] houses be vacated and that everything in them be collected for the heroes. The "heroes," that is, were fighting at the front and one had to do something for them. And thus, the police went from house to house (avoiding Catholic homes) and requested donations for the heroes. When the Jew was cunning, he would open the door right away and say: "I'll give everything to our brave warriors, I'll spare nothing." And he would give them a few pieces of soap, ribbons, mirrors, and other trifles. But meanwhile he would say to himself, "May the devil take them!!"

A stupid Jew would say instead: "What should give? I have nothing!" Such a person would have his store taken apart and anything of any value looted from it. On the streets people had their shoes taken off their feet, their clothes stolen, their hats removed from their heads, and if anyone said even one word, they would learn what a rifle butt feels like. I personally saw how the shoes were taken from the feet of several Jews, as well as their pants, if they were still in good condition.

Bochurkiv and Luchkiv were gone and people said that they had fled to the Poles. Luchkiv's wife was a Pole from the Krimmerów family. In the past her father had a big business for rubber goods in Hotel Zorsa in Lwów. When she married Luchkiv she was already a widow with

grown children. Luchkiv had once been chairman of the Polish Sokół
association in Lwów. More recently a portrait of [Taras] Shevchenko[60]
was hanging in his office, but his wife removed it and hung a portrait of
Piłsudski instead. Luchkiv protested, but eventually had to submit to
his wife's wishes. Moreover, he even took into his own home two [Polish]
people condemned to house arrest! During Easter he then changed completely and wanted to have nothing more to do with the Haidamaks.
That is why they began to suspect him. Bochurkiv's wife is also Polish.

In the evening the two of them [Bochurkiv and Luchkiv] returned to
the city, but no one knew where they had been. The following morning,
the Wednesday before Easter, I saw a new company of Haidamaks on
the street, heading out to the front with Luchkiv at their head, riding
on horseback with a huge black hat on his head. The Jews shut all the
stores, because it often happened that the heroes would begin plundering with no warning and grab anything that fell into their hands, while
the store owner was compelled to remain silent. It would also happen
that after such looting the heroes would split the plunder and flee in all
directions ....

The plundered goods taken from Jewish homes and stores by the
policemen and the heroes were not used at all by the heroes. In fact,
a bunch of young women from the nearby villages came to Buczacz,
all dressed up like puppets in lacquered shoes, with colorful kerchiefs
on their heads and elegant skirts. None of them had bought these
things; rather, they received them as presents from their lovers, and the
heroes got absolutely nothing! Then all of a sudden, an order was given:
"Plundering is forbidden!" The astonished inhabitants walked through
the streets and no one stopped them. Poles and Ruthenians greeted each
other politely, chatted with each other and complained: "Ach, if all this
business with that cursed Ukraine would finally come to an end, we've
simply had enough of it!"

On Easter Sunday a large group of people, Poles as well as Ruthenians,
came to church for the Feast of the Resurrection, and everyone they
sang together: "Through Your Holy Resurrection." In the Easter procession Luchkiv walked next to me. It had not been long since he escorted
a company of troops to the train station with a huge hat on his head and
looked like a savage from Africa. On this day he was modestly dressed,
and no one would have believed he was the same person.

In the city we had the usual thefts. Mr. Berger's hog was stolen
from his barn. Two thieves sneaked into the home of the pharmacist
Czerni, but they were caught and fled. Then we heard the terrible news:
in Złoczów the Haidamaks murdered twenty-three Poles, completely
innocent people, among them the engineer Niecia. During the execution

of these men, they were first beaten with rifle butts, and tortured before they were shot. As it turned out later, this story was entirely true.

26 April 1919

On street corners posters were put up warning that anyone speaking about the Bolsheviks drawing closer would be tried by a military court and shot. This announcement was meant primarily to warn unscrupulous people, especially Jews, who deliberately spread such news in order to obtain a higher price for their goods and to squeeze money out of people. That may be true.

On the same day another notice was posted, which caused a stir throughout the city. It said: "On account of the important events on the western front [of Galicia] all soldiers on vacation are hereby called upon to terminate their vacation and go to the front. All Cossacks from eastern Ukraine are called upon to vacate this region right away. Civilians among them should report to Równe, and the soldiers to Dubno to a certain [Symon] Petliura.[61] Additionally, all types of entertainment, theater performances, cinema and even private celebrations are forbidden. All taverns are to be closed at 8 p.m."

We speculated about what might have happened on the western front. Buczacz, known for its rumors and false reports—which sometimes proved to be true—went silent all at once. In the afternoon we heard news that the Poles had broken through the front at Bóbrka [120 km northwest of Buczacz] and that the Haidamaks had panicked and were fleeing with great dispatch. It also became known that they wanted a peace agreement with the Poles, but that the Poles would hear none of it. As far as celebrations went, only the Haidamaks were celebrating, holding joyful feasts in Polish Sokal [215 km northwest of Buczacz], while the Poles were starving. The Haidamaks were allowed everything; they plundered estates, stole horses from Polish peasants, handled hogs and cows as if they were their own property, and asked permission from no one, neither the administrators nor the owners.

But why did they order troops on vacation back to the front? For the Greek Catholic Easter, a large number of soldiers had returned from the front to their families in the villages. Each of them had a rifle and ammunition, and so they made use of their guns, even with live ammunition. In Buczacz too there were such shoot-ups, in which they mostly aimed at the windows of Jewish houses, and it was fairly dangerous to stand by the window. They killed a Jewish woman in this manner and the Jews called out: "gevalt!" One such volunteer came to Petlikowce, bringing with him a loaded weapon. When he was asked why he had brought a weapon with him, he replied: "Am I not worthy enough to do a little shooting during the Easter holidays?" (The same soldier joined the Polish army with his weapon the following month).

A certain Mr. Fir came to Buczacz from Koropiec with provisions in his car, driven by a youth named Antek. They stopped in front of Piotrusz's bakery and Fir went in for a coffee. At that moment the spy Hanczakowski showed up and tried to requisition the supplies on the car. The youth began to shriek, the Jews came running, and the street filled with noise. Fir heard the noise, went out to the street, and asked who had the right to take the supplies away from him. Hanczakowski displayed his documents, at which point Fir pulled out a Browning [pistol] from his pocket and pointed it at Hanczakowski, who began to flee; Fir shot at him, hitting [instead] a Jew called Falashuk in the stomach. Half an hour later Falashuk was dead and Fir had driven off in his car. No one even asked for the name of the murderer. The following day a Haidamak showed up and struck the Jew Rottenberg with his bayonet and murdered him on the spot. Not a single Jew uttered a word about this murder. Such were the times; all thefts and murders went unpunished.

During this war many poor townspeople and peasants made good profits. Before the war, they did not have enough linens to cover their beds, now they pile them up to the ceiling. They stroll through the streets like members of the gentry. The young women from the villages hang out in town wearing the finest materials, but since their clothes were cut by village tailors, they look like pigs in leg cuffs for horses. But on the street one can also encounter many boys and girls cheaply selling shoes, clothes, samovars, irons, and other items not needed in the village. No one asks, where these things come from. This is war booty.

Whole formations of soldiers are retreating from the front, telling us as they march through the city: "They are finished, they and their Ukraine; I am personally Ruthenian, my mother is Polish, my sister is Polish, all good people—it would be best to kill the people who sent us into this war, then we'd have our peace." Frustrated men were fleeing to Koropiec, taking with them their weapons and ammunition, even a machine gun. The police were sent there in order to reintegrate those men, who had so pompously called themselves volunteers, back into the army.

At this point I would like to describe the men in the [Ukrainian] police. These were normal laborers from the estates, who did not own a sliver of soil; they were a bunch of slobs, often men who had been thrown out of school, losers and good-for-nothings, incapable of doing anything without directions from a master. Such types as those policemen did well at the time, since no one interrupted their plundering, they received a salary, and instead of going to the front, they seized children on the estates and sent them to the war. In one case twenty policemen were sent to Koropiec but did not return. One only heard some rifle shots from the distance. Then sixty more policemen were sent from Buczacz. The following day only the sergeant returned. What happened? The mayor of Koropiec had decided not to let youths go to the war. He set up an armed guard and ordered them to sound the alarm as soon as the police approached. When they arrived, they were surrounded and told that they had no business coming there. The policemen put down their arms and dispersed. Some went home, others stayed in Koropiec. The same happened with the second unit. Only the sergeant came back to Buczacz, since he could not really stay in Koropiec.

In Buczacz there were already one hundred people under house arrest, among them Mr. Szczerbar, a teacher at the gymnasium, who had lost an eye in the war and was also ill. On the street several people were standing, and then one of the Haidamaks said: "On one side the Poles, on the other side the Bolsheviks, oh, we are in dire straits." "Why don't you reach an agreement?" asked Szczerbar. "Why are you interfering," yelled the Haidamak; he then arrested Szczerbar and sent him to Jazłowiec. Count Korytowski, whose estate had been totally plundered, was also in local custody. Korytowski had traveled to Buczacz in order to complain about his losses to the military commandant, but they laughed in his face. The desperate Korytowski said to them: "You are thieves, robbers, and villains!" For this he was put into custody, where he sat for twenty-one days. Finally, he was released, and he said again: "Although you have released me, you still remain thieves, robbers, and villains."

Today my son Zygmunt went out to the street wearing boots. A righteous Ruthenian walked up to him and said: "Go home, because today they are stealing shoes off the people on the street. They'll also take your shoes off right away." Zygmunt took his advice and went back home.

Soon thereafter an order was issued to print new money notes that were called hryvnia and karbovanets .... No one wanted to do business with this money. The commissariat and finance department accepted only crowns and paid with crowns. The Jews and peasants refused to take this money at all because it was worthless .... And so, an order was issued that refusal to accept hryvnia would be punished by confiscation of the business and a heavy fine. The soldiers would then buy some trifle in the store, for which they paid, say, 1,000 hryvnia, and then demanded the change in crowns. Consequently, many Jews closed their stores. Then the police came up with another idea. They positioned themselves in groups on the street, stopped Jews passing by, searched through their pockets and took away their crowns .... This was nothing but theft ....

At about 11 a.m. several internees were driven through the city. All were in a very bad state, hungry, ... close to death .... Jews with anxious expressions were standing on the street. These wretches were brought to the train station and were supposed to be transported to Kosaczów [internment camp in Kołomyja]. The military commandant of the train station was the teacher Symovonyk. He was an affable man, who tried to help these poor people as best he could. He allowed their acquaintances and others to help. This did not sit right with the Haidamak power and consequently he was transferred to Czortków.

In the city the Poles bought food, baked bread, and brought it to the train station. Among the donors was also Miss Ziobrówna from Rzeszów, who brought them two loaves of bread. Under one of the loaves a card was glued on which it said: "Don't be fearful, soon everything will be over. Lift up your spirits!" The note was badly glued and fell off. The Haidamaks found the card, read it, and struck the women with their rifle butts and cursed in a manner she had never heard in her entire life. They brought her to a court martial in Czortków. Her father heard about this, ... drove to Czortków, and after four days managed to liberate the child from the hands of the Haidamaks.

8 May 1919

In Buczacz every Thursday was market day. Masses of wagons would come to the marketplace bringing hogs, geese, calves, cows, and horses. The market opened. But the peasants sold the fruit of their labors for crowns only. Prompted by the Haidamaks, the Jews paid for the cows they bought in crowns, but they did it so ostentatiously that everyone could tell the reason. Once the peasants had the money in their hands the police arrived and confiscated the crowns from the peasants, giving them hryvnia instead. This created a great tumult in the market, because the peasant is no fearful Jew. Suddenly the peasants rose, picked up their wagons' crossbars, and surrounded the policemen, who threatened to shoot; but the peasants yelled: "Just try, shoot, but not one piece of you will remain!"

Just before it came to bloodshed, the more reasonable women pushed in and within ten minutes not a single wagon remained in the marketplace, nor hogs, nor cows. A couple of stones were thrown, but that was about it. Only when the square was empty did the policemen start shooting, but only in the air. I have seen columns of wagon convoys in retreat, but a scene such as this I had never seen. The horses were running, the pigs were grunting, the cows were mooing, the women were screeching, stones were falling, peasants cursing, Jews fleeing, and the policemen could not recover from the shock and had no idea how to stop this flight. [Following this] the karbovanets and the hryvnia dropped in value ..., and whoever bought hryvnia wanted it only as a memento.

As I was going to the commissariat today, in order to register [as a former detainee], I saw a group of people reading an announcement. This was a new decree by the military commandant in Czortków: "To all gentlemen riflemen—the Bolsheviks and legionnaires have exploited the fact that our heroic riflemen went home for the Easter Holiday and have attacked us from the east. The Poles have attacked from the west, and our heroic army has been compelled to flee. Go to the front, for if you do not, you are no gentlemen!" One might have thought this was a joke, urging people not to go to the front but to flee. The Poles laughed, the Ruthenians shook their heads and said: "To hell with you and your Ukraine, have you not stolen enough?" The women screeched with all their might: "Thieves, thieves!"

The following day a new announcement appeared on the street with the following content: "Ukrainian riflemen have on occasion carelessly left their positions and gone to their families at home for the holidays during this most difficult time for the Ukrainian nation .... The Poles have thrown vast forces into the front, in order to exterminate us, and have been simultaneously supported by the Bolshevik gangs in the east. For us an important moment has arrived, in which we either 'rule' or 'kneel!' Ukrainian riflemen, you cannot be so unwise as to give up the future of our nation for a couple of days. For such stupidity you will have to pay for many years thereafter. Come to your senses, as long as there is still time, and return to the ranks in order to fulfill your duty .... Chortkiv [Ukrainian for Czortków], 23 April 1919."

This announcement should have really been placed in a satirical journal. Or was someone in the commandant's office having fun? ...

Two peasants are walking down the street and talking about the military command: "How stupid can they be? Were things worse for us before? Those who were a bit richer worked on their own field, while the poorer ones worked as laborers on the estates, each person was his own master, as long as he worked, and these rebels play with our blood and our lives and things are good for them. They should go to the front themselves, since they want to rule and yet don't do anything in return."

On Sunday Mass was celebrated at the Greek Catholic church in Trybuchowce. The policemen surrounded the church and wanted to seize the young men coming out as volunteers. The young women began to shriek in order to warn the men. The policemen opened fire and wounded five women .... Altogether sixty men were brought to Buczacz and were locked up in the Sokół building. But ... one of the guards showed them a window that was blocked with wooden planks, and they did not ponder the issue too long, dismantled the planks and fled ....

23 May 1919

We received news that the Poles were already in Stanisławów and heading toward Niżniów. Bochurkiv and Vynar were crossing to the market. The "commissar," pale and stressed out, was gesticulating wildly with his hands; he was clearly very agitated, or as we say, his heart fell into his pants [that is, he was terrified]. At about 10 a.m. some two hundred wagons full of bed linens and other new materials arrived. Perched on top of each wagon were women wearing hats and coats. The entire camp was moving toward Czortków.

The Jews were behaving ever more politely to the Poles; no trace was left of their arrogance. A certain salesman I knew, in principle not a bad person at all, came to me and said: "Could you lend me some money?" I laughed and said: "Now you want to borrow money from us, but only recently you yelled in the Sokół: 'Long live Ukraine, down with Poland!'" The Jew leaped up in shock and said: "That was not us or anyone smart, that was the stupid students, who called out because they were afraid, believe me." The Jews are the best barometer, they knew better than us, but they were afraid to speak out—they too waited impatiently for the Poles, because they knew that the Poles would not loot their businesses or open fire on the streets ....

Despite the war couples were getting married in the Roman and Greek Catholic churches, including couples of mixed religion. That very morning some ten wagons of guests arrived for a wedding in Podzameczek. Suddenly the policemen showed up and, saying nothing, requisitioned the horses and the wagons, ... and the wedding guests and married couple had to walk on foot to their homes. The policemen also requisitioned horses in the villages, especially in Polish ones. The Haidamaks came to estate owner Jakób Kulasz's barn in Dźwinogród in order to requisition a horse, but Mrs. Kulasz refused to hand it over. In the midst of the quarrel Mr. Kulasz came out of the house and the Haidamaks shot him from behind, killing him on the spot. The wife was beaten up and the horse was requisitioned. When he heard about this, the Greek Catholic priest of that congregation said: "He had it coming, he should have handed over the horse." The Greek Catholic priest in Jaworów spoke in precisely the same spirit. These men were supposed to be representatives of the Christian spirit, but instead they pursued a politics which is not grounded in Christian ethics, for although they had once studied it, they had banished it from their hearts ....

28 May 1919

... From the direction of Jazłowiec artillery fire could be heard. It was said that the Poles would remain on the banks of the Dniester and not cross over. The Ukrainian secretariat moved to Buczacz, including [Olexander] Pisetsky, [Sydir] Holubovych, and [Olexander] Hrekov.[62] In the city there were many officers, but they could only speak German; one heard absolutely no Ruthenian or Polish. There was a bunch of policemen and NCOs in the city, but without command; all the volunteers had already fled. Cows and pigs were being arbitrarily requisitioned from the peasants and city inhabitants. They were slaughtered right away for the army. The peasants and townsfolk in Nagórzanka similarly had their hogs and cows slaughtered. In Nagórzanka all the pitchforks were removed from the peasants' houses, for fear that the peasants would defend their property with them.

Two teachers, Bokład from Petlikowce and Sohabowski from Rawa Ruska, who were under house arrest, were standing on the Palace Bridge over the Strypa. As they saw this tumult among the Haidamaks, they said: "It somehow doesn't seem to be working out for them." Someone overheard this conversation and reported it immediately to the military headquarters, where a certain Kusma—a former student in the sixth grade at the Buczacz gymnasium—was now serving as Ataman. He ordered to arrest the two of them and punish each with one hundred cane strokes!

It was forbidden to walk around town in threes, or even in twos. The young gentlemen Sadliński and Bohumiewicz went together to complain that again they had no soap to wash their collars. They were taken to Kusma and were held there until their families bought their freedom for 200 crowns each, which at the time was a major undertaking. The plundering on the streets started again. Old Salewicz had his shoes removed on the street and walked home barefoot. Mr. Szawłowski from Przewłoka was driving to Buczacz in a cart. On the way Haidamaks attacked him and ordered him to go back home by foot. They got on the cart and have not been seen since ....

Hrekov was the commander of the Ukrainians, but they did not trust him, because he supposedly said that at the first opportunity, he would change sides and join the Poles. There was great unrest among the senior Haidamaks. They stuffed their pockets with money and wanted to flee, but where? None of them knew anything precise about the situation. There were no men of ideas among them; they were only interested in their own pockets …. Any Jew simply standing on the steps of his own house or business had to show his documents right away and was arrested on the spot if could not produce them. Apparently, it was all about grabbing as much money as possible …. The Ukrainian officers and Haidamaks have whole crates full of hryvnia and karbovanets, but what can they do with them, after all this paper is worthless and no one wants it.

30 May 1919

Two hundred wagons came to Buczacz, but because there was no room for them here, they were sent on to Soroki [8 km south of Buczacz]. In the morning a Polish airplane appeared over the city; it flew very low and surveyed the surroundings. The Jews are happy and rub their hands, because the Haidamaks have greatly bothered them. Now not only the soldiers but also the peasants are looting. The brothers Marcinkowski, one eighteen, the other fourteen years old, made their way on foot to Jazłowiec. In the village of Trybuchowce they were attacked by shepherds and their clothes and shoes were torn off them. By coincidence an honorable soldier happened by and chased away the shepherds, and then accompanied the youths back to Buczacz. How many years will it take for these people to regain their balance and return to the path of virtue?

Again, an announcement was posted: "People, have you gone totally insane? Have you lost your reason? We have given you this noble piece of land. Why are you fleeing?" As the Polish and Ruthenian peasants read this, they said: "These are bandits, we don't own any piece of land, we are dying of hunger, and now they steal our pigs from our barns, they want to take over property that is not theirs and then, ha, ha, to distribute it as gifts."

31 May 1919

In the morning an order was issued: "We appeal to all soldiers not to plunder homes on your own initiative; whoever does not obey this order will be shot." What's the point of such an order when the military commanders themselves have set an example of how to loot, have stuffed their own pockets, and now, when there is nothing left to plunder, they issue a humanitarian order. How perfidious! Despite this "order" no Pole dared go into the city, for fear of being attacked right away by a Ukrainian. From the direction of the Złota Lipa River in the west, powerful artillery fire could be heard. Those in the know estimated the distance at about 4 miles.

All through the night guns, supplies, and wagons travelled through the city; I could not see them, because it was forbidden to go out to the street, but the noise of the wagons could not be missed. The next morning a cavalry unit rode through the city on beautiful horses, stolen from the estates in the districts of Sokal, Rawska, Żółkiew, Jaworów, and Radziechów [185–240 km northwest of Buczacz]. The unit numbered about two hundred men. I was standing on the sidewalk, as always in a coat of Kraków cloth [a symbol of Polish nationalism], and one of them saw me and said: "You are another one of those patriots." But he did nothing to hurt me. Six canons drove by behind the cavalry.

News was spreading about various murders in the district. In Jazłowiec the two brothers Piwoworski, former students of mine, were murdered in a gruesome manner; ordered to dig a grave, they were then shot and stabbed with bayonets. In the village of Pochorowa the Haidamaks attacked the Roman Catholic parish church and dragged the provost Dziurkiewicz out of bed. This seventy-year-old man, who was wearing only his dressing gown, was hanged from a tree and disemboweled with bayonets. The eighteen-year-old youth Józef Kramarski was murdered in Podzameczek without any reason. He was stabbed thirty times with a bayonet, and his head was crushed with clubs.

Two honorable Ruthenians were living in Buczacz—the construction worker Khoretskyi and his next-door neighbor Rohatynskyi. Their sons worked at the train station selling iron pots. Filk Khoretskyi was a beloved boy because he was helpful and obliging. The two youths were confronted by Captain Hessel, a Haidamak of German descent, who ordered to stab them with bayonets. Before their death he made them dance and meanwhile shot them with his Browning [pistol]. The older brother Mykola Khoretskyi was also wounded with the bayonet and they tried to kill him as well, but he begged for his life, saying that he had a wife and children, and they let him go (he was sick for three months after that). I was at the funeral of these unfortunate youths, and there I heard that it was Major Kraus, also a German, who had killed the Piwoworski brothers.

Mrs. Brogowska, the wife of a councilor from Jezierzany, was beaten black and blue with clubs, paying no heed to the fact that she was still nursing a child. Her sixteen-year-old daughter was likewise beaten and robbed of 6,000 crowns. A Dominican priest was brutally beaten directly in front of his church in Potok Złoty for having delivered a political sermon.

Two students came to me and said: "Perhaps we should arm ourselves and attack the Haidamaks from the rear?" "How many of you are
there?" "About fifty." "How many guns do you have?" "Fifty." "Are they
good guns?" "Not all." "Have any of you served in the military?" "No."
"How many bullets do you have?" "A thousand." "Well, my dears, wait
for a few more days. Forget about setting up an ambush, because with
a thousand bullets you can shoot for only an hour and without much
result, since one needs to learn how to shoot. You will be defeated very
quickly, and this concerns not only you but also your families, because
there will be terrible revenge. Have patience and everything will turn
out well." And so, they went away.

In the afternoon many dozens of infantry soldiers marched again
into town from the direction of Czortków. They passed through the city
singing, but they did not loot. A sixteen-year-old priest's son wanted
to leave his home and go to war, but his mother, an energetic woman,
shook this idea out of his head: "Son, sit quietly and don't move from
your spot!" And she was right.

In the city we could no longer get any milk or meat even with a
medical prescription.

In the building of the Polish Sokół Association 154 Poles were being
held prisoner by the Ukrainians, among them Major Rybiński. They
were kept under heavy guard and were given nothing to eat; even the
town residents were forbidden to bring food to the prisoners. These
poor people were very close to death from hunger. At the last moment
a Ukrainian Ataman intervened and ordered that soup be made for the
prisoners. I write this here in order to demonstrate that even among the
Haidamaks there were some honorable people.

In the Ukrainian commissariat there was a debate over what to
do with the [former] Polish prisoners. Many of the people there were
scared and shaken, so that they could not think clearly. Some of them
shouted: "Intern them! If we don't do that, they will intern us." The
new Commissar Kryzhanovskiy, a reasonable man, said: "Let's not talk
nonsense, since if we harm Poles even at the end of the war, they will
have a right to take revenge." But there were also voices against, and
it went so far that Kryzhanovskiy threw books on the floor and yelled:
"Am I the boss here, or you?" Everything that happened in the commissariat was reported to us right away by the Ruthenians. Since we now
knew precisely what was being debated, we prepared a backpack with
bread and clothes in order to flee at any moment, so that what happened
to us during our imprisonment in Jazłowiec would not be repeated.

The following morning, during Sunday Mass, the Haidamaks surrounded the church, arrested the young men, and incarcerated them

in the Sokół building. My sons, who know every nook and cranny in Buczacz, managed to flee. A large number of young men were captured. This hunt caused a great deal of agitation among Poles and Ruthenians; most agitated was Kryzhanovskiy himself, since this action had occurred against his will. It was clear that they had bungled things up and that very afternoon everyone was released.

1 June 1919

... A group of policemen was walking down the street and talking [in Ukrainian]: "Who is still fighting at the front?" "Stupid intellectuals and nurses." They burst out laughing. "The nurses, they are good girls, until now we had friends among them, now the Poles are standing in line." "But I tell you, when the devil gets hold of our intellectuals, things will be better for us, since the Poles have not hurt anyone and won't do it in the future."

From the West we could hear powerful artillery fire. In the military hospital there was no more food left for the wounded and they were starving. The medics had gone home.

Luchkiv went to the engineer Ostrowski and suggested to him that the Poles create a militia. My son Józef had come up with the same idea, but it was not taken seriously, first and foremost because it was Luchkiv's proposal. No one trusted him any longer—neither the Poles nor the Ruthenians, not even the Haidamaks.

3 June 1919

At 2 p.m. the last Ukrainian patrols passed through Buczacz. At 4:30 p.m. two Haidamaks went toward Nagórzanka, but they were real bandits. I saw them with my own eyes as they walked past me toward the watermill, which stands right next to St. Nicholas' church. There they threw a hand grenade right in front of a Jewish woman. This miller's wife did not know what this was and looked at it closely. Suddenly the grenade exploded, all nearby houses shook, and the Jewish woman was very seriously injured, although she recovered a few days later. The two bandits ran down to the marketplace and stole the shoes from one Jew who was passing by. A few minutes later I was informed that Luchkiv had singlehandedly shot two bandits, and that they were the same men.

Once the Haidamaks fled, Luchkiv took command over the city; I don't know whether he had any subordinates, but I believe that no one was left. A curious chap this Luchkiv, and I don't even know whether he had the right to shoot those two bandits. It was said that they had raised their weapons against him. I don't know that; ultimately, God will judge them. These two murdered people were buried right away, by the street, near the Black Bridge, and one can see their grave to this day.

Soon thereafter the Poles in the Sokół building were also released, since their guards had fled. Suddenly someone shouted: "The Poles are coming!" Anyone who had legs ran to the entrance of the city, but nothing could be seen. Night was coming and the anxious feared that this was a trap, because the Ukrainians had done everything to stay in the city. The nightly silence descended on the city, but no one slept.

4 June 1919

At 7 a.m. I stepped out of the church and walked up Potocki Street. I raised my eyes, and there I saw simple cars driving by with Poles holding bayonets sitting in them. We couldn't believe our eyes, yet these were real Poles. Happy and smiling faces, courageous eyes, and a noble soul. We greeted them enthusiastically. People threw flowers to them, and with this welcome, they drove to the marketplace and stepped out of their cars. There were some seventy soldiers, led by commander Maczek, a man of small stature but exceptional courage: dark, sunburnt, and wearing worn-out clothes; no wonder, for this was war. The oldest officer was appointed city commandant—Major Rybiński, a former prisoner of war. The Poles stood in two rows on the marketplace, surrounding the soldiers. Our Polish and Ruthenian women prepared for them sausage, ham, cooked meat, coffee, and tea. Everyone was happy that the guests they had yearned for were finally there. Just then Luchkiv arrived at the marketplace, dressed in the uniform of a lieutenant, and handed over command of the city to Rybiński. The major looked at Luchkiv, smiled, and then said: "You don't have to hand over the command, it's in my hands in any case." He ordered the arrest of Luchkiv right away and for him to be taken to his own house. The question is, what would have the Haidamaks done had someone like that fallen into their hands?

The entire youth of Buczacz and Podzameczek assembled right away and organized a militia. We thought that Maczek and his unit were only a forward patrol, and asked him, where was the rest of the formation: "They are coming but are still far away."

Around the marketplace there was a large gathering of Jews. One of the Jews spoke to a soldier in Ruthenian, and the latter pulled the Jew's beard and said: "And you, mutton, don't you know how to address a Polish soldier?" The shocked Jew answered only: "I did not know; I had no idea." Right away another Jew called out: "Schilder [signs]! Schilder!" Right away the Jews sprang into action—even though it was Pentecost [or the Jewish Holiday of Shavuot, the Feast of Weeks]—and began putting up white-and-red signs over their stores. Within half an hour the city acquired Polish colors and five thousand new Poles, among them the attorney, Dr. Ausschnitt. And a miracle occurred! All the Jews forgot the Ruthenian language in an instant and spoke only Polish.

My eldest son Józef took over command of the militia, as befit his military rank as a second lieutenant. As soon as the sinister elements [Ukrainian troops] left the city in the direction of Trybuchowce Forest, through which the road to Czortków passed, he took with him twelve youths, whom he had armed with old rifles and a dozen bullets each. Once they reached Trybuchowce Forest, they positioned themselves in a trench facing a guesthouse. All of a sudden, they heard loud voices and yells coming from the guesthouse. Then someone called: "Who is there?" My son recognized that these were the voices of the Haidamaks, who were positioned with 150 men above the inn on the serpentine road, perhaps ten paces from the Polish patrol in the woods. Two students, Adam Wagner und Jaś Kochanowski, were lying on the forest floor and ready to fire: "Lieutenant, should we shoot?" He ordered them to be silent. Then one of the Haidamaks walked over to the forest and stood next to the hospital, which was located at the foot of the hill. After a few moments he went back and said: "There can't be too many Poles in the city, since they have not sent out even one patrol." "Be quiet, you idiot. Don't you hear that the forest is speaking?" said another. They all looked fearfully toward the forest on both sides of the inn and returned very quietly to the road leading to Dżuryn [and onward to Czortków].

Meanwhile the situation in the city was deteriorating. Someone had seen these Haidamaks and reported in the city that the Polish patrol had been captured. That whole night no one shut their eyes, but in the morning all the youths returned to the city without any injuries. Command over the military in the city was taken over by Józef Potocki, with Józef Sluzinski and Gottwald as his deputies. Those who had been interned until recently now ruled the city, and the decision over the life and death of the captured Haidamaks was now in their hands. While searching suspected houses, Professor Vynar, the citizen Lishchynskyi, and the miller Füllenbaum were discovered. A soldier led them with his bayonet to Józef. All three of them had known precisely what was going on, yet we knew them as good people; especially Vynar had to be saved, he was after all my sons' teacher. They were held in the municipal offices for hours and after a protocol was written up were released to their homes.

Lieutenant Maczek drove with a vehicle all the way to Dżuryń. In the firefight that ensued he captured four artillery guns, and because he lacked enough men, they harnessed horses to the guns and towed them to Buczacz. But Maczek's company had four wounded men, including an officer, and had to leave one of the wounded behind, because the Haidamaks had launched a major counterattack. The Ruthenian soldiers carried the Polish soldier into a shack on the side of the road, but when a real Haidamak wanted to shoot him, these honorable soldiers would not allow this crime. Then another policeman showed up, but the soldiers threw him out of the shack, saying [in Ukrainian]: "The Poles don't kill the wounded but instead save their lives." The following day the Poles went again to Dżuryn and brought that wounded soldier back to Buczacz ....

As I noted at the beginning of my memoirs, not a single man from the villages of Podzameczek and Podlesie volunteered for the Polish Legions in 1914. Generally, the inhabitants of these villages, although they were Polish, were not particularly patriotic .... But now, when things were going very badly, and they were suffering from poverty, they grasped their error. Already on the first day forty youngsters from Podzameczek stood up like oaks, along with young people from Podlesie, and reported to the army, and each day fresh contingents of recruits arrived. And in other villages even Ruthenians reported to the Polish army, because they had had enough with this Haidamak state and its economy.

But the war was not over yet. The Haidamaks knew very well precisely how weak the Polish forces in Buczacz were. They themselves possessed about thirty thousand men, who were certainly not highly motivated, but nevertheless numerous .... Already when the Poles marched into Buczacz, my son Józef went to the city commandant and said: "To be sure I am not a member of the [Polish] military and stayed in Buczacz during the [Polish-Ukrainian] war, but I tell you, be careful, because here in the woods a large number of soldiers are hiding, they even have artillery, and there are so few Poles here that in the case of an offensive, which is imminent, you'd have no chance."

The eighth of June 1919 was a market day in Buczacz and many residents, as well as people from the area, gathered in the marketplace. Suddenly at around 10 a.m. two artillery shells were fired from the woods near Żyznomierz. The first shells were directed at Trybuchowce where they struck a large house, in which women and children were hiding. The shells exploded and buried fourteen people. After that the artillery fire was aimed at Buczacz. I was at that time close to the ruins of the Buczacz castle, but the shells went over our heads and although they flew quite low, they fell further behind the city and caused no damage. One shell struck near the train station, one hit the house of Mazur, fell directly on a bed, but did not explode.

Altogether I counted twenty-five shell strikes. People were fleeing from the marketplace, the Jews shut down their businesses with all dispatch, and the city was thrown into unnecessary panic. This artillery fire made no sense at all, was entirely aimless, and actually harmful to the Haidamaks, because it betrayed their positions. It was rumored that the shells were deliberately fired to show the Poles from where they face a threat. The artillery attack brought the rapid arrival of help from the direction of Monasterzyska. About a thousand infantry troops and many artillery pieces arrived. They were led by Major Heinzl. The army marched forward rapidly, the men were in a good mood, and Major Heinzl was in the best spirits and optimistic. The Poles could finally see things coming to an end.

But then, I don't know why, came an order from the top to stop the attack and in fact to retreat all the way to the heights of the Złota Lipa River. This was an unpleasant order for victorious troops, but soldiers should not philosophize and follow orders. The Polish side was preparing for a counter-offensive, but first they retreated to the west. By midnight [other formations of] the Poles had reached Czortków and were marching triumphantly forward. But they too received the order to stop their battle operations and retreat.

Among the Polish soldiers in Czortków was a certain sergeant called Urban. His father was treasury commissioner in Czortków. The young Urban visited his parents, for what kind of son would he have been had he not visited his parents after years of being away. Following the retreat of the Poles from Czortków the Jewish woman Tiszterówna informed the Haidamak authorities that the young Urban had visited his father. The Haidamaks seized old Urban on the farm and ordered him to dig a grave. Mrs. Urban begged the Haidamaks for mercy, noting that her husband had not become involved in anything. But this did not help, and he was executed in front of his wife, on the farm where he lived. He was beaten to death with clubs. This is the consequence of dehumanization. "The tiger is frightful when its angry, the rage of humans is even more brutal."

At the same time of the Polish retreat to the West, the Haidamak army returned to Buczacz.[63] An honest Ruthenian policeman came to me and said: "Inspector Ostrowski, Father Wracha and Principal Siewiński should flee right away." Someone warned us, I don't know who that was, perhaps Professor Vynar, perhaps Bochurkiv, but whoever it was, the warning came from the Ruthenians themselves. We didn't contemplate this long, got dressed, took the most important things with us and headed on foot to Monasterzyska, and then further to Korościatyn. There we jumped on a freight train that was passing by and traveled to Stanisławów. An hour later my son Józef came there, but on foot, whereas Zygmunt traveled directly to Warsaw ....

Fleeing with us, wonder of all wonders, was also Ataman Viktor Luchkiv, who was the first to come to his senses. He brought along his wife and child. He came to me at the train station in Stanisławów and said: "Principal, I admit that I hurt you, but I had orders from Czortków to keep an eye especially on you. Please forgive me." Well, how should have I responded to that? I stretched out my hand and forgave him. People joked about me afterwards, but I was pleased and knew that any Pole in my position would have behaved in the same way .... We then traveled to Lwów, where my sons reported to the army, joining it as officers ....

The army of the Haidamaks was largely made up of gangs that operated arbitrarily, without being responsible to anyone; they murdered with impunity, not only Poles but also Ruthenians .... But about a month later news arrived that everyone who had worked with the Haidamaks had surrendered and gone home.

The uprising ended as quickly as it had begun, the population returned to work, especially the villagers, who had never dreamed of a West Ukraine. That had been an Austrian idea, meant only to incite them against each other, children of the same Mother of God .... The uprising caused transgressions of the law, but was the population guilty of that? "No." Was it perhaps the priests and the others, who led the people? "Not them, either." The House of Habsburg and their followers had tried ever since the first partition of Poland to sow hatred among the population, ... but the honorable and reasonable Ruthenian people refused to be incited into such a crime. They tried again and again to bring the Ruthenian people, who are of our blood, into conflict with the Poles, which they partly succeeded in doing. Our descendants will be ashamed of us for having allowed ourselves to be provoked in this way by the Austrian and Prussian Germans, even if now love and reconciliation predominate among the people ....

Today we see that our trust in God has not been disappointed. The great and devious Austria lies in ruins, and one day historians will write that this state was a giant with clay feet. So too the swaggering Germany-Prussia and its ideas and policies—of which we, here in the distant East, were the perpetual victims—was destined to collapse, because it was not founded on love for God and one's neighbor. But we continue to strive, as the Ruthenian poet Platon Kostetskyi[64] wrote: "In the name of the Father, the Holy Spirit, and the Son. This is our prayer. Like the Holy Trinity—Poles, Ruthenians, and Lithuanians."

On the Bolsheviks

… Following the pacification of the land and after a terrible civil war I returned to my old position in Buczacz. The school building over the Strypa was totally destroyed, without windows, desks, and any school materials. In the school building on the so-called barracks, which was also destroyed, I found a military hospital. After a temporary reorganization of the school I notified the students and offered a seven-grade education. This was a peculiar group of students. In the first grade were children aged between seven and thirteen. In the higher classes there were also significant age differences.

One does not need to be a teacher in order to understand what hard work this implied for the teachers. Additionally, during the war the youth had learned to focus only on survival, saw numerous armies marching in and out, and observed arbitrary looting and unpunished theft; such youth could not maintain a sense of morality. In the classes there were daily thefts, and the little thieves were so refined that it was difficult to catch them in the act. They even managed to get the glass out of the window frame and to take it home, where the perpetrator was actually praised by his parents. The locksmith inserted locks into the school doors but within a few hours all the keys had been stolen.

Under such circumstances we taught school until almost mid-June 1920, at which time we received the terrible news: "Our army has begun to retreat. The Bolsheviks are already in Kyiv, our soldiers have retreated all the way to Proskurow" [170 km northeast of Buczacz]. The order was given for all teachers and officials to go to the West, and thus I had to flee for the third time and once more the most important things had to be left behind. It was indeed high time, because for the previous few days we could hear artillery fire from the East, coming ever closer, evidence that the enemy was also advancing toward us. We boarded the train and traveled to Przemyśl.[65]

Przemyśl

I had hardly arrived in Przemyśl when it was proposed to me to work as a military instructor and teach the troops history, geography, love for the fatherland, and respect for the law. I immediately agreed and did it for free, because I still received my pay as a teacher. Thank God I am still healthy and despite my sixty-three years of age (in 1920) I have a powerful voice and can still lecture to five hundred students, and I can also adapt to their spiritual educational level .... I taught at this school from 15 June to 15 October 1920, and I count the time among the soldiers among the most beautiful periods in my life.

My superiors called me back to Buczacz. I took over the post of principal of a seven-grade boys' school with eleven classes. I had eleven teachers and three teachers of religion. In the classrooms there were no benches, tables, blackboards, or chairs; the windows were shattered, the doors smashed, the city poor and plundered; nevertheless, the mayor of the city, Władysław Prusak, was keen to at least restore the school building so that the teaching would not have to suffer .... The youth were poorly educated, no wonder, because for seven years they had watched the plundering, murders, battles, and other immoral events, and had been in the company of soldiers from different countries and nations. One could still write a great deal about this today, but it is better to keep quiet. Our task is to strive to heal these wounds of our youth as swiftly as possible.

I learned from the inhabitants of the city how the Bolsheviks had behaved here recently. From these stories I concluded that the Bolsheviks proceed systematically. The head of the town and district was a Galician Jew named Seidler. He was friendly and polite to all the inhabitants of the city, yet he sent soldiers who called themselves "comrades" into all the houses and apartments, and they registered what and how much each person owned. Of course, they would have loaded all this, as one does among comrades, on wagons and would have taken it all to "Rossiya" [Russia in Russian] as had happened in the districts of Tarnopol and Brody. Unfortunately for them, following the "Miracle on the Vistula"[66] no time was departed, and so they departed as quickly as they had come and will surely try again to invade our land. May God protect us. Amen.

Kołomyja, 14 March 1939, Antoni Siewiński

Notes

"Pamiętniki buczacko-jazłowieckie z czasów wojny wszechświatowej od roku 1914 do roku 1920: pamiętnik rodzinny," Biblioteka Jagiellońska, Kraków, BJ Rkp. 7367 II. Transcribed and translated from Polish by Frank Grelka. Additional translation and editing by Omer Bartov. Text and photograph courtesy Jagiellonian Digital Library: https://jbc. bj.uj.edu.pl/dlibra/publication/332145/edition/317515/content; digital copy identifier: NDIGORP004848.
1. A derogatory name for Russians.
2. *Buczyna* or *buk* means beech in Polish.

3. Podolia was a historical province that straddled parts of Galicia east of the Dniester River and a greater expanse of land east of the Zbrucz River, which became the border between the Austrian and Russian Empires in 1772 and between Poland and the Soviet Union after World War I.

4. The new "fortress" synagogue was built in 1728, under Stefan Potocki, who indeed supported Jewish life in the city; his son Mikołaj inherited the city from him in 1733.

5. The eccentric Mikołaj Potocki (1712–82), owner and benefactor of Buczacz for much of his lifetime, was also known for his violence. He was immortalized by the poet Zygmunt Krasinski as a "governor, who shot women on trees and baked Jews alive." See more on this early history in Bartov, *Anatomy of a Genocide*, 6–15.

6. Meaning Roman Catholic Poles and Greek Catholic Ruthenians (later known as Ukrainians).

7. Stern was in fact the town's only Jewish mayor. He was elected in 1879 and remained in that position until the end of World War I, i.e., for thirty-nine years, but Siewiński may be excluding the war years in which the mayor's role was very limited, especially under Russian occupation. Stern also served for a while as head of the Jewish community and as member of the Austrian parliament.

8. He was in fact Bosnian.

9. It seems that no one read these memoirs; Siewiński's sons did not add anything and the manuscript was deposited in an archive where it remained untouched for many decades.

10. The Polish educational system at the time provided the option of entering an 8-grade gymnasium divided into a junior gymnasium at grades 1–3 (ages 11–14) and senior gymnasium at grades 5–8 (ages 14–18). Most children attended a conventional 7-grade primary school, and many dropped out after the 4th grade.

11. Siewiński's derogatory term for Germans.

12. Hardly unknown, Piłsudski (1867–1935) was leader of the Polish Socialist Party before World War I, a fighter for Polish independence, and a fierce opponent of Imperial and later Soviet Russia. He formed the Polish Legions under Austrian auspices in 1914 to fight Russia and advance Poland's national cause. Appointed commander in chief of Polish forces in November 1918, he declared Polish independence, and served as Chief of State (being appointed marshal in 1920), relinquishing his socialist loyalties, until 1922. During that time, he led the country in the Polish-Ukrainian War (1918–19) and the Polish-Soviet War (1919–21), inter alia. After a short stint as Chief of the General Staff, Piłsudski retired from politics in 1923, but returned to power in a coup d'état three years later, remaining Poland's authoritarian head of state until his death in 1935, by which time Polish democracy had been thoroughly dismantled.

13. Formerly the quasi-independent part of Poland left over from the partitions but later taken over by Russia.

14. The Riflemen's Association was a Polish paramilitary organization formed in 1910 in Lwów.

15. Napoleon Bonaparte and Swedish king Charles XII were both defeated after invading Russia.

16. The first is dance music originating in the Hutsuls, a Carpathian ethnic group; the second is a Polish dance from the region of Kraków and Galicia.

17. Named after 3 May 1791, on which the Polish-Lithuanian Commonwealth adopted a constitution meant to strengthen and liberalize the kingdom, shortly before the Second and Third Partitions of 1793 and 1795 wiped Poland off the map as an independent political entity until the aftermath of World War I.

18. The Kachkovsky Society was organized by Ruthenian Russophiles in 1874 in response to the Ukrainian nationalist Prosvita (Enlightenment) Society founded in 1868.

19. Leading out of Buczacz over the Strypa toward neighboring Czortków.
20. Siewiński uses the Polish derogatory term żydek.
21. This is Siewiński's attempt to indicate that they were calling out numbers in Yiddish, "eyns, tsvey," or "one, two."
22. The first, "Boże coś Polskę," was a close competitor for Poland's national anthem; the second, "Mazurek Dąbrowskiego," later did become the Polish national anthem, and is known especially for the verse: "Jeszcze Polska nie zginęła," or Poland has not yet perished. Ironically, the Ukrainian national anthem has the same verse: "Shche ne vmerla Ukraïna," Ukraine has not yet perished.
23. This term may come from the Yiddish/Hebrew word that means literally house-owner but refers to an established person, a bourgeois.
24. Lucius Licinius Lucullus was a Roman senator known for serving lavish meals.
25. The reference is likely to ethnic German peasants.
26. The Polish version of the name given in the diary is Święcki, pronounced Shvientsky, which is similar to Siewiński, pronounced Shevinsky; its most likely Russian equivalent is Savitsky.
27. The Polish version of the name given in the diary is Szeptyłycz, whose Russian rendering would be Sheptelich.
28. Referring to the Haidamak Cossack paramilitary bands of the eighteenth century, who fought against Polish rule in right-bank Ukraine.
29. Appears in the Polish version as Medyński.
30. The reference is to the secondary fictional character Andrzej Kuklinowski in the historical novel by Henryk Sienkiewicz (1846–1916), *The Deluge* (Potop, 1886) about the Swedish invasion of Poland in the mid-seventeenth century. Kuklinowski is a cynical, cruel, and ruthless mercenary, deprived of conscience and feelings, a Pole who renounces his national identity and thus serves as the stereotype of a traitor.
31. There were 100 heller in a crown.
32. Tadeusz Kościuszko (1746–1817) was a Polish military leader who fought in the American Revolutionary War and the Polish uprising against Russia of 1794; Adam Mickiewicz (1798–1855) is considered Poland's (as well as Lithuania's and Belarus's) national poet and is celebrated as a major proponent of Polish independence.
33. The original is: "Ask, and it shall be given you; seek, and ye shall find; knock, and it shall be opened unto you." Matthew 7:7, King James Bible.
34. Both towns were located in the pre-World War I, Russian-ruled Polish-Ukrainian province of Volhynia and had large Jewish populations.
35. Matejko (1836–93) was a Polish painter from Kraków known for his works of historical and military figures and scenes; Grottger (1837–67) was a Polish Romantic painter from Eastern Galicia. Sienkiewicz's *With Fire and Sword* (1884) is a historical novel about the Cossack uprising of 1648 and the first volume of the Trilogy that includes also *The Deluge* (1886) and *Fire in the Steppes* (1888).
36. Vereshchagin (1842–1904) was an acclaimed Russian war artist known for his graphic depictions.
37. Grand Duke Nicholas (1856–1929), grandson of Tsar Nicholas I, was commander in chief of the Russian Imperial Army at the front in the first year of World War I. He published his "Manifesto to the Polish Nation" on 14 August 1914, promising the reunification of the Polish lands under the aegis of the Russian Tsar.
38. From Samara in southeastern European Russia.
39. Siewiński writes in German: "Man muss zum bösen Spiel eine gute Miene machen."
40. Bayram is a Turkic word for holiday.
41. Yiddish: literally "violence" but used as an exclamation in view of a threat or exercise of violence; from the German word for violence, power, and authority, Gewalt.

42. In the Battle of Limanowa in December 1914 a Russian advance toward Kraków was beaten back by Austrian and German formations; in the First Battle on the Masurian Lakes in September 1914 the German army pushed the invading Russian army out of German territory.

43. The Austrian garrison in Przemyśl surrendered to the besieging Russian army on 22 March 1915, after holding out for 133 days.

44. In the battle in Sieniawa, located 275 km northwest of Buczacz in western Galicia, German forces pushed the Russians out of the town as part of the major German-Austrian counter-offensive of May 1915.

45. Lessing (1729–81) was a major German Enlightenment writer and philosopher, perhaps best known today for his play "Nathan the Wise" (1779), advocating religious tolerance.

46. Mechnikov (1845–1916), later known as Élie Metchnikoff, left Russia in 1888 and spent the rest of his life working at the Louis Pasteur Institute in Paris. The child of a Russian father of Romanian ancestry and a Jewish mother, he was one of the pioneers in the field of immunology and shared the Nobel Prize in Physiology or Medicine with the German-Jewish physician and scientist Paul Ehrlich in 1908.

47. This is likely a reference to "Big Bertha" (*Dicke Bertha*), fielded by the Imperial German army, which fired caliber 42 cm (16.5 inch) shells; the gun is not known to have been used in this region, but the name came to be commonly attributed to all super heavy guns used by the Germans and Austrians in World War I.

48. Austrian troops wore blue uniforms at the time.

49. In fact, 320,000 Jewish soldiers, including 25,000 officers, served in the Austro-Hungarian Army in World War I. See Derek J. Penslar, *Jews and the Military* (Princeton: Princeton University Press, 2013), 157.

50. Haller (1873–1960) served as an officer in the Austrian army and commanded the 2nd Brigade of the Polish Legion; while in exile in France, he subsequently formed the Blue or Haller's Army, which inter alia participated in the 1918–19 Polish-Ukrainian War in Galicia.

51. Dmowski (1864–1939) was leader of the right-wing and antisemitic National Democracy (ND, also known as "Endecja") political movement.

52. Colard (1857–1916) was appointed military governor of Galicia on 1 August 1915, and died on 8 April 1916, aged fifty-nine.

53. Austrian General Remen (1855–1932) subsequently served as governor of Austrian-ruled Serbia between July 1916 and the end of the war.

54. Here, Siewiński is confusing the Brusilov Offensive of June 1916, during which Buczacz was captured once more by the Russians, with the Kerensky Offensive of July 1917, which ended up with the return of the Austrians to Buczacz on 26 July after another year of Russian occupation. Aleksei Brusilov (1853–1926) employed innovative offensive techniques that enabled the Russians to reoccupy much of Galicia but at a tremendous human cost, which in turn demoralized the Russian army and the population, contributing to the fall of the Tsarist regime. Alexander Kerensky (1881–1970) was head of the post-revolutionary Russian provisional government formed following the February Revolution of 1917, and was the moving spirit behind the disastrous July offensive that ended up in a major withdrawal, the ouster of his government, and Soviet Russia's eventual decision to reach an armistice in the aftermath of the Bolshevik October Revolution. Kerensky spent the rest of his life in exile.

55. The Austro-Hungarian Empire was officially dissolved on 31 October 1918, and the very next day the West Ukrainian People's Republic (ZUNR) was proclaimed, leading to a brutal war with Poland over the territory of Galicia, replete with massacres of

civilian populations on both sides and pogroms against Jewish communities, lasting until July 1919. See Bartov, *Anatomy of a Genocide*, 64–71.

56. This is Siewiński's term for a Ruthenian claiming to be a Ukrainian, which to his mind was a false identity.

57. Siewiński seems to have written this and several other paragraphs under Ukrainian rule, while other comments in the diary were likely written in 1922.

58. *Caesar's Column: A Story of the Twentieth Century* (1890), a dystopian novel by Ignatius Donnelly, who also authored *Atlantis: The Antediluvian World* (1882), depicts the destruction of a ruthless capitalist oligarchy in New York City in a bloody populist uprising.

59. Palek, who had taught at the Buczacz gymnasium before World War I, established in Buczacz a Jewish secondary school with Polish-language instruction in 1927 because of growing restrictions on admitting Jewish students to the state gymnasium. See Bartov, *Anatomy of a Genocide*, 90, 325–26 n. 14.

60. Shevchenko (1814–61), considered Ukraine's national poet, was also a writer and a painter and a key figure in the creation of modern Ukrainian literature and language.

61. Petliura (1879–1926) was supreme commander of the Ukrainian army and president of the Ukrainian People's Republic from 1918 to 1921, fighting for Ukrainian independence after the fall of the Russian empire and before the takeover by Soviet Russia. He was accused of being responsible for the tens of thousands of Jewish victims in pogroms during the civil war in Ukraine. Petliura was assassinated as an exile in Paris in 1926 by Sholom Schwartzbard, whose family was murdered in Odessa. In the subsequent trial, Schwartzbard was acquitted by a French jury. In Ukrainian lore, Petliura is remembered as a national hero.

62. Pisetsky was secretary of post and telegraph; Holubovych was secretary of justice; Hrekov (1875–1958) was commander in chief of the army of the West Ukrainian People's Republic.

63. On these events see Bartov, *Anatomy of a Genocide*, 70–73.

64. Kostetskyi (1832–1908) was a Ruthenian-Galician journalist, writer, and poet who wrote in Polish and described himself as "gente Ruthenus, natione Polonus" (of Ruthenian ethnicity and of the Polish nation).

65. On the San River, the current border between Ukraine and Poland. On these events see Bartov, *Anatomy of a Genocide*, 73–74.

66. The victory of the Polish Army over the Red Army at the outskirts of Warsaw in August 1920 that ended to Polish-Soviet War. The war began with the April–June 1920 Polish offensive, in alliance with Petliura's Ukrainian army, which attempted to seize Ukrainian territories that had come under Soviet rule following the Bolshevik Revolution.

Viktor Petrykevych in 1925. Source:
Petrykevych private papers, courtesy of Bohdan
Petrykevych, Ivano-Frankivsk, Ukraine.

VIKTOR PETRYKEVYCH

WRITTEN IN STANYSLAVIV AND BUCHACH, 1941–44

WITH ADDITIONAL NOTES FROM STRYI, DROHOBYCH, AND KOLOMYYA, 1944–56

Stanyslaviv: Under Soviet Rule

9 September 1939

I must frankly admit that when the Germans launched their campaign on 1 September, and when France and England declared war against Germany on 3 September, I had no intention of writing a diary. Why should I? I am not in the military, and although I am a citizen of the Polish State, I do not participate in public or political life. I am just waiting for the war to end. Yet today, nine days after the war began, I decided to write something down. There are no newspapers, and even if any reach us, the information in them is completely out of date; as for official communiqués, nobody believes them. Only those who have a radio can receive information about the current state of affairs.

On 31 August I returned from the village of Yamne [Polish: Jamne, 45 km northeast of Lviv] after I heard the dispiriting news about the first mobilization. When I got home to Stanyslaviv [Polish: Stanisławów, now known as Ivano-Frankivsk] at 2 Issakovycha [Polish: Izakowicza] Street, I observed a great deal of military traffic. Following the experience of the previous war, the population began to stock up on food and other supplies. Already on 2 and 3 September it became impossible to obtain sugar, petrol, kerosene, and so forth, or more generally, any goods that had to be brought from elsewhere. One could see that the railroad had been taken over by the military.

In the city ditches were being dug for protection from aerial bombardment. Ditches were dug in the park and in the city square near Mitskevych [Polish: Mickiewicz] Street, and in other squares. One wonders whether they will be of any use. An order was issued: as protection from chemical weapons, everyone must prepare a safe room in every apartment. People have glued strips of paper across their windows ..., so that when walking down the street, one can see where they would be hiding from a gas attack. Every block of houses has its own watchmen. They wear a yellow-green armband and when the siren goes off their role is to stop the traffic on the streets. Passersby run into the shelters, wagons are stopped, the horses are unharnessed and led into backyards. In general, all traffic is halted, and only policemen, civil guards, and soldiers are out on the streets.

The city is now filthy and unwashed, filled with dust and dirt. A good and pleasant autumn has begun. Unfortunately, there are no clouds in the sky and the air is clear. Since 4 or 5 September airplanes have been appearing daily, usually at about 10 a.m. Yesterday there were eleven or twelve of them. It is said that the area of Yamnetsya [Polish: Jamnica, 8 km north of Stanyslaviv], where explosives are stored, was bombed—bombs were dropped somewhere near the manor house. Yesterday afternoon at 4 p.m. the alarm was sounded. Our family gathered in the safe room prepared as a shelter for a gas attack. However, at 4:10 p.m. there was a terrible explosion. Everyone began screaming "bombs!" There was terrible panic .... When all calmed down, I learned that a plane had dropped bombs on the airfield in Yasyhory. In fact, they attacked Dubrava, destroyed inspector Pikulsky's villa, and wounded six people. The windows in the houses were damaged and the windowpanes were cracked. Today people are inspecting the school and picking up bomb fragments.

The Poles are in a very gloomy and resigned mood. One can see no manifestations of joy and the like. All the faces look sad. Despite the newspapers' exhortations of their countrymen, everybody knows that the information in these newspapers is completely out of date and mostly cannot be trusted. Yesterday's evening papers reported that the Germans were 50 kilometers north of Warsaw and that in the east the front line was between Tarnów and Tomaszów; this afternoon I learned that the Germans were already in Warsaw, and a German communiqué was issued yesterday from Warsaw indicating that in the east the front line was between Wisłok and Sandomierz, and that the Germans were already reaching the Vistula River. [Polish Foreign] Minister [Józef] Beck left for London by airplane or train. What will happen next? What will happen to Poland as a result of the war?

Personally, I do not believe in Poland's demise and Germany's complete victory. True, the Germans can smash and occupy Poland in a month, but the final victory is still far. The last world war demonstrated the superiority of England and France over Germany. Poland now has powerful allies, and I do not believe in Germany's complete victory over England and France. The Germans will crush Poland, just as they crushed Serbia, but the victory of the Allies will restore Poland, and it might become even stronger. A disaster will befall Poland only if England and France abandon it, or if Hitler reaches an agreement with England and France at Poland's expense. But for now, all this is mere fantasy and conjecture ....

10 September 1939

... Last night at 2 a.m. there was an alarm, then at 5 a.m., at 8 a.m., and at lunchtime, and again now, while I am writing, at 3 p.m. People are at their wits' end, running to the shelters in the beerhouse cellars. Will that even help?

When I meet my [Ukrainian] friends, I am surprised by their optimism. Probably all of us feel Schadenfreude.

During their rule, did our [Polish] vanquishers not do everything to arouse the hatred of both the intelligentsia and the peasantry? Do we need to recall all our martyrdom, especially during the last few years? Despite our politicians' declarations of loyalty, each of us, whether educated or common men, has personally witnessed our annihilation; and this experience prods us to rejoice over their defeat. For instance, here is a story told by a tailor, a dressmaker. A certain woman tried to flee from Communist Ukraine with two infants. The military caught her, killed the children, and then killed the mother. Is this really true? One can't say. But their abuse of us has created an atmosphere conducive to such feelings and images.

With this background, our [Ukrainian] people are making plans, organizing their lives, etc. It is still too early. People say that the Germans are dropping small maps from airplanes, in which Poland appears only as an ethnic entity. It is said that Nazi Germany is going to make Galicia into a separate state—its protectorate—and that Volhynia and Polesia will go to the Bolsheviks. They [the Bolsheviks] are already mobilizing. People say that today the Germans occupied Yaroslav and Peremyshl [Polish: Jarosław, Przemyśl]; that one Polish general was killed, and another was taken prisoner; that the military is demoralized and in retreat, and so forth. People obtain some of this news from the radio, from German broadcasts, while the other part is fiction.

I consider this big news premature and currently harmful. One must not forget that England and France are Poland's allies, and that in the last war these states proved to be invincible. Germany is again almost surrounded by neighbors who are waiting for and believe in the eventual destruction of their enemies, but even in alliance with the Germans, they still cannot prevail over the union of England, France, and Poland.

We, or rather our politicians in power, whether by tradition or because they are somewhat familiar with the German language, their periodicals and the strength of their cultural, are always linking our future prospects to past German victories. They barely take into account England and France, because they do not know them and do not appreciate their might and resilience. These states seem too far from us. Even though the situation of Poland at the moment is tragic, we must not forget the fate of Serbia. At the moment, we should wait patiently.

The mood in the city is very bad. Polish circles are very gloomy and silent. Groups of Jews converge on the streets, whispering. It is said that the authorities arrested a hundred Germans from the German colonies. One or two were shot. These are rumors that cannot be verified.

11 September 1939

Today, the school principal announced the opening of the school year. But the gymnasium and the hospital are occupied. So, the school year is postponed. On Thursday, I just went to attend a parents' conference; they have to decide whether the teaching should begin despite the danger. There is great commotion in the city. In front of the city bank there are long lines of people trying to draw out money. One store is selling oil in the morning; a large crowd in front of the store is pushing into it. Policemen restore order. It is impossible to get oil, sugar, gasoline, coal and, in general, the goods that are sold there. But the goods are not there, because they are sold out, or because the storekeepers are hiding them. Everything is distressing and uncertain. One of the teachers mentions that the conference has been postponed to Thursday, because it is not clear whether the Germans would be here by then.

Yesterday and today there were no newspapers from Lviv [Polish: Lwów; German: Lemberg; Russian: Lvov]. I went to the kiosk next to the main post office, but only the local newspaper can be found there.

Last night I inspected the devastation caused by the German bombers in Dubrava. The air pressure damaged the roofs, blew out windows, and there was a two-meter deep crater in the ground. But the aircraft hangar did not collapse. Clearly, it's not that easy [to destroy it].

Life here is hard; every two or three hours the air raid alarm goes off. Life on the street stops, everyone goes into hiding under the staircases in the buildings or in their cellars.

My neighbor, the wife of an army major, heard somewhere on the radio that the Germans were threatening to impose statements of loyalty on our envoys and citizens. Is that true? And in the case of noncompliance, who will protect us from our rulers? One Polish woman related to the major's wife how the Poles treat captured Germans. The POWs have all sorts of benefits, good food, clean washing, etc. The Poles are probably afraid of punishment and revenge for maltreating captured Germans. What would have happened to the Ukrainians? ...

It is said that according to Bolshevik Radio the Polish government and its ministries have retreated to Kremenets [Polish: Krzemieniec]. Just as our government had escaped in 1919. History repeats itself. People say that the Bolsheviks are mobilizing but explain this differently: some say they are against the Germans, others that they are against the Poles and will unite the Ukrainian lands.

12 September 1939

The mood is very grim. Numerous refugees are coming from the west, and army vehicles have been driving through all night. No newspapers have arrived from Lviv. Earlier this morning, I saw two or three radio transmission vehicles. It is said that the communication station will be mounted in the apiary near the railroad station. From the radio people are learning about the actual slaughter of the Polish Army. The Germans captured twenty-four thousand soldiers and three generals yesterday on the bend of the Vistula. Peremyshl has been bombarded in many sites. In Kiasarna, eighty soldiers were killed, and 150 civilians perished in their homes. The Germans have crossed the San River in several places. The Polish Army in the Poznan area is surrounded by the Germans. Warsaw is still holding out, and although here the radio is boasting about the great zeal of the inhabitants, nobody believes that the civilians' zeal and dedication can save the city. Rather, the Germans have so far not occupied the city for tactical reasons.

In our city ration cards have been issued. There is chaos, panic, and uncertainty about what will happen tomorrow. Constant air raid alarms. A rumor has spread that the government has escaped with the treasury to Kremenets and from there to...

At 1 p.m. an air raid on the airfield. We hear the sound of bombs. We go into the cellar. One dead or wounded person is carried away on a stretcher.

13 September 1939

It is said that the Germans have surrounded Sambir and Yaniv [Polish: Sambor, Janów] in the Lviv region. Today, at 9:30 a.m. German planes bombed the airport and destroyed four Polish aircraft. We had to hide in the cellar. In three or four days we expect the Germans to arrive. No one believes in the Polish Army anymore. They mock it and recall how it had abused the defenseless populations and carried out pacification [the repression campaign of Ukrainian nationalists in 1930].

Men of my age are not called up for war because there are neither uniforms nor weapons for them. Chaos and mindlessness. There are no newspapers. There is talk about France and England encouraging Poland.

15 September 1939

Yesterday the Poles were in good spirits. There were reports that Lviv was defending itself and that the Poles had destroyed a few enemy aircraft. Today there is a report that the Polish army has been largely defeated, that the retreat is disorderly, that the soldiers are fleeing home, and the officers are dressed in civilian clothes, etc., that the Poznan Army is surrounded, that the Germans took sixty thousand prisoners, that the Germans are in Brest, and that the French are just approaching the Siegfried Line.[1]

For now, one has to rely on this [rumor], since we have no newspapers, and the announcements and accounts on the radio are very one-sided and distorted.

The airplanes appear daily from 9:30 a.m. to noon and from 2–4 p.m. Everyone hides in the cellar and everything comes to a standstill. The airplanes strafe vehicles and drop bombs on military targets, airfields, and bridges.

16 September 1939

Today at 6 a.m. we were still asleep when the air raid siren sounded. We had to get out of bed and run to the cellar. At 8 a.m. there was another alarm: happily, it lasted only half an hour. It is said that the Polish government is in Zalishchyky [Polish: Zaleszczyki, 112 km southeast of

Stanyslaviv]. The Germans know that and are dropping bombs there. [Polish] President [Ignacy] Mościcki and his ministers have to hide in a cellar. The Romanians do not want to let them in, and the border [less than 50 km south of Zalishchyky] is sealed with barbed wire .... At night long freight trains are heading in the direction of Nadvirna [Polish: Nadwórna, 40 km southwest of Stanyslaviv].

17 September 1939

At 6 a.m. there was an alarm, and everybody ran to the shelters. At noon there was another alarm. On Wojciechowski Street, on the hill, a bomb hit a house; people there were wounded and killed. The hospital is full of wounded civilians.

Today I learned that the Polish government had already fled to Romania. The same fate of the government of the ZUNR [the short-lived West Ukrainian People's Republic, Zakhidnoukrayinska Narodna Respublika, of 1918–19] has also befallen it. They [the Poles] even had to flee to the same neighbor! People say that the Bolsheviks declared on the radio that since there was no government in Poland, and there was no one to talk with, they would occupy Ukrainian and Belarusian lands. On the radio the Germans declared that if the population of Warsaw failed to disarm by the deadline they issued, the Germans would destroy the city.

In our city some stores are already empty, shoe and textile stores; there is no firewood and no matches. So far, there is still some bread, butter, and flour.

Some officials have already been paid a three-month salary [in advance], just in case; we, the teachers, have already been registered and the school principal has told us that we would also be paid in the event of an evacuation. People say that behind the park the military are digging ditches and trenches, since the Polish defensive line will be located there. Others are talking about a line along the Bystrytsya [Polish: Bystrzyca] River [just west of the city]; still others speak about a line next to the village of Drahomyrchany [Polish: Drohomirczany, 10 km southwest of Stanyslaviv].

At 7 p.m. I was summoned along with other teachers to the school principal with the news that we would be paid a three-month salary in advance. I went to the principal's house and learned that the Polish bank was being evacuated, and that the principal had not received the money for us, although the principals of other gymnasiums had obtained the money at the last moment. At the principal's house I learned that this morning the Bolsheviks had crossed the Polish border and were demanding the return of three districts.[2] At home my neighbors spoke of a rumor that the Bolsheviks had occupied Chortkiv [Polish: Czortków, 107 km northeast of Stanyslaviv]. Nobody knows in what capacity the Bolsheviks are coming: as a friend or as an enemy of Poland? But on the way home I saw military aircraft and army units heading to the east. In the east one could see flashes of light. We could not tell whether the light came from artillery or from lightning.

18 September 1939

This will remain a memorable day in the history of Stanyslaviv and Galicia in general. In the morning we were informed that we would be paid a six-month salary. As I went to the city, I learned that the Polish military was leaving Stanyslaviv and retreating to the west, and that the Bolsheviks were approaching. City Mayor Kotlyarchuk appealed to the public, stating that the Bolsheviks were coming, and urging people to stay calm for the sake of Slavic solidarity and to await their arrival. In the city I heard that the Ukrainians too were going to issue a proclamation greeting the Soviet army. In the streets there is extraordinary traffic. Cars, buses, motorbikes, military trucks are constantly driving through, all heading to the west. The Jews and the communists have formed a volunteer unit [sotnia] (lacking any weapons); they are marching down Sapizhynskiy [Polish: Sapieżyński] Street, wearing red armbands and flowers (dahlias or roses); only the kike in the lead is carrying a rifle. Polish rule is over. The police can still be seen, but it no longer interferes with the communists. I stayed on Sapizhynskiy Street until 11 a.m.; Polish cars were driving away, but one couldn't yet see any Bolsheviks. People say that yesterday evening they were already in Buchach [Polish: Buczacz, 70 km northeast of Stanyslaviv]. The Ukrainian proletariat is also on the move, and they are preparing to greet the Bolshevik army at 4 p.m.

In the city there is calm; the only sporadic shooting is coming from groups of young soldiers, apparently trying to loot the army depots.

In the morning a rumor spread in the city that [Adolf] Hitler and [Hermann] Goering were killed.[3] So far, people do not believe in it, but there is no denial either. We are facing the unknown.

The stores are closed today; even the post office is completely closed.

19 September 1939

This was a very restless and dangerous night. The volunteer guard, formed in the city, was too weak, and came under attack by deserters and remnants of the Polish army fleeing via Vorokhta [Polish: Worochta, 90 km south of Stanyslaviv] to Hungary.[4] Reportedly up to sixty of our people were wounded, and some were killed, but this number is probably exaggerated. Yesterday the Bolsheviks did not arrive, although people were expecting them.

Today, at about 9 a.m., I went into town to obtain some information about what was happening in the city. In town I learned that [the commander-in-chief of the Polish armed forces Edward] Rydz-Śmigły had fled to Chernivtsi [German: Czernowitz; Romanian: Cernăuți, 135 km southeast of Stanyslaviv]. *Sic transit gloria.*[5] As I approached Sapizhynskiy Street, I again saw masses of people, mainly Jews, who were standing on both sides of the street, forming a dense crowd as they waited for the Bolsheviks who were coming from the direction of Tysmenytsya [Polish: Tyśmienica, 11 km east of Stanyslaviv]. At the junction of Sapizhynskiy, next to the post office, the workers' organizations were gathered, holding red flags with Polish inscriptions. In front of this human barrier, on both sides of the street, recently released political prisoners were standing. There were about a hundred of them, or slightly more. The prisoners included Jews, but there were probably more of our people [Ukrainians]. Their faces were pale, their hair closely cropped—evidence of Polish violence against us. At 9:30 a.m. a car carrying soldiers arrived. The assembled people began applauding and threw flowers at them. They [the Bolshevik military] inquired where the post office was located and went to secure it. The postal employees handed them their weapons, since they had been serving as the armed guard of the post office. Behind the car came a tank. The assembled Judeo-communists were seized by a triumphal mood. The tank was covered with flowers and garlands; some people leaped onto the tank, which stopped for a moment, and began to ride with the soldiers and to kiss them [calling out]: "Long live the USSR, long live Voroshilov, long live Stalin; long live Soviet Ukraine!"[6] After this tank a second one arrived. The same scene was repeated. Then the third tank came, and then hundreds more. Altogether some two hundred tanks drove by, and they were all welcomed with cheers, applause, flowers, and garlands. All this was mostly the doing of the Jewish proletariat; here and there one could observe a Ukrainian or a Pole. The Jews quickly found their bearings and adapted to the situation. Today we saw the power of the Jewish element in the cities. The Jewish bourgeoisie and plutocracy strolled calmly on the sidewalks, rejoicing that Hitler had not come to the city.

The soldiers, riding on trucks or in tanks, talked to the locals. The soldiers have a star on their helmets. They speak Ukrainian and Russian.

They say they are from Podolia.[7] There were some cars with officers. This welcome lasted until noon. In the afternoon I returned home and therefore did not see any more military units. Today the stores are closed. The city is calm. In the sky there were apparently two Soviet airplanes ....

21 September 1939

There are difficulties with supplies. Milk is hard to get today. The Jews intercept the peasants and pay exorbitantly for each liter. There are long lines in front of food and textile stores. A soldier is keeping order in front the oil store and one can get a small amount. Many products are sold out completely and it's impossible to get them at all. Everything has gone up by 50 to 100 percent.

Today an ordinance by the military authorities in Ukrainian and Polish appeared on city walls. The commandant of the garrison is Captain Harbuz [Russian: Garbuz]. All weapons must be surrendered, stores must be opened, and there is a curfew at 10 p.m ....

Yesterday, accompanied by many workers, two workers who were allegedly shot by Polish soldiers were laid to rest. They were later described in the news as victims of fascism. It is said that the Germans will retreat to the demarcation line, presumably along the San and Vistula Rivers, making this the territory of the USSR [Union of Soviet Socialist Republics]. Bolshevik troops have probably already occupied Lviv. They say that trains are already running to Peremyshl. No newspapers are available and conflicting pieces of news are circulating.

The Jews are beginning to organize in trade unions. We, Ukrainian teachers, are also organizing into a professional union.

The National [Ukrainian] House has hoisted a red flag. From Tsarist-philia into Soviet-philia. What mendacity.

22 September 1939

There is a long line in front of the oil store, hundreds of people are waiting to get a quarter of a liter oil; there is no meat and no firewood. People are buying everything to get rid of their money. The prices keep going up, so money has little value.

Today, at 11 a.m., there was a gathering of educational workers, teachers of all schools; the assembly took place in the hall of the Ukrainian state gymnasium. So many came that there was not enough room and they gathered in the courtyard. But there was no program for the assembly. There were only exclamations in honor of the USSR and statements of hatred toward the Polish lords. One teacher proposed that we meet at 3 p.m. We agreed to that and at about 3 p.m. we gathered in the hall. The head of the assembly was selected, and we were ordered to register ourselves on a card: our full name, where and what we teach. Then the meeting ended, and the chairman of the meeting or the secretary stated that further instructions for the purpose of establishing a professional union of educational workers would be provided in the Ukrainian teachers' information sheets.

It is said that [former Polish] policemen have been arrested and imprisoned. The [former Polish] Public Prosecutor for Political Affairs was also arrested and detained. In some villages, the population has fiercely punished the police, which had mercilessly abused them for years. Everyone is talking about this, but I cannot confirm the facts. Policemen who had not maltreated and offended the population were allowed to go home.

25 September 1939

In the city you can see the following scene: a Bolshevik soldier surrounded by simple people, with a few scattered intellectuals here and there. The soldier tells them about life in the USSR. People ask questions, and he answers. The soldier, armed with a long bayonet, is there to keep the order, but is in fact an agitator. Somebody asks him how the peasants live, what are the collective farms like, etc. He answers, "Our men plow, sow, and reap together, and then each person takes as much grain as he needs." Another asks if people go to church or whether there are any churches at all. He answers, "There are churches and you can pray. But who wants to go to church? Of course, the old people go but the young rarely do."

Two peasants who had served in the Polish army visited an acquaintance of mine. He listened to their story all night. They related that during the war they never fired a shot but fled from the Germans without stopping. The commander of the army was General [Bernard Stanisław] Mond.[8] He was captured. The Germans broke through the first line, after which the Poles did not dare put up any more resistance. The Poles were defeated because of their underestimation of tactics, their inferior weaponry, and the lack of courage and unpreparedness of the higher ranks.

Today, one of the tenants [in Petrykevych's building] bought two heads of cabbage for 110 złoty when they usually cost 15. There are no newspapers, no news reports.

27 September 1939

Today, a meeting of teachers from the district of Stanyslaviv took place in the hall of the Sokół [Polish gymnastic society] building.[9] The assembly was scheduled for noon, but the meeting was opened at 12:35 p.m. by the teacher Chervonyakov. A presidium was elected, which included M. Lipky, Boytsun, Chervonyakov, Hirnyak, a Jewish teacher, and two others whom I don't know. A senior officer—a representative of the army—made a political speech. It is hard to convey its content: it clarified the struggle of capitalism against the USSR and the truce between Germany and the USSR. The Soviets are invincible and have brought salvation to Ukrainian and Belarusian lands from the unbelievable pogroms perpetrated by Poland. He declared that all national groups would study in their mother tongue, that the authorities would not interfere with religious instruction, and that history would not be taught yet, because following the destruction of Poland there was no need to teach the history of the Polish lords and magnates. The study of history was for now irrelevant. The report was discussed. Comrade Chervonyakov elaborated: everyone should immediately resume work in their positions! The school authorities would issue instructions and orders and normalize school affairs, appointments, etc. The army spokesman said that the teachers should organize in a professional union. Finally, he read out a telegram to [Joseph] Stalin, the genius of mankind, which was approved by the assembly.

The entire hall was full of teachers, up to a thousand people. It is not known whether they were all teachers and teaching trainees, or whether some were non-teachers.

All workers, laborers, craftsmen, and intellectuals are organized in professional unions.

In the city the first issue of the newspaper "Soviet Ukraine" came out on 23 September, but it carries little news. There are no other newspapers. The mail does not arrive.

Civilians and soldiers are buying up all the supplies in the stores. The locals are buying because they are afraid of the currency devaluation; the soldiers are buying because our prices are very low for them. It is said that the karbovanets [a Ukrainian Soviet currency similar to the Russian ruble] had a quarter of the value of the Polish złoty; but due to the equalization of both currencies, the value of the złoty has fallen sharply.

People say that the Bolshevik authorities have arrested several Ukrainians, but we don't know why. Among those arrested are

Y. Olesnitsky (a lawyer), the student Yasenytskyi, and others whom I do not know. Is this a misunderstanding?

Tomorrow the teaching of science begins at the Skarbovsky girls' gymnasium.

P.S. A representative of the Red Army has said that private schools would become state-owned (he means Ukrainian and Jewish schools).[10]

The peasants have divided the noble estates and partitioned them between the landless and land-poor. They share the lords' cows, horses, and so forth among themselves. The landless received 10 morgues [2.5 hectares] of land.

And so, we have resolved the land issue. As for the factories, their owners have become their managers.

28 September 1939

Today is the first day of school. I teach at the girls' gymnasium. First the students went to church, and then there was a school assembly.

In the city, announcements are posted that all complaints against citizens, government officials or institutions can be lodged with the military prosecutor. People say that it is the GPU [Soviet secret police].

It is said that Warsaw is already in the hands of the Germans. The Germans took a hundred thousand prisoners there ....

It's hard to find a maid. Village girls return to the villages, lured by [the newly available] land.

29 September 1939

Former political prisoners are living in the building of the gymnasium. These are young people, mostly peasants, whom the war has liberated.

Bolshevik airplanes frequently pass over the city. They fly low and buzz very loudly.

30 September 1939

The students are told that they have full freedom of religious practice (prayer, worship in church, etc.).

The city administration consists of the following persons: the head of the city administration, comrade Chuchukalo, and members Tarasovsky, Chervonyak, and D. Shpunder.

1 October 1939

Today in the "Warsaw" cinema a court-martial was convened against merchants who had overcharged for their merchandise. Three were sentenced to 10 years and two to 7 years in prison. These merchants are Jews. Will these sentences help? The price of commodities continues to go up because it is impossible to buy anything. Supplies are meager.

5 October 1939

Our senior leaders know how to deal with the current conditions. In the schools, small portraits of Stalin have appeared, red flags have been hoisted from schools and government buildings, and our school's management addresses letters to Comrade Chervonyakov. Is everybody adjusting to the spirit of the time?

Different instructions are being issued by the city administration for schools to prepare for enemy air raids. Who would carry out such a raid and where would it come from? Bohdan [Petrykevych's son] says that the schoolchildren and staff found some flyers printed in Ukrainian and in Polish, promising a raid by British aircraft. There is no end to the hardships.

This evening there was an assembly of teachers in the building of the Ukrainian Sokil [gymnastic society], addressed by Comrade Hrushetsky, regarding the convocation of a People's Assembly in Lviv. The Red Army liberated Western Ukrainian lands from the Polish landlords' yoke. We, the laboring intelligentsia in Stanyslaviv, support the proposal of the Lviv Provisional Authority to convene a West Ukrainian assembly. At that meeting, the working masses would choose deputies, representatives of the working masses. The task of the People's Assembly is to decide on:

1. Establishing a Soviet government on the land of Western Ukraine.
2. Uniting the land of Western Ukraine with the USSR.
3. Transferring land from the landlords to the peasants.
4. Nationalizing banks and factories.

The meeting adopted these resolutions and decided that the duty of teachers was to work among the people in that direction.

Comrade Chervonyakov made a proposal that the assembly put up as first candidates for the position the genius of humanity Comrades Stalin, [Vyacheslav] Molotov, [Mikhail] Kalinin, Voroshilov, and [Nikita]

Khrushchev.[11] This proposal was accepted without opposition. There were several other speakers who did not say anything new and the meeting was closed.

7 October 1939

The anniversary of the October Revolution has begun. All state buildings and private houses are decorated with red flags. The red flag is also hoisted from episcopal palaces and seminaries.

Yesterday, today, and tomorrow the Kamyanets Podilskyi [Polish: Kamieniec Podolski] Theater is performing [Oleksandr] Korniychuk's play "Truth" at the Monyushko [Polish: Moniuszko] hall.[12]

More trouble with supplies; there is no oil, no fuel. In front of the stores there are long lines.

9 October 1939

In the conference hall portraits of Stalin and Molotov are hanging from the wall. The teaching of Ukrainian has been introduced in Polish high schools. There are three hours of Ukrainian per week. But there are no textbooks, grammar books, or teaching plans. Up to now no one had worried about this and everyone taught as they saw fit, because during its tenure, the Lviv Curatorium [board of education] published no new textbooks and frequently issued only terrible reprints.

At the gymnasium today people said that the Bolsheviks had occupied or taken over Carpathian Ukraine in the Hungarian region.

It is said that Rector [of the Jan Kazimierz University in Lviv, Polish archaeologist Edmund] Bulanda was detained in Lviv and threatened with execution within twenty-four hours if he did not divulge the names of those who had killed Jewish students. The killers could not to be found. Bulanda finally stated that the killers were the sons of the [last Polish provincial] Governor [Alfred] Bilyk and former Mayor [Stanisław] Ostrowski. These worthy men's two sons were shot ....

It's reported that Hitler proposed a ceasefire to England and France on the condition that Poland would be a state within its ethnic boundaries. Four provinces (out of sixteen!) would be included in it, i.e., only a quarter will remain of prewar Poland.

The [cultural-educational club] Ukrainska Besida [Ukrainian Conversation] has ceased to exist here. There are no newspapers, there is no firewood to heat the halls.

10 October 1939

Today the first snow fell. We have been granted an early winter. People are anticipating it with some anxiety and fear. How will they survive this winter? We have no fuel and no fur coats. So far, there is meat, said to be coming from the cows and calves on the estates. No factories are producing coats and other winter clothes. In front of the stores that carry such products there are long lines as early as 7:30 a.m. Today a politruk [Soviet political officer] came to the gymnasium and lectured on the USSR.

13 October 1939

Next to the post office on the western side of the street propaganda slogans have been posted: "Long live the USSR"; "Long live Stalin, the father of the workers"; "Long live the Soviet Army"; "Long live Marshal Voroshilov." There are banners in Polish and Hebrew [likely in Yiddish written in Hebrew script].

Our principal (at the Skarbovsky Gymnasium) has told us that the politruk and the board meeting have adopted some reforms. The politruk demanded the elimination of the title "pan" [Polish and Ukrainian equivalent to Mr. or Sir]; teachers would be addressed as "comrade professor" or just "professor." Bowing is forbidden, but there should certainly be greetings such as "Good day, goodbye." All images of saints must be removed from the classrooms.

I have no radio, from which one might still get some information, since there are no newspapers. It is said that in the war with Poland, a hundred thousand Germans were killed. How many Poles were killed and how many have been taken prisoner by the Germans is unknown.[13] Along the main streets of the city there is heavy traffic of military trucks, artillery, infantry, and cavalry. It is said that the Bolsheviks have closed down and reinforced the border with Romania.[14]

17 October 1939

Typhoid fever and scarlet fever are spreading in the city.

The Bolsheviks know how to agitate and influence the masses. Everything is prepared for the elections. Voter lists are inspected. Yesterday evening in the Basilian [Ukrainian Greek Catholic religious monastic order] school there was a gathering of teachers to select candidates for deputies. The meeting was called for 5 p.m. and opened at about 6. The Jews proposed the teacher Fink as a candidate, the Ukrainians chose the teachers Petrunova and Chervonyakova, and the army put up Comrade Hrushetsky. The last three nominations were approved. Each candidate had to tell his or her autobiography. In general, those autobiographies were remarkably pallid because Petrunova and Chervonyakov claimed that they were non-party, but they had worked for peasants and workers in the Prosvita [Ukrainian Enlightenment Association] reading rooms, in the Ridna Shkola [Ukrainian Native Schools Association], and in the Union of Ukrainian Women [all nationalist organizations].

It is said that the Bolsheviks allow the Basilians to maintain their schools, but the Basilian teacher nuns must come to class in secular dress rather than their monastic clothes.

Since the arrival of the Bolsheviks, contributions to national institutions and membership fees have ceased. For a long time, this was a monthly expense of 8 to 10 złoty. Now the bill does not come. "Besida" no longer exists ....

19 October 1939

The military needs many apartments. The senior officers take rooms from those who have more than two of them. For the troops they took over the seminary. And part of the bishop's residence has been allotted to officers.

Today it's a month since the Bolsheviks came, but it seems as if it happened a long time ago. How everything has changed, how slowly time passes from day to day.

21 October 1939

Major preparations are being made for the elections. All teachers, regardless of age and nationality have become agitators. The city is divided into electoral districts. Streets or parts of streets in each district are allotted to agitators, so that they can inform the voters, explain to them the "Regulations" (the ballot pamphlet on the elections), verify them on the lists, and encourage them to vote. Everywhere the walls are covered with slogans, paintings, portraits of Stalin, Molotov, etc. The electoral commissions have lists of voters in Ukrainian, in some districts also in Polish.

As an agitator I have been assigned Kosharova [Polish: Koszarowa] street. Fortunately, there is only a tobacco store there. Yesterday afternoon I explained the "Regulations" to the official and the workers there.

It seems that in connection with the elections several Poles were detained. The two principals of the Polish gymnasiums, formerly members of [the right-wing interwar Polish party] Ozon [Camp of National Unity: Obóz Zjednoczenia Narodowego, known also as OZN], were arrested. Imprisoned were also the Roman Catholic priest Szwed and the clergyman Menziński, who had worked in the jail.

Today, at about 3 p.m., there was a huge election campaign rally ([by members of] institutions). All national and secondary schools were obliged to participate in the rally. There was military music, banners with slogans, and a speech.

22 October 1939

It is a cloudy, gloomy autumn day. It is Sunday. Today from morning until late evening we have elections. I also went [to vote] with my wife. Everywhere there was heavy traffic, especially in the afternoon. I showed my passport and received a ballot with the name of Comrade Chervoniakova (District 9). From there they sent us to the room where we made a check sign next to [the name of] the candidate. My wife and I inserted the ballots into the ballot box.

The communists are confident of their victory. After all, there is no other candidate. The issue is [to ensure] that the number of voters is as high as possible and equal to that of all eligible voters. Then, the government will be able to say: we were elected, for instance, by 80 to 85 percent of all eligible voters. I did not notice any abuse. Everywhere there was peace and order.

Students over eighteen years of age vote. Indeed, these elections are very democratic and embrace the broad strata of the people.

24 October 1939

The communists won an easy victory in the polls. Of the fourteen deputies elected, there are ten Ukrainians, three Jews, and one Polish woman. Over ninety percent of eligible voters took part in the elections.

25 October 1939

To be honest, proper and serious studies have not yet begun in the gymnasium. Everything is provisional and tenuous. The curriculum is being altered constantly, and therefore teachers have not yet been assigned permanent classes. Many students who enrolled before the vacation have not returned to school. Principals have been instructed to accept all students from other cities. In the gymnasium there are now students from distant Poland; there are even children of refugees from Warsaw [likely Jews who fled the German occupation].

The curriculum has undergone major changes. The study of religion has been abolished. Religion is no longer one of the school's disciplines. Priests cannot come to the gymnasium. Prayer before and after classes has been abolished. If students—boys or girls—want to pray, they can pray before the teacher arrives. The number of Ukrainian language hours has been put on a par with Polish. But what can be taught? What can one study? We do not even have Latin textbooks. And what about the Ukrainian language? At the moment, I still teach Ukrainian in the first-grade class at Gymnasium No. 1. Sixty students have enrolled. Of those about seven or eight are always absent. For the entire class, we have only two textbooks .... The students have never treated Ukrainian seriously until now .... Some of the students have never studied Ukrainian before.

New students are still arriving, either to enroll or to check out the school.

Also, consider the study of Latin or German. Here too we do not have any textbooks; how is it possible to teach a foreign language without a textbook?

Moreover, recent events have affected the psyche of young people. There is a notable decline in attention, neglect of school chores, and debauchery. After all, when every family is trying hard to find some bread, firewood, lamps, matches, butter, shoes, and clothes, how can the youngsters concentrate on their schoolwork? The youths are undernourished, because there are long lines in front of the stores, and it is impossible to purchase any supplies. Thus, the youths have no energy for schoolwork. Many of the schoolgirls do not come to class because they have to wait in line in front of the stores.

27 October 1939

At the girls' gymnasium a certain Red Army officer or "politruk" lectured to the older schoolgirls, those in the third grade and above, about the organization of communist youth, the "Komsomol." This is the world of new ideas.

A couple of days ago, a teacher from Gymnasium No. 1, a Pole, was arrested. It is said that he had once lived in Soviet Ukraine and wrote a book in which the communist system was falsely and maliciously depicted.

People say that some of the prisoners have been taken somewhere in vehicles, and that the rest of the detainees are prohibited from seeing their relatives.

In school we may not use the word "zhyd" ["Jew" in Ukrainian and Polish but derogatory in Russian] and instead should say "yevrei" [commonly used in the USSR]. The word "zhyd" never had a derogative meaning for us; on the contrary, "yevrei" was considered derogative. But after some time "yevrei" will become a respectful term. A few days ago, the parents of the students in Gymnasium No. 1 had to write statements indicating in which language they would like their sons to study.

The gymnasium is decorated with communist slogans on red banners. The classrooms are adorned with them. The youth must see the slogans of communism always and everywhere. These slogans are in the city, in government, in stores, and so forth.

29 October 1939

Today, Sunday, as I was walking down Sapizhynskiy Street, I encountered senior students standing around and smoking Russian cigarettes. In conversation with one of the teachers, I learned that the school authorities would soon examine the level of education in the schools and tighten discipline. We live under conditions in which one cannot require a high level of education and discipline is declining.

At the elementary school, where [Viktor Petrykevych's son] Bohdan is studying, a student in his class lit a Russian cigarette in the hallway. This was reported to the principal, and he called the student's parents to the office ....

1 November 1939

Today at 6 p.m. a lecture for teachers on the significance of the October Revolution, whose 22nd anniversary is approaching, was held in the hall of the Ukrainian Sokil building. The speaker was from the education section of the Red Army. It must be admitted that the Communists have good agitators, speakers who can appeal to the masses. The hall was full: besides the teachers there were many others, mostly Jewish members of the public. There were also senior school students (seven to eight hundred people). The lecture lasted more than two hours. The speaker described the present state of the USSR, its progress, culture, and politics. Then he moved on to history, to the history of the Bolshevik Party, its leaders, [Vladimir] Lenin, Stalin, etc., before the uprising in St. Petersburg, then the fighting against [leader of the Russian revolutionary provisional government Aleksander] Kerensky's troops, etc. The enemies of the Bolshevik revolution were the national armies of [Ukrainian leader Symon] Petliura and the Ukrainian Galician Army, which showed up in Ukraine; it joined the army of [White Armies General Anton] Denikin, and then let the Poles in. This was a gang of officers, a counterrevolutionary force, and the enemies of the working people. With the collapse of Austria in Galicia, a bourgeois power emerged with the support of the Entente, which stood in defense of the landlords and manufacturers. When the Entente conceded Galicia to Poland, its national politicians turned against the interests of the peasants and the workers and betrayed them in favor of their masters... The remnants of the officers, the nationalists, and the henchmen of the bourgeoisie are now hiding. But let them remember that every Chekist [meaning here member of the Soviet secret police Cheka and its various successors] has not two, but millions of eyes. The communist government will crush and destroy the enemies of the people root and branch. The happiness of the peasant and the worker is ensured by the communist party, which is the only patron of the people.

This speech was often interrupted by applause.

4 November 1939

Yesterday at about 4 p.m. a meeting of teachers was held in the hall of the Ukrainian Sokil. The purpose of the meeting was the establishment of a professional union of teachers. As usual, there were numerous attendees, likely more than one thousand people. The meeting was chaired by Comrade Klymenko. Comrade Mikhailov reported on trade unions in the USSR, and said that Poland, as a land of landlords and capitalists, had persecuted and destroyed trade unions. The Ukrainian SSR [Soviet Socialist Republic] has organized, developed and supported the unions...

After the report there was a discussion in which the speakers were asked for clarification of unclear points. Moreover, we talked about the work of the teacher, his duties at school and outside the school, the dissemination of the idea of communism, and the dissemination of the ideas of Marxism-Leninism and Stalin.

Finally, members of the Trade Union Council were elected: Ukrainians, Jews, and perhaps one Pole ....

6 November 1939

Today marks the 22nd anniversary of the October Revolution. All buildings, especially those that are state-owned, are decorated with Stalin's image on a red background, with red flags, banners, slogans, etc. All windows have stickers with Comrade Stalin's portrait. A large portrait on a red background is prominently displayed and lit up with flashing electric lights on the first floor of the Ukrainian gymnasium. The same is in the commercial school, and in general all schools are festively decorated, as are all the apartment blocks. On the square in front of the Gartenberg Palace, a large tribune has been built, covered with red cloth.

Today, the students came to school at 9 a.m. The teachers gave their home classes an account of the October Revolution. Then everyone went to a free performance at the cinema, where they watched a film on the events that have occurred since the revolution.

At 3 p.m. a commemoration of the revolution was held in the academic hall of the gymnasium. A representative from the education department opened the festivities. He spoke well and accessibly. Of course, these speeches are similar, the approach to historical events is the same, and they all end up stating that socialism is leading to communism, which is the peak and culmination of human social progress. Then [Ukrainian national author Ivan] Franko's poem "The Bricklayers" ["Kamenyari," aka "The Pioneers"] was recited, as well as a sort of Polish declamation written by a student.[15] The musical quartet played the Bolshevik anthem, which was sung at the end of the event ....

7 November 1939

To be sure, in the last twenty-five years power has changed hands in Galicia four times; but never before has Stanyslaviv seen such a demonstration (what we call manifestation). Everything was well thought out and organized according to plan. Columns of people waited in designated streets and, when instructed, marched to Sapizhynskiy Street, where on the square facing the arcade a large stage had been erected, on which the commandants stood. Hundreds of thousands of people, old and young, children, girls, women, ordinary folk, intellectuals, peasants, workers, and so forth, marched down this street. The rally included not only the residents of Stanyslaviv, but also peasants and youth from the nearby villages. The brass orchestra was amplified through megaphones, into which Bolshevik slogans were also called out, to then be picked up and repeated by the marching columns. And each column carried many banners with slogans, images of Stalin and Lenin, etc. Everywhere there were Bolshevik stars on poles (the color red is everywhere and is so intense that it hurts one's eyes). I saw the peasants' division, which had the appearance of a church procession. At the front were a couple of girls who carried a great image of Stalin, decorated with flowers and wrapped in red ribbons, followed by a second pair of girls carrying a similar image of Molotov, then of Khrushchev, and behind them two pairs of girls carrying the image of Lenin on poles, just as they would carry the images of saints in the Epiphany procession! Everything appeared holy, cheerful, full of life. The marching columns sang Bolshevik Ukrainian songs.

The insignia, slogans, and emblems—the hammer and sickle, banners of different schools, organizations, trade unions, etc.—were written mostly in Ukrainian; only now and then could one see some written in Polish or Yiddish. Everywhere there were large portraits of Stalin, decorated and lit up with electric light bulbs. The houses of the military commanders were festooned with slogans and signs in Russian, because Russian is the official language of the army.

Two trucks drove down the street. On one truck stood a Polish officer, apparently a captain, looking wretched, dressed in rags, whose apparent wound was wrapped in a kerchief; at his side stood two other Poles. In front of these three stood a Bolshevik soldier, aiming his rifle at them. On the benches of the second truck sat young men and women: peasants, a worker, and working intelligentsia—all of them laughing and looking very pleased. The sight of the first truck deeply upset the Poles. I was standing near students from the girls' gymnasium and saw that some of the girls were crying. Why mock those who suffer? Such trucks should drive only through Ukrainian villages.

The stores and offices are closed today.

People say that the military prosecutor in our city is a Jew, and that's why the Jews, who had been Poland's greatest lackeys, are not being arrested.

8 November 1939

Today is a holiday: the government does not work; the stores are closed.

15 November 1939

This afternoon there was a rally of young people from all schools to display their joy about the unification of Western Ukraine with the East. From now on Ukraine is united in one republic.[16] The youth gathered in the square near the post office. There were speeches, resolutions, and reports in honor of the leaders, and telegrams sent to Father Stalin ....

27 November 1939

The military commanders are bringing their families from the USSR. There are daily transports of furniture to registered homes... Whoever has more than two rooms must give one or two to the military. It is said that a thousand wives of Bolshevik commanders or soldiers have come from Arkhangelsk [in the north of European Russia].

28 November 1939

Today after 6 p.m. the principal gathered the students in the gymnasium hall: "Comrades! We are gathered here to discuss the attack by Finland on the USSR. Elect comrades for a Presidium Meeting." This speech was given by the principal (himself from Krosno [in Subcarpathian Poland and the former western Galicia]) in Ukrainian. The presidium was nominated: comrade principal, one of the teachers, and three students of the upper class. A spokeswoman for the school department then spoke about the Finnish attack on the Soviet Union and the killing of three soldiers and one junior officer.[17] One student read the resolution, in Ukrainian, another in Polish. Then the rally was adjourned. The resolutions of the students in the gathering were circulated [in the school].

29 November 1939

Today, after 5 p.m., the council of activist students had a small meeting. At the meeting I was elected chair, along with three students. The students decided to fight the smoking of cigarettes in the gymnasium and to eliminate breaches of discipline by the students. It was decided to arrange a ball at the end of the year.

Yesterday's rally at the girls' gymnasium lasted two hours. After the report by the political department, the girls asked questions. The girls took the perspective of Polish patriotism and raised questions such as the following: "The speaker said that the Red Army had liberated us. Why then are some of our parents sitting in jail and others being dismissed from office? Why are there lines in front of the stores?" I did not witness this; I know from what I was told.

Today the inspector came to the office and wrote a report.

1 December 1939

The lines in front of the stores are such a disaster! Those who have not seen them or stood in them cannot imagine what they are like! In Romanovsky [Polish: Romanowski] Street where people were queuing for sugar, a poor girl was suffocated. In another line, a woman was struck so badly on the temple that she died on the way to the hospital. People sometimes stand in line day and night, freezing, hungry, and distraught. Some treat each other with respect, others fight, and occasionally a knife is pulled, and someone is stabbed. Here is one scene: some people waited the whole day to reach the store only to find that there were no goods left.

Underhanded trade is underway. It's quite clearly carried out by the Jews, who first hid the merchandise and now brought it out and are selling it at extortionist prices ....

Today I learned at a shoemaker's that there is no more leather to be had, old or new. Stores are shutting down, but new ones are not opening. The population is suffering and tormented.

We are returning to a primitive life, or rather existence. For example, you cannot buy a toothbrush or shoelaces in any store. Students write their assignments on cardboard because there are no notebooks. In front of the store with leather goods there is a small line, seven or eight people. I go and ask what they are selling there, since the line is so small. They are selling shoe polish.

3 December 1939

Going downtown we hear the radio playing everywhere non-stop. The authorities have placed loudspeakers in the most important points of the city, and they broadcast reports on events, news, concerts, and more. In the city there is constant noise and tumult. Opposite the Jesuit church there is a store with journals and tobacco. It too has a radio loudspeaker. The storefront is painted red: at the top there is a sign in Ukrainian: "Workers of the world unite." Below it is a sign in Russian: "Tobacco store," and a Polish sign: "Religion is the opium of the masses." This is the fraternity of peoples.

The authorities have opened a Russian gymnasium in the building of the Ursulines [monastic order], from which they were removed. The Ursuline nuns have afternoon lectures in the German gymnasium.

4 December 1939

As of 1 December, every gymnasium has a Bolshevik comrade "politruk" or commissar, who oversees the political spirit of the gymnasium, and educates the youth in the Bolshevik spirit. Ultimately, the function of this comrade remains unclear: he walks into our principal's office, talks with him about this and that, and collects information. It appears to me that he is one of us [Ukrainian], and he looks and speaks like a simple person.

Today, after 5 p.m., the anniversary of the Stalin Constitution [of 1936] was celebrated. The politruk made a speech about the Constitution, and later there was an artistic event consisting of recitations ... singing, and music. The event ended with the communist anthem. Tomorrow is there is no teaching ....

8 December 1939

Today is the Roman Catholic Feast of the Immaculate Conception. More than half of the students did not attend school. The Jews and several Ukrainians came but very few Poles.

10 December 1939

Today many people have gathered around the post office. I asked one of them why they were there. He replied that German delegates had arrived by car. They are creating a commission that will assess the property of the local Germans-colonists. These Germans will go to Germany, and the USSR will pay them for their real estate.

At 5 p.m. Ukrainian citizens of the city gathered in the Ukrainian Sokil to welcome Ukrainian writers who came to visit Galicia. The gymnasium janitor had come to my home after dinner with a note that a meeting with the Ukrainian writers would be held at 5 p.m. and that we should attend that meeting. I went to the Sokil. The audience arrived slowly, mostly foreigners, Jews, several Polish teachers and a few Ukrainians. Most of the intellectuals and even the simple people were Jewish men and women. Altogether there were about five to six hundred people there. At about 5:30 p.m. the curtain was raised and a comrade from the school administration opened the meeting and proposed a presidium. The presidium was elected, and four writers were introduced: Ivan Le, [Alexander] Kopylenko, [Andrei] Holovko, and the poet [Pavel] Usenko.[18] Prompted to speak, Le recalled how difficult past years had been for Ukrainian writers and outlined current developments and opportunities. He took note of the emergence of Bolshevism among Ukrainians. Kopylenko spoke about children's publications and children's literature, Holovko read excerpts from some of his novels, and Usenko read his still unpublished poetry dedicated to Western Ukraine ....

As of 1 December, the study of the Polish language has been abolished in Ukrainian and Jewish gymnasiums. It will surely soon be replaced by Russian.

12 December 1939

This afternoon a meeting of teachers was held to select the municipal teachers' committee. There was a long debate about the currently unfavorable working conditions for teachers. What kind of professional association will result from this remains unknown.

13 December 1939

There was a vote on members of the board for the teachers' trade union, which now has as many as 579 registered members.

14 December 1939

Here are some small examples of the difficulties we are experiencing now in the city: the electricity goes on and off, and there is nothing to make light with, because nothing can be bought in the city. Oil is available, but one cannot use it for lamps, because no oil lamps can be found. It is said that a light bulb costs 25 złoty.

When you walk into any store, the merchant treats the customer rudely, because the customer will surely buy his merchandise. Merchants eventually sell goods to their old customers only, but nothing to newcomers. Today I wanted to buy toothpaste in the pharmacy. The pharmacy is already state-owned. "There is no toothpaste, but it has been ordered, and when it arrives, we will sell it." With such words the pharmacist tried to comfort me.

20 December 1939

Today it was announced in [the official journal] "Soviet Ukraine" [Radyanskiy Ukraïni] that as of 21 December only Soviet currency would be accepted; government offices, cooperatives, cinemas, etc., will only take karbovanets, not złoty, the Polish currency.

The Polish currency is exchanged in the "Bank Polska" (the old Polish Bank) for Soviet money.

But this unexpected order has caused a great deal of commotion, because the officials had paid the last salary in złoty, and it was impossible for all account holders to change their money in twenty-four hours. The next decree of the Bolshevik Government then caused the ruin of many people, not only those property owners, profiteers, speculators, etc., but also working people. Whoever has savings in the bank, no matter the amount, receives only 300 karbovanets, and the rest is confiscated by the state. Whoever changes 300 złoty will get 300 karbovanets. This government decree is contrary to article 10 of the Stalin Constitution. It has destroyed not only the rich but also the working people, who, thanks to their thrifty nature, had put aside for themselves at least a few thousand złoty for the purchase of something for themselves and their family. Everything I had saved for ten years was lost because of this decree.

21 December 1939

This morning as I was going to school, I saw a crowd of people in front of the Polish Bank, who had gathered there to change money. The militiamen dispersed the people. Will the city die? The stores are empty; there is no merchandise on the shelves. You walk into the store and the storekeeper looks at you coldly like a wolf, as if you were about to take from him his last bit of merchandise. Still, here and there one can find a few goods. The stores are empty. Only in front of the "Dairy Union" national store there are long lines. There are still very few state stores, some with bread, or meat, and one with tobacco and candies on Sapizhynskiy Street; and in front of them there are lines. Stores with leather are not always open. There are two bookstores, but they have only a few books. In the arcade there is a state store with cotton and wool, and in front of it a line. There is a co-operative workshop that makes coats from materials brought to it, but where would one get such materials? There is a shoe cooperative, but outsiders are not allowed entry. People can acquire goods "under the table" for three to ten times as much as before the war. The price depends on the demand for such goods.

The storekeepers have removed the nice signs from their stores and now there is just a gray wall. It's so heartbreaking! On the street kikes are selling toiletries for an exorbitant price. There are still not enough state stores to accommodate buyers.

23 December 1939

Today the first semester ended. Students read their grades from the lists, and did not receive certificates, because none were available for this semester. The semester ended with difficulty. What we found was that we had no consistent curriculum, and everything changed from day to day. And what sort of learning this was! There were no books, and the students wrote their assignments on cardboard. About five to ten missed class every day. They justified this by the fact that they had to stand in lines, or that they had no shoes or coats. There were no meals, as in the past, because food was hard to come by. As for discipline ... please, God! The principal and the teachers have lost much of their authority and the students behave badly. They stroll down the main streets smoking cigarettes or hang out with girls. When teaching a class became impossible because of the behavior of the students, the teacher would complain not to the principal but to Commissioner Shkarupy. He would enter the class and admonish the students. The students do not know what kind of person he is, nor what his rights and responsibilities are (the teachers also don't know that), and are therefore afraid and respectful. He speaks to them in Ukrainian-Russian. The function of the principal is the maintenance of the office ....

The principal of the Ukrainian gymnasium, Levitsky, and the principal of the Polish girls' gymnasium (where I worked until recently), Kopitov, have been removed. The reason for Levitsky's removal is unknown. Kopitov was removed because the students had behaved badly during the speeches of the "political leaders" and had demonstrated their Polish patriotism rather than contentment with Bolshevik ideology.

25 December 1939

Local Germans are leaving to Germany. This is by agreement between Hitler and the Soviet government. Along with the Germans, some Ukrainians, who do not like the communist government, are leaving legally. Everyone is selling everything and leaving their homes ....

28 December 1939

By order of the head of the city council signs in cooperatives, stores, etc. must be in the Ukrainian language.

One maid who found work here told my maid that in Buchach the Bolshevik authorities have seized many Ukrainians in the city and young people in the villages. Recently, someone hung a Ukrainian national flag on the Buchach castle, at another time a Polish flag was hoisted; she has also come across flyers with anti-communist content ....

31 December 1939, New Year's Eve

This will be a memorable year in history. This year, the Red Army liberated us from Polish captivity. For six hundred years we suffered under Poland (and under Austria we were also still under Poland). But just as Poland was preparing for the anniversary of the conquest of Galicia, nemesis turned the wheel of history and Poland collapsed. Western Ukraine has joined with the rest of Ukraine. No Ukrainian speaks well of Poland and nobody wants it to return. It has wrought destruction on us for centuries, in all sorts of ways, and it did not conceal its goal to wipe us out and take over our land. But Poland fell victim to its own pride, conceit, treachery, deception, and mischief. It has fallen and I believe that it will never rise again in our land. If it ever rises again, then only on its own ethnic lands.

Although it was difficult for us to live under Poland, our people did not succumb; we nourished our vitality, created our organizations, societies, cooperatives, banks, etc., and resisted the Poles. We had such societies and organizations that our enemies envied us: Prosvita, Ridna Shkola, the Union of Ukrainian Women; three very beautiful and well edited journals; and over one hundred (up to 150) other publishers, with at times highly respected publications; as well Ukrainian stores, merchants, co-operative, and farms. Generally, it was clear that we would react to Polish harassment and would not surrender to oppression. Still, everything has come to a halt now, has disappeared, ceased to exist, or has been nationalized. Everything has become state-owned, there is nothing individual, personal, everything is controlled by the state. Private initiative and entrepreneurship provide room for creativity, for competition. All the societies have ceased to exist.

Pessimists say that we were caught in the rain—under the gutter, as has always happened in our history. I do not agree. Things are not good now, because the new system is just beginning, and the apparatus has not been installed. To build a social system on new foundations, one generation does not suffice, for this is a long-term business. From this perspective what does a single year mean, or rather just a few months... Right now, we live badly, it's hard, I must say, very hard. Lack of everyday items, the ghost of hunger, long lines in front of the stores, the decline in the value of money, the loss of savings—all these are painful pages from today's life for many—a tragedy. But are there any unblemished pages? We are united with our brothers, we live in Ukraine, an integral part of the USSR, the Ukrainian language is dominant in government offices, teaching in the villages is in Ukrainian, and unemployment has declined. It's too early to say what forms of life will evolve. We must monitor and understand the new system. Only at a distance of time will it be possible to say what was vital and what was an illusion. I am of the opinion that no state can manage to take over all aspects of life, all branches of trade, manufacturing, crafts, many of which must be left to private initiative and entrepreneurship. With this thought, one must allow the people and society to create their organizations, their associations, unions, and so on. Without that the whole nation or its national energy will freeze up and be completely deprived of life.

1 January 1940

The Bolsheviks have adopted a new calendar and began the year in the new style. Yesterday and today there was a New Year's supper in the gymnasium. Last night there was a ball for young people beginning at 6 p.m. I was not there, but I heard that it was not a great success, since there was no one to dance with. The students did their own entertaining.

Today, at about 11 a.m., some young people from the lower grades gathered in the gymnasium hall (it might have been about twenty-five to thirty students and several teachers). The politruk spoke about the achievements and successes of Soviet power in our region and ended his speech by hailing Stalin. Then there were two choral pieces and a declamation (all in Ukrainian). Afterwards the students were handed out Christmas presents (candies in a tube of paper). In the middle of the hall a beautifully decorated Christmas tree was placed, a symbol, according to the politruk, of Bolshevik youth and life.

What will the new year bring us? How is our life progressing? What forms will it take? What experiences, surprises, joys or sorrows, what erosion or improvement of our future will it bring us? Everyone is preoccupied with these questions.

2 January 1940

Today, in the Franko cinema theater, formerly called "Ton," there was an assembly of teachers from the city and the district. The purpose of the meeting was to become acquainted with Bolshevik pedagogy and the school structure, ahead of the second semester.

The meeting was opened by Klymenko, head of the local school department, who provided an overview of school pedagogy. He made a note of the terrible education under Poland, when the Poles oppressed the Ukrainian and Jewish schools, and he lauded the growth of schools under Bolshevik rule. There are no unemployed teachers, as long as they want to work. Private schools have become public schools, and the overall number of schools has increased. He also discussed schools in the city. The spirit in the schools must be communist, providing an education in the materialist ideology of Marx-Engels-Lenin-Stalin. In high school No. 4, the students demonstrated against the screening of Bolshevik films, on account of which the principal was fired. Klymenko also criticized the teachers for their grading (strange idea!) and registered their names.

After that there was a meeting with representatives of the People's Commissariat, followed by a discussion and questions. The participants complained about the difficult work conditions, and the lack of books in grammar and science. (There were up to seven hundred people at the meeting). The event ended with a screening of a cinematic production of [Aleksandr] Ostrovsky's [nineteenth century play] "Storm." A Russian movie![19]

3 January 1940

This morning and afternoon several comrades presented a lengthy report on the Bolshevik school, the principles of education, and the role and duties of the teacher. The lengthy presentation was a torment for everyone. Earlier, one comrade spoke in Russian about the need for communist education and about the remnants of the bourgeois spirit in Western Ukraine. He noted that the Poles had created legions in Romania, whereas here members of [the interwar Ukrainian National Democratic Alliance] UNDO, the Polish People's Party, and the [Jewish socialist] Bundists are hostile to Soviet rule. Somewhere the peasants had hoisted [Ukrainian World War I nationalist leader Symon] Petliura's banner. When Bolshevik guards tried to remove it, a bomb exploded and killed or injured several people. Where and when this happened was not reported.

At noon, elections of union delegates took place at the conference of the unions of the region. Afterwards there was a performance at the cinema for participants in the meeting.

4 January 1940

The teachers have been divided into sections and each teacher listens to presentations in his section. I belong to the Ukrainian section. In the morning there were three presentations, in the afternoon another three. The papers are read by Ukrainians, mainly from Ukrainian gymnasiums, and discuss curricula and instruction in the USSR. Then the papers are discussed ....

During the break some teachers said that in Stanyslaviv there would be fourteen or fifteen gymnasiums; of these, four would be Polish, two Jewish, and the remaining eight would be Ukrainian. As of 10 January, I will begin teaching the Bolshevik curriculum. Male and female students (co-ed) will be assigned to new gymnasiums. Will everything be prepared this time, will there be books, textbooks?

5 January 1940

Today, from morning until 2 p.m., there were presentations. A comrade from the Poltava region [in left-bank eastern Ukraine] spoke about teaching in Ukrainian schools and about learning Russian; another comrade spoke about Ukrainian textbooks. In the afternoon, all the participants in the conference gathered in the state theater named after Franko (formerly named after Moniuszko). The head of the school division Klymenko reviewed the work of the congress. Subsequently, section leaders gave brief statements. Then the teachers of the Dnieper region were given prizes. One of them said that he had been a laborer for the past seventeen years, and that thanks to the communist system he had acquired higher education. The meeting greeted them sincerely. The Stalin region invited the Stanyslaviv region to take part in a socialist race.

The meeting ended with a report by Comrade [Mykhailo] Hrulenko, secretary of the local communist party. Describing the state of Western Ukraine under Poland with figures, he demonstrated the accomplishments of the Soviet Government in the field of schooling. These achievements are truly great. He ended his speech with the following statement: "Whoever thinks that the past will return, whoever dreams of Poland, of lords and capitalists, whoever conceals his nationalism yet wants to cleverly disseminate it to the youth—should not be a teacher here, and has no place among us at our school." ...

7 January 1940

The Bolshevik press is state-owned. [The USSR is] a one-class state, or rather a classless society, and a single press serves society, but is also in the service of the state. This is useful for the state, but it is somewhat disadvantageous for society: there is no criticism, the topics are directed from above, and everything is unanimous and gray. Previous newspapers relied on the ruling class which provided them with material support and direction. Now the papers are very cheap (5–10 kopecks [cents]), but monotonous, the articles in all newspapers are very similar to each other or are simply reprints. This press differs greatly from the old one, not least because it is so inexpensive (there are no advertisements by merchants, stores, or manufacturers in the press).

People are informed about actual events by the radio, or they fantasize about them. The combination of guessing and imagining has no limits. Most times these fantasies cannot be trusted, but they still spread. Senseless or hilarious fantasies are shared by simple people and the intelligentsia. Who can believe this stuff? ... [Such as] that the Bolsheviks in Finland suffered huge losses in the hundreds of thousands and that the Finns are already fighting inside Russian territory? ... Or that a war between the USSR and Germany is about to break out?[20] The Poles dream about rebuilding Poland... It is clear to them that West Ukraine belongs to them, what else! The Poles owned these lands for six centuries, and then suddenly they fell apart! ...

8 January 1940

Today I walked across the whole city and could not buy matches. In the oil and petrol store I was told that in the afternoon there would be fuel for lighters. Now one cannot get a toothbrush ....

10 January 1940

Today is the last day of the winter vacation and the principal has convened a conference. The teachers, the principal, head teacher Protsenko, and Commissar Shkorupa all attended. The principal opened the conference in Ukrainian and stated: the Romanovsky Gymnasium no longer exists and has been transformed into the Ukrainian comprehensive secondary school No. 16. Some of the current students would remain, but more than half would be relocated to other gymnasiums. Students whose parents live in the neighborhood of our gymnasium will come to us from other gymnasiums. The gymnasium will have sixteen sections. There will apparently be morning and afternoon teaching. Some of the old teachers will stay, others will be new: altogether twenty-four teachers. Two are identified as teaching the Russian language. They do not know it (one of them is a Pole). Tomorrow we will begin to work at 9 a.m. according to Moscow time (our old 7 a.m.).

A severe frost has come. The temperature in the morning is 30–32 [Celsius] below freezing. And there is not enough firewood ....

11 *January 1940*

The teachers were gathered today at 7 a.m. in the hall. A thousand students were waiting in the vestibule. But at about 8 a.m., it was announced that there will not be any schoolwork because of the extreme cold (-30).

12 *January 1940*

They say that spotted typhus is spreading in the villages. The reason for this is lice that cannot be destroyed due to lack of soap.

My maid visited her mother in Kuty [100 km southeast of Stanyslaviv]. [She reported that] along the Romanian border the Bolshevik army is digging trenches against Romania.

15 *January 1940*

Today, at 7 a.m. (9 a.m. in Moscow), we were to begin teaching at our secondary school. But this ended up in a great mess because there is no curriculum and there are no books. Yesterday, at the conference of principals, it was announced that for now things would remain as they were: that is, in our gymnasium instruction would temporarily be in Polish, and the old curriculum would remain. Polish students do not want to attend a Ukrainian gymnasium. Our gymnasium is made up predominantly of Jewish boys and girls. All schools are now co-ed. Our gymnasium has taken students from the Ozheshkova [Polish: Orzeszkowa] Gymnasium.

An indescribable chaos. I came for the Ukrainian lesson. I see female and male students mingling and sitting together. I am a class leader. I want to seat them separately and learn that the Komsomol [Communist Youth Organization] activists sit separately from the rest of the students and that they had been put in their places by the "komsorg" [Komsomol organizer]. The komsorg has instructed that students of the 8th grade and higher use the formal term of address. Some students call their teachers "comrade teacher" while others use their patronym.

The Jews say that the Germans will come here soon, probably to discuss the situation on the Romanian border with our army ....

19 *January 1940*

Today is Epiphany. We work normally at school; all the teachers as well as the students ....

During the Ukrainian lesson at our gymnasium the students spoke unbelievably rudely. It was necessary to lodge a complaint to the "head teacher." Students are still changing schools. There is no permanent list of students.

20 January 1940

In the morning before 8 a.m. the teachers gathered in the conference hall. A comrade arrived with the head teacher. The head teacher said: "This is the new principal." Everyone was shocked, because Principal Yun had not even known about this. When he walked in, Principal Yun discovered that he was no longer the principal. He accepted the news calmly. It seems that he will be in high school No. 1. The new principal is called Koval and, according to him, teaches history.

The purchasing power of the karbovanets keeps shrinking... Many things can be bought only "under the counter" at exorbitant prices. What will happen next? How can government officials live on their salaries? ...

21 January 1940

Today at 11:30 a.m. the 16th anniversary of Lenin's death was commemorated at the gymnasium. The head teacher spoke about Lenin's life, then there was singing and recitations. One short recitation was in Russian. Tomorrow there is no school ....

24 January 1940

Yesterday evening we had a parents' meeting. The purpose of the meeting was to decide on the language of instruction. The speakers, the principal and others, advised parents to vote for Ukrainian, because completing a Polish gymnasium without learning Ukrainian and Russian would affect the future course of a student's life. He would not be accepted either to a higher school or to a government position, because he would not know the government's language. These arguments had little effect on the Polish parents. The Ukrainians voted for Ukrainian and possibly so did some of the Jews, whereas the Poles voted for Polish. In our high school there are many Poles in the lower classes, but in the higher classes there are probably more Jews. I do not have accurate statistics. One does not know how the authorities will decide this issue. For the Ukrainian language there were probably forty-two votes, for Polish twice as many.

29 January 1940

... In front of the state stores there are long lines; people are freezing. They say that in one line a peasant was killed or injured, and a child suffocated. There is no fuel. All look dejected, everyone sees the ghost of hunger. The peasants have a lot of money and want to change their produce for cloth, soap, and so on. But where would we get them? In smaller towns, such as Buchach, things are cheaper and you can buy more, but there are inspections on the trains and at the stations and everything is confiscated. My maid and her friend brought 3 kg of butter and 3 kg of flour from Buchach. One of them was lined with those products, pretending to be pregnant. She was happy to have succeeded. People say that the Bolshevik authorities vehemently appeal to the merchants to open their store. It is obvious that the government itself is powerless in the fight against speculators. Speculation is bad, but things would be worse without it. If the goods could not be bought at a high price, then there would already be a famine. High prices still save us from hunger.

Teachers in the gymnasium must register precisely at what time they come to school on a sheet of paper in front of the clock: for example, at 7:45 a.m. What is the purpose of this? ...

Coming from the trade union meeting at 8:15 a.m. I see on the street in front of the store a long line of sixty to seventy people who have been waiting all night, twelve hours, for the store to open. There they will get one kilogram of sugar and half a kilogram of soap and some cereals... People suffer so much in order to not die of hunger.

Some students in the 6th grade have defiled Molotov's portrait. The case is under investigation.

2 February 1940

Today, after 4 p.m., the youth of our school welcomed Ukrainian writers in the gymnasium sport hall. One of the writers was a Jew. They read poetry, paeans in honor of the Soviet Union and Stalin. Among these writers were [Teren] Masenko and L. [Leonid] Smiliansky (from Galician Zolochiv [Polish: Złoczów]).[21] The Jewish writer read his poetry in Yiddish and in Ukrainian translation.

3 February 1940

From now on, our gymnasium has converted to using Ukrainian as the language of instruction. According to national statistics, there are 63 Ukrainians, 333 Jews, and 36 Poles in our gymnasium. Jews are the most numerous, and that Jewish element has voted in favor of Ukrainian, which has now been introduced as the language of teaching. The Polish language is not taught at our gymnasium. Some students have left the gymnasium and gone to Poland.

12 February 1940

I have not written any observations, because I was looking for wood. The house is freezing but there is no firewood. Where can I get it? I went to the government sawmill with a certificate from the trade union and the school board that I have no wood for the fireplace. There I received a permit for five-hundred weights of wood. Now I had a permit but still no wood, since there wasn't any. Every day I went to 84 Sapizhynskiy Street where they distributed wood. Finally, I got the wood. Transporting and cutting the wood cost as much as the wood itself.

The currency is losing its value …. There is no meat to be had at all; at home we have not eaten meat for a month. We have some beans and cabbage. Bread, albeit black and mixed with corn and beans, can still be found after standing in line. We no longer eat enough. As of January, we were supposed to be paid according to Soviet regulations. But until now we have received only an advance. There is an "accountant" working in the principal's office who calculates our salaries ….

14 February 1940

Yesterday, after the fourth lesson, the principal gathered the students in one of the classes, made a speech and provided them with information. He pointed out to them that the Soviet government had deported Polish settlers and Ukrainian and German kulaks, and generally counterrevolutionaries, to the Far East for reasons of security.[22] Although it is now extremely cold there, the settlers are provided with accommodation, and they can take clothes, bedding, etc., with them. Then the principal complained of a lack of discipline in the high school and threatened the students with punishment.

For several days now there has been talk of some kind of unrest or conspiracy in Chortkiv; there have been rumors that three hundred students had "rebelled," and that the police were called in, even from Stanyslaviv. This is meaningless and thoughtless nonsense.[23] …

Money has no value for thieves either. They no longer steal money, but rather clothes, shoes, firewood, linen, food, etc. They break into apartments in broad daylight. To keep them away, one must always stay at home, because you cannot trust the locks. We were sitting at home, and someone quietly went into the kitchen and stole a shawl. This is a great loss, because where would we buy a new one? ...

29 February 1940

People are whispering that yesterday the court sentenced Krushelnytsky (junior) to death for nationalism. My sister, whom I met by chance, confirmed the news and said that this was for something he had said against the Bolsheviks in a lecture. His family will file a petition for pardon. The sentence was commuted to seven years in prison.

10 March 1940

Two hundred wealthy merchants have been ordered to leave the city at once. They will be moved to somewhere else in Ukraine, 100 kilometers away from the border.

Yesterday our school celebrated [Ukrainian national poet Taras] Shevchenko's birthday.[24] In the afternoon the youth gathered in the gym. The Komsomol leader opened the meeting with a brief speech, then a presidium was elected, and then we had a presentation on the life of Shevchenko, as well as a recitation and violin music. It was a modest program. The local newspaper, Soviet Ukraine, published my little article about Shevchenko. But how they changed it! The end is not mine at all. I'm surprised that the editorial staff could make such changes to this article.

The names of the streets in Stanyslaviv have been changed. Not all the streets have new signs yet, but the main streets have already been signposted. Sapizhynskiy Street is now called Soviet Street.

15 March 1940

Almost every day one can observe the following parade on the city streets. At the front a handsome fellow is riding on horseback, holding aloft a red flag. Behind him, either marching or sitting on vehicles, are peasants holding up the images of the leaders or of Shevchenko decorated with corn ears. They are followed by singing girls marching or riding in vehicles. Then come sleds piled with sacks of grain, sometimes also carrying cages with hens, as well as cows being led. These peasants are taking their grain to the warehouses and bringing their fowl to the cooperatives for the price set by the government.

16 March 1940

In Western Ukraine, the election campaign is in full swing. Everyone takes at least a small part in the elections, whether as an agitator or in some other role. No one is idle. The Bolsheviks know how to control and mobilize the masses. Everything is written down, checked, and approved. Apparently, no voters have been left out. This is an admirable election apparatus. I'm a man far from politics. However, they now made me member of the editorial board of the newspaper. It's not a lot of work... but I have already dedicated one afternoon to it. There is no doubt that the government will win a brilliant victory in the elections and that all the selected candidates will be elected. What is the government afraid of? It fears apathy and indifference by the population toward the elections, as well as the public's lack of trust that they [the government] will improve its fate. It is for that reason that the entire electoral apparatus is organized.[25] ...

24 March 1940

Today is Election Day. Everything is done to ensure that everyone votes. The polling booths are clean, well-organized, with everything in place. There is only one list and no doubt that the elections will turn out as the government wishes.

Roman Catholic Easter has arrived. The snow is still piled up, it's cold, and we have no heating at home because there is no fuel. There is no expectation of warmth.

Yesterday we ended the third quarter of the school year. In the Soviet system, the school year is divided into four quarters. The students did not receive certificates, but a record of grades that parents need to sign. Many of the grades are bad. We now have spring recess until 1 April ....

31 March 1940

The Jews say that instructions will be issued for the eventuality of air raids. Relations between the Soviet Union and Romania are uncertain.

4 April 1940

Instructions have been posted on the city walls as to what should be done in the event of an air raid. People make various comments about this...

13 April 1940

Today, under our windows, there were carts filled with people who, in the view of the Soviet security authorities, need to be deported. The wives of Polish officers are being taken out. There is turmoil and terror in the city. They say dubious people are being taken regardless of their nationality. Somewhere a postman was seized who, as it turned out, was a Polish Major.

A Jew told me that in one line a woman was again smothered. There are long lines in front of stores selling threads and needles.

It is said that the authorities are evacuating the population of Kuty in the Carpathian region of Kosiv [Polish: Kosów]. It is obvious that there are fears of an attack on this side.

There is no chalk in our school. There is nothing with which to write on the blackboard. There are enough rolls, meat, sausages in the state stores, but the price is too high for us...

1–2 May 1940

May First: The city is cleaned up, everywhere there are portraits of Bolshevik leaders and communist slogans. It's a holiday—there is no teaching. The entire garrison has gone to the parade. A large parade of youth, organizations, etc., passes before the podium.

6 May 1940

It's hard now to travel by train. It's hard, because the ride is almost free... The cheapness of the railroad means that the majority of the passengers, 90 percent of them, are Jews, who go to buy from and sell to the peasants, to exchange goods, and so on. They are cleverly hiding goods under the benches and transporting mass amounts of them. Railcars used to be empty at night, now they are full. When the train arrives, the passengers rush into the carriages to occupy them: simply Dantesque scenes. The railways are cheap so one can profit from trading. It's hard and upsetting to ride the train now.

On 5 May we buried our mother.

31 May 1940

And I have no desire to write... People are fantasizing about what will happen next. It is said that Hitler will return to Galicia, turning to the east after vanquishing the Western powers. Again, those dreams of German sympathy for us... these are the remnants of an Austrian upbringing ... .

In Lviv there is a German commission charged with bringing [ethnic] Germans into Germany. Already sixty-seven thousand have registered as wishing to move to Germany.

During the winter unrest in Chortkiv, Polish rebels had disarmed the guard and killed six soldiers. It is strange that none of them were caught and that the authorities did not know anything about their intentions.

10 June 1940

A malicious joke being told now is that all peoples are happy because they have achieved their desires. The Ukrainians have Ukraine; the Jews, who had always complained that they could not get government positions, now fill government offices everywhere; and the Poles, who lamented that they had no trade of their own, are now selling their belongings in the flea market.

11 June 1940

This morning news spread that Italy had declared war on France and England and that Soviet troops had crossed the Romanian border. The merchandise disappeared quickly from the stores. Although there was not much there anyway, that too is gone. Everything is more expensive...

[The diary entries spanning the period between early July 1940 and June 1941 are missing. They were torn out by Petrykevych's son Bohdan after Viktor's death and following a visit by the KGB, the main Soviet security agency, for fear of compromising him and his family as the son of a Ukrainian nationalist. During this time Petrykevych lost his job in the school in Stanyslaviv, returned with his family to Buchach—where he had taught and purchased a house in the interwar period—and found a teaching position in a nearby town.]

Buchach: Under German Occupation

Late June 1941 [no precise date indicated: continuation of a missing entry]

On Sunday [22 June], as I was reading the Saturday issue of "The Communist"—which carried not a single word about the possibility of war—suddenly, like thunder on a clear day, it was war. Molotov and Stalin made speeches on the radio and explained the causes of the war to the people.[26] Germany had attacked first. Its position is now hopeless. With a few differences, the events of 1914–18 will be repeated. People learned about the outbreak of war from the radio. When they heard about the war, they rushed into the stores and began buying everything—those who had some money. Within a single night the prices rocketed; one kilogram of meat, which had cost 7 karbovanets, was selling already on Monday for 14 karbovanets; one liter of oil costs 40 karbovanets. There is no bread. Before Sunday one could buy five or six eggs for 1 karbovanets; now two eggs sell for 1 karbovanets. People are alarmed. Different rumors are being spread; that the Germans have bombarded Stanyslaviv, Lviv, Chortkiv; that the Germans have occupied Horodok [Polish: Gródek, just west of Lviv]; and then again, that Soviet troops have occupied Kraków, even Warsaw. There is panic among the Jews; they fear pogroms, they have become that hateful to the population. There were no newspapers on Monday or Tuesday. Everyone subsists on speculation.

The news is that the Poles are now joining the Soviet Union; a statement to this effect was issued on the radio by [exiled Polish Prime Minister in London] General [Władysław] Sikorski. Today people are saying that the local Poles are not being drafted into the army, because they will be formed into Polish legions to fight the Germans. Our people [Ukrainians] had already noticed earlier on that this was the policy favored by politicians committed to the Poles.

27 June 1941

All kinds of rumors are being spread, whether as a result of provocation or of military psychosis: that in Monastyryska [Polish: Monasterzyska, 18 km west of Buchach] the entire Ukrainian intelligentsia was arrested; that they were subjected to torture in prison; that some leaflets were distributed there; and that last night several Ukrainians and a Pole were arrested in Buchach. Everybody is again filled with indescribable fear. One of the residents in my building is a doctor. Under the impact of these widespread rumors he cannot sleep at night. He expects to be arrested. The same applies to his wife. Anything is possible, because this is war, but one must keep self-control. There are no newspapers from Kyiv; only the local paper is being published. All day long airplanes are flying low overhead, single planes or three to four together, heading in the direction of Chortkiv. All day long vehicles keep driving through.

28 June 1941

All night long columns of vehicles with artillery and tanks drove through town in the direction of Chortkiv. People say that the Germans have already occupied Lviv and are approaching Stanyslaviv. Soviet officials have packed up and are ready for departure.

1 July 1941

Since 3 a.m. there has been non-stop traffic: cars, tanks, and the like. As of today, Soviet government offices no longer exist. The same applies to the NKVD [Soviet interior ministry and police]; its officials have already left or are in the process of leaving.

2 July 1941

Since early morning tractors pulling artillery and trucks filled with soldiers have been driving through town toward Chortkiv; they return empty, heading in the direction of Stanyslaviv. There are also vehicles with officials coming from the other bank of the Zbruch [Polish: Zbrucz] River [east of Chortkiv and the interwar border between Poland and the USSR]. But traffic is thinner than yesterday.

Living is tough. In the evening we are forbidden to turn on the light. But that's a mere trifle. There is no supply of food: no bread, milk, meat, or vegetables. The peasants won't bring their produce to the city because they are scared; and it is impossible to buy anything. Prices for supplies have risen .... We have no newspapers. We live entirely cut off from the rest of the world.

In the afternoon the movement of vehicles picked up. All were going in the direction of Chortkiv. In the morning mobs looted the stores. The city is full of soldiers.

3 July 1941

Tractors towing artillery and trucks with soldiers keep driving through all day long.

In the city there is fear and confusion. Soldiers have been breaking into stores, forcing doors open with crowbars, and people have been looting the goods. In the afternoon soldiers emptied about a hundred sacks of flour into the Strypa [river that runs through Buchach]. People salvaged some flour; the rest went with the stream. In general, the soldiers have been destroying food supplies. Mobs have been looting government offices. They have even carted off the telephones.

There is no authority. In the police station someone was killed. The body lies there, and nobody bothers. There are murders in the villages. Twenty people are said to have been murdered in Ripyntsi [Polish: Rzepińce, 10 km southeast of Buchach]. People who had suffered under the Bolsheviks wreak ferocious revenge on the heads of village Soviets, informers, and others of that ilk.

People say that the Germans have occupied Leningrad or Moscow (?). There are no newspapers, and people are whispering to each other and fantasizing. They say that the Germans will come tonight. A few dozen Jews left with the Soviets to the Zbruch River.

4 July 1941

All night long trucks, artillery, and other vehicles drove through the city. In the morning I came out to the street. The stores had been smashed and looted. The artillery keeps withdrawing, but now they have only horses to pull the guns. They must be retreating from the front. Far away, from the direction of Stanyslaviv, one can occasionally hear the hollow roar of the guns. The indigent and the peasants are milling about in small groups; they are carrying sacks, hoping to find something to loot.

At about noon we heard an explosion from the south, perhaps two. Was a bridge or a gas storage facility blown up?

The body of a young man is lying in the old courthouse (in the room that had served as a jail); he is said to be the victim of police mistreatment. They beat him with rifle butts, and then they shot him. Today a soldier shot a fellow who was carrying two military overcoats. People say that the building of the former bank, the office of the executive committee, and even the former Basilian Institute [college], where the NKVD had some offices, have all been rigged with explosives.

There is no news. Because the power plant was destroyed, the radio does not operate. People say that the Germans have crossed the Berezina River [in Belarus]. At 4 p.m. we heard another explosion.

Some people are looking for cloth or dresses ... to sew ...[27]

Yesterday and today the Jews sent a delegation to the abbot of the Basilian monastery, asking him to influence the population and restrain it from attacking the Jews.

As they retreated, the Bolsheviks put up posters stating that fascism is the source of people's misery. People say that in the morning flyers

inciting violence against the Jews and the Poles had appeared. I have
not seen any of them.

5 July 1941

Saturday. It was a difficult, anxious, sleepless night. The Soviet units
have already retreated, and only small groups remain. At about 9:45
p.m. according to the old [Soviet] time, a terrible ...

[The entries for the period between 5 July and the end of 1941, covering the establishment of German rule in Buchach and Petrykevych's
early involvement in the Ukrainian administrative-educational apparatus, are missing. They were torn out by his son Bohdan under the
circumstances described in the section "11 June 1940."[28]]

Late 1941 [no specific date given: continuation of a missing entry]

... those who have some German ancestors are being given certificates
testifying that they are ethnic Germans, from which they derive much
benefit. Those who become ethnic Germans receive six times more food
than ordinary citizens (for example: we get 600 grams of lard, ethnic
Germans get 3.6 kilo, and so forth). Among the Poles, two hundred
people have declared themselves to be of German origin; they received
positions and better living conditions.

1 January 1942

What will the New Year bring us? ...

   Will the misery and deprivation of the population end? Will the war
end and will our fate be resolved in a manner favorable to us?

8 January 1942

Christmas holidays. The youths from the National Committee are
singing Christmas carols. Everybody is troubled by the difficult living
conditions... Prices are rising every day. Many items are impossible to
get; it is prohibited to bring them into the city, and the police confiscates
them. The peasants are selling their produce in exchange for furniture,
clothes, leather; they usually bring their produce to the Jews, because
the Jews still have something to exchange. But what can I exchange?
The Jews apparently get more food from the villages than we civil
servants do. Life may be easier only for those who have managed to find

positions in economic organizations, cooperatives, farm management, and so forth.

People say that Ukrainian prisoners of war have a high death rate. In Rymanów [in southeastern Poland, 350 km northwest of Buchach] there was a camp with ten thousand Ukrainian POWs, but only two thousand are still alive; the rest have all died. The [Ukrainian] National Committee is collecting money and donations, but it's a drop in the ocean. Where can they acquire underwear, shoes, clothes, and so forth for them?

11 January 1942

What is true and what is fantasy in the matter of the Jews? People say that between a month-and-a-half and two-and-a-half months ago, the Gestapo assembled 15,000 Jews in Stanyslaviv and shot half of them, as well as 700 Christians who were hiding Jews... Half of those 15,000 Jews were allowed to leave, because there were no graves for them!...[29] People say that in Stanyslaviv there is already a Jewish ghetto, separated from the rest of the city by a fence. The ghetto is in Belveder [Polish: Belweder] Street. A similar ghetto will also be established in Chortkiv, and the Jews from Buchach will be taken there. It is also said that in Stanyslaviv almost all Polish teachers were arrested several months ago. Some Ukrainian teachers were also arrested. There has been no news about the prisoners, and nobody knows what has happened to them ....

22 February 1942

... Since 20 February there is a two-year Ukrainian trade school in Buchach. Young people enrolled in large numbers; 250 students were formed into four classes ....

Both in the whole of Galicia and in Buchach a collection of winter clothes for the German army has been announced. This was proclaimed by the [Ukrainian] National Committee, which appointed a commission to handle this issue.

Initially, the commission was skeptical about the collection, saying that the people would not give anything. After a week they were persuaded that the villages would provide a mass of coats, treated and untreated furs, clothes, etc. So far, more than two thousand items have been registered... Apparently, the fear of abuse by the Gestapo influenced this collection. But these items will be useful for the army for the very next winter.[30] ...

I had a conference with the school principals of the district; in the evening there was a banquet in their honor.

23 February 1942

They say that [the German] Governor [of Galicia, Karl] Lasch was bribed by the Jews and that he shot himself.[31] Buchach should have a ghetto.

25–26 February 1942

Horses are being requisitioned. Again, there are complaints of gendarmes beating people for being late, etc. The National Committee has asked where to lodge a complaint. The Germans say that the beatings are educational! The beatings teach the peasants precision, order, and discipline ....

When you go through our villages, you meet some travelers there: some come with carts, others walk, pulling sleds behind them. These are people from the Pidhirsky [Polish: Podhorce] district who have come to the Buchach district for clothes, leather, and so forth. These are people from districts where the fall flood destroyed the harvest. We call them Hutsuls.[32] People say that they get clothes, cloths, linen, and household items from the Jews, exchanging them for grain.

5 April 1942

Resurrection Sunday. Easter. Although it should already be spring, people are still wearing furs. Next to the school, in the ditches, the shaded spots are still full of snow. The rooms still need to be heated, but with what? Outdoors, the roofs are still covered by ice and snow.

This past winter was terrible. It lasted almost five months. The extreme frost left its mark on everyone. Many people, especially the young, suffered frostbite in their fingers, ears, etc. There was no coal at all, and very little firewood. People who had no firewood cut down rafters, fences, and enclosures. At home it was cold, and in school it was also winter. Additionally, there were no good shoes, we did not get any galoshes, and the food was without fats. People froze like dogs... We will remember this great winter for a long time.

Anyone who has not been to Buchach for several years would not recognize the city upon coming here.

A row of stone houses on the bank of the river and beyond it was destroyed. Next to the river, where the tenements had stood, there will be an area for automobiles or a park. These were Jewish houses, and there was also a Ukrainian Bank there. The Ukrainian Bank will be given another nationalized Jewish house. The city looks better now.[33]

12 April 1942

They say that in Chortkiv [35 km east of Buchach], in the Ukrainian gymnasium, the authorities uncovered some kind of secret student organization. They have threatened to shut down the gymnasium.

The rail line going to Kopychyntsi [Polish: Kopyczyńce, 50 km northeast of Buchach] was sabotaged, apparently by the Poles; the train was derailed, and many soldiers perished.

Speaking of the war, one can say that it will not end this year. Another decisive offensive has not begun, and people do not see the end of the war.

29 April 1942

It is said that the Poles are preparing banners.

The German gendarmerie imprisoned twenty-five students from the Ukrainian gymnasium in Chortkiv as Banderites [militant followers of Ukrainian nationalist leader Stepan Bandera] and sent them to forced labor [presumably in Germany; but as it turned out, this was a false rumor].[34]

Bolshevik aircraft have bombed Ternopil [Polish: Tarnopol, 70 km north of Buchach]. In the evening we have to block the light in our windows, and we must keep buckets of water and sand on the top floor.

13 May 1942

Boris Babiy, secretary of the Landkommissariat [county commissariat] in Buchach, was buried in a splendid ceremony today. A hard-working and honest man, he drowned last night. Whether it was a suicide, an accident, or a political assassination, cannot be determined or confirmed. Anything is possible. The deceased served as an official since the Germans came; the Ukrainians loved him, and he did all he could to help his countrymen.

15 May 1942

Yesterday Professor [and head of the collaborationist Ukrainian Central Committee, Volodymyr] Kubiyovych, Colonel [and founder in 1943 of the

Waffen-SS "Galicia" Division, Alfred] Bisanz, and Secretary [General of the UCC, Vasyl] Hlebovitsky visited Buchach.[35] They spoke about the (above-mentioned) destruction of the Banderites by the government (the death of the Banderites) and said that our city would not have a gymnasium, but most likely a teachers' college.

They say that the Germans are using gas in the east. We have to cover the windows in the evenings.

Horribly high prices ... For the third month the teachers have not been paid. Since 1 May we belong administratively to Chortkiv; nobody cares about us. I give private German language lessons to some students and they pay me with flour ... Without this option, I would simply die. There is no meat, no fat.

The students who had been imprisoned in Chortkiv by the Germans were kept for an hour to perform some work and then sent home. Youth politics is strictly forbidden.

21 May 1942

Yesterday [the German] Governor [of Galicia Otto] Wächter came to our city.[36] The city was decorated, and government officials and youth stood at designated spots. The city mayor offered him "bread and salt" as welcome. The governor then continued on to Chortkiv.

1 June 1942

... Bread is not being delivered, because there is none. In the villages, there are requisitions from the peasants, leaving 15 kg of rye per person until the next new harvest. There are no potatoes ...

When will this horrible war end? People are speculating that by the end of the fall ... Whoever wants to, let them believe it! ...

7 July 1942

... It is said that the Germans released all the Banderites from prison.

In the villages we have famine. They took the grain, there are no potatoes, the milk and eggs have been requisitioned ... Many people become horribly swollen from hunger ...

11 July 1942

People say that [the leader of OUN-B, the radical faction of the Organization of Ukrainian Nationalists] Bandera[37] is in London now;

[Andrii] Melnyk [the leader of the more moderate faction, OUN-M] has disappeared somewhere.[38] There are good prospects for the harvest ... Some people see this as a sign that before long there will be peace, and life will become easier. In Chortkiv there is already a Jewish ghetto. A gendarme shot one young peasant woman who had come to the Jewish ghetto and was talking with Jewish women. He also shot two Jewish women.

14 July 1942

The Germans need many people for work in their country. Those among our people who have no jobs here are leaving for Germany "voluntarily." But this does not suffice. The gendarmes force young girls (apparently from the age of twelve), and young and mature men to go to Germany. They do it by surrounding a village and seizing young women and men. Terrible scenes! Girls and boys are hiding in the fields and woods for weeks. They don't want to leave their parents' homes.

19 July 1942

In Chortkiv the Gestapo arrested about twenty students of the Ukrainian gymnasium; some were released, others were detained in prison.

27 July 1942

For several days now trains are going from Buchach to Stanyslaviv, and from Pyshkivtsi [Polish: Pyszkowce, 7 km east of Buchach] to Chortkiv. The railroad tunnel and bridge in Buchach [blown up by the Soviets when they retreated] have not yet been repaired. In the city people say that the Jews have again bribed some influential person, and that is why there is no ghetto here, and the Jews are free to move around. When the German army arrived, the Ukrainian district administration [to which Petrykevych belonged at the time] wanted to issue a proclamation to the population that emphasized the liberation of the people from Jewish exploitation—but the Landkommissar [county commissioner] did not allow it to be published.[39]

Driven by hunger, the poor have been looting vegetable gardens, digging out potatoes and cabbages. Last night my garden, in front of the house and in the back, was also destroyed.

8 August 1942

Today was graduation day in our school. It was hard work under difficult conditions. The teachers were saved from hunger by giving private lessons in the afternoons and thereby earning 15–20 kg of flour or a pound of butter. Without these earnings, there would be famine. Up to twenty students stopped coming to school, because they could not live in the city; others walked barefoot 10–12 km from nearby villages .... .

30 August 1942

The German authorities are devoting a great deal of energy to collecting the assigned "quotas" [requisitions] of crops .... . Teachers, government officials—everyone is working on collecting the quotas. Under the signature of Hitler himself, punishments were issued, including the death penalty, for failure to deliver the quota .... . Today, Sunday, during the morning service, the priest proclaimed that there would be no Mass, because the authorities banned it, so that people would go to work in the fields. It is said that yesterday the gendarmerie drove pilgrims away from Zarvanytsya[40] [Polish: Żurawińce, 24 km north of Buchach] and sent them to work in the fields to collect the quota. People complain again about beatings for sluggish and sloppy work.

For several days now the Jews have been agitated because they have heard that Jews were shot in Chortkiv.

3 September 1942

This is the first day of the fourth year of the war with England. And the end cannot be predicted. People say that the danger for the Jews has passed. The Jews gave a beautiful gold box [to the Germans] as a gesture of gratitude.

In Buchach the teachers' college has opened.

12 September 1942

It is said that the Germans are vigorously collecting the [food requisitions] quota because they have to hand Galicia over to the Hungarians. (It's not known whether temporarily or for longer. Some Poles are happy.) People are afraid that the famine would begin even before winter .... .

This morning the assistant to the Landkommissar and former underground member Mykhailo Chaikivskyi was arrested and taken to the Gestapo.[41] Two or three days ago Soviet aircraft bombed Lviv, Drohobych, and Stryi [Polish: Stryj]. They also flew over Chortkiv and Buchach. Lights are now forbidden throughout the city. In one school the light was left on in the middle of the day. The German police and gendarmes came and gave the school principal a dressing down.

29 September 1942

An accidental fire destroyed Osivtsi, part of Bilyavyntsi, and Bobulyntsy [Polish: Osowce, Bielawince, Bobulińce, villages about 15 km north of Buchach]. It is said that up to five thousand people were left homeless. Several people perished in the fire. They say that in the chapel and in Polish homes ammunition exploded in the fire.

3 October 1942

Yesterday Polivtsi [Polish: Połowce, a village 20 km southeast of Buchach] burned down; today there was a fire in the marketplace. They say that some gas bombs were dropped from airplanes. The gas disperses and then ignites.

19 October 1942

Yesterday was a terrible day for the Jews. Up to now such actions [or roundups; Ukrainian: aktsia; Polish: akcja; German: Aktion] as had happened with Jews in other cities had not occurred in Buchach, and people said that Buchach was a paradise for the Jews. But in the last few days the Jews did not feel safe. They begged to be let into Christian houses. The day before yesterday the Gestapo arrived. Yesterday morning they started assembling the Jews in the square by the river. Those who tried to escape were shot. They shot sixty people. They broke into houses and took everyone out (we live in a house with Jews and they took them too). The Jews—young, old, women, and children—stood in the square until evening. In the evening they were led to the railroad. Nobody knows where they were taken. Some say they were shot in Stanyslaviv; others say that were taken to Bełżec and killed there with electric current in Bolshevik [?] prison cells. What the truth is, nobody knows. It is said that 960 people had been assembled in the square. The rest of the Jews hid in the woods and fields. The Gestapo will stay here for another two days.[42]

In some villages, dysentery is spreading and has taken the lives of hundreds of victims.

Autumn drought. There has been no rain for a long time. It is impossible to plow and sow winter crops.

20 October 1942

Studying in the teachers' college has begun.

26 October 1942

Great displacement in the city and in the villages. The Germans are seizing the unemployed between the ages of fourteen and sixty, and deporting them to work in Germany. People are hiding.

12 November 1942

The first snowfall: General Winter is on the offensive.

The German gendarmerie here has arrested several (six or seven) Poles. The reason is unknown for now. People say that this is related to some kind of Polish unrest in Warsaw.[43]

The German gendarmerie seizes people on the street and deports them to work in Germany. Today they caught 150. People are fleeing.

27 November 1942

Yesterday there was a new roundup of Jews. Several were shot; they were seized and taken away, probably about a thousand of them. Jews who learned about this in time fled to neighboring villages.[44]

It is said that on 11 November at the cemetery in Lviv two or three Germans were shot. The Germans killed twenty-five to thirty Poles for this. In Warsaw, a train with Germans was blown up and a bomb was thrown into a German restaurant. Several thousand Poles were jailed, and two to three hundred were shot.

The Jews and the Poles are disseminating a rumor that in two to three months there will be a revolution. German fortunes have deteriorated significantly in view of events in Africa and the East. There is talk about unrest in Italy and Germany.

In the villages people are being taken to work [in Germany]. People are fleeing. On 26 November there was to be an inspection of everyone between the age of eighteen and thirty-five, but the order was later withdrawn.

29 November 1942

There is a rumor that in Chortkiv the Germans shot Ukrainian political prisoners (forty people).

8 December 1942

This is what is said about the shooting of Ukrainians in Chortkiv. Recently, Lviv underground members had a secret meeting. Twenty-four people were present. But the Gestapo already knew about the meeting and sent in two gendarmes. The underground members, taken by surprise, killed one or two gendarmes. In retaliation, the Gestapo shot all the underground members who were caught, and additionally shot a hundred completely innocent prisoners. The prisoners in Chortkiv, sick with typhus, were forced to lie outside in the cold for two hours. After that, with some of them already half-frozen, they were thrown into a truck, transported to Yahilnytsya [Polish: Jagielnica, 40 km southeast of Buchach], and shot next to a pre-dug pit that was then covered up. Among those executed, they say, was a priest, Father Vytvitsky, an engineer, and Dr. Kosso, an attorney from Kolomyya [Polish: Kołomyja].[45] I do not know for what reason they were in jail. Fifty-two people were shot, including two Poles.

Others say that the Gestapo found the archive of the Banderites, which was hidden somewhere in St. George's Cathedral in Lviv. From the archive, they learned about the main figures and obtained lists of people and anti-German appeals. Those who were shot in Chortkiv came from Kolomyya and were already imprisoned. It is said that the Germans, having found this material in St. George's Cathedral, do not trust the Metropolitan.[46]

18 December 1942

Today the people accompanied Prefect Mykhailo Chapkivskyi, a member of the underground,[47] who died yesterday, to eternal rest in Monastyryska. The Landkommissar and Father Melnyk bid him farewell. He died from a carbuncle. From 19 December to 20 January we have Christmas break. The reason for this is typhus, which is spreading in Buchach and the villages. It is said that nine hundred people are sick with typhus. It is prohibited to hold any meetings as well as to show any discontent.

1 January 1943

Everyone wonders whether the coming year will bring reconciliation between the warring parties, or will there still be war? What will end the war? What will it bring to us Ukrainians? The powers are fighting for world domination and the world is dominated by unprecedented calamity ....

Apparently in two weeks the railway will again go to the train station in Buchach by the bridge and tunnel as before. One will not need to go to Pyshkivtsi to catch the train, but only to the Buchach station.[48]

All the population is to be vaccinated against typhus in Chortkiv ....

24 January 1943

An order has been issued for the departure of youths over the age of sixteen, for work in Germany.

3 February 1943

The Central Committee has withdrawn the order; the Buchach Delegation reported this to the Directorate ....

... only a few students attend school. Classes are consolidated.

Again, news of German setbacks. The Bolsheviks have recaptured Voronezh, and near Stalingrad a German army, along with six or twelve generals (there are different versions), was taken captive. Some German officers shot themselves so as not be taken prisoner. In Africa, too, things are not good.

Yesterday and today there was an anti-Jewish roundup. The Jews who are caught (yesterday 250, today 200 or more) are taken to the Fedir [Polish: Fedor, a hill located several minutes' walk southeast of the town center], where a few days ago the Baudienst [German forced labor service for non-Jewish Polish citizens] dug pits; they are shot in the back of the head and thrown into the pit; those who are well-dressed are first told to take off their clothes. There is much despondency among the Christians. Our militiamen let some Jews go; our people hide them in the hay, in their barns.[49]

The common people say that some kind of Mihalda [popular books of prophecy] has predicted that the war will end by Easter, because this year our [Ukrainian Greek Catholic] and the Roman Catholic holidays occur on the same day, hence there must be peace...[50]

4 February 1943

The anti-Jewish roundup ended yesterday evening. It is said that more than a thousand Jews died (some say up to thirteen hundred).[51]

19 February 1943

The German defeats (the loss of Kharkiv) have caused panic; Ukrainian and Polish leaflets have been circulating around the villages. I have not seen them, but it is said that they are in the hands of the [Ukrainian] Delegation [representing the UCC].

They say that Professor Kubiyovych went to Berlin with a colleague to initiate measures toward the formation of a Ukrainian army. Generally speaking, as far as the creation of a Ukrainian army is concerned, a drowning man will clutch at straws.

27 February 1943

It is said that Polish organizations are carrying out a great deal of sabotage. Their base is in Lublin. In Poland, a train with Italian troops was blown up; a tram was blown up in Warsaw. In the villages no injustice is being carried out [by Ukrainians]. The Poles, especially the Polish settlers, are being expelled from the villages. The formation [apparently the Ukrainian Insurgent Army, Ukrainska Povstanska Armiya (UPA)] that is carrying out these expulsions was established in Volhynia, and assisted the Germans for a long time, but has now broken with them. The Germans do not deal with it.[52]

29 July 1943

The fall of Mussolini has stirred people. The Poles rejoice, hoping that the British will come here soon; Jews who live somewhere in the woods, come in the evenings to the houses that are far from the bridge and threaten Ukrainians with revenge.

Once again, some partisans have appeared in the Chortkiv district (in Dzvynyach [Polish: Dźwiniacz, 60 km southeast of Buchach]). People say that they are Poles. According to them the Hungarians destroyed [Taras] Bulba's formation, and he killed himself. Bulba is [the nom-de-guerre of nationalist Ukrainian resistance leader Taras] Borovets.[53]

O. D. [Petrykevych provides only the initials of this person's name] from Chortkiv has recounted that Bulba's partisans are up to forty thousand men strong. They print flyers against the Germans and disseminate

them. They are strong in Volhynia. Their goal is a Ukrainian legion ....
They have a national ideology. Poles from Volhynia are being driven
away. The [other] partisans, who appear in the vicinity of Chortkiv,
Zemshchyk [?], and Buchach, and spread out toward the Carpathians,
number up to fifteen thousand men. They keep close to the woods and
attack the Germans. The nature of their policy is unknown.

The English army took Palermo without a shot. The Italians do not
want to fight. Two German officers were killed [by Italians] slitting
their throats. (According to English radio).

Last night the Germans executed with machine guns a group of the
Jews who emerged from somewhere under the ground in the city (up to
two hundred people).

30 July 1943

It is said that Bulba ordered the Poles to leave the city of Ternopil.

6 August 1943

Again, the partisans' operations can be heard every day. The partisans
are clustered in the mountains that surround Nadvirna. From there
they attack the farms and take the cattle and whatever else they need.
Among them are Jews, Bolsheviks, and others of that ilk. They are
dressed and armed in every possible way. Their commandant is a certain
[Sydir] Kovpak.[54] Their orientation is Bolshevik. The Germans attack
them with airplanes, dropping bombs on them.[55] ...

These are difficult times for the Germans; hoping for decisive events
before winter.

12 August 1943

Someone who has come from Germany recounted that the Germans
have fortified their Alpine front. In Germany there are terrible bombing
attacks. Some cities have been completely destroyed.

Again, several [partisan] bands have appeared. A few days ago, a
Polish band, which was organized by a sergeant of the old [prewar
Polish] army, killed a Ukrainian—a forester—robbed people, and the
like. The bands are hiding in the woods; the Germans drive vehicles to
the forest, but do not go into the woods, probably because they don't
have enough troops ....

There is talk about changing German policies in view of the events
at the front.

20 August 1943

The German authorities are confiscating church bells. All the bells were removed today from the Basilian bell tower. On Sunday, church bells are no longer heard at all.

9 September 1943

Today the radio reported that Italy had capitulated. This was predictable. Serious events are about to happen. The partisans are in the villages. For the last few days Buchach is full of trucks and tanks, which occupy various squares and the gymnasium courtyard. Part of our house is occupied by the army. They leave and come back. They say they are fighting the partisans. I had a chance to speak with one of them. This Wachtmeister [NCO] said that the partisans commanded by Kovpak fight bravely and are well equipped with weapons, but those partisans that do not belong to the legitimate armed forces of any state are poor hungry scum. They say that there are Bolshevik, Polish, and Ukrainian partisans. They appear in small units. It is said that some partisans even come to the city in disguise to buy supplies: they can be recognized by their language, a mishmash of Ukrainian and Russian. Fighting them is hard. The Germans do not have enough troops to force their way into the forests, and the partisans keep to the woods.

They say that a few days ago the Germans arrived at the village of Uhryniv [Polish: Uhrynów, 40 km northwest of Buchach], Chortkiv District, to punish the peasants for the undelivered quota of grain. The peasants were punished with ten strokes. The peasants fought and killed six Germans. The partisans do not allow them to deliver grain and warn the peasants against doing that.

Conditions in our school are difficult. Although it is said and reported that we have a Ukrainian school, our hands are tied. Before the break, we became accustomed to teaching college classes of up to 300 students. This time we accepted only 57, because an order came from above that this should be the number for each grade. The same applies to the trade school. Before the break, 150 students took the exam; so many that we had to form two classes. Now there is an order to create only one class, and to dissolve the other. In Galicia only 1,000 students are assigned to each school. Where will the rest of the young people study? It is difficult to be admitted to the gymnasium, and the same goes for the teachers' college and the trade school. The vocational schools, they say, are already crowded. But they cannot accept students above the allotted number. Young people are demoralized, and teachers who are unemployed because of the shrinking demand have to look for other sources of income. Teachers are paid as much as [they were] in Poland. What can one live on? Teachers give lectures and work as private tutors to students who attend school. These days this is allowed.

Many people subsist on trade under the counter. I would not be able to survive without it. After all, a civil servant or a teacher cannot live on his income.

It is said that in Koropets [Polish: Koropiec, 35 km southwest of Buchach] and neighboring villages, Polish partisans killed ten Ukrainians.

13 September 1943

The assassinations of our innocent and most prominent people, especially in Lviv, but also in the provinces, are causing great alarm and commotion among our citizens. Hardly a day goes by without a newspaper report on the death of a prominent citizen, claiming that he died tragically or unexpectedly (unreliable)! Many of those killed served in the police. But people who do not take any part in political life are also killed, such as scholars, industrialists, merchants, doctors, cooperative employees, teachers, principals, and others. Their only fault is that they are Ukrainians working with Ukrainians. Many have died in Poland while working there for the [German] government. Polish fighters are calling for them to be killed as revenge for the action of Bulba in Volhynia.[56] Apparently the killing is so easy that none of the killers has been captured yet. The German authorities are not interested in these murders, because they do not hurt them [the Germans], and consequently they do not retaliate. For the murder of one German, many innocent people perish, but who will take revenge for the murder of a Ukrainian? P. H. [Petrykevych provides only the initials of this person's name], who came from Lviv, recounted that Ukrainians were thinking about self-defense and revenge for those crimes. We'll have to see how this turns out. In the meantime, the assassins continue to kill Ukrainians ... .

18 September 1943

Yesterday or the day before yesterday partisans or some bandits in automobiles attacked Tovste (Polish: Tłuste, 40 km southeast of Buchach). They took with them two Roman Catholic priests, killed them, and threw them into a ditch outside the town. The chief of the post office and his wife were stabbed. (It turned out to be a fabrication!)

It is said that some eighteen people from Buchach received threatening letters from the Polish militants.

21 September 1943

German gendarmes found a machine gun and other weapons at some Polish peasant's house in Puzhnyky [Polish: Puźniki, 55 km southwest of Buchach]. The village has been punished: the villagers were evicted, and the peasant in question was apparently shot.

23 September 1943

The Germans are collecting grain quotas with draconian brutality. They beat up people, destroy their stoves or entire houses, take away everything from the houses, and confiscate the cattle. There have been cases of peasants, men or women, who were wounded or killed while fleeing from their houses. People have been unable to provide the quotas: they have had no time to thresh the grain and deliver it, and partisans have threatened punitive actions.

Once again, people are being seized on the streets and in the villages for forced labor in Germany. In the villages, there is crying, groaning, and grief.

Some people had thought that the establishment of a Ukrainian army division [the Waffen-SS "Galicia"] would change the Germans' attitude towards our population, but there has been no improvement. (These are naïve expectations).[57]

The coming winter will be terrible. There is no fat and there will be no firewood. In the woods, no one is cutting down trees; people are afraid to work in the forest because of the partisans.

28 September 1943

The Bolshevik troops are approaching the Dnieper. Although the radio broadcasts news favorable to the Germans, nobody believes it. The Germans remove everything; day and night, trains are going from Chortkiv to Stanyslaviv. In our city, there is dismay; some people have begun packing their possessions. People say that in Lviv there are numerous refugees from Kyiv. The Kyiv Theater has moved to Lviv. The Bolsheviks wreak ferocious revenge on those who collaborated with the Germans. On this issue there is much fantasy and exaggeration. One lady who works in a hospital in Lublin related that many people who had been terribly tortured were brought there from Kharkiv. The

Germans, who had recaptured Kharkiv (quite a while ago), brought the victims to Lublin. (All of this is a lie!) People say that October will be a critical month for the Germans...

[Date Missing]

... Officially the Jews no longer dominate the city. But every week, by chance or through denunciation, their bunkers are discovered; from there, they are taken to the police. Now the Germans kill even Jewish doctors. Jews are still hiding in the woods and in some villages. People say there are still up to two hundred of them in Yazlovets [Polish: Jazłowiec, 17 km south of Buchach]. During the day they hide, at night they go to fetch some food and so forth.

2 October 1943

For several nights now already, one can hear trains passing one after the other. These are the Germans transporting all kind of goods (probably also grain quotas) to the West. It is said that they are also evacuating the ethnic Germans; others say that they are taking away young men capable of military service and leaving behind only the elderly, women, and children. For the Bolsheviks they are leaving behind only ruins.

People have noticed that the freight cars are carrying whole train-loads of electric power equipment. They explain that these are materials from the Dniprelstan [Dnieper Hydroelectric Station].[58]

14 October 1943

Somewhere in the Pidhaitsi area [Polish: Podhajce, 40 km northwest of Buchach] the (Polish) gang of Nyedzvetsky or Nyevedomsky [in Polish likely Niedźwiecki or Niewiadomski] has committed outrages.[59] It attacked a certain village, disarmed the police and whipped them severely. A German gendarme who pretended to be a Pole was only stripped of his clothes. In the Landkommissariat, somewhere in Monastyryska, typewriters have been disappearing from the offices of the district authorities. Whether they are stolen for profit, or they vanish because secret [underground] organizations need them—is impossible to tell. People offer different explanations.

Kyiv has been heavily damaged. The city was destroyed, the population evacuated. One can hear voices saying: "Kyiv is burning."

20 October 1943

About a week ago there was talk about peace negotiations between Germany and the USSR. Now such talk has ceased. Even the terms of the armistice were mentioned, namely: Germany would hand the territories up to the San River to the Soviets and provide them with eighteen million people, mainly craftsmen, to rebuild their country (!!) (What nonsense?).

Things are getting worse rather than better. There is no security or tranquility in the land. Gangs pretending to be partisans are constantly roaming about and attacking the agricultural estates, taking away cattle, horses, and food products. The estate employees steal their property and ascribe the loss to the partisans. The partisans rob cooperatives and workshops. German gendarmes pretend that none of this matters. In fact, they are very thin on the ground, because only a few of them are left in the city, and they feel powerless. Everything is uncertain and unstable; one does not know what the future may bring at any moment. People expect changes. The Poles rejoice, hoping that things will be better for them, but I think Polish optimism is unfounded.

23 October 1943

Today the Kreishauptmann [District Chief] issued an announcement that people are allowed on the street only until 8 p.m.; anyone walking out later would be shot.

It is said that in Chortkiv more than fifty Ukrainians were being held in jail for political reasons. Recently, they were taken somewhere: perhaps they were shot.

In our city traffic begins at night. Some unknown people walk in the streets. These are probably Jews, who leave their bunkers at night, and perhaps also some members of the underground. A few days ago, there was a burglary at the house of the former Landkommissar, and other people were also robbed.[60] Probably the district chief's announcement [of curfew] was in response to these events.

When the sun goes down and darkness prevails, the fields also come to life. Jews and partisans appear in the fields. It is generally dangerous to venture out to a field or a wood at night. Recently a peasant from Nahiryanka [Polish: Nagórzanka, on the outskirts of Buchach] forgot some rug or blouse in the field. He went to pick it up and never returned home. When it gets dark, all civilian traffic and activities stop. Then those who cannot be seen during the day can come out.

31 October 1943

It has been announced in the city that Ilchuk, the owner of a plaster mill, who committed sabotage against the state by grinding people's grain, was executed in Borshchiv [Polish: Borszczów, 70 km southeast of Buchach]. He was convicted by a summary court in Ternopil.

Yesterday some Jews attacked the house of Ch., who lives on Pidhaitskiy [Polish: Podhajecka] Street.[61] The attack took place at 6 p.m. [... The attackers] threatened all the people present in the house (including two guests) with revolvers and took away whatever they could carry with them (mainly cloths and linen).

1 November 1943

People quietly commemorated 1 November [the proclamation of the West Ukrainian People's Republic in 1918].[62] A collection of donations for disabled veterans took place in the churches, and in the evening, there was a service for the fallen and a sermon at the Basilian monastery. Our school and the teachers' college commemorated this anniversary modestly, by reading essays and recitations during the last class of the day.

People say: first, there was the devil (Poland), then came the demon (Germans), and now we no longer know what will happen.

3 November 1943

Today and yesterday the "citizenry" has "seen off" recruits leaving for military training. More than three hundred of them left for the [Waffen] SS ["Galicia"] Division. The Germans mercilessly seize grain quotas. In the villages, people are beaten, imprisoned, and abused in their farms and households.

5 November 1943

Yesterday, on market day, German gendarmes seized people for forced labor in Germany. First, they broke up the market, confiscated agricultural produce, and announced that there would be no more market days as long as the peasants did not deliver their grain quotas. Then they began to seize young women and men. People were running away, fleeing, hiding wherever they could. It was said that some fellow plunged into the Strypa, was shot and drowned in the river. Only in the evening did things calm down a little.

It is said that the deputy director of the Ukrainian Central Committee, Dr. [Kost K.] Pankivskyi, visited our city yesterday. He addressed delegates of the communities and the citizenry. He complained about the Banderites, who cause unrest among the youth in the land, and announced that the UCC would continue to exist for another three to four months.

Yesterday, while another group of SS recruits was leaving, the soldiers who accompanied them noticed a man hanging around them. When seized, the stranger pretended to be an ethnic German, but after checking his belongings, he was found to be a provocateur or a spy. He was carrying hand grenades and flares. People say that he intended to use the flares as a signal to attack the train or to blow it up.

7 November 1943

Mrs. H., who was in Lviv, brought news that a German was killed in Lviv. In retaliation, four Ukrainian and four Polish hostages were shot.

9 November 1943

Yesterday afternoon, the police seized twenty to thirty Jews in Zolotyi Potik [Polish: Potok Złoty, 20 km south of Buchach]. They were not shot there but driven to the train somewhere further down the line (to Chortkiv).[63]

It is said that in view of the military situation, camps are already being prepared in Germany for evacuees from Galicia.

The Jews, who are hiding in bunkers, are getting bolder. At night some of them, armed with weapons, go to families that other Jews had previously asked to store their belongings, and demand to hand them back. They bring with them lists of items of Jews who are already dead, and they take them away because these items are Jewish property. Anyone who refuses to hand over those goods is warned that the Jews would punish him later. During these encounters the Jews emphasize that in due course action will be taken against the Christians.

People say that Hitler is moving two million troops to the east to save the situation. The front is about 350 kilometers away. Total uncertainty and frightening rumors. (Even those who believe in Germany see that it is declining).

12 November 1943

It was rumored that on 11 November the Poles would create some kind of unrest or even stage an uprising. In the villages, our youth was getting ready to respond to them. Did the authorities notice that?... In the evening of 10 November, several cars (two or three) and two or three armored vehicles arrived. The soldiers occupied part of our school. The day passed calmly.

13 November 1943

Yesterday at 3 p.m. three men showed up at the office of Mr. Rudovskyi, director of the Buchach county, located at the house of Shcherbonevych, near the Landkommissariat. They threatened him with revolvers and took away a typewriter with a Latin keyboard. They did not take the typewriter with a Ukrainian keyboard. They spoke Polish ....

16 November 1943

The Germans are having difficulties with the partisans and the Banderites. People say that in Nadvirna the Banderites killed two or three German Gestapo officials. In retaliation, the Germans arrested up to 700 (seven hundred) Ukrainians, mainly members of the intelligentsia and [politically] conscious peasants and workers. It is not known what has happened to them.

German gendarmes came to Truskavets [Polish: Truskawiec, 200 km west of Buchach] to arrest three Banderites. They seized two of them and tied them to a telegraph pole. The third killed two Germans and released the prisoners. Now the Germans arrest both the guilty and the innocent. It is not known whether this is just a rumor or there is some truth to it.

People say that in the Buchach district the partisans are also organizing. In Perevoloka [Polish: Przewłoka, 10 km north of Buchach] they are strong, but they are also present in other villages. They come to the villages at night. Their commandant is a certain Lohush from Yazlovets. (There are many people named Lohush living in the vicinity of Yazlovets.) Right now, the partisans are confronting the Germans, but when the Bolsheviks come, they will fight them (!). Lohush and his comrades approach the richer Ukrainians, especially those who have enriched themselves during the war, and demand from them bigger contributions for the partisan organization.

The successes of the Bolsheviks and the German retreat have frightened some (of our bourgeois) "citizens." Some of them have already packed up in order to flee to the west as soon as needed. But it is said that the Germans will not take in our people, except for the ethnic Germans.

People say that 25 to 30 percent of the Jews escaped the mass shootings and live illegally either in bunkers in the city or in the fields, forest, and villages.

17 November 1943

Near Yahilnytsya two Germans with bullet wounds were found in a field: one of them was dead but the other was still breathing. The Germans surrounded the town in order to punish the people. The wounded soldier regained consciousness for a moment and said that they had been shot by Jews. This saved Yahilnytsya.

In Barysh [Polish: Barysz, 13 km southwest of Buchach], some partisans took a mare from a peasant but left the foal behind. A few days later, the mare returned to the foal with a saddle on her back. Later the police followed the mare, and she led them to a Polish peasant. There they found all kinds of loot and the uniform of a German gendarme who had been killed.

In Buchach, two Roman Catholic priests from Warsaw were arrested, along with an official from the Polish Agricultural Society, a female teacher from Pidzamochok [Polish: Podzameczek, 5 km northeast of Buchach], and possibly two or three other people. The reason for their incarceration is unknown.

18 November 1943

Terrible news has reached us. In Stanyslaviv, the German police surrounded the theater, conducted a search among the students and citizens present there, and found thirty-eight revolvers. They [the suspects] were shot right in front of the theater, in full view of their friends and comrades. Some say that the Poles tossed in the arms and informed the Gestapo. Others say that the students were Banderites. The father of a girl who attends a gymnasium in Stanyslaviv confirmed that the shooting had occurred.[64]

In Kalush [Polish: Kałusz, 100 km west of Buchach] eleven students (among us people say seventy) from the commercial school, who were caught with arms and leaflets, were shot. Some of the students were only fourteen or fifteen years old.

It is said that Polish members of the organization POT (Polish Terrorist Organization) were arrested.[65] Evil events have been taking place in our villages, especially those in remote locations. Horrible anarchy. People and militiamen are being killed. Niedziałkowski's [for alternate Polish spellings see above, entry on 14 October 1943] Polish gang is operating in the district; there are also Ukrainian partisans ....

23 November 1943

It is said that in the village of Pomoryany [Polish: Pomorzany, 90 km north of Buchach] someone killed two Germans. In retaliation, all the men—members of the intelligentsia and commoners—were arrested. There are no more government officials in the public administration, the post office, and so on: everybody has been incarcerated.

6 December 1943

In our area the Germans have rebuilt Soviet airfields as bases for their own aircraft.

People say that just as the Jews here went to Bełżec, so too in Poland the Poles went to Auschwitz. "Pojdziesz do Oświęcima" [you'll go to Auschwitz] has even become a figure of speech.

It is said that some air force units will be coming here and taking over schools as their quarters.

The city council has written off brass door handles, and window handles, as raw material needed for war production.

10 December 1943

An awful message has come from Chortkiv. Yesterday the Germans shot ten of our young people in the city. It is not known if they were Banderites or partisans or [if they were shot] for another reason.

11 December 1943

Today we were told that the shooting of ten (or, as others say, twelve) young Ukrainians and Poles in Chortkiv was in revenge for the murder of a Gestapo man. They were shot in the presence of the Ukrainian and Polish Delegations.[66] Armed Germans came for the Delegation, and Delegation members thought they were about to be shot. However, they only had to witness the terrible tragedy of the young prisoners. In retaliation for [the assassination of] one German, ten political prisoners—five Ukrainians and five Poles—were publicly executed. Because it is not known who killed the Gestapo man, five Ukrainians and five Poles were shot.

21 December 1943

A list of the fifteen Ukrainians shot in November (five) and on 2 December (ten) has been issued in the city. One of them was a woman.

It is said that large Jewish hideouts were discovered in Komarivka [Polish: Komarówka, 90 km north of Buchach] with up to two hundred Jews. They were killed inside these bunkers with hand grenades.

People say that a large bunker with four hundred Ukrainian partisans was discovered in Korostiatyn [Polish: Korościatyn, 25 km west of Buchach]. In the bunker they found a sewing machine and a typewriter. This bunker must have been a natural cave. Some of the partisans were killed, while others escaped. It is not known whether they were Banderites or Bolshevik partisans (pretending to be Ukrainians).

26 December 1943

Yesterday a Gestapo court came to Buchach and sentenced six people to death. They led them to the "Fedir," where previously the Jews had been shot, and executed them there. Before being shot, they were ordered to undress.

It is said that the leader of the Polish partisans, a certain Niedźwiecki, sent the German gendarmes a map of the Buchach area indicating the locations of Ukrainian partisans' hideouts. With [the help of] this map, the gendarmes uncovered these hideouts.

27 December 1943

From 27 December to 21 January there are no classes. Today Wehrmacht units occupied our school and the school in the "barracks." Many troops arrived in vehicles.

28 December 1943

These are in fact units of the Schutzpolizei [uniformed police, rather than Wehrmacht troops].[67] Somewhere behind Chortkiv or in the area of Kopychyntsi partisans have appeared, and these units were sent to fight them.

It is said that Ukrainian partisans killed the Polish partisan leader Niedźwiecki.[68]

29 December 1943

Buchach is now a miserable sight. Because previously the Jews populated the city, and the Germans killed them, many houses are left uninhabited. The Christians—petty merchants, craftsmen, and workers—have moved into the best houses and keep them as well as they can. But the empty houses, in which nobody lives, are in ruins. The windows are broken, the window frames have been torn out, the doors, the floors, and so forth, have all been removed. Wood from the houses has been serving as fuel for the poor. The houses are without doors and windows, full of rubbish and dung, so dilapidated that they are hard to look at. War devastation? Yet, strangely, although many houses are uninhabited, it is hard to find a good residence. Nobody wants to take the apartments in the destroyed houses, because nowadays where would you find the craftsmen and materials to repair and clean them up?! This calls for a great deal of money, and even more work and effort. The old clay huts have been razed to the ground. The multistory buildings look terrifying. The city council wants to sell them, but even those who profited from the war do not want to buy them, since nobody knows how the war will end and whether, after the war, they will be forced to return the houses to their former owners, or generally to those who have a right to these homes. German families live in the best houses.

1 January 1944

The citizens welcome the New Year in a pessimistic mood. This is the fifth year of the war, but there is no hope that it will end soon. Both sides are strong and solemnly declare that they will defeat their enemy. And the nations endure, suffer, and agonize as never before. Life has become so hard that it is impossible to describe; and what will come next? The unknown awaits us... The front has come closer to us. It is said that a few days ago Bolshevik aircraft attacked a train near Husyatyn [Polish: Husiatyn, 75 km east of Buchach] and killed two passengers. The Germans have designated all schools, dormitories, even the house of the former Sokół—which now accommodates the office of the "Relief Committee"—as quarters for the troops. They even inspect private apartments and record the [number of] rooms. It is said that five thousand German soldiers are about to be dispatched to the district. Food is very expensive now and will get even more expensive. Buchach, which is not located on a main road, but on a secondary route, has still not been the site of fighting. This may well change now.

4 January 1944

Because of the holiday vacation I have more time and can therefore provide some information about daily life [in Buchach]. Our present existence is destitute; we live in unprecedented poverty, even considering the conditions of a world war. But this is not the same for everybody... Because some people are living well, making profits and buying everything that that one can buy these days. Surely, the war destroys and ruins some, and gives too much to others, often undeservedly. War transforms all values. Today, the official and the employee are the poorest, and among them, the teacher is probably the poorest of all.

Why are government officials so poor? The war has wiped out the value of money. The price of goods has risen by a factor of between ten and one hundred or even more. For instance, a lumberjack demands twenty times more for his work ... the same applies to other workers. And what does the official earn? The state, behaving as if it does not see the real situation, pays the official as much as Poland did, although living conditions have changed and this salary is totally unrealistic; even the most frugal person cannot get by on it .... So how do the officials survive? To avoid starvation, they provide for themselves in any way they can. Teachers save themselves through tutoring, preparing students for elementary school and for the gymnasium. Rural teachers prepare the young for city schools. Some communities help teachers with firewood, milk, and other food items so that they can keep teaching ....

... Many families of the intelligentsia subsist by providing lodging to students—girls or boys—and accept food as a fee for room and board. Sometimes a whole family subsists on this food. In my home, for example, four female students have been living with me for more than a year already.

Teachers in the countryside, who have a plot of land (2.5–5 acres), a school garden, cows, pigs, poultry, and so on, know no hardship: they live well, and can buy shoes or clothes in exchange for food.

Government officials in the cooperatives receive at least a part of their salary in kind, so they have the least reason to complain. According to gossip, they speculate with products, so that instead of reaching people, these products end up in the hands of profiteers in all kinds of obscure ways. Recently, the head of the city's cooperative was removed from his position. People say that he made a fortune. Now he has opened a store and is doing good business. Government officials in other institutions, such as the post office, the railway, the tax office, are destitute or try to earn something on the side. At times, their wives engage in petty speculation, and go elsewhere to find some products and resell them. Nowadays, an official's position is worth nothing; often an official will request to be dismissed so as to be able to earn something in private commerce or speculation. State service is slavery, worse than ancient slavery insomuch as one starves faster .... No wonder that a youth graduating from the gymnasium does not want to study philosophy or law in order to find employment in a gymnasium or a court, but studies subjects which allow him to make a living independently from the state service .... Because of the officials' penury, one sees all kinds of corruption. When you carry some products on the train, you must pay the conductor in kind: butter, flour, and so forth. Then he will help you to hide your supplies. When you buy something with coupons, you must give something to the salesperson so as not to wait too long and to get better products .... Everybody must have a side income, apart from their salary, or else they will not get by. The war has destroyed the government official's integrity .... Often people who had earned very little before the war, now profit and earn more than they would have ever dreamt possible, even under the present circumstances.

Merchants and artisans earn well. Nowadays they have no Jewish competition. They adapt their work practices to the present material conditions. It is true that there are not many products now, but if they manage to find something and acquire it, they sell it quickly and for a high price. Products are sold very rapidly, because everybody, whether in the city or in the countryside, lacks all kinds of goods. There is no cloth or leather in stores (only the state can distribute such materials), but there are fancy goods, all kind of household things, products of tin and iron, glass, and so forth. All the stores are always full of people; sometimes it is hard to squeeze in. It is said that some merchants have made big fortunes. Some craftsmen, house decorators, and masons have gone into trade, or opened cafeterias, restaurants, and so on. Clearly, this is where one can earn more.

Both merchants and craftsmen earn well. Tailors and shoemakers are the most important. One tanner (apparently the only one in the city) is said to earn 200–250 złoty daily. In addition, he opened a store for selling lime. Such people fare well and do not feel the burden of the war. On the contrary, they make more money than ever in their lives.

Masons have streamed to the landed estates and work there. If one wants to hire a mason for a day of work, he demands 70–80 or even 100 złoty …

Members of the intelligentsia, doctors, veterinarians, and dentists also earn well. It is said that lawyers fare no worse, because even though there is not much litigation, lawyers charge 100–150 złoty for submitting a suit or indeed any letter to the court.

The peasants are pressured for grain quotas. But the peasants have incomes independently from the quotas. A diligent peasant who, apart from cultivating a field also has a good farm, with cows, goats, and poultry, as well as a garden and a beehive, will have a good income. People say that peasants with more money than they can spend buy whatever they lay their eyes on. There is a lot of drunkenness in villages: in every village there are people who make moonshine. Many peasants buy it, resell it, trade with it, and profit from it. Many peasants send their children to school; they pay in kind, and it costs them relatively little, barely half of what it would have cost before the war. Members of the intelligentsia are happy to take peasant children into their homes, because this helps them get by. Food and board usually costs 25 kilograms of flour or cereals; 2 kilograms of lard, 1–2 kilograms of meat, and 100 kilograms of firewood.

10 January 1944

The teacher Ya., who was recently in Chortkiv, saw a German officer with a partisan newspaper called "To Arms!" He was unable to tell whether it was written in the spirit of the Bolsheviks or the Banderites. In the vicinity of Borshchiv, Zalishchyky, and Kopychyntsi [all 50–70 km east and southeast of Buchach] there are said to be up to three thousand partisans.

Precisely on Christmas Eve, the Germans shot sixteen young partisans in Polivtsi [Polish: Połowce, 20 km southeast of Buchach]; another sixty were arrested and transferred to a military court.[69]

17 January 1944

This morning we could see fugitives and exiles from the East: they carry their belongings on sledges or in carts. Among them are ethnic Germans and our own people [Ukrainians]. The Ukrainians of Buchach shake their heads and think: what will happen to us next?

At night, one can hear the whistles of trains carrying people and goods from the east.

All the schools have been ordered to vacate their premises: our school, the elementary school, and the school in the barracks. Only schools located in private homes have not received this order .... Their facilities are unsuitable for the army. Some other buildings must also be vacated.

18 January 1944

It is "secretly" said that the Germans shot fifty-seven Ukrainians in Chortkiv. It is not said whether the victims were partisans or accused of something else.

The elderly compare World War I with the present conflict, saying: "The first war, compared to the present one, was a mere military exercise." This total war has left a strong imprint on everybody's memory.

23 January 1944

It is difficult to record events. What is happening in the villages of our district and in the neighboring districts should be recorded in every single village, because by the time the news reaches Buchach one can no longer tell what is true and what is fantasy. The partisans come to the villages—sometimes they are Ukrainians, then Poles, and then again Soviets. The Polish partisans attack the Ukrainians; then when the Ukrainian partisans come, they punish the Poles for the Ukrainians who were murdered or beaten and robbed. What is happening in the remote villages of the district, close to the forests, can be described by one word only: anarchy. It is said that Ukrainian partisans attacked a village in the Monastyryska or Pidhaitsi districts and murdered or destroyed fifty Polish families. Is this true? Even the name of the village is uncertain.[70] It is said that the German Gestapo again shot numerous people (up to forty) in Chortkiv. The German authorities fiercely punish villagers for partisans who kill Germans. The Gestapo men herd people into a school or a library, select ten to twenty and shoot them. Absolutely innocent young men perish, in dozens of villages, without trial or investigation.

People are fleeing from Ukraine through the city, some on carts, some on German vehicles. Sometimes they lead a herd of wretched-looking horses that can hardly be ridden. A dozen horses are given to our villages to be fed.

A few families from Chortkiv have already left for the west.

Again, Polivtsi is mentioned; it is said that it is a true Sodom and Gomorrah there. Part of the village is populated by Latins [presumed ethnic Ukrainian Roman Catholics] or Poles, and they informed the Gestapo that Ukrainian peasants were supporting the partisans. The partisans attacked the Poles. The Gestapo came to the village and began shooting people. The school principal and a teacher were arrested, and it is unknown whether they are still alive. Apparently, they wanted to arrest the priest, but he fled to Buchach. Terrible news!

25 January 1944

The Ukrainian Delegation is moving today from the former Polish "Sokół," which will be occupied by the Germans, to a house on Franko Street.

It is said that the German authorities are trying to bring the Poles over to their side. The commander of the Southern Front [Army Group South?] is now General Bravshits [*sic*], who once had some broad agenda for the Ukrainian issue. Does he have it now, when the Germans occupy only a part of Ukrainian territory…?[71]

That's what people say, but it's fantasy.

26 January 1944

Today final examinations were held at the teachers' college. Everybody passed the exam (during a single afternoon).

2 February 1944

Today our school moves to a new home. The building of the former gymnasium had to be emptied. All the houses on the street of the former gymnasium must be evacuated because the army will occupy them. A hospital will probably move into our building. It is said that four thousand patients will be housed in Buchach. There is much traffic in the streets: these are the inhabitants of the houses near the gymnasium, the commercial school, and the elementary school who are moving out. The streets are muddy. This winter has been surprisingly mild. Up to now, there has been no frost or snow. January felt like March.

Yesterday one of the teachers brought a flyer that she found somewhere near the railroad. The flyer, printed in Russian, contains anti-German propaganda …

[Two to three lines cut out.]

5 February 1944

Our school and the teachers' college have been housed in the buildings of the industrial school. The college conducts classes in the morning, and our school in the afternoons (after 1 p.m.). The rooms of this residential house are inappropriate as classrooms; there is no schoolyard. Our school is situated next to the post office.

People say that the Germans are digging trenches around Zbarazh [Polish: Zbaraż, 90 km northeast of Buchach].

The partisan movement is growing. The partisans in Perevoloka decided to shoot or slaughter the Ukrainian intelligentsia, because it supports the Germans (!?). This news may be just a provocation. The fact is that some Ukrainians in Chortkiv, who occupied more important positions or made some fortunes, have already sent their families westward to Kraków. Panic among the peasants in the villages and the intelligentsia in the cities is widespread. This is fertile ground for a provocation.

8 February 1944

It is said that the Hungarians are to blame for the [Red Army's] breakthrough between Dubno and Rivne [Polish: Równe].

[A few lines cut out.]

In the villages, Ukrainian partisans are wreaking revenge on the Polish population for the murder of Ukrainians, and then Polish partisans punish the Ukrainian peasants.

They say that the Bolsheviks are punishing our people terribly, especially the intelligentsia. After they capture a city, they conduct mass shootings, torture people, cut off their arms and legs. They herd people into minefields and make them shout "Hurrah." This is a fabrication. German provocations!

26 February 1944

In Chortkiv somebody killed the commandant of the Criminal Police.[72] The killer was not caught. The Germans again shot ten or more of our young men. Others say that they shot a hundred young people—hostages or prisoners. Still others speak of up to twenty executions. They were shot on the spot where the German was killed.[73]

The name of the Ukrainian partisan leader Bulba is often mentioned nowadays. He has moved from Volhynia to Galicia and is expelling Poles from the villages. The Poles flee to the cities; those who stay behind in the villages do not sleep at night and are armed. There are cases of murder, arson, and robbery.

People say that in Medyka near Peremyshl [250 km northwest of Buchach], the partisans seized a whole train full of arms, and that other partisans captured Rava-Ruska [Polish: Rawa Ruska, 220 km northwest of Buchach] but were pushed out by the Germans.

3 March 1944

Winter demonstrated its might in February: we had frost and snow-storms. Now there is a great deal of snow on the ground.

Ukrainian partisans passing through Korostiatyn (Monastyryska district) ran into a Polish ambush that opened fire and killed one or two of them. As revenge, the partisans burned down the village and killed more than a hundred people with guns and hand grenades.

There are reports of an attack and murders in Nyzkolyzy [Polish: Niskolyzy, 35 km west of Buchach] and Huta [120 km southwest of Buchach].

The Polish population is fleeing from the villages to the larger cities. The Poles in Nahiryanka [on the outskirts of Buchach] have installed window shutters, double doors, and so forth.

Yesterday before noon ...

[A page missing from the diary.]

... the teachers' college handed diplomas to the students. Our school had no forms for diplomas and just handed out certificates.

12 March 1944

There is a steady flow of trucks and personal automobiles [through Buchach]. Things have calmed down a little, but there is still uncertainty. This Sunday morning only a few people attended church; there were almost no members of the intelligentsia, they have left. Yesterday it was said that Bulgaria and Turkey had declared war on the Soviet Union.[74] Today those who own a radio speak only about tensions. (These are naive words!)

As far as one can tell from scattered conversations, the Poles are pleased [with the turn of events] and are not fleeing. They expect to gain from an Allied victory.

14 March 1944

We have only bad news. Since before dawn, caravans of vehicles and carts have been moving westward. Only a few vehicles are driving to the east. German aircraft have been flying over the city toward the east for several days already. They fly low, aggravating the panic. There are no newspapers, and the post office and other government offices are not operating. People are depressed about what awaits them. Some are still leaving for Stanyslaviv [70 km southwest of Buchach], Kalush [100 km west of Buchach] or even farther away. These cities have become crowded and the prices there are soaring.

The partisans move through the villages: in Hubyn near Zolotyi Potik they killed eighteen people, including four Ukrainians; in Ustya [-Zelene, Polish: Uście Zielone, 38 km west of Buchach] eleven, and in Bobulyntsi [16 km north of Buchach] twenty-two Poles and six Ukrainians were murdered. Human blood is flowing. The latent thirst for revenge for all kinds of injustice cheapens its value.

Hungarian units retreating to the west are spreading panic. They say: "We are going to defend our homeland; the Germans are finished." The Hungarians are hostile to the Germans.

15 March 1944

Yesterday evening the Pole Pis. bought some hand grenades from a certain Hungarian. The Pole bargained and paid. Upon leaving, he said something (apparently abusive) to the Hungarian. The latter pulled out a revolver and shot Pis. People assume that the Hungarian understood Slavic languages. This episode shows that the Poles are stocking up weapons.

People are talking again about peace negotiations between Germany and England, and between Germany and the Soviet Union. They mention the Curzon Line, which would become the border between Poland and the Soviet Union.[75]

There are no newspapers and the stores are closed. The peasants are exchanging their agricultural products or handmade goods for oil, matches, and the like. We get information about events either from someone who has a radio, or from those who come from Lviv or Stanyslaviv. Those who acquired wartime wealth have left the city; the poor, mainly teachers from the intelligentsia, have stayed. They sit at home all day. In the morning, teachers will meet somewhere on the street and exchange news. The streets are not pretty: full of puddles, which the passing vehicles splash at pedestrians. Walking outside of the city can be dangerous. My wife and children have left for Kolomyya (75 km southwest of Buchach). Only I stay at home.

16 March 1944

Yesterday six people were killed in Ripyntsi [Polish: Rzepińce, 10 km southeast of Buchach].

18 March 1944

Six Ukrainians were killed in Hubyn (30 km south of Buchach).

20 March 1944

Eleven people were killed in Soroky [Polish: Soroki, 8 km south of Buchach]. The Germans found nine Jews in a bunker [in Buchach] and shot them on the Fedir.

21 March 1944

Ten or eleven people were killed in Osivtsi [Polish: Ossowce, 15 km north of Buchach]. (These numbers are uncertain!)

There are now no people in the city at all. The Germans are seizing young people for work; and for this reason, there is barely anyone on the street. Those seized work either in the airfield in Ozeriany [Polish: Jezierzany, 9 km to the northwest], or in Buchach, where they chop wood for the kitchens, clean the streets, and so forth.

Some of those who fled to the west have already returned. They say that the Germans take the carts and the horses from the fleeing Ukrainians and deliver them to the army camps. The same will happen to the Galicians.

It is said that Hungary has rebelled [against the alliance with Germany] and that the Germans have occupied Hungary and that even [Hungarian dictator Admiral Miklós] Horty has been arrested.[76] Apparently, the Germans will put up fierce resistance against the Bolsheviks in the Carpathians.

22 March 1944

Our people complain about the Hungarians. The Hungarians are sympathetic to the Poles and, where they can, settle scores with our people. Three or four days ago they arrested eight of our people and killed two of them on the way; it is unknown what happened to the others.

Following the recent developments in the war, people, merchants, artisans, and so forth, who were living in houses that were formerly Jewish, but had since been nationalized, are moving out of these Jewish homes. They fear Jewish revenge.

In connection with these events, looting has become widespread in the city. Since our intelligentsia left hastily, they had no time to entrust their belongings or apartments to somebody else. Within a couple of hours, the poor looted these residences. Today one can see here people from the city and its vicinity going from house to house with sacs on their shoulders in order to steal or plunder something. The city council no longer functions; since panic set in, power has been taken over by the Wehrmacht, which concerns itself with its own affairs, not with those of the city.

There is still some trade but only as barter. One can hardly buy anything for money. The peasants bring milk, eggs, cheese, butter, and so forth to the city, and exchange these products for oil, sugar, salt, clothes, and so on. But where would someone like me acquire these goods? Those who worked in stores still have some stocks of goods.

Today there is much traffic of trucks and tanks to the west. During the night, aircraft flew over the city. The mood is grim.

23 March 1944

Noon. In the morning news spread that last night the German gendarmerie and the Ukrainian police left the city. Walking through the city this morning, I found out that this was true: there is no trace of the "security guards." The city is crowded with lads and young women, all types of poor people, who walk into abandoned houses and apartments and take from them whatever they can. The poor have looted the mill: I personally watched the inhabitants of Muliarska Street with sacks of flour on their backs, carrying this valuable booty across the Strypa despite today's chill and snow. Other people break into stores, grab the merchandise, firewood, packages, and so on. Most vehicles are driving to the west, only a few are heading to the east. The Germans are still in the city, but they are clearly packing their belongings. The hospital (the former gymnasium) has been evacuated, and so has the former cinema. It is said that the buildings of the former gymnasium and the Gestapo lockup, where there was a hospital kitchen, have been mined; that the bridge on the way to Chortkiv will shortly be burned down, and the railway bridge will be blown up. But what will happen to the tunnel? Will the Germans do the same as the Soviet army did when it retreated?

Those citizens who have remained in the city, especially members of the intelligentsia (I am not sure that there are even ten of them), are uncertain and fearful. There is nothing to live on, and life is precarious.

It is said that the Bolsheviks have occupied Mykulyntsi, Terebovlya, and Strusiv [Polish: Mikulińce, Trembowla, Strusów, all 50–60 km northeast of Buchach]; others say that they have already captured Pidhaitsi.

24 March 1944

This was a hard, terrible night, and the day that followed it was no different. At 3 a.m. a fire broke out in the gymnasium as well as the houses of Shcherbanevych, the photographer Niemand, the house near Feierstein's villa, and the wings of the villa. The Germans who were living in those houses and had offices there started the fire. Nobody tried to save these houses; everybody stayed indoors. In the morning, the urban poor and children started grabbing from the burning houses whatever the Germans had left behind. At 2 p.m. Shcherbanevych and Niemand's houses burned down, and the gymnasium's roof was on fire. There was a great deal of smoke in the building, and flames could be seen on the roof. At 1 p.m. there were several explosions. Some say these were mines exploding in the gymnasium, but it seems to me this was artillery fire, because one could hear the incoming shells. Apparently, the Bolsheviks' advanced units are approaching from Trybukhivtsi [Polish: Trybuchowce, 7 km southeast of Buchach]. Only half an hour earlier a German armored car was driving to the west.

25 March 1944

The buildings of the former gymnasium, the Polish "Sokół," and the elementary school are still burning. Only smoldering ashes remain from the stone houses and tenements. People are standing mostly next to the gymnasium, shaking their heads in regret that such a beautiful and large building has burned down.

Yesterday at 4 p.m. the first Bolshevik tank entered the city from Pidzamochok [5 km northeast of Buchach]. Today more tanks have been moving westward. Now and then one can hear machine gun fire and explosions. The infantry is also marching through.

In the city the German gendarmerie offices have been taken over by the Bolshevik militia, consisting chiefly of Jews. They walk around with armbands and weapons. They are greeted by their acquaintances.

In the afternoon columns of carts traveling to the west could be seen.

27 March 1944

Yesterday and today, Bolshevik tanks and troops have been moving westward.

That the retreating Germans did not destroy all the bridges, the tunnel, and the most important buildings, is explained by the fact that the vehicle carrying the explosives broke down in Trybukhivtsi. Then a

Bolshevik unit arrived and opened fire on the Germans. One German was wounded, and the rest jumped out of the car and fled. The wounded German hid among the peasants and was treated by them (?!).

The gymnasium building and the houses next to it are still smoldering. All manner of paupers, from the city and from the countryside, have been looting the burned houses, or breaking the locks and bolts of the houses abandoned by their owners and plundering their furniture, utensils, paintings, and so forth—items both useful and useless to the poor. The wave of destruction has aroused the mob. People rob unhindered, for there is nothing to stop them.

In the villages, the partisans are torching the manor houses: along the line from Trybukhivtsi to Yazlovets all manor houses have been burned down.

The Jews still stay in the city. They do not dare go to the villages. Mostly young Jews were saved; the children and the elderly died. One Jewish woman told me that on the territory of the former Poland up to five million Jews perished. Not only Polish Jews are gone, but also German Jews, Czech Jews, and others died.

There is talk about peace negotiations between Romania and the Soviet Union. If the Bolsheviks reach the Carpathians or the Dniester, Romania will have to surrender.

29 March 1944

The fire that destroyed the houses has finally died down. The medical insurance office on Kolejowa [Railroad] Street has burned down (there was a German hospital there), as has the building of the printing house. The Jews are walking in the streets and greeting their friends. They carry beds and tables for their dwellings. Some Jewish houses have been destroyed, and have no doors, floors, or windows; others are in good shape. They say that there are already eight hundred Jews in the city.

After the arrival of the Bolsheviks, a rally took place in the city. The Bolsheviks were surprised that there were no Ukrainians to occupy government offices; there are only Jews and Poles. The Poles threatened the Ukrainians, but the Bolsheviks forbade harming them. Later the NKVD would investigate the matter.

The Bolsheviks occupied Monastyryska before Buchach. In their confusion, the Germans burned down the warehouses. But they left three or four wagons full of barley and lentils in the synagogue, and a large amount of flour in the mill. The Bolsheviks seized the supplies from the synagogue; the mill was looted by the poor. The Masurians

[Poles considered locally as non-indigenous] from Pidzamochok were especially active in plundering the houses whose owners fled from the Bolsheviks.

1 April 1944

The whole month of March was cold, full of snow and wind. Today it is snowing, almost a meter [of snow accumulation], and the blizzard is continuing.

Yesterday one could hear artillery fire or bomb explosions from the northwest. People say there is fighting near Pidhaitsi. During the night, Hayi Buchatsky [Polish: Gaje Buczackie] apparently burned down.[77] In the villages, there are fires and murders. For the last three days the sound of aircraft circling over the city can be heard at night.

Representatives of the authorities are already in the city. There is a director of education (Heller), a chairman of the executive committee, a prosecutor, a police chief, and a city Mayor. The board of education announced that all teachers and teacher candidates must register.

This morning, Mr. Semk came to me and announced that he had been appointed inspector by the board of education. The board would be opening the secondary schools: a Ukrainian school in the building of the Basilian Fathers [the monastery], and a Polish one in the house of the "barracks." I am to become the principal of the Ukrainian secondary school, and the teacher Bok would be the principal of the Polish school. I declined the position on account of my age.

The representatives of Soviet power are very courteous to the clergy, and generally to the Ukrainian population as a whole. Distrustful people consider this to be a tactical maneuver. Recently, it is said, there was talk in the police about arresting several hundred Ukrainian citizens, of whom about a hundred men would be executed, as well as of deporting the women and children to Siberia! (These are stupid fabrications!) People are scared; they sit at home and wait to see how events will turn out.

4 April 1944

All night long one could hear the sound of airplanes. From the noise it was possible to tell that some were very big. These were probably German airplanes supplying the divisions encircled near Ternopil with war materiel or food.[78] Things calmed down a little only toward morning.

The chairman of the city council has issued orders to hand over all radios to the city council. A proclamation signed by Khrushchev and

[Mykhailo] Hrechukha,[79] condemning the collaboration of Ukrainian nationalists with Hitler, has been plastered on city walls. The poster propagates against the supporters of Bulba, [Andriy] Melnyk, and the formations of the UPA ([Ukrainian] Insurgent Army) and the UPRA [Ukrainian Insurgent Revolutionary Army] and warns Ukrainians against [working with] them.[80] Soviet Ukraine is free and has representatives abroad. All the others do not serve Ukraine but only its occupiers and foreign invaders.

5 April 1944

Overnight there was again aircraft traffic. In the morning the Jews in the city panicked. They learned that a German division encircled by the Bolsheviks near Ternopil had broken through the front lines and was advancing to Buchach via Chortkiv. The Bolsheviks now have three lines of defense: one in Dzhuryn [Polish: Dżuryn, 17 km east of Buchach], a second in Trybukhivtsi, and a third in Buchach. They are quickly reinforcing them: in Buchach, they are dragging artillery to the Okopyshche [in Polish: Okopysko, the hill of the Jewish cemetery and a site of mass killing of Jews by the Germans] and digging trenches.[81] In the afternoon, the Jews visit Christian homes and ask to be sheltered during this time of danger. Others flee to the forest. People are grim and uncertain as to what will come next. Far to the west and the east one can hear artillery fire or bomb explosions. In the city there are firing and machine-gun positions.

6 April 1944

A terrible, sleepless night followed by a terrible day; hardly anyone slept last night. Throughout the night artillery fire rattled the windows: explosions, machine gun fire, the rumbling of tanks. Only in the morning did things calm down a little. The Bolsheviks are entrenched on the Fedir Hill slope facing Trybukhivtsi and are targeting it with their guns. At 2 a.m. there were two or three big explosions. They probably blew up the bridges: one explosion in the city, another one on the road to Chortkiv. Before noon about six to eight airplanes passed overhead in the direction of Trybukhivtsi. The engines were very loud; apparently, they were Soviet. Although today is a Thursday, no one can be seen in the city. Everybody is sitting at home, terrified. It is unknown whether the Germans are approaching or have turned in another direction. Yesterday I heard that the German division is heading toward us not from Ternopil, but from Skalat [Polish: Skałat, 80 km northeast of Buchach], to which it came from Ukraine.

7 April 1944

The night passed calmly. There were only airplanes circling over the city and its outskirts. In the morning, German tanks rumbled near the town hall. Yesterday evening an acquaintance told me that between 3 and 4 p.m. German advanced guards were in the city. The artillery fire is continuing.

Hundreds of German vehicles are driving to the west. At 4:30 p.m. Soviet aircraft bombed Nahiryanka; one could see a column of smoke rising from it and hear the explosions. (Is it the railway station?)

8 April 1944

Last night the glare of large fires was visible from the direction of Trybukhivtsi. All night long there was movement of Bolshevik vehicles and anti-aircraft searchlights illuminated the city.

This morning at 6 a.m. Bolshevik airplanes bombed the city. One bomb fell not far from the roof of the former post office and destroyed it. Two people were seriously wounded. At 7 a.m. there was second raid. German anti-aircraft guns and cannons fired from Fedir Hill.

Around noon there was another bombing raid; by evening, there had been two more raids. The afternoon raid was terrible for us: one bomb fell in the courtyard of the Basilian monastery and destroyed the right wing of the building that served as a school. All the windowpanes were shattered; a part of the roof was destroyed. In my house there is shattered glass. One bomb fell on the gymnasium building. Bombs fell in the city. Near the former forestry office, a house was burned down. The number of victims is unknown.

The aim of the raids is to destroy the columns of [Wehrmacht] vehicles that stretch along the Strypa and to destroy the remains of the bridge. The houses by the Strypa are under grave threat.

9 April 1944

Sunday. It is the Roman Catholic Easter. At 6 a.m. an air raid, the bombs dropping somewhere near the forestry office. The house is shaking.

At 7 a.m. there was a terrible artillery barrage. The train station, railway, and forestry office have been bombed. Clouds of smoke and fires everywhere.

The same occurred at 2 p.m.; one bomb fell on the Roman Catholic rectory. It is unknown whether anybody died.[82] There is a fire in Nahiryanka. Today we had five consecutive raids.

10 April 1944

A sleepless night: at least every half an hour one airplane after another flew over and dropped bombs. The German artillery did not respond in order not to betray its positions at night, so the aircraft could calmly go about their business. A bomb destroyed half of the dome of the [Greek Catholic] St. Pokrova church. There are probably also casualties.

11 April 1944

The night passed relatively calmly. I sat in the cellar for a while, and then slept in bed. In the morning at 6:30 a.m. and at 9 a.m. there were air raids. The German air defense drove them off. Apparently, the Bolsheviks were afraid of German fighter planes and stayed away for a while.

12 April 1944

Yesterday evening at about 5 or 6 p.m. I saw endless columns of trucks and tanks moving westward. Later I learned that the [German] divisions started retreating to the west. All night long I heard the incessant roar of engines and the clanking of tank tracks. The shouts of people, whistles, and rumbling vehicles intermixed in succession. Then I could hear explosions, one after the other. I thought the army was blowing up government offices and the like. It turned out to be a horror. The soldiers living in my house left at 3:15 a.m. The whole city is flooded with troops. It is morning. The traffic does not stop anymore. They say it will continue the whole day, and maybe also tomorrow.

The Bolsheviks have not responded so far. There were no bombing raids yesterday evening and during the night.

It is said that up to seventy civilians were killed in the bombing of the city. Yesterday a bomb fell on the garden of the Basilian monastery. Four windowpanes in my house facing the monastery were shattered.

13 April 1944

Yesterday evening a Bolshevik airplane appeared over the city. The same happened today before noon. Columns of vehicles, infantry, and prisoners of war have been moving to the west. Now and then one or two vehicles drive to the east. North of the city one can hear the powerful roar of artillery.

It is said that the Germans seized people today to dig trenches on the heights facing Fedir Hill, above the Jewish cemetery. People, in general, have been hiding; only occasionally does someone appear on the street.

Behind the columns of military vehicles caravans of peasant refugees on horse-drawn wagons are dragging along. They come from as far as Vinnytsia [300 km east of Buchach]. The wagons carry women and children, or the women walk behind their wagons. Now and then one can see a cow or a horse walking next to the wagons. These refugees look truly pitiful.

Today a Bolshevik airplane was repeatedly spotted over the city. It does not appear to have dropped any bombs, but I had to hide in the cellar. The whole afternoon passed in this manner; I would be sitting in the room or walking near the house, then run to cellar, and, once the alarm was over, return to where I had been before.

14 April 1944

It was a tough night. At about 8 p.m. an aerial bombardment began. There was a roar, and then a crash. I sat in cellar until 3 a.m. and could not sleep because of the cold. At 3 a.m. I went to my room and dozed off for a while. At 5 a.m. I was woken up by the sound of two bombs exploding elsewhere in the city.

At night, columns of vehicles were on the move. In the morning I noticed vehicles carrying supplies driving to the east. People who live in locations exposed to gunfire seek shelter in the Basilian monastery. Some people spend their nights in the monastery's cellars. Some spend nights in the tunnel side-by-side with cows and horses. Others sleep in the bell tower, under the church, and so on.

It is still cold everywhere.

In the afternoon, at about 5 or 6 p.m., Bolshevik aircraft dropped bombs. A piece of shrapnel penetrated our window from the side of Ulvanska Street and smashed three windowpanes. At the Basilian monastery, the glass windows facing our side of the house were shattered.

An airplane has dropped leaflets in German. One of them fell in the Basilian garden, and I read it. The Bolsheviks boast of their successes in March. Two hundred thousand Germans were killed or taken prisoner (only an eighth of the total losses). Four thousand artillery pieces were destroyed, and so forth. The flyer calls to take the side of the Bolsheviks, because Hitler's defeat is certain.

15 April 1944

I slept in the cellar. Last night, not many bombs were dropped.

It is said that the Germans lost hundreds of troops in the bombing raids on Buchach. About a hundred were killed in the school "at the barracks," which was bombed several times.

16 April 1944

Easter. It's a beautiful sunny day. Some snow still remains in the ditches.

The night passed without any bombing raids. About 100 to 150 people attended the church of the Basilian monastery, mostly women.

Between 9 and 11 a.m. there was a powerful artillery barrage to the north: apparently, in Medvedivtsi and Pyliava [Polish: Medwedowce, Pilawa, 8 and 12 km northwest of Buchach, respectively]. Behind the hill of the Jewish cemetery something is burning.

They say that three to four days ago the Germans took all the men from Trybukhivtsi and placed them behind barbed wire in Ozeriany. This is in order to prevent them from being conscripted later by the Bolsheviks.

An acquaintance living in the [railroad] tunnel said that several thousand people from Nahiryanka and Pidzamochok were sheltering there. There are no cows or horses. At times, German soldiers also hide there; at one time there were twenty of them, at another time two hundred. Inside the tunnel it is damp and cold. During the day you can still sit somewhere, but at night you have to stand, because there is no space to sleep or sit down. The air is stuffy, there are lice, and there is not enough food. It is a true Sodom.

In the afternoon an acquaintance told me that the Bolsheviks had encircled the Germans. There is a new wave of fear that the Germans will destroy the city.

In the evening, news spread that the Germans had taken all the men from the tunnel and forced them to dig trenches.

17 April 1944

The night passed calmly. The Germans cleared the people from the tunnel: the explanation is that it will either be mined or that the Germans need it for military supplies.

It is said that the Bolsheviks have encircled the Germans and are tightening the ring around them. The Germans have removed their artillery from Nahiryanka and the "Bashty" [Polish: Baszty, the Jewish cemetery hill].[83]

The Germans keep taking people for work, to carry weapons to the front. They are also requisitioning cattle.

The soldiers of the German units that fought in Ukraine are very demoralized and destitute. They have lost their field kitchens and their supplies and are leaving their weapons behind and straggling along the road in small groups. They live on whatever they can beg for or take away from the people.

In the evening, the news spread that the Germans had mined the house of the former gendarmerie office. Supplies of food, beans, flour, and so on, were distributed to the people.

18 April 1944

All night long vehicles and tanks were driving through town. Somewhere in the east, apparently in Chortkiv, there were powerful explosions. It seems that the Germans were blowing up the bigger buildings. During the night, a Bolshevik airplane dropped bombs somewhere near the forestry. As a result, a hut burst into flames, and the glow of the fire could be seen all night.

In the morning there were powerful explosions (I don't know whether of artillery shells or aerial bombs) north of the city. Vehicles are driving to the west and to the east.

In Buchach, a rumor has spread that recently, on 9 April, General [Field Marshal Erwin] Rommel was in the city. The Bolsheviks learned about it and dropped bombs on the Roman Catholic parsonage, where he stayed for a while (?!).[84]

19 April 1944

The night passed calmly. During the day, vehicles and tanks have been driving westward and eastward. Yesterday there was one raid by Bolshevik airplanes. They dropped bombs somewhere in the distance and caused no damage in the city.

It's spring. We are having beautiful days. But people are hiding in cellars and bunkers, and no one is to be seen in the gardens or on the streets. The Germans seize people and take them to camps surrounded by barbed wired in Ozeriany, allegedly to prevent the Bolsheviks from recruiting them later to the army or for work. People are afraid of the Germans and so go into hiding.

20 April 1944

The night passed calmly. Nahiryanka is crowded with the military and supply elements. It is said that Rukomysh [Polish: Rukomysz, 5 km north of Buchach] has been evacuated, and that other villages as well as Buchach will be evacuated too. People from Rukomysh have been transferred to Ozeriany. The Bolsheviks are firing from the woods of Petlykivtsi [Polish: Petlikowce, 11 km north of Buchach]. People say that Medvedivtsi, Zvyniach, and Novostavtsi [Polish: Zwiniacz, Nowostawce, 33 and 8 km northeast Buchach, respectively] have been evacuated.

The mood is grim; we do not know what will happen to the city.

21 April 1944

Last night I slept in my room rather than in the cellar. All night I could hear vehicles; this continued into the morning. At 10 a.m. we learned that Pidlissya and Peredmistya [Polish: Podlesie and Przedmieście, just across the Strypa east of Buchach] had been evacuated.[85] Generally, all the villages north of Buchach have been evacuated. Peasants from the evacuated villages are walking through the streets and crying; mothers are holding their children by the hand or carrying them. We in Buchach have no idea what will happen tomorrow or even a few hours from now. Sodom and Gomorrah are coming, and for the evacuated have already begun. Those who have stayed behind now regret that they had not left for Stanyslaviv when it was still possible to do so ...

22 April 1944

We are like dead people walking. We are waiting for the evacuation. Where can one flee, by what means, how?

People say that [the villages of] Polivtsi, Kryvoluka [Krzewółuka, 25 km southeast of Buchach] and Dzhuryn in the vicinity of Chortkiv have been evacuated.

24 April 1944

At midnight, airplanes dropped bombs somewhere north or east of Buchach. Apparently, these were German planes, because they did not bomb the city. I spent the night in the cellar, expecting an attack on Buchach.

Today, Pidlissya and Petlykivtsi were evacuated. The mood is grim, because they say that in a day or two the city will be evacuated.

25 April 1944

Today the suburb on the other side of the Black Bridge and Trybukhivtsi were evacuated. There is fear in the city. Many houses have now been taken over by the troops. Yesterday some sort of headquarters was established in my house. A big loss for me: German soldiers robbed many dishes, two carpets, a watch, and so forth. In the afternoon, the news spread that the Germans would take all the men with them and leave behind the women, and that there would be no evacuation.

26 April 1944

It was a terrible night. It seems that the Germans are retreating. At 11 p.m., an artillery exchange began, lasting almost until morning. German artillery is located somewhere nearby, perhaps a kilometer away. The roar from Trybukhivtsi was so powerful that windows were rattling.

In these days of horror and suffering, the Basilian Fathers have earned great appreciation and respect for their Christian love for those subjected to misery and woe. They were sheltering the evacuees in their buildings: when the city was shelled, some people spent the night in the monastery's cellars. They gave a bowl of oats, potatoes, or beans to the hungry. Yesterday, when the men panicked, fearing that the Germans might take them to work, the Basilian Fathers hid them in the church or the bell tower, and they remained there during the alarm. One must acknowledge that the Fathers help people however they can.

It is quiet in the city. Now and then a car drives by or a soldier walks down the street. Occasionally artillery fire can be heard.

27 April 1944

Today, at the Germans' initiative, there was a meeting about appointing the city council and the mayor. At 11 a.m. people went to the representatives of the German gendarmerie and the Ortskommandantur [local headquarters], and the abbot had to submit a list of members of the city council. One German announced that there was a German order for a compulsory evacuation of Buchach, which would begin on Saturday, 29 April, by forcibly sending groups of four hundred people in the direction of Olesha and Pidhaytsi [Polish: Olesza, Podhajce, 15 and 37 km northwest of Buchach, respectively]. For all of us, this felt like a death sentence.

28 April 1944

All night airplanes were dropping bombs. I spent the night in the cellar. Tomorrow we are leaving. People are in despair. We are leaving everything behind and going into the unknown.

29 April 1944

We will be leaving the house between 10 and 11 a.m. Will I ever return here? All I have earned since World War I will be lost. The days of drifting and wandering begin.

Stryi and Drohobych: Under German Occupation

4 May 1944

Stryi [160 km west of Buchach]. From Buchach, I went with my bundles along with the teacher K. to Zhyznomyr [Polish: Żyznomierz, 7 km south of Buchach]. Our plan was to hide in some village for a week until the situation clarified. Zhyznomyr was crowded with soldiers and refugees. The village itself had become a battle site; fifty-three huts had burned down. There were frequent air raids. On Tuesday, 2 May, we left with a military truck in the direction of Halych, [Polish: Halicz, 60 km to the west] and arrived in the afternoon. We spent the night at the house of a former student of mine, and on Wednesday we left in the direction of Lviv. But, the day before, Lviv had been heavily bombed: several hundred people were killed. We got off at Khodoriv [Polish: Chodorów, 60 km northwest of Halych] and took a freight train to Stryi, where we arrived in the evening. Here by chance we found accommodation at the home of the teacher Kotelko. We spent the night there and reported to the [Ukrainian] Relief Committee. In fact, however, the Committee does not exist anymore; because of recent events, everybody has fled. Only two or three clerks remain. I bought a coupon for the Committee kitchen. A bowl of soup costs 1 złoty; this is the whole lunch, nothing else. About fifty people were having lunch there. Many citizens of Stryi fled to the west when the panic began. The prices are terribly high. One liter of milk costs 15 złoty, an egg costs 4–5 złoty. And the teachers here are penniless. There is no work, because the schools have closed down.

Saying that there were Dantesque scenes in Zhyznomyr among the people who were evacuated from villages over Strypa River does not fully describe what I saw there. People had been evacuated at the last moment. Children lost their parents. Many people had taken nothing with them and were living on alms. The Germans seized their cows and horses, as well as the people themselves, especially the young, for work in the camps. People did not want to go and tried escape. They were emaciated, lice-ridden, and so on. But although the region is a battlefield, people want to return home, and try to sneak back on side roads.

In Stryi, three people who fled from the Baudienst were shot. This was announced to all the civilians.

10 May 1944

I have been living in Stryi for almost a week now. The schools in the city are not operating. In the countryside, it is possible to find a job. I board at the Committee kitchen. There is just enough food so as not to starve: breakfast (coffee), lunch—soup and a few potatoes, and dinner (coffee), at a total cost of 4 złoty. But it is impossible to demand anything more for this money. There are lots of evacuees and refugees from the front line here. Many soldiers, especially Hungarians, are taking quarters in the houses. There are some evacuees from Buchach. One lady visited Buchach two or three days ago. She said that the city was empty, and that the houses of the evacuees, including my own, have been "cleansed" of their furniture.

11 May 1944

I went from Stryi to my relatives in Drohobych [Polish: Drohobycz, 200 km west of Buchach]. I reported to the Schulamt [school department] and to the principal of the Ukrainian gymnasium.

14 May 1944

Yesterday a list was issued of six Ukrainians who were shot by the Gestapo for joining the partisans.

15 May 1944

Yesterday between 9 and 11 a.m. Soviet aircraft raided the city. There were four or five airplanes, which dropped up to thirty bombs. Apparently, their aim was to destroy [the oil refinery of] Polmin, [the factory] "Galicia," and Boryslav [Polish: Borysław, 11 km southwest of Drohobych].[86] Since it was a dark night and the area had to be lit by flares, and because German anti-aircraft artillery opened fire, the airplanes were badly oriented and dropped their bombs on the houses of the city residents, on civil servants. Bombs fell on Stryiska [Polish: Stryjska] Street, Holy Cross, and St. John's Church. Four or five bombs fell in the square by St. George's Church, killing a horse and wounding some people. In the building of the Ukrainian gymnasium (the former elementary school opposite St. George's Church), all the windows were shattered; the building, the roof, and so on were damaged. School instruction was halted. Close to the city there is a Ukrainian trade school. A bomb destroyed a neighboring house and damaged the school. Instruction has been stopped for a few days. Two or three people were killed and several wounded. People are hiding in their cellars and so on.

19 May 1944

Today I began teaching at the gymnasium. I teach Latin in the first, second, and third grades. There are only a few students—they are scared of air raids. In first grade over seventy students are registered; today sixteen showed up. The teaching takes place in the elementary school on Holy Cross Street. I attended this school fifty-odd years ago. The windows are shattered; a bomb hit a neighboring house, and three bombs fell on the square near St. George's Church.

24 May 1944

Although air raids on Drohobych, as compared to Buchach, have been rare so far, and the damage has been relatively limited, the inhabitants are scared and usually do not go to sleep until midnight, 1, or 2 a.m., in order to keep watch in case of enemy airplanes. Some people have become very nervous because of all this waiting and watching. Everybody thinks that because of the proximity of Polmin, "Galicia," Boryslav, and so forth, hard times can be expected for Drohobych. Indeed, the Germans will not forget about the oil wells, refineries, and so on. People think that the Germans will hold on to Galicia until the end of the harvest; then, taking all the grain with them, they will retreat. Even now everybody is already afraid of starvation.

In these difficult moments, people seek solace in divination! ... The "intelligentsia" often mentions [the West Ukrainian stigmatic] Nastia Voloshyn. She declared that the Bolsheviks would not capture Lviv, but vice-versa![87] They repeatedly mention the name of a certain Pylypok—a clairvoyant peasant from the Stanyslaviv region. These prophecies link people to the future of Ukraine: that Ukraine will soon rise up, and that those who are wrecking the world will fall. (This is all nonsense that does not deserve to be recorded) ....

26 May 1944

Yesterday afternoon five people broke into the bank near the marketplace, threatened the officials there with revolvers, took 36,000 złoty in cash, got into a car and drove off. The locals say that a similar raid occurred recently on the railway ticket office in Rykhtychi [Polish: Rychcice, just northeast of Drohobych]. There is no trace of the culprits.

A week ago, nine people, including two German officials and several ethnic Germans, went by cart to fish somewhere near Dorozhiv [Polish: Dorożów, 20 km north of Drohobych]. They never came back. People are still searching for them, but it is doubtful they are still alive.

27 May 1944

Our gymnasium is being transferred today to the building of the Basilian nuns in the city.

Professor Mak from the Abteilung für Unterricht u. Wissenschaft [Department of Education and Science] has arrived from Lviv. At 9 a.m. the students of the fourth to seventh grades were summoned, and the principal explained to them Dr. Mak's assignment. Youths from the age of fifteen (!) have to "volunteer" for the army. They will be grouped in another city, possibly in Zakopane or Nowy Sącz [in Poland, 350 and 250 km west of Drohobych, respectively]. There, the youths will continue their school education under the direction of teachers. In the afternoons, the youths will do military training, specializing in anti-aircraft guns. The aim of these youths' training is to free up older soldiers for the front: our youth, once they have been trained, will replace them. A Ukrainian soldier from the SS-division ["Galicia"] also spoke, providing explanations. If the Bolsheviks come here, the parents of the youths being trained will be given an opportunity to leave. (This blatant attempt to make nice with Ukrainians shows that the Germans are faring badly.) The principal has summoned the parents for tomorrow to relate this business to them.

It is said that there is a revolution in Russia; Ukrainian partisans have already captured Kyiv! ... In Ternopil, an epidemic is spreading, either cholera or the plague. (These are tall tales and fantasies!)

30 May 1944

It is said that German units in the city had rigorous training today. Partisan units penetrated Lyshnya [Polish: Lisznia, just northwest of Drohobych], from where they were then driven out. The Germans are entrenched in Turka near Stanyslaviv [200 km southeast of Drohobych].

In Boryslav, two oil wells were set on fire and burnt down. These are actions by paratroopers [likely Soviet partisans parachuted into the area].

3 June 1944

Yesterday morning the Germans shot twenty partisans on the market-place square. People watched the execution.

8 June 1944

Today, another ten people were shot at the marketplace. It is said that the overall number of those shot there by the Germans is in the hundreds.

11 June 1944

Yesterday I talked with Father P-koy—a monk who came from Buchach. He informed me about the fate of the city. By 10 June everybody had to leave the city by train or on foot. Even the handicapped and beggars and so on were evacuated. The evacuees were taken by a train that came from Stanyslaviv to the [Buchach] train station, loaded the evacuees, and returned to Stanyslaviv. The evacuees were allowed to take their personal belongings, linens, underwear, and clothes on the train with them. They were not allowed to bring furniture. German trucks drove to the houses of the evacuees and took the furniture and whatever other belongings were left in them. There were only a few air raids [in Buchach] recently, because the city had already been destroyed. Nahiryanka has also been evacuated. Only those who work for the Germans have stayed in the city. As the priest said, soon the towns and cities along the Buchach-Stanyslaviv line, namely, Barysh and Monastyryska, will also be evacuated. After this, it will be Stanyslaviv's turn.

In Buchach, the Germans have been building a bridge over the Strypa, which connects the Fedir to the city. Evidently, they will need it in case of a retreat. Chortkiv is under the Bolsheviks, and the front line runs, perhaps, through Dzhuryn. A common opinion is that if the

Germans have to retreat, they will destroy the cities completely, mine or burn the houses and leave only ruins for their enemies. They acted this way in Left-Bank Ukraine; Right-Bank Ukraine has not been destroyed only because the Bolsheviks did not leave [the Germans sufficient] time for destruction. It is not known whether the Germans will spare even monasteries and churches.

Such a way of waging war, such destruction of the country and the population, provokes hatred among our people. You can often hear: "We are not on the same path with the Germans." The Germans do not respect even churches; they take away carpets and altar covers. German soldiers everywhere check whether the evacuees have not hidden or buried their belongings. They have iron rods, with which they search for hiding places and so on; they break and destroy furniture and all kind of items and use broken chairs as firewood. The Germans have a single goal—to leave only ruins for the Bolsheviks. In pursuing this goal, the Germans destroy our people: the peasants and the intelligentsia lose their belongings. In the area close to the front the land has not been plowed or sowed; people are threatened with famine. It is said that the Germans will hold on to Galicia until the end of the harvest. Once they have harvested the grain, they will slowly retreat to the Carpathians.

16 June 1944

Today about twenty people were shot on the marketplace square. As I was passing there by chance, I saw corpses of men and women strewn about. A German soldier stood guard nearby. People had been standing on the sidewalk and watching the execution. The reason for the execution will apparently be announced tomorrow. People are guessing that this was done in revenge for two Germans who disappeared somewhere in Dorozhiv, as I noted above.

26 June 1944

The German authorities have provoked hatred among the peasants with these draconian measures. One can often hear people saying, "Who is exterminating our people more [relentlessly], and who is causing it greater destruction?" … The Germans shoot our people en masse (among them are members of the intelligentsia; two of those who were shot on 8 June were teachers), evacuate cities and villages, and take away all property.

The situation of the peasantry today is simply tragic. At night, the villagers do not sleep: the peasants walk in the streets, listening to every sound. They are afraid of robbers and partisans. Threatened by the partisans, they are compelled to give them food or some clothing. Then the Gestapo arrests and shoots the peasants for this, charging them with helping the partisans, being allied with the partisans, or being partisans themselves. So, the peasants are threatened by both sides, caught between two forces, and their lives are very bitter. On the whole, people in the countryside envy the city dwellers for having more security ....

At 3 p.m. [Soviet aircraft] appeared over the city. They dropped between ten to twenty bombs, which destroyed the Drohobych [railroad] station, where ammunition was stored, and set the "Polmin" [oil refinery] on fire. Clouds of black smoke covered the sky. By evening, the entire city was covered with clouds of smoke. The smoke is drifting westward. Up to forty people were killed or wounded. It is said that the Germans shot down two or three enemy airplanes. They say that these were American aircraft, not Bolshevik. In the evening, the news spread (it was reported by phone) that a new squadron of airplanes had crossed the border.

30 June 1944

Today the school year ended. Due to the present circumstances, the students were evaluated very indulgently: some will have an additional exam after the vacation; others received passing grades.

Drohobych is in mourning: the air raid of 26 June was horrific. What I wrote down immediately following the raid needs to be supplemented and corrected.

The bombers, up to forty altogether, were in fact American. They could be recognized by the accuracy of the attack and by the bomb craters on the ground. The bomb craters were large, about ten meters in diameter, much bigger than Bolshevik bomb craters. Three bombs hit the railway station and destroyed it, many hit "Polmin," but the refinery survived. In the railway station, up to twenty people perished. Even now there is no exact count of those killed by the bombs. It is said that 350 have been counted, but they say that shelters and cellars with dead bodies are still being uncovered, and the numbers will rise to four or five hundred dead. Yesterday a shelter was uncovered that contained forty live but terribly emaciated people. People who had suffocated in the shelters from smoke or gas or oil are being discovered. All kinds of tragic scenes are reported. A mother perished from a bomb, and her fifteen-year-old daughter was badly wounded. A certain worker fell on the ground when the bombs were dropping and that saved his life. The poor man turned gray out of terror. For three days, funerals made their way to the cemetery one by one; today a mass funeral for the victims took place.

They say that now it's the turn of the "Galicia" [factory]. Almost every day sirens signal the alarm; last night at 11 p.m. the siren went off, and no one could sleep for almost an hour.

They say that in a village in the Mykolaiv [Polish: Mikołajów, 50 km northeast of Drohobych] region partisans or peasants killed twenty-six Germans. In retaliation, the Germans burned down two villages, and shot all of those who were trying to flee from them.

When you walk through the marketplace or on the main street, you can see the store windows displaying meat, sausages, and so forth, and here and there also butter and cheese. But a sign on the window says: "Nur für Deutsche" [Only for Germans]. Our people can merely look at the food and be satiated by watching.

The priest D. from Peremyshl, a refugee from Chortkiv, said to his acquaintances here that he was moving to Drohobych or Stryi. Starting in Podolia, Polish underground organizations have been killing members of the Ukrainian intelligentsia, and not a day goes by without somebody being killed. The Germans, who so [mercilessly] decimate villages for the murder of a German, are indifferent to these murders [of Ukrainians], since they consider them to be an internal Polish-Ukrainian issue. *Tertius gaudens* [Latin: the third party benefiting from conflict between two others].

1 July 1944

The district chief issued the following announcement: all men born between 1903–30 must appear before a commission and will either be drafted into the army, so as to fight Bolshevism with weapons in their hands, or they will be assigned to labor detachments. The time and place will be announced later. The announcement refers to Ukrainians and Poles.

Almost every night between 11 and 12 p.m. the alarm goes off as a warning that enemy airplanes are approaching.

9 July 1944

It is said that last week three or four Poles who had mined [the factory] "Galicia" were arrested. Their landlord cut his veins; their landlady fled.

19 July 1944

Fortunately, the number of victims in the air raid on 26 June turned out to have been exaggerated ten-fold. After the raid, many workers from "Polmin" and the Baudienst fled. An order was issued for everybody to return to work. Those who fled were presumed killed, but they have been slowly returning to work. About forty to forty-five people were killed, including those who subsequently died from their wounds. Still, this is a considerable number.

For the last two days there is terrible panic in the city. This morning news spread that the Bolsheviks are already fighting near Lviv. Others say that the Bolsheviks are fighting along the Zolochiv—Zhovkva—Kamianka Strumylova [Polish: Żółkiew, Kamionka Strumiłowa] line [130–200 km northeast of Drohobycz].[88] On the whole, the situation of the Germans is considered hopeless. Many of our people are leaving to the west. Some have already transported their furniture, have relocated their families to Sanok and Krynica [135 and 270 km west of Drohobych, respectively, across the San River and inside Polish territory], and are now preparing to leave themselves.

Hardly a night or a day goes by without an alarm. Last night, aircraft dropped flares and the anti-aircraft artillery fired back. One could hear two bombs exploding. In the afternoon the alarm was sounded again.

It is said that the "Galician SS Division" was fighting against the Bolsheviks. Many people from our city were killed, many were wounded.[89]

It is already said that soon the city will be evacuated. Ethnic Germans from Ukraine, who had received plots of land in the countryside and farmed them, have been ordered to go to Germany.

20 July 1944

Today the newspapers from Lviv did not arrive. German officers are packing their belongings; the Gestapo officials are burning their documents. People say that the Bolsheviks want to cut off the German retreat route to the west: they have captured Horodok [56 km north of Drohobych], and paratroopers are preparing to sever the Lviv-Peremyshl line. Trains are running only to Stryi [30 km southeast of Drohobych]. German officials in Lviv are fleeing or have already fled.

The Bolsheviks have the best weapons. The Germans have transferred their forces to the west; this is the reason for the great breakthrough [in Galicia].[90]

In the evening, news spread that there had been an assassination attempt on Hitler in the Reichstag; a few generals were killed, Hitler himself had burns on his hands. Everybody feels that the long-foreseen demise of Germany is approaching.

22 July 1944

It is said that there is a revolution in Germany. Today the German Schulrat [superintendent] advised the teachers to escape to the west. Again, there are no newspapers. There is a great deal of traffic in the city.

An acquaintance has said that the Germans took thirty Ukrainian and about a dozen Polish prisoners to the Jewish cemetery and shot them there.[91] The rest of the prisoners were released.

24 July 1944

People say that the Germans have mined [the factory] "Galicia"; its workers have already been dismissed, and the factory has stopped operating. Today there was no electricity; there is no water either. The price of food has rocketed. The Germans have been retreating; trucks are taking away all supplies, all hospitals and offices are being evacuated. The trucks leave mainly in the direction of Sambir] 30 km northwest of Drohobych] while some are heading southward to Siltse [Hungarian: Beregkisfalud, Czech: Selce, in Subcarpathia, 215 km southwest of Drohobych].

The Ukrainian Relief Committee has left, while the Polish Relief Committee has stayed behind. In the evening, news spread that Hitler had been killed and that there were peace negotiations between England and Germany. [Rudolf] Hess is participating in the negotiations.[92] It is impossible to tell if there is any truth to this.

Two to three hours later. The news has spread that Hitler died of burns, that Hess has appointed a new German government, and that England and Germany will start a war against the Bolsheviks! ... People rejoice as if the war is already over (and believe all kind of nonsense!)

25 July 1944

The troops of the [Ukrainian Waffen] SS [Division "Galicia"] from the Drohobych area are returning in a wretched state. They say that the Germans sent them to the front near Brody without tanks or artillery. The Bolsheviks crushed them. Some of them broke through the Bolshevik encirclement.

The Bolsheviks have dropped leaflets in German from airplanes. In two of them they urge German soldiers to lay down their weapons and flee to their side. The third leaflet is issued by a certain Deutsches Nationalkomitee [German National Committee] and signed by a certain colonel.[93] The leaflet describes the hopeless situation of the German army in the east and reports that the front was breached along a 600-km stretch within eighteen days. The Germans lost more than three hundred thousand troops, of whom half were taken prisoners, and half killed. The leaflet urges [German soldiers] to renounce Hitler and unite around the National Committee.

The Germans brought to the "Galicia" [factory] machines that were removed [from elsewhere] and have re-activated the factory. We already have [electric] lighting and water.

The news about Hitler's death and Hess showing up turned out to be mere Polish rubbish. A certain Pole, listening to the radio in German, did not understand it well, and interpreted the news of the death of two generals who were killed in the assassination attempt against Hitler as saying that Hitler had died. Hitler is alive and is wreaking ferocious revenge on his adversaries in Germany. Some say that he has brought to trial twenty-five hundred officers, others say that the number is five thousand. Many have already been shot.[94]

30 July 1944

Life is hard in Drohobych. The Ukrainian intelligentsia has left; only a few, those who do not trust the Germans, have stayed behind. The Polish intelligentsia has stayed. There are no newspapers; prices are exorbitant ... There is no traffic in the city; the stores are closed, and there are no goods. The Germans have ordered to open the cooperatives and the stores, but what can one find there? There are few people in the city; here and there somebody walks by. In the streets, military trucks, tanks, and so forth are driving to Sambir, Stryi, and Siltse, so many of them that the ground is shaking. It is said that Eastern Galicia has already been occupied by the Bolsheviks. The Germans still hold Stryi, Drohobych, and Sambir and are retreating to the Carpathians. In this time of transition, the poor come from the countryside to the city with sacks on their backs so as to make some profit. The Germans have proclaimed that looting would be punished by death, and it is said that yesterday twenty people were shot for looting.

Last night American or Bolshevik planes appeared over the city. There is no more anti-aircraft artillery in the city. The airplanes dropped a few bombs. One of them destroyed the house opposite the former Austro-Hungarian bank; another fell on Viytivska Hora [Polish: Wójtowska Góra] Street and killed seven people who were running to a shelter.

31 July 1944

A tough night with little sleep: from 10 p.m. until 4 a.m. Bolshevik planes were flying overhead and dropping bombs. They dropped up to fifty bombs, maybe more. Some houses were destroyed. The German anti-aircraft artillery has left, and there was nobody to shoot at the Bolshevik planes. People can hardly sleep; they worry, what will come next?

2 August 1944

This morning before dawn, at 4:45 a.m., I woke up at home because the Germans set their depots on fire. A huge cloud of smoke rose from the military barracks near the small station. Some houses in Boryslavska [Polish: Borysławska] Street were burning. At about noon I inspected the sites of the fires. In Boryslavska Street two houses used as German depots had burnt down, and the stables just behind them, which apparently were [also] used as depots, had similarly burnt down. People were saying that the Germans were retreating, but in the early evening German trucks and cars drove by in the direction of Siltse, which indicated that the retreat would apparently take place later.

In the early evening there was an air raid on the city. The planes dropped bombs on the small [train] station and killed one or two people. Above our house a machine gun was firing, and the cartridge shells fell on the roof. There was great panic among the people.

3 August 1944

There is news that the Bolsheviks have bombarded Stryi and have driven the Germans out of the city. The retreating Germans seize people in the villages, load them on trucks and drive in the direction of Siltse-Turka [70 km southwest of Drohobycz, on the eastern slopes of the Carpathians]. It is a pitiful sight, these people taken from the villages against their will. The Germans will apparently use them for labor, for digging trenches, repairing roads, and so forth.

4 August 1944

All day long we could hear shots and explosions, especially in the evening. It is said that the city hall has been mined, and that the Germans will blow it up. Likewise, the train station has been mined. The people are frightened and hide their belongings underground.

5 August 1944

Until late last night the Germans were destroying the rail tracks with explosives. At night military units and supply trains were moving southward.

Before noon and at midday we heard powerful explosions. It is said that the "Galicia" factory is being blown up. At 10 p.m. a large cloud of smoke rose from Stryiska Street. People say that the Germans have poured gasoline on the Sasyiv mill and set it on fire.

Drohobych and Kolomyya: Under Soviet Rule

6 August 1944

All night long we could hear detonations. In the morning, there was a big roar and a cloud of black smoke. The Germans were blowing up a bridge over the river: the bridge in Boryslavska Street. At 7 a.m. a tank with a machine gun, on top of which Soviet soldiers were riding, drove through Truskavetska [Polish: Truskawiecka] Street. Then another tank arrived. At 9 a.m. I went to the city and saw many tanks driving in different directions from Stryiska Street. One tank had a female driver. In the marketplace, I saw two shabby and miserable Jews.

At 10 a.m. we could hear Soviet artillery firing in the direction of Boryslav or Sambir. The German artillery fired back; shells were coming down somewhere in the suburb and a dozen people were wounded.

At 11 a.m. the artillery moved in the direction of Boryslav. The guns were being pulled by horses.

The population does not lament the Germans' departure: they will always remember the German conduct of war. People say that in the last days the rye was burned in the fields. But we must admit that Drohobych was not destroyed to the same extent as Buchach. There, they burned down the best buildings; here they destroyed the railway, bridges, and what remained of the "Polmin" refinery.

The town hall, the schools, the "Galicia" factory, and the oil factory have remained. Apparently, the Germans were in a hurry. To the joy of the city's inhabitants, there was no evacuation, which would have meant complete ruin.

At noon the German artillery began firing on the city. I do not know whether there was any damage. One or two Bolshevik long-range artillery batteries drove to Viytivska [Polish: Wójtowska] Hill and began firing at the Germans. It is said that the Bolsheviks have occupied Boryslav and Skhidnytsia [Polish: Schodnica, 25 km southwest of Drohobych], and that Boryslav was occupied before Drohobych.

7 August 1944

A German aircraft is said to have dropped a bomb yesterday afternoon on one of the buildings of the "Galicia" factory and set it on fire. It is still burning today. A Soviet officer has summoned people with buckets and spades to fight the fire.

Last night there were alarms because of a German air raid; Soviet artillery was firing.

8 August 1944

The night passed calmly. Soviet units are heading in the direction of Boryslav. Their motorized artillery makes a good impression; apparently, it is an American make. The morale of the troops is very high and optimistic; they are elated by their victories and feel self-confident.

It should be noted that Drohobych, as compared to Buchach, has seen much less destruction by the Germans. It seems that they had no time. They destroyed the railway and wooden bridges (one next to the hill, and a smaller one on the way to Boryslav).[95] Military barracks, schools, gas depots, the mill, and the hospitals have remained [unscathed].

The stores are closed. A Militia has been formed from Jews and Poles and has been stationed in the house of the former Gestapo (on Mitskevych [Polish: Mickiewicz] Street opposite the public girls' school). At this point, nobody cares about the civilians.

In the Soviet units, especially among the supply troops, but also among the infantry, one can often see women: they ride vehicles along with the [male] soldiers. Some wear medals for bravery on their chests. The army makes a good impression: the troops do not loot the population and do not arbitrarily take away anything. Now and then a soldier enters a house and asks for some vodka or a cigarette.

Plastered on the city walls are appeals to the fighters of the UPA and the UPRA, signed by Hrechukha and Khrushchev. The same appeals were also put up in Buchach.

It is said that up to two hundred Ukrainians have been arrested. Nobody says who [they were]. It seems to be a rumor. Some people say that two or three were arrested.

9 August 1944

I registered as a teacher with the Department of Public Education. Only three of us gymnasium teachers have remained. It is said that four Ukrainian and three Polish secondary schools will be established.

On the city walls propaganda posters are being plastered. For example: "All Workers for the Reconstruction of the City!" and so on.

A few teachers met at Department of Public Education. The secretary of education, a certain young woman, told us that teachers would receive rations like factory workers while the schools would have cafeterias, and that the discipline in Soviet schools would be tightened. Let's see.

10 August 1944

People say that the Jews appealed to the NKVD to give them a free hand with the Ukrainians for an hour. The NKVD declined and ordered them to leave the Ukrainians in peace. (This is a naïve rumor).

A Soviet officer at a barbershop said that the Soviet Army would not stay here for long. 1.5 million (?) Polish troops are on the way and will soon occupy Poland. The officer apparently did not know that he was in Western Ukraine.

11 August 1944

Overnight vehicles were moving southward, and artillery fire was heard from a great distance, possibly from Staryi Sambir [Polish: Stary Sambor] or Turka.

For the past two days, there has been conscription into the Soviet Army. Men between the ages of eighteen and fifty are being conscripted. Although the Germans already took away many people, one can again see long columns of conscripts marching through the city. So far, the villages have been providing the recruits.

13 August 1944

This afternoon a certain Bolshevik general, who was killed in battle, was buried near the city hall. During the parade, when salvoes were fired [in his honor], one soldier was killed by a machine gun bullet, and two were wounded.

14 August 1944

The principal of the secondary school No. 1, where I will work, reported to the teachers about the reforms introduced in Soviet schools. There will be no more coeducation, but [separate] girls' and boys' sections; discipline and the authority of the teachers have been restored. Teachers and students will wear uniforms. Well, time will tell.

15 August 1944

An acquaintance, a shoemaker from Stebnyk [Polish: Stebnik, 9 km south of Drohobych], told me that our people had been digging trenches for the Germans near Roliv [Polish: Rolów, 15 km northeast of Drohobych]. When the Bolsheviks advanced, the Germans shot those people with machine guns so as to prevent them from crossing over to the Bolsheviks. Did this horrible crime really take place, or is it a fabrication? It is impossible to verify.

People talk about the defeat of the Bolsheviks in the Carpathians. The Germans pushed the Bolshevik front back to Sambir and Maidan [Polish: Majdan, northwest of Lviv] and took a few dozen Bolshevik prisoners. (This is nonsense!)

19–21 August 1944

A meeting of the teachers in the region took place in the gymnasium hall. About 150–180 teachers were present. Reports were delivered.

The school year for grades 1–4 begins on 1 September and for grades 5–10 on 1 October, because the older students have to work in the fields.

20 August 1944

In the garden on Truskavetska Street, a podium has been put up and decorated with flowers. Today, Sunday, a big rally took place here on the occasion of the liberation of our city from the fascist occupiers. Many speakers, Soviet and local, gave speeches; all hailed the victory of the Red Army. The secretary of the regional party organization also spoke. He said: "We won because our politics, our worldview, proved stronger than the political worldview of the enemy." The commander of the Drohobych Division, General Petrov, also spoke. Children gave the victors flowers and greenery. A telegram was sent to Stalin. Everything went according to plan. The speeches were in Ukrainian; the general spoke in Russian. One speaker spoke Polish. Many people were present, up to three thousand.

The national policy of the Bolsheviks is incomparably better than that of the Germans. The motto is: "Friendship of the peoples." Conscription is underway these days. Polish conscripts march in the streets as separate units, singing Polish songs. Then, they are sent to the Polish Army, which is being created.

At present schools are being established. In Drohobych, according to national statistics, five Ukrainian secondary schools are being formed (two with a 10-grade program), three Polish schools (one with a 10-grade program), and one Russian. I do not know whether there will be that many Russians here, or if this is a gesture to Moscow. The same concerns the district: every nation will have its own schools.

These are all nice slogans, but the reality is harsh. The currency we used under the Germans has still not been exchanged, and possibly will not be exchanged at all. Again, a loss for poor people: those who saved some money will lose it. Teachers are literally penniless. We have received no salaries, and the Polish złoty is worthless. How can one get by? Nobody cares [about us].

The school year has begun. There are no books, no notebooks, and no school supplies. The school buildings are in ruins. There is no whitewash. Workers do not want to work for 3–4 karbovanets (for this money, a worker can buy a glass of milk).

28 August 1944

Yesterday evening detachments of Polish recruits marched to Sambir, then to Peremyshl, to join the Polish Army. They sang patriotic songs as they marched. In front of the column they carried the Polish emblem (the eagle) [painted] on a long piece of cloth. People say that the recruits asked the Bolshevik authorities to allow them to hold a field religious service. But the authorities refused.

I have not noticed any animosity toward the clergy or religion by the Bolshevik authorities. The clergy and nuns walk freely in their garbs. Nobody is paying attention to them.

6 September 1944

We have been under Bolshevik rule for a month. The Bolsheviks have not exchanged Polish money for Soviet currency but have ordered to hand it over to the banks in return for certificates, without any compensation. People who have a great deal of Polish money sell it on the black market. This money still circulates on the other bank of the San River [the border with Poland]. The worst is that we have still not received a salary. We live either on our families' generosity, or by selling our belongings. A whole month without a penny; nobody cares. Speculation and the black market are on the rise. Everything is becoming more expensive ....

Near the city hall, where the Soviet general is buried, a concrete monument has been erected, into which a small canon is embedded.

Polish conscripts are being dismissed. There are all kind of guesses about the reason for this.

Yesterday a one-month course for teachers was opened. About 150 candidates showed up. Many teachers have been conscripted; hence there is a shortage of teachers in the countryside. There are complaints that woodcutters in the forest are being relieved from military service, but teachers are not. It is said that in some cases teachers go to chop trees in the forest so as to be released from conscription.

The city authorities have ordered to hand in the furniture of those who fled with the Germans. Their furniture and belongings are state property.

Walking through the city you can see store window displays of soap, sugar, flour, and so forth. The prices are surprisingly low. But next to the goods there is a sign: "Only members of the NKVD can buy in this store." Great disappointment! ...

7 September 1944

Finally, a month after the arrival of Soviet power, we have received a salary. We will also receive a quarter of a loaf of bread daily. People already say that there will be famine in the winter. Even now, in the fall, a kilogram of potatoes costs 6 karbovanets.

10 September 1944

This evening we celebrated a solemn opening of the school year. The youth and teachers gathered in the sports hall (the gym of the former "Native school" [Ridna Shkola]).[96] The guests included heads of local government offices. The festivities began with a speech by the principal (previously a principal in Kharkiv). Then came greetings and good wishes from various organizations and chiefs. The second part consisted of performances by the youth: dancing, a choir, and a declamation. The celebration had a purely Bolshevik-propagandistic nature.

Our secondary school for boys is school No. 1. The girls' school is on Shevchenko Street and is called school No. 2.

11 September 1944

This morning there were three hours of work. We made lists of the registered students and divided them into classes.

15 September 1944

Today after 4 p.m. there was a meeting in the sports hall. A long letter to Stalin (a poem) expressing gratitude for the liberation of Ukraine was recited. All teachers, workers, students from the fourth grade and higher, signed the letter. The same occurred at a meeting of civil servants, citizens, and so forth.

17 September 1944

Many Poles intend to go to Poland, taking advantage of the agreement between the governments of Poland and Ukraine regarding the transfer of Poles to Poland and Ukrainians to Ukraine.[97]

It is not known how many Ukrainians left Galicia to go west before the Bolsheviks arrived. But there must have been many of them, perhaps fifty to sixty thousand, and maybe far more. Some of them had occupied important positions, made political pronouncements, and so forth. Obviously, they had to leave. But if I were to estimate their number ...

[About fourteen lines deleted.]

... the people leaving to the West were not involved in anything, they were completely apolitical, average, and unremarkable people. The reason for their departure is the panic that took hold of everyone, the fear evoked by the terrible stories the Germans were spreading about the Bolsheviks. All sorts of military personnel left, as well as speculators, thinking they could save their wartime profits in this way. Nobody knows where these people live today and what they live from. Whether they or some of them will come back to us is also unknown.

Conscription is still continuing. Long columns of conscripts march down the streets every day ....

19 September 1944

Panic among the people. The authorities are arresting former ethnic Germans [apparently local Poles and Ukrainians who claimed German ancestry in order to gain benefits under German rule ...]

Here is a pattern we often see: groups of twenty to thirty men and women surrounded by soldiers armed with loaded rifles. These prisoners are partisans [presumably OUN-UPA fighters]. They are being taken to [the] Brygidki [prison in Lviv].[98]

30 September 1944

An acquaintance summed up the nature of this war as being about "race, mass, and cash" (?!). (This is what he heard people say.)

Tomorrow, Sunday, male and female students from our school will collect shovels and spades and go to work in the [train] station ....

The authorities are arresting more ethnic Germans.

Every night artillery or machine gun fire can be heard.

5 October 1944

Today a comrade from the eastern regions said in the teachers' room: yesterday our army fought with two hundred Banderites, 12 km from the city.

On the street in the windows of the best stores you see good fruits and vegetables. There is nothing else to trade, so people try to at least sell these. A kilogram of pears or apples costs 20-25 karbovanets. This is the equivalent of a government official or junior teacher's full-time salary.

The NKVD has imprisoned the teacher S. from our school. The reason is unknown.

7 October 1944

There was a meeting of students to collect gifts for the army division that liberated us from the invaders.

Hitler appealed on the radio to the Polish government in London (?). Among the Poles there is great joy and excitement.

It is said that in the Bronytsya [Polish: Bronica] Forest [15 km north of Drohobych] the Germans shot up to twenty thousand Jews and non-Jews! Others say it was up to thirty thousand.[99]

15 October 1944

A big rally in the city park on the occasion of the liberation of Ukraine from the German invaders. There were speeches and greetings, followed by a festival for the people.

On the walls of the city, announcements in Polish have appeared. Poles and Jews who wish to go to Poland need to let the representatives of the commission dealing with this matter know by 15 November. This announcement has been the cause all sorts of interpretations: the borders of Poland and the Soviet Union have not yet been determined, and yet the relocation is already beginning! What is the purpose of this and what deceits may be behind it?

21 October 1944

A rainy afternoon. What seem to be ethnic Germans are being led down the road. They are taken away as Germans: old and young men and women. Hatred for the German invaders is directed at them.

8 November 1944

Anniversary of the October Revolution. Big parades, speeches. Concerts.

10 November 1944

News has spread that Metropolitan [Andrei] Sheptytsky died and was buried with great honor on November 5.[100] ...

Horribly high prices; famine has already begun ... We still have coffee with milk, but no sugar. The merchants and sellers make money. Government officials are in great trouble ....

It is said that Banderite bands are fighting with Bolshevik units. Somewhere near the village of Volya Yakubova [Polish: Wola Jakubowa], the Banderites killed two Bolshevik soldiers. For this, the peasants of this village were jailed.

It is said that the commission, which relocates Polish families to Poland, has declined the request of thirty families to relocate to Poland. This is a small number.

20 November 1944

So far, 360 Poles have elected to depart to Poland.

In villages close to the city, they are seizing families whose sons or parents had served in the SS ....

25 November 1944

It is said that someone killed eighteen Ukrainians in Dobrivlyany [Polish: Dobrowlany, 13 km north of Drohobych]. Whether this was an attack by the Poles, or a settling of accounts among Ukrainians, is unknown.

5 December 1944

Yesterday evening I came by car to Kolomyya [200 km southeast of Drohobych, 100 km southwest of Buchach. That is where Petrykevych's wife and children were living since they evacuated Buchach]. After all sorts of events in the city of Drohobych, I was fired on 1 December, and, having received a pass from the NKVD, went by rail to Stanyslaviv. But there was no connection to Kolomyya, so I got on a car to Kolomyya. But the car drove only to Nadvirna and left us there. The next day I reached Kolomyya by car. On the way, I saw many villages whose huts were destroyed and burned down. In Kolomyya, I went to the municipality, but there were no positions for me as yet. I was told to come back in a week.

It is said that the Banderites and some Vlasovites[101] are operating in the mountains. The roads are not safe. From Nadvirna we had driven via Delyatyn [Polish: Delatyn], because the road through Krasna is dangerous.

Thirty railcars with children and women have come from the eastern regions [of Ukraine] to Kolomyya. The difficult food conditions in Ukraine and the devastation left by the Germans are forcing them to seek rescue in Galicia.

Compared to Drohobych, Kolomyya is 20 to 25 percent cheaper, depending on the product. It seems that there are more goods here.

8 December 1944

As for the Banderites, some are telling horrifying things about them: that there are many of them in the forests, that masses of young people flock to them, that they have artillery and tanks; others are somewhat skeptical about them, noting: "Ukraine cannot be built in the forests." It is said that the Banderites killed two or three "Soviets" or locals serving the Soviet government. All those rumors are unverified and unreliable.

11 December 1944

I have now begun teaching at a Russian secondary school on Copernicus Street [in Kolomyya]. I teach eighteen hours a week in grades 5 to 7. The classes are small, with six to twelve students from all over the Soviet Union. The teachers complain about discipline. The school is attended by boys and girls.

16 December 1944

Yesterday a comrade lectured in the theater on the topic "Ukrainian Nationalists and Hitler." The lecture had a propagandistic character. Interestingly, the speaker said that [Ukrainian nationalist leader Yevhen] Konovalets was killed by the Germans themselves.[102]

Yesterday there was a big deportation to the east of those who had worked with the Germans or whose menfolk had evacuated with the Germans.

20 December 1944

The deportation railcars are back. This time, they are here for the Poles who have elected to go to Poland (there are up to three thousand people). They will be taken to the west in batches.

People are filled with dread when word arrives that the railcars are ready. Everyone is afraid.

It is said that there are sixteen to seventeen thousand Banderites. Entire villages have gone to the mountains instead of being conscripted into the Soviet Army. Under interrogation, prisoners declare that they are fighting for "independent Ukraine," but this does not prevent them from being shot. The "Appeal to the Population of Western Ukraine" [to welcome Soviet rule] has reappeared.

22 December 1944

Overnight, 200–250 armed men in 50–60 carts attacked the mill at Pyadyky (Polish: Piadyki) and took away all the flour (forty tons). Then they went to the brewery and took all the beer. The watchman was killed.

Overnight, someone killed an NKVD official.

1 January 1945

Today is New Year's Day. All institutions are celebrating. Yesterday in school there was a Christmas tree for the students. As usual, the principal made a speech and there was a performance by an amateur club. Our thoughts concern the future: will the war end in 1945, when will our grief and misery come to an end?

Last year was a turning point in the World War. The German armies were crushed, the East was liberated from the invaders, any chance of a German victory was eliminated. Germany can expect what it deserves. And what will happen to Ukraine? When his fellow countrymen complained about our tragic situation, [Ukrainian historian and nationalist activist Mykhailo] Hrushevsky said: "Ukraine has been, is and will be." Twice already our short-sighted politicians had linked the future of Ukraine with Germany. That was a fatal mistake, because the Germans did everything to disown our people and aroused their hatred. Thousands of innocents executed, others tortured in prisons, the land plundered, the cities destroyed: the ruin of the people and the country is the work of the Germans. What common path do we have, what do we share?

As expected, the Galician-Bukovynian[103] conception of Ukraine has failed completely. West Ukraine has united with its mainland and will endure its future destiny with it. This is a historical process that nothing can hold back. And although our people live in difficult conditions, the story is not over. The east has just begun to live, and it is not possible to predict where this evolution will turn. There is no doubt that when Ukraine finds itself in conditions favorable to the development of its national existence, its relations with its neighbors will determine whether it is prepared for state independence or must live in the Soviet Union with other peoples. As long as Ukraine does not have the capacity to develop, to create the preconditions for a viable state, all its impulses and efforts will end in failure. Galicia is not enough to give direction to the whole of Ukraine. The worldview of the Galicians was formed differently from that of the Ukrainians of the eastern regions.

Last year also decided the fate of the Poles in West Ukraine. The Poles, as a dominant nation, ceased to exist and to oppress us. It is not known whether they will, in general, live in West Ukraine, or will be expelled to Poland. Sic transit gloria. Skeptics say: "The Poles are heading to the west, while we Galician are going to the east." The destiny of both nations is unfathomable. But this is what the pessimists say.

4–6 January 1945

A conference of the city's teachers took place. It was directed by the head of the city council. Many teachers and principals were reproached ... .

One issue was not mentioned: the terrible life and living conditions of the teacher. They forgot about it.

The conference sent a letter to Stalin, with a statement of fidelity and love.

Our teacher B., a Pole, has been jailed. It is said that many Poles in Galicia were imprisoned (in Lviv). There is some conspiracy among them. It is impossible to verify whether this is mere gossip.

16 January 1945

A teacher has arrived from the eastern regions [of Ukraine]. She will be teaching Ukrainian in the Russian school; I will teach German.

18 January 1945

I will record here a small but characteristic detail of our time. The glass on my lamp broke. Replacing it cost me more than I earn in three days ... .

21 January 1945

Yesterday afternoon a theology student was hanged in the main city square. He was imprisoned by the Germans in Pechenizhyn [Polish: Peczeniżyn, 14 km west of Kolomyya], and then joined the Banderites. He was wearing Hutsul [Carpathian ethnic group] garb. Today (Sunday) his corpse is still hanging, and they say it will hang for a few more days.

22 January 1945

Yesterday NKVD men led fifty to sixty young Banderite trainees through the city. The lads were wearing [Ukrainian nationalist] "mazepinka" caps and had embroidered tridents [Ukrainian national symbol] on their chests.[104] A young woman marched in the front.

It is said that the hanged man had collected money for a Soviet tank as head of the village council and handed over the money collected (a large sum) to the Banderites.

26 January 1945

At night, toward morning, we heard two explosions, like a bomb or artillery fire. At school, the comrades said that two bridges had been blown up near Stanyslaviv. It is unknown who blew them up. Some said it was the Banderites, others that it was the Poles.

11 February 1945

The police have arrested two teachers and two or three students ...

11 March 1945

It turned out that the son of a teacher had hidden weapons. He escaped; his mother was imprisoned. The second teacher (the first teacher's brother) was released from prison .... It is said that by June or the end of June all Poles must leave Kolomyya to the west. Hence this week the pastor's sermon reproached those who present themselves as Poles so as to go to the west!

Today, the priest appealed to the people to help their countrymen [who were deported] from Peremyshl and its region. These people had to leave everything behind to save their lives and traveled from their native land to come here to the east.[105]

14 March 1945

Yesterday our school commemorated [Ukrainian national poet Taras] Shevchenko with a modest ceremony.

Again, three students from school No. 1 were imprisoned. Five students from the pedagogical school and four from school No. 2 were also imprisoned.

28 March 1945

Taking advantage of the recess after the end of the third quarter, I will mention something about our living conditions. They are really horrible. Ultimately, no one is interested in our living conditions, nobody pays attention to them, no one speaks about them, although we are all tormented and tortured by them. The past winter was very difficult: there was no fuel and no light .... I slept with Bohdan in an unheated room ... I went to sleep early, because there was no light ....

And food? Although we receive ration cards, no one can survive on them ... I have not heard anyone mention our condition at meetings or rallies, nor have I read any articles or announcements about it; you get a salary and do whatever you want with that money. My wife and I work, and my mother-in-law has a small pension, but we cannot make ends meet. On some days for breakfast we drink black coffee without sugar and eat a piece of bread, for lunch we eat potatoes and beans, and for dinner we have again what we had for lunch or breakfast. We rarely see a piece of meat, sometimes milk .... Teachers earn less than a woodcutter or a washerwoman .... In the past, teachers could survive on offering private lessons, and parents brought wood to the teachers in winter, but now all this has come to an end ....

Buying clothes or shoes is unthinkable. What will happen when they are completely worn is impossible to imagine! ...

Government officials, and especially teachers, are terribly malnourished. They go hungry without knowing what to expect. We live in the midst of devastation and graveyards (left behind by the Germans). There are only a few state stores, and everything needs to be bought on the free market, but with what? Maybe a change will happen when the war ends, but it has not happened yet. For now, we are in great trouble.

People often ask: if the Soviet armies are winning such glorious victories, and the value of the Soviet currency is falling, why are all the goods more expensive?[106] How can this be explained?

1 April 1945

For several days now the sound of guns can sometimes be heard in the daytime, such as the rattle of a machine gun. It's at a distance of 5 to 10 km. It's not known who is shooting. Yesterday afternoon there was the sound of anti-aircraft fire.

17 April 1945

Today at school it was said that units of the 4th Front were dispatched to destroy the Banderites. Yesterday, some of the tanks of this front drove through the city.

22 April 1945

Since morning gun fire can be heard from a distance of no more than 5 to 8 km.

27 April 1945

It is said that Soviet units captured eight hundred Banderites.

29 April 1945

I have been fired from my position as a teacher at the Russian school. The reason is lack of discipline in the classroom. The Russian school gave me the sack because of the behavior of my students. In my entire life I have never seen such students.

8 May 1945

As of today, I have been transferred to school No. 4 (Polish).

9 May 1945

Early today we learned that yesterday Germany surrendered and that the war ended. Great joy, a rally, a day off from school, a parade, festivities.

Postwar in Kolomyya

20 May 1945

In the villages typhus and scabies epidemics are spreading and taking many lives. These are the consequences of war and poor living conditions.

I go out to the street. NKVD men armed with loaded weapons are leading a group of forty to fifty people. Who are these people? Banderites or disobedient citizens? People are asking each other.

The government has once again issued an appeal to the Banderites and is giving them a deadline of 20 July to repent. Will this help? Under the current conditions why is this Banderite insurgency [banderivsh-china] occurring?[107]

25 May 1945

At around noon there was gunfire. Are these shots at Banderites? They say they again killed several NKVD men. The retribution by the NKVD is to worsen the treatment of imprisoned peasants ....

16 July 1945

It is said that after the 20th things will go badly for local Ukrainians, even those not involved with the Banderites: they will be sent east.

In Stanyslaviv, a Jewish woman gave a loaf of bread to the German POWs working there. They ate the bread, and they all died: the bread was poisoned.

Though the war has ended, there is suffering and privation among the working people: there is no bread, no money; there is nothing to cook, everything is expensive, all of it beyond a teacher's means .... None of us eat, we have all dried up. Some people keep talking about political change, but they are deceiving themselves ....

Who can live and subsist today? Anyone who has a farm, several acres of land, a pretty garden, a cow, a pig, a goat. Well, all sorts of merchants are living well—speculators, traders, peddlers, and so on. Those who have a state office, but who have a side income, or engage in fraud or just theft ... can live. But teaching! ... No one wonders what we eat, whether we have any clothes or shoes ....

People who travel for various reasons say that in the villages in the Carpathian region there are numerous troops, soldiers are positioning artillery, digging ditches, etc. It is clear that the authorities are serious about eliminating the Banderites ....

9 August 1945

Yesterday at 10 p.m. the Soviet Union declared war on Japan.

14 August 1945

Japan has capitulated.

23 August 1945

Polish school No. 4 has been closed down because the Poles are going to Poland. Since the 20th I have been working at the forestry Engineering school (which was established this year).

The departing Poles are selling furniture, libraries, etc., very cheaply for these times. But the wage-earners who need these things most cannot afford to buy them. They are bought by people with gardens, speculators, etc.

26 August 1945

So far, thirty-three students have applied to our school. The principal sends teachers to other areas to campaign for our school. In the district of Kolomyya, parents are brought together and encouraged to send their children to our school.

29 August 1945

In Kolomyya there are fugitives ... telling horrifying stories about how the Poles treat our people. Polish gangs rob and murder and attack people, shoot them, loot, kill even children.[108] It is strange that the Soviet authorities do not interfere and do not punish the perpetrators. The people on the left bank of the San leave their land and flee to the east ....

1 September 1945

According to the newspapers we receive, altogether twenty-six million people were killed in the German concentration camps. Most were killed in the Dachau camp. Twelve to fourteen thousand people were killed every day, and on 10 June 1944, twenty-four thousand people were killed. So, this is the "culture" of the twentieth century!

1 November 1945

... When Soviet Power came in 1939, everywhere the official written and spoken language in government offices and institutions was Ukrainian. Today all this has changed in favor of Russian. On the street you rarely hear Ukrainian. Ukrainians from the eastern regions of Ukraine or Russians speak Russian. Our school is Ukrainian. But we have teachers who know only Russian and teach in it .... All instructions, certificates, and so on, are written in Russian .... The Ukrainian language has therefore been pushed to the background, although the institution in which we work is Ukrainian and the clerical work should be in the Ukrainian language. The accountant, the cashier, all use Russian. It is the same in other institutions: in banks, transportation, mail, Russian is heard more often than Ukrainian.

7–8 November 1945

The anniversary of the October Revolution. We had dinner for students and teachers, then festivities. On the second day there was a trip and a rally. Most importantly, we received food cards for 6 kilograms of meat at the state price (8 karbovanets per 1 kilogram) ....

Again, they are talking about Banderites who attacked a train somewhere, attacked a leather factory in Stanyslaviv and took the leather, destroyed Bolshevik monuments, and placed crosses in their place.

The Bolsheviks wanted to remove the crosses, but they were boobytrapped and one or two people were killed. This story needs to be verified.

1 December 1945

... It is said that Banderites in Stanyslaviv attacked a jail and released all prisoners. The head teacher said he had been told that the Banderites send their people to the school to listen to the teachers' lectures to the students. If a teacher praises Soviet Russia, he will be punished for it.

23 December 1945

Although half a year has passed since the end of the war, the lives of working people have not improved. Everything is still very expensive, and there are no goods in the state stores ....

31 December 1945

Today we buried the deputy principal of the school. This young man had recently been discharged from the army and began working in our school. Yesterday or the day before yesterday he drove to Ispas [14 km south of Kolomyya] to bring firewood for the school. In front of a bridge the vehicle came under fire by four Banderites or bandits (the villages are now full of bandits). The deputy principal was mortally wounded in the head; the driver was wounded in his finger. The driver was allowed to run off and the car was set on fire, but only the driver's cabin burned down.

1 January 1946

We have no joy in greeting the new year. Will our future be easier? Will life be possible? Will a person feel like a human being? Many promises are made, much verbiage, but what will be the reality? The war destroyed all properties, all savings, cities, regions—will the rule of law be reestablished, will the wounds be healed? Will there be real peace and security in the land?

When will we no longer live like beggars? When will the extreme poverty that torments us come to an end?

9 February 1946

A wave of arrests. It is unknown whether this is because of the elections that will take place tomorrow, that is, on 10 February, or for another reason. The prisoners include several members of cooperatives, a few teachers, and seven actors. Everyone is filled with fear: who's next? In the villages the persecution is even more terrible. At the gate of the NKGB (Soviet state security) prison many people stand every day with food or other necessities for their imprisoned husbands or relatives.[109]

The authorities have launched a great deal of propaganda around the elections. Almost all intellectuals are included in the list of agitators. Everywhere there are posters and leaflets.

3 March 1946

Five of those arrested have died: two teachers, one engineer, two theater workers. The rest were released. They say that the prison is infested with lice. The five deceased likely died from typhus.

Why they were imprisoned—no one knows yet.

9 May 1946

The first anniversary of the victory over Germany. Although a year has passed since the victory [... missing lines ...] .... Six hundred people have died from disease (especially typhus), ... [figures missing] 00 people were imprisoned, and up to six hundred were killed.

This is a very dry spring: there has still been no rain. Crops are not sown, and if they are, they do not grow because of the drought. People are grumbling now that everything will be expensive and that there will be nothing to eat ....

4 June 1946

Today I finally received my salary for April. No one was interested in how we made ends meet this month! Unprecedented poverty! ...

20 June 1946

In the Soviet Union, two kinds of prices exist side-by-side: the state prices and those of the market. The difference between them can be dozens of times higher, even a hundred times or more. For example, a newspaper costs 20 kopecks by subscription. But in the market, the same newspaper sells for 2 karbovanets. The peasants buy it, not in order to read it, but to use it instead as paper for rolling cigarettes. But newspapers are hard to come by: in front of the stores there are long lines, since there are not enough copies for everyone ... You can buy a local and regional paper, but it is difficult to buy a newspaper from the capital.

5 July 1946

The exams are over. This year altogether 272 students enrolled in the technical school; of them 102 first-year students took the exam ... Only 68 passed the exam [and] 34 students failed ... This is due to the difficult conditions of work and, in general, the difficult conditions of existence ... Some students were barefoot, weary, and hungry. The dorms were a horror. In the school since the new year, the hall was not heated as the firewood had vanished. The doors had no handles, and some window-panes were missing ... The teachers and students were malnourished and freezing. At home and in the dorms, there was no light or heat. In the dorms there was no bucket or pan.[110] Sheets were not changed during the second semester: dirt, bad temper. There were no notebooks, no paper, no chalk. All year long we wrote on the board with pieces of broken plaster. The students wrote on the other side of sheets of paper used in Austrian or Polish times. The food was very meagre, insufficient to survive. There were no books, of course—just one book for the teacher.

Let's hope that next year will be better.

24 July 1946

Many people came to Kolomyya from Bessarabia. They were selling carpets and lambskins. Others went to the villages and asked for bread. We were told that there was a terrible famine in Bessarabia, that this year nothing was growing, because the drought had destroyed everything. People were merciful and gave what they could. Suddenly yesterday a rumor spread that the Bessarabians engaged in cannibalism and killed two or three children; the police detained many of them. They have already vanished from the bazaar.[111] ...

14 October 1946

An impossible existence—we live in permanent malnutrition, a half-starved existence. There is not enough bread, no flour, groats, fat, even potatoes. We eat just enough so as not to die of hunger. Everything is worn out and torn, but there is nothing new to buy. Worst of all are shoes. In the Russian school I received a coupon for boots. But they have not been made yet. When the yard is flooded, I walk in German wooden clogs; my wife is even worse, she has holes in her boots, and each boot belongs to another pair, one higher than the other. We are wearing our only remaining clothes. What will happen next?

24 October 1946

Although the government claims to have destroyed the German-Ukrainian nationalists, Banderites, etc., they still show up every once in a while. Somewhere they kill a representative of Soviet Power, then they gather the villagers and some nationalist makes a speech against the Soviet government, then they distribute leaflets against Stalin and hand out their anti-Soviet newspaper. Today, the head teacher assembled the staff and said that the authorities had noticed that German-Ukrainian nationalist ideas were spreading among the school youth. In their homework they show sympathy for the German-Ukrainian nationalists. This must be countered. We should examine all books about the Germans. Check the students' bags [for such materials]. Every class must demonstrate the superiority of the socialist system over the capitalist one. In each group, we must appoint an activist head youth who will inform the teacher about everything. In general, we must strengthen our ideological work ....

17 December 1946

It's now -20 degrees [-4 Fahrenheit]. The classrooms are unheated. There is no fuel, not even for the kitchen. Today, in some classes there were only one or two lessons. Our school is sad, unwelcoming, gloomy. Today, automobiles with students went to the forest to fetch firewood ....

Although it is freezing, we do not heat the rooms. There is a fire only in the kitchen. I am getting tired of ever more poverty! We groan in unheated rooms.

Our food is scant and uniform. In fact, we eat just once a day: lunch. Usually, we eat soup, potatoes, a piece of meat. Early in the evening there is coffee colored with white milk and a piece of bread. We have forgotten when we last had sugar in our coffee. ...

1 January 1947

Pessimistic about the future. We hear that instead of improving—things are getting worse. Food products are more expensive, and the threat of hunger looms over us. We often hear it said: we will die of hunger. ...

7 January 1947

[Greek Catholic] Christmas. For four days we have not received any bread at all.

26 January 1947

These days it is difficult to receive medical treatment. In the pharmacy most medicines are lacking ...

9 February 1947

Today we have elections to the Supreme Soviet of the USSR. The elections are well prepared. Agitation [propaganda] points are identified, agitators are allotted to the streets, rallies are arranged. Kolomyya candidate General Halitskiy will, of course, receive all the votes. One Union, one leader, one list of candidates for deputies ....

20 February 1947

From my brother's letter, I learned that my sister Julia died on 7 February. She was seventy years old ... I could not attend the funeral because I found out about her death only two weeks later.

In the school several members of the staff (the librarian, the cashier, cooks), and one of our teachers, were arrested for fraud concerning bread ration cards. The results of the investigation will show whether this was slander or true.

P.S. Within a few days, apart from the cashier who escaped from prison, everyone was released (but the teacher G. was re-arrested).

10 March 1947

Everyday life is ever harder. It is inadequate to say that there is not enough to eat—we are hungry. I cannot afford to buy bread; it is too expensive .... And my salary has not changed .... At the market you can buy everything, but the prices are too high for our salary ....

13 April 1947

Easter Holiday, and we are starving. There is no bread ... no meat, no milk. I bought a few potatoes and flour for bread. We are so exhausted and weak that we suffer from headaches ... Black thoughts come to mind. Famine! What is the way out, how will we be saved? ...

1 August 1947

Between 25–31 July I was in the city hospital with a dystrophy (hunger). But how can the hospital help me, when they cannot provide milk, fat, or meat? ...

5 October 1947

How are things now? Is there still hunger? This year brought an unprecedented harvest. So, there is no hunger as there was in the spring .... Prices have fallen, but they are still high enough to make life impossible. This year I had enough apples: I exchanged them for newspapers in the market. I recovered a little and then was eating potatoes with apples .... We all worked hard—most of all my wife—but there are just potatoes, beets, beans, tomatoes, and the like. We don't need to buy all this in the market [i.e., they were growing them in their own garden].

19 October 1947

There was heavy snow that destroyed many trees, breaking their branches. Trees that still had leaves broke from the weight of the snow.

22 October 1947

Yesterday there was a big deportation. Today, at school, comrades from the eastern regions said that thirty families were taken from the city. Those of the eastern regions, who do not have apartments, are appealing to the municipality to acquire apartments that had belonged to the deported families.

There were even larger deportations from the villages. A peasant from Isakiv [Polish: Isaków, 40 km northeast of Kolomyya] reported that sixty families were taken from there ....

12 November 1947

Fifteen bodies of Banderites were brought to Kolomyya. They were killed in fighting with NKVD men in the area of Tovmachyk [Polish: Tłumaczek, 16 km miles northwest of Kolomyya].

25 December 1947

In the city cemetery near the old church stood the grave of a Rifleman [like Petrykevych, a member of the Ukrainian legions of World War I and the Polish-Ukrainian War of 1919], who was buried there in 1920. The Bolsheviks called him a Banderite (!). The authorities ordered the grave to be dug up. Yesterday and the day before, our students and college students worked there, in the evening and at night.

There is news that the graves of Riflemen are being dug up in the villages. The people are very angry about this ....

1 January 1948

What will the new year bring us? When will our misery end? The monetary reform and the transition to open trade have somewhat reduced the prices of some commodities, but these changes are far from improving our lives. Milk and butter are cheaper ...; bread ... can be purchased in stores, but there is no sugar, flour, or groats. And long lines form in front of the store with manufactured goods already at 5 or 6 a.m., or even earlier. It's hard to satisfy people's desire to buy essentials: everyone is crowding in, there are no clothes, shoes, utensils, etc.

2 May 1948

Easter, a state holiday. How do we live? Compared to last year, when we were in terrible shape and starving and ate nettles in the spring, life is better: we do not eat nettles, we still have potatoes, although our stock is about to run out ... But in the state stores there is no fat, no sugar, and it is necessary to buy them in the market ... By and large only potatoes, corn, and wheat ... are cheap enough for a teacher to be able to buy. These make up our main food ....

1 July 1948

School graduation. The first graduating class. Eighteen students sought to gain a diploma (one of them was ill and did not receive his diploma).

There were 172 students in the three courses, two of whom did not pass the exams. Local students are at most only 15 percent of the student body. There are no local girls ....

And what about the language of instruction, what about Ukrainianization [of instruction]? ... Nothing has happened. All technical subjects are taught in Russian; all office work and accounting are written in Russian; the principal writes instructions and speaks also in Russian, likewise, the teachers. We are only two local teachers, a teacher of chemistry teaching in Ukrainian [and Petrykevych]. Head teacher Nykolayenko, a Ukrainian, speaks and writes in Russian ....

12–14 August 1948

I have finally visited Buchach. I traveled with some difficulty to Tyshkivtsi [Polish: Tyszkowce] and from there had to continue on foot [since the distance would be 50 km this seems unlikely; perhaps he meant Trybukhivts, Polish: Trybuchowce, 7 km away]. I inspected my house: in the cellar the owner keeps a cow and three pigs. I went to the rayon [district] executive committee and made a statement requesting the transfer of the house [to his ownership]. The head of the executive committee told me that the house would not be returned, because it had been more than three years [since Petrykevych left it].

The city itself is totally ruined. The street leading to the station is the most severely damaged. All my belongings: furniture, books, etc. have disappeared. Some of them were kept in the cellar of the monastery and have disappeared from there ....

1 January 1949

We enter the new year with much uncertainty. Clouds are gathering on the political horizon, there are tensions between the USSR and the capitalist states .... The newspapers report about the instigators of a new world war.

In the meantime, we continue to lead a difficult life (we are becoming used to it). Products are cheaper .... But it's a miserable existence; I can't afford to buy shoes. My two children are studying at the medical institute.

There are citizens who are convinced that they will be deported. They are always nervous, at night they cannot sleep, the sound of a passing car sets them running. They spread all sorts of rumors, exaggerate trivial facts, and draw wild conclusions from anything they hear on the radio ....

8 July 1949

The nationalist underground has once again made its presence felt. Two or three weeks ago a blue-and-yellow [Ukrainian] flag appeared on the ruins of the gymnasium in Kolomyya. The same happened in some villages. In Spas [Polish: Ispas, 12 km south of Kolomyya], a leaflet was left at the door of each house with a caricature of the leader [Stalin] and corresponding content. In another village, the underground hanged the head of the village council, and in another, the village council head was sentenced to death. There is no peace in the villages. People are hoping for change, and some of the peasants, the [wealthier] kulaks, are hostile to the collective farms ....

30 October 1949

Today a rally of workers celebrating the reunification [of Ukraine] was held on the square near the city council. There were, of course, speeches and greetings. A telegram was sent to Comrade Stalin. The rally lasted two hours. The store had white bread for the occasion of the holiday. But the line was so long that I could not buy any.

21 December 1949

There is great fear among the townspeople. Everyone says that towns-people will be deported to Siberia ....

12 March 1950

Today we had elections to the Supreme Soviet of the [Soviet] Union and the Upper Soviet of Nationalities. At 5 a.m., the agitators (I am an agitator of Lysenko Street) had to be at their agitation center, and then went to their streets and prompted voters [to vote]. At 6 a.m. the elections began. Next to the room where the voting takes place there is a room with a buffet, then a hall where amateur artists perform, the voters dance, etc. Vehicles transport the elderly and the handicapped. Everywhere there is movement, people are rushing about, there is excitement everywhere. There will probably be 99 percent participation in the elections.

11 April 1950

Today, the city's general secretary Makarets presented an interesting report on Ukrainian nationalists. After speaking about their origins ...

he went on to their misdeeds in Kolomyya. Nationalist cells were created among the school youth last year. At school No. 2, a certain student called Pitak formed a nationalist organization .... They had a typewriter and distributed leaflets .... The authorities exposed their activities and they were sentenced to prison (twenty-five years). In the school, twelve members of the organization were punished.

21 June 1950

Bread is again hard to come by. Early in the morning there are long lines in the stores. There is not enough bread for everyone.

1 July 1950

Yesterday at school No. 2 graduation certificates were awarded and the occasion was to be celebrated with a ball. But someone was handing out anti-government leaflets in front of a distribution line on the street. The police took away the leaflets and the ball did not take place.

A red flag has again appeared on the ruins of the burned-down gymnasium.

1 August 1950

I went to Buchach, where a court considered the case of my house. The prosecutor declined to return the house to me, because I had appealed to the court in 1950, six years too late. ...

1 January 1951

The issue that concerns everyone is what will the new year bring us: peace or a third world war? The Soviet Union and all progressive humanity are at peace. But the enemies of peace are also powerful and, wherever they can, they pursue hostile policies.

10 April 1951

It is said that a large deportation just took place. The deported were members of the Baptist sect. Other people mistrustful of Soviet power were also deported. They say that seventy-two railcars (with twenty-five to thirty people each) went to the east ....

[1952]

During the last schoolyear, 1951–52, I worked (six hours weekly) in the evening school and with the money I earned there I bought myself an autumn coat and some clothes ....

22 February 1953

The elections to the local councils have been unbelievably successful: 99 percent cast their votes for the official list of candidates. Such unity is possible only in the Soviet Union.

5 March 1953

On 5 March at 9:50 p.m. Stalin, the maker of the socialist state, died of a stroke—he was one of the greatest people of the twentieth century.

9 March 1953

Today at noon Stalin was buried.

In our churches prayers and sermons were held, in which his love of peace and commitment to the working people were praised ....

28 June 1953

We are undergoing a new Ukrainization. In mid-June, newspapers reported that the Central Committee of the Communist Party of Soviet Ukraine had declared that the first secretary of the Central Committee [Leonid] Melnikov had distorted the Leninist-Stalinist national party policy in order to Russify the entire state apparatus in the western regions, and that people from the eastern regions had been appointed to leadership positions in the western regions. Melnikov was dismissed from the position of secretary and replaced by [Oleksy] Kyrychenko.[112]

The reality is that Russian dominates government offices, courtrooms, institutions. Our technical school ostensibly uses Ukrainian, but in fact everything is in Russian—administration, accounting, diplomas, and so on. All assemblies of students, speeches, and reports are in Russian. Of the teachers (fourteen people) only four teach in Ukrainian. The students in many classes do not know any Ukrainian, having come here from Russian regions; even some Ukrainians, starting from Principal Zherdova, teach in Russian, because that was the language of instruction at the institute [where they had studied]; hence they know Russian terminology and it is easier for them to use Russian than Ukrainian, whose own terminology they don't know. Our students are accustomed to Russian and the graduates prefer diplomas in Russian. Among the subjects of the class in general education, Russian language and literature occupy the first place.

Therefore, within two days of becoming head of personnel in the technical school, [the newly appointed] Kovalev ordered all slogans to be written in Ukrainian or in both languages and instructed that as of the next school year all subjects would be taught in Ukrainian. Those teachers who do not know Ukrainian must learn it.

Kovalev said that although the language will change, the ideological direction will remain the same. Kovalev himself spoke in Russian.

What brought about this change? They say that the Central Committee of the Communist Party in Moscow received hundreds of appeals from the western regions of Ukraine complaining that while under Austria we had German, and under Poland it was Polish, now we have the Russian language. But this is probably just a guess. Perhaps the reason for this is deeper—the national issue [in the USSR as a whole].

Yet in my opinion, Ukrainian will be recognized here only when it becomes part of everyday life in the eastern regions [of Ukraine], and when it is used consistently and not only on occasion ....

10 July 1953

Today the newspapers reported that the Plenum of the Central Committee of the Communist Party of the Soviet Union had dismissed [Stalin's fearsome long-term chief of the NKVD, Lavrentiy] Beria from the position of member of the Central Committee of the CPSU and expelled him from the CPSU as an enemy of the Communist Party and the Soviet people.

The Presidium of the Supreme Soviet of the USSR dismissed L. Beria from the position of Deputy Chairman of the Council of Ministers of the USSR, and from the position of Minister of the Interior of the USSR; the case of Beria's criminal actions has been referred to the Supreme Court of the USSR.[113] ...

25 December 1953

... The case of my house in Buchach has already been resolved: I completely lost it .... I was called before a city party committee and a government official explained to me that it was impossible [for Petrykevych to regain the house] and advised me to discontinue the case. ...

21 March 1954

... Although it is the first day of spring, the fields are still covered with snow and the ground is frozen in the morning. This was a very severe winter. It was very hard to find fuel .... We suffered and froze a great deal. The potatoes in the cellar were frozen. We all lived in the same room ....

7–8 November 1954

Celebrating the October Revolution. A great parade. There is only black bread and it is difficult to come by. In the past it was possible to buy a few kilos of white wheat flour, but this year I could not buy a single kilogram: there are long lines for ration cards, and one must stand there for hours.

10 January 1955

What will this year bring us? In the postwar years, apparently, the world was not as threatened as it is now. The Paris and London decrees, ratified by the French and Italian parliaments, allow the remilitarization of West Germany. The arming of West Germany will greatly increase the danger of a world war, stop the unification of Germany, and accelerate the arms race between all states. The world is threatened.

1 May 1955

May is the holiday of the working people. What are our weekdays like? Compared to the year after Stalin's death, today it's harder to live. Clearly, this is all due to the political situation and the threat of world war. You can get bread in the morning, although there are long lines. But there is no sugar, flour, semolina, noodles, and if there is any, then the crowds are so thick that it is impossible to breathe .... There is no cloth, manufactured goods, or shoes in the stores. If they appear for a moment they immediately sell out. There is no meat either; it's rare for anyone to bring some home ....

3 July 1955

The peasants have no bread and go to buy it in the city. In front of the bread stores the lines stretch for a mile. There is chaos and disorder of a kind that I have not seen before. Recently a great rain- and hailstorm passed over the villages. The water tore down bridges and destroyed the mills. The people do not have grain to grind into flour, which is why there are so many lines for bread ....

12 July 1955

... all sorts of rumors are circulating, sometimes outright ridiculous, such as that Galicia will be handed over to Poland, and that the Germans will get Prussia and the provinces across the Oder from Poland. Who is spreading this nonsense? There are still a few Poles in Kolomyya, and they may be distorting the news they hear on American radio or just inventing them ....

13 August 1955

If a policeman keeps order during the distribution of bread, then things are not so bad. Today there was no policeman and there were unimaginable scenes. I was knocked down to the ground and was trampled and barely managed to get back on my feet. I did not get any bread. In the second store there was a policeman and I struggled and finally got some bread.

1 September 1955

The opening of the school year. Children, girls and boys, go to school decorated with flowers. I'm at the technical school this year. I will teach ... German to the third year. I found a job at a medical college, where I teach Latin in three classes ... and Ukrainian in one class ... Latin is taught only in the first semester ....

8 October 1955

After three years of waiting I was given a state apartment, consisting of a room and a kitchen on 4 Chervony [Red] Street ....

1956

Thanks to the wise policy of the Communist Party of the Soviet Union, we have reached a turning point in international politics. The cause of peace seems to have triumphed and the threat of a war has diminished. [Soviet Premier Nikolai] Bulganin and [First Secretary of the Communist Party of the USSR] Khrushchev's policy toward Asian states has been a great success. They have dealt a great blow to the colonial powers.

On 5 January my eldest brother Mykola died in Drohobych from a stroke and was buried on 7 January. I was at the funeral.

On 14–25 February, the 20th Congress of the Communist Party convened to discuss the sixth Five-Year Plan. The congress was a great, unprecedented success. The reports by Khrushchev and Bulganin took center stage. The citizens of Soviet Russia look confidently and boldly into the future.

2 June 1956

Molotov has been relieved of his duties as Minister of Foreign Affairs, a post he held for many years. There is hope for a change of policy ...

Priests, monks, and the like are returning from [deportation in] Siberia.

1 July 1956

The medical school has graduated 180 of its students: paramedics, nurses, midwives.

9 August 1956

I am ill with cardiac asthma [a symptom of congestive heart failure].

23 August 1956

[I was taken] to the hospital. There my condition improved a little, but I am still sick. On 10 August I left the hospital.

Added note:
Petrykevych Viktor Ivanovych
Born 13 January 1883 in Drohobych
Died on 14 October (Sunday)
At 6:30 p.m., 1956, in Kolomyya
from a hemorrhagic stroke [bleeding of the brain]
In eternal memory,
His son, Bohdan

Notes

Text and photograph courtesy of Bohdan Petrykevych. Transcribed and translated from Ukrainian by Sofia Grachova. Additional translation and editing by Elena Medvedev and Omer Bartov. The headings in this chapter were added by the editor in order to help readers orient themselves geographically. The dates were in the original manuscript.

1. Also known as the Westwall, this was a German defensive line built in the 1930s opposite the French Maginot Line along the border between the two countries.
2. Presumably the three districts making up the former eastern Galicia under interwar Polish rule, namely Lwów, Tarnopol, and Stanisławów (Ukrainian: Lviv, Ternopil, and Stanyslaviv).
3. Goering was Hitler's deputy, commander of the Luftwaffe, and minister in charge of the Four Year Plan.
4. These "volunteer units" were likely Ukrainian nationalist militias.
5. The full Latin phrase is "sic transit gloria mundi," meaning, "thus passes the glory of the world," traditionally used in Papal coronations and indicating the transitory nature of earthly powers and honors.
6. Marshal Kliment Voroshilov was a prominent military and political figure, former commissar for defense, member of the Soviet state defense committee, and member of the presidium of the central committee.
7. A historical province straddling the southeastern part of Galicia and the adjacent territories of Soviet Ukraine in the interwar period, now entirely in Ukraine.
8. Born in Brody, Galicia, Mond was a practicing Roman Catholic of Jewish extraction.
9. Sokół, meaning falcon, and Sokil, its Ukrainian counterpart, were patriotic nationalist youth organizations modeled after the Czech Sokol that promoted physical health and national values.
10. Under Polish rule public schools were mostly Polish or bilingual Polish-Ukrainian but dominated by Polish language and content. This led to the establishment of Ukrainian and Jewish private schools.
11. Molotov (1890–1986) served as minister of foreign affair between 1939–49; Kalinin (1875–1946) served as nominal head of state of the USSR from 1919 to his death; Khrushchev (1894–1971) was the long-term first secretary of Soviet Ukraine and succeeded Stalin, after his death in 1953, until his removal in 1964.
12. Korniychuk (1905–72) was a popular and much lauded Soviet playwright of Ukrainian origins; Stanisław Moniuszko (1819–72) was an admired Polish composer and conductor.
13. The Wehrmacht lost in fact between 10,000 and 16,000; Poland about 65,000.
14. On Romania and Hungary in World War II see Holly Case, *Between States: The Transylvanian Question and the European Idea during World War II* (Stanford, CA: Stanford University Press, 2009).
15. Franko (1856–1916) was a highly influential Ukrainian-Galician socialist and nationalist writer, poet, critic, and political activist.
16. See further on this in Jan T. Gross, *Revolution from Abroad: The Soviet Conquest of Poland's Western Ukraine and Western Belorussia*, expanded ed. (Princeton: Princeton University Press, 2002).
17. This was apparently a covert Soviet operation intended to legitimize a massive Red Army attack against Finland on 30 November.
18. All Soviet Ukrainian authors, mostly of peasant origins: Le (1895–1978) was a social realist writer; Kopylenko (1900–58) was known especially for his children's stories;

Holovko (1897–1972) was an acclaimed novelist; Usenko (1902–75) was a journalist and a poet.

19. Influential Russian playwright Ostrovsky (1823–86) wrote "The Storm" in 1859; it was made into a film by Vladimir Petrov, five-time winner of the Stalin Prize, in 1933.

20. The Red Army did in fact suffer heavy losses in Finland, and Germany was indeed preparing to attack the USSR.

21. The poet and journalist Teren Masenko (1903–1970) authored numerous poetry and essay anthologies glorifying everyday Soviet life, and is remembered especially for his verses for children, many of which were set to music by Ukrainian composers. The prolific Jewish writer and journalist Leonid Smiliansky (1904–1966) is known for his two-volume work on the poet Taras Shevchenko and a drama that was made into the 1956 film "Ivan Franko."

22. Kulaks in Russian or Kurkuls in Ukrainian refers to more affluent peasants (often by a very small margin) who actually or allegedly resisted Stalin's collectivization campaign or were perceived as enemies of the state and were deported to gulags.

23. The uprising in Czortków did in fact happen and to this day is lauded in Poland. See: https://www.tvp.info/35648734/pierwszy-zryw-zapomniana-historia-powstania-czortkowskiego.

24. Shevchenko (1814–61) was a Ukrainian poet, writer, and painter considered to be a key figure in the creation of modern Ukrainian letters and the modern Ukrainian language.

25. On this see Gross, *Revolution from Abroad* and Bartov, *Anatomy of a Genocide*, 129–57.

26. The so-called Molotov-Ribbentrop Pact was a non-aggression treaty between Nazi Germany and the USSR signed on 23 August 1939, by foreign ministers Molotov and Joachim von Ribbentrop. The treaty enabled Germany to invade Poland without Soviet interference and its secret protocol divided Eastern Europe between the two powers, which meant, inter alia, that Poland's eastern territories would come under Soviet rule.

27. Some words have been blotted out. Presumably people were searching for cloth to sew the blue-yellow Ukrainian national flag.

28. The word "terrible" must refer to some horrible event surrounding the withdrawal of the Soviets and the arrival of the Germans. Entries for the subsequent days likely reported anti-Jewish violence by local Ukrainians soon joined by the Germans (as described in detail in Moshe Wizinger's diary), as well as the Ukrainian nationalist attempt to seize power, and the discovery of the mass executions of mostly Ukrainian political activists incarcerated in the Chortkiv prison by the NKVD. Petrykevych's son Bohdan reported in an interview several decades later that the diary described how the Ukrainian population greeted the Germans, adding that his father became the director of the district education department in the Ukrainian nationalist "government" for some two months in 1941. This is confirmed in Nestor S. Myzak, *Za tebe, sviata Ukrayino* [For You, Holy Ukraine] (Chernivtsi: Bukovyna, 2004), vol. 4, 94–96 where the author lists the members of this Buczacz "government." This appears to have been the only time in Petrykevych's life when he was a person of regional importance beyond his role as a teacher.

29. On the events of the "bloody Sunday" massacre in Stanisławów on 12 October 1941, in which up to twelve thousand Jews were murdered, see Dieter Pohl, "Hans Krueger and the Murder of the Jews in the Stanisławów Region (Galicia)," *Yad Vashem Studies* 26 (1998): 239–65, and https://www.yadvashem.org/odot_pdf/Microsoft%20Word%20-%202292.pdf

30. On the "winter collection" of clothes for the Wehrmacht from the Jews see Wizinger's account.

31. Lasch was removed from office as governor of Galicia in January 1942 and arrested on charges of corruption. He was convicted by the Sondergericht Breslau in May 1942 and executed in his cell on Heinrich Himmler's order on 3 June 1942.

32. The Hutsuls are an ethnic group in the Carpathian regions of Ukraine and Romania.

33. On this see also Bartov, *Anatomy of a Genocide*, 216.

34. The Banderites are known as Banderowcy in Polish and Banderivtsi in Ukrainian.

35. Kubiyovych (1900–85) was a geographer of mixed Polish-Ukrainian background, a Ukrainian nationalist activist who supported cooperation with Germany during World War II, and a proponent of Ukrainian culture and independence in postwar exile in France. Bisanz (1890–1951) was a military officer in World War I and the Ukrainian Galician Army, who closely collaborated with the German occupation in World War II, commanded the Waffen-SS "Galicia" Division, and was arrested and subsequently executed by the Soviets. Hlebovitsky (1904–?) was a Ukrainian Galician journalist, editor, religious and public figure, who emigrated to Germany after the war and disappeared in 1947. On the Ukrainian Central Committee see further in the Internet Encyclopedia of Ukraine: http://www.encyclopediaofukraine. com/display.asp?linkpath=pages%5CU%5CK%5CUkrainianCentralCommittee.htm

36. Wächter (1901–49) was a veteran Austrian-German Nazi, who succeeded Lasch as governor of Galicia in January 1942 and retained this position until the loss of the province to the Soviets in July 1944.

37. The name was blotted out in the diary. Bandera (1909–59) cultivated ties with Nazi Germany, was arrested by the Gestapo when he declared Ukrainian independence after the German invasion of the USSR, and remained an influential radical nationalist leader during the war and later in exile until his assassination by the KGB. He is still revered by Ukrainian nationalists especially in West Ukraine.

38. Melnyk (1890–1964) was the more moderate head of the OUN, from which Bandera split in 1940, and was largely overshadowed by the latter during the war. He played an important role in promoting Ukrainian nationalism in exile after the war.

39. The Landkommissar was mostly charged with developing the economy of his county to the benefit of the German occupiers.

40. A famous Greek Catholic pilgrimage center about 25 kilometers north of Buchach.

41. In a footnote Petrykevych adds: "It is said that an anonymous denunciation by a Pole from Monastyryska led to his imprisonment." A later note adds: "On 19 October Chaikivskyi was released from prison thanks to the intervention of his friend, the Landkommissar." Petrykevych uses the name in its Russian version, Mikhail Chaikovsky. See also Bartov, *Anatomy of a Genocide*, 355–56, n. 58.

42. This was the first action, or roundup of the Jews of Buchach, in which approximately 1,600 Jews were transported by train to the Bełżec extermination camp near the Polish-Ukrainian border and several hundred killed on the streets and in their homes.

43. Note by Petrykevych: "They say that Polish saboteurs blew up two buildings with Germans in Warsaw. They [the local Poles] were released ten days later."

44. This was the second "action" in Buchach in which some two thousand Jews were deported to Bełżec or shot in their homes and on the streets.

45. Note by Petrykevych: "It is said that among the executed in Chortkiv was Hanushevsky, director of the dairy, who had spent some time in Buchach as chief of police and then as a prosecutor. (A hybrid!)." Petrykevych seems to imply that Hanushevsky worked for both sides, the Germans and the Ukrainian underground.

46. Andrei Sheptytsky (1865–1944), was the Metropolitan Archbishop of the Ukrainian Greek Catholic Church from 1901 to his death; a Ukrainian nationalist who welcomed the Germans in 1941, he protested against the murder of the Jews, encouraged his clergy to help them, and himself sheltered many Jews. See, e.g., Shimon Redlich, "Metropolitan Andrei Sheptyts'kyi," 39–51.
47. Apparently, the reference here is to the prewar Ukrainian underground OUN.
48. The railroad bridge and tunnel were rebuilt with Jewish forced labor.
49. On the nature of the shootings and the largely but not entirely false claims of local Christian attempts to help their Jewish neighbors, see Bartov, *Anatomy of a Genocide*, esp. 232–62, 277–84, 289–95.
50. The Roman Catholic Church follows the Gregorian calendar while the Greek Catholic and Orthodox Churches follow the Julian calendar.
51. This was the third "action" in Buchach, in which approximately two thousand Jews were shot on Fedor Hill.
52. The UPA was formed in late 1942 as the armed branch of the OUN-B and was engaged primarily in ethnic cleansing of the Poles in the provinces of Volhynia and Galicia and later in an insurgency against the returning Soviets. Its fighters included former Ukrainian policemen and members of the auxiliary police units that supported the German genocide of the Jews as well as former members of the Waffen-SS "Galicia" Division.
53. Taras Borovets (1908–81), who took up the name Taras Bulba from the eponymous novel by Nikolai Gogol, was a Ukrainian partisan leader who cooperated with the Germans and established the first Ukrainian Insurgent Army that was then replaced and largely crushed by the OUN's better known UPA. He died in exile in Canada.
54. Sydir Kovpak (1887–1967) was a legendary Soviet partisan leader whose formation operated deep behind German lines in Ukraine. He later held senior positions in the Soviet government.
55. Note by Petrykevych: "It is difficult for the Germans to destroy the partisans, because the Germans don't know the language, the forests, or their way of warfare. The partisans flee before the fight and hide in the woods. Their plan is to reach the forests in Yugoslavia."
56. The reference is to the ethnic cleansing of Poles by Ukrainians led by Bulba and the UPA in Volhynia, which later occurred in Galicia as well, and to which Poles often responded in kind. As many as one hundred thousand Poles and twenty thousand Ukrainians are estimated to have died in this fraternal conflict, which had little to do with German occupation policies. See Bartov, *Anatomy of a Genocide*, 266–71, and literature cited therein.
57. The 14th Waffen Grenadier Division of the SS (1st Galician), made up primarily of Ukrainian volunteers from Galicia, was formed in 1942 and destroyed in the battle of Brody in July 1944, although it was later reformed and fought in Slovakia, Yugoslavia, and Austria.
58. Located in Zaporizhia, Ukraine, at the Dnieper Rapids in the lower reaches of the river.
59. This is in all likelihood the resistance group led by Edek as described in Moshe Wizinger's account, although he never provides the leader's surname.
60. On this event see also Bartov, *Anatomy of a Genocide*, 218.
61. In the text "some bandits" is crossed out and replaced with "some Jews."
62. In the text the date is corrected to 7 November—the anniversary of the October revolution.
63. "(To Chortkiv)" added to the text.

64. On this event and the memorial currently in the renamed Ivano-Frankivsk, see Bartov, *Erased*, 79–81.

65. Note by Petrykevych: "Several members of the organization were arrested in Kovalivka [Polish: Kowalówka, 22 km northwest of Buchach]. They had a list of Ukrainian priests in villages, whom they wanted to kill once the Germans retreated, and a list of Ukrainian organizations they wanted to destroy." There is no other evidence of an organization with that name operating at the time in the region.

66. The "delegatura," or the Government Delegation for Poland (Polish: *Delegatura Rządu Rzeczypospolitej Polskiej na Kraj*) represented the Polish government in exile within the Polish underground government in German-occupied Poland.

67. The Schutzpolizei was also employed to hunt down and kill Jews. See, e.g., Christopher R. Browning, *Ordinary Men: Reserve Police Battalion 101 and the Final Solution in Poland* (New York: HarperPerennial, 1993).

68. See Wizinger's account of the killing of this local partisan leader, to whom he refers only as Edek, by a group of ethnic German villagers near Buchach.

69. Note by Petrykevych: "Later it was said that somebody had killed a Gestapo official there."

70. Note by Petrykevych: "Markova?" (located 30 km northwest of Buchach).

71. Petrykevych is apparently referring to Field Marshal Walther von Brauchitsch. But Brauchitsch went into forced retirement in late 1941 and never commanded Army Group South, whose commander at the time was Field Marshal Erich von Manstein.

72. The local agents of the Kriminalpolizei, or Kripo, were members of the Security Police (Sicherheitspolizei, or Sipo) outpost in Chortkiv, which murdered sixty thousand Jews in the Chortkiv-Buchach region. Although a Kripo official was assassinated elsewhere in the region, there was no Kripo commandant there since its officials were under direction of the Sipo.

73. Note by Petrykevych: "In Chortkiv I was told that twenty-eight Ukrainians were shot, including three women."

74. Bulgaria was allied with the Axis Powers from March 1941 but never declared war on the USSR; in September 1944 it declared war on Germany. Turkey was neutral during the war and only declared war against Germany and Japan in February 1945.

75. The Curzon Line, proposed by British Foreign Secretary George Curzon, was intended to demarcate the border between Poland and the Soviet Union after World War I but was not implemented at the time. It was then employed to partition Poland between Germany and the USSR in 1939 and was reestablished with minor modifications as the border between Poland and Soviet Russia in 1945.

76. Horty served officially as "Regent of Hungary" between 1920–44 and led it into an alliance with Nazi Germany and participation in the invasion of the USSR, as well as partial compliance with German demands to deliver its Jewish population. Fearing that the Hungarians would change sides as the Red Army drew near, the Germans invaded Hungary in March 1944 and managed to deport the vast majority of its Jewish population to Auschwitz, with considerable assistance from the fascist Hungarian Arrow Cross Party. In October Horty withdrew from the alliance and was forced to resign, but while he testified at the Nuremberg Tribunal, he spent the rest of his long life in exile in Portugal.

77. On this location see also the account by Wizinger.

78. The Wehrmacht's First Panzer Army was encircled by the Red Army in the "pocket" of Kamyanets Podilskyi, southwest of Lviv, in late March 1944, and while the Germans managed to break out of the pocket (thereby also recapturing Buczacz in early April), the Panzer Army suffered significant losses and lost most of its heavy and armored materiel.

79. Hrechukha (1902–76) was a Ukrainian-Soviet politician who served on the Presidium of the Supreme Council of the Ukrainian SSR from 1939 to 1954.

80. Known also as the Polissian Sich, the Ukrainian People's Revolutionary Army, and, confusingly, as the Ukrainian Insurgent Army, this was the force led by Taras Bulba-Borovets that later clashed with the OUN-B's UPA and was eventually disbanded in October 1943. Its men were also known as Bulbivtsi or Bulbashi.

81. This traditional local name for a Jewish cemetery is derived from the word for trench and is associated with fortifications on hills surrounding medieval and early modern towns in the region, where Jews also buried their dead.

82. Note by Petrykevych: "One priest was lightly wounded, and three or four German officers were killed."

83. This was the location of the Jewish cemetery and the site of mass killings in spring and summer 1943. The name of the hill, which means towers, comes from the fortifications that were on the hill in the early modern era. Nahiryanka was a village near Buchach and is now a suburb of the town.

84. There is no evidence or likelihood that Rommel, who was then in charge of the Atlantic Wall in France in anticipation of the Allied invasion, ever visited the Buchach region.

85. Petrykevych note: "The next day it turned out that Peredmistya across the Black Bridge [over the Strypa] had not been evacuated."

86. On the oil industry in this region, see Alison Frank, *Oil Empire: Visions of Prosperity in Austrian Galicia* (Cambridge, MA: Harvard University Press, 2005).

87. Lviv was captured by the Red Army on 27 July 1944.

88. Petrykevych note: "Newspapers, according to a report from 17 July, write about the line Lutsk-Ternopil. But nobody believes official newspapers these days."

89. After encircling the German-Ukrainian forces in the Brody area in mid-July 1944, the Red Army eliminated the pocket on 22 July; only 3,500 men out of the original 11,000 members of the Waffen-SS "Galicia" Division managed to break out and escape capture.

90. In fact, the Wehrmacht had transferred significant forces to the Eastern Front during the Soviet offensive of March 1944, which were sorely lacking during the Allied landing in Normandy on 6 June.

91. Petrykevych note: "Some say thirty Ukrainians and seventy Poles were shot; others, that a hundred Ukrainians were shot, and there were no Poles among the executed. People say that Ukrainians were shot for [taking part in] partisan warfare, Poles for participating in some conspiracy."

92. Hess (1894–1987) was Hitler's deputy since 1933; he flew on his own initiative to Scotland in 1941 in an attempt to negotiate peace, and spent the rest of his life in prison, committing suicide at the age of ninety-three.

93. The National Committee for a Free Germany (Nationalkomitee Freies Deutschland, NKFD) was an anti-Nazi organization founded by German prisoners of war in the USSR in July 1943. The reference is possibly to General Walther Kurt von Seydlitz-Kurzbach, who fell into Soviet hands at Stalingrad and was among the founders the League of German Officers (Bund Deutscher Offiziere, BDO) in September 1943, which joined the NKFD soon thereafter.

94. On 20 July 1944, a group of conspirators tried to assassinate Hitler. The failure of the coup lead to the execution of close to five thousand people, including senior army officers and other prominent figures.

95. Note by Petrykevych: "A certain railway man said that in total the Germans destroyed six bridges, wooden and iron ones."

96. The Ridna Shkola Society, founded in Lviv in 1881, promoted Ukrainian-language education in Galicia and organized Ukrainian private schools in the interwar period as a response to the Polish government's policy of closing Ukrainian public schools.

97. The Soviet "repatriation" policy meant a population exchange between Poland and what became Soviet Ukraine, as a result of which by 1947 there were almost no Poles left in the former eastern Galicia.

98. The Brygidki Prison in Lviv was the site of a mass execution of mostly Ukrainian political prisoners by the NKVD following the invasion of Nazi Germany in 1941 and the site of beatings and killings by Ukrainian militiamen and German soldiers of local Jews, brought in to exhume the bodies.

99. About half of Drohobych's fifteen thousand Jews were taken to the Bełżec extermination camp or killed in the deportation roundups; most of the rest were murdered in the Bronica forest. It is not known that any Gentiles were killed in these operations.

100. On Sheptytsky, see note 46, this chapter.

101. Andrey Vlasov (1901–46) was a Red Army general who was captured by the Germans and formed the Russian Liberation Army under their auspices. He was tried for treason and hanged by the Soviets. The term Vlasovites ostensibly described followers of Vlasov but in fact was popularly attributed to any Red Army troops that ended up fighting for the Germans, often former prisoners of war.

102. Konovalets (1891–1938) was the leader of the OUN between 1929–38 and was apparently assassinated by the NKVD in Rotterdam in 1938.

103. Bukovyna or Bukovina lies south of Galicia and straddles the eastern Carpathians and the adjoining plains. It was under Habsburg rule before World War I and under Romanian rule in the interwar period. Northern Bukovina, including the city of Chernivtsi (Czernowitz), was annexed by the USSR after World War II and is now in independent Ukraine.

104. The Mazepinka or Mazepynka is a traditional Ukrainian military cap, first used by the Legion of the Ukrainian Sich Riflemen in World War I. It was modeled on the headgear of the Hetman Ivan Mazepa (1639–1709), who ruled Left-Bank Ukraine from 1687 to 1709. The trident was adopted in 1918 as the coat of arms of the short-lived Ukrainian People's Republic and was officially adopted again by independent Ukraine in 1992. It bears the colors of the Ukrainian flag (a yellow or golden trident on a blue or azure background) and is associated with the medieval ruler of Kievan Rus Volodymyr the Great.

105. See note 97, this chapter.

106. Petrykevych is speaking here about a command rather than a free-market economy; hence his apparent expectation that if the value of the currency drops, the government would also lower the prices of basic staples.

107. See note 52, this chapter.

108. Petrykevych note: "There were 'actions' against Ukrainians similar to those the Germans conducted against the Jews. Masses of them were killed." While there were indeed mutual massacres by Poles and Ukrainians, the number of Polish victims far exceeded that of Ukrainians. The genocide of the Jews was on an entirely different scale.

109. The NKGB (the People's Commissariat for State Security) operated separately from the NKVD from 1943 to 1946.

110. Petrykevych note: "Students in the dorms often had scabies."

111. This case has all the hallmarks of a blood libel event similar in some ways to what occurred in the Polish town of Kielce in 1946. On the latter, see Jan Gross, *Fear: Anti-Semitism in Poland after Auschwitz. An Essay in Historical Interpretation* (New York: Random House, 2006).

112. Melnikov replaced Khrushchev as first secretary of the Communist Party of Ukraine when the latter was promoted to secretary of the Central Committee in Moscow in December 1949. Melnikov led a hard-line Russification drive, identifying Ukrainian nationalism with collaboration with the Germans, and turning against the remaining Jewish community as part of an "anticosmopolitan" campaign. Shortly after Stalin's death, Melnikov was removed as first secretary for "deviations in nationality policy" and replaced by the Ukrainian Kyrychenko.
113. Beria (1899–1953), of Georgian origin, headed the NKVD during World War II and administered a wide range of areas, including the expansion of the Gulag system, the postwar communist takeover of state institutions in Eastern Europe, and the Soviet atom bomb project. He was removed from office by Khrushchev shortly after Stalin's death and then executed.

Moshe Wizinger. Organization of Partisans
Underground Fighters and Ghetto Rebels in Israel.
Public domain.

Moshe Wizinger
Written in Cyprus, 1947

I remember those evenings. Your figures are alive before my eyes. Your voices still whisper in my ear. You often asked: "Will anyone know after the war what we went through here? Will anyone be left to tell the world about our fate?"

I am alive. It has been three years since the war, and I am alive. In Cyprus. At the gate of the Holy Land. The only thing I took with me was my life. Apart from my life I can offer my country nothing else. I will not forget your dying wish, Nacio: "Kiss the Holy Land for me." I will never forget your loud lament the day before Salu died. I will not forget Dolus's emerald eyes, just as I will never forget any of you who suffered and lived together with me. I have often considered copying the loose, overwritten scraps of paper, my only memories of those days. But every time I was about to begin, I gave up in despair. At last, here in Cyprus, behind a double row of barbed wire, I managed to overcome my emotions and to describe what to this day does not let me sleep at night; today I completed this task.

I do not know yet whether I will be able to bring this with me. Perhaps a British soldier at the border will inspect me and, upon finding these scraps of paper filled with unfamiliar writing, will suspect they contain some secret that might hurt the whole British Empire and confiscate them. Perhaps I will manage to hide and carry them with me through the gate of the Holy Land. Then you should know—it is to you, the ten thousand eternally sleeping on Fedor Hill; to you, my mother and brother; to you, my "grandmothers" Elżbieta and Staszka;

and to you, whose name is unknown to me, the "Bearded Lieutenant Colonel"—that I dedicate this book.

[Added later] Hero of the Soviet Union, Major General Pyotr Vershigora.[1]

Part I

The thunder of the guns could be heard coming closer and closer, blocking out every other sound, even the chirping of the birds that always brought everything back to life at this time of year—early summer— bringing a smile to even the most dejected face with their songs. The boom of the heavy artillery was rolling through the streets of the small town of Buczacz with such intensity that windowpanes were shattered. At other times there were tanks, or troops riding in trucks, carts, and often, on foot. The soldiers' faces were tired, besmirched by dirt and sweat. Their eyes, mostly flashing with anger, peered out from under their helmets.

The soldiers did not readily talk to civilians and, seemingly because they knew that they could not answer this question, avoided being asked: "Why are you going to the East? After all, the Germans are approaching from the West..." Some of them responded curtly and even with a smile: "We are not afraid since we have faith." At the same time, their eyes, when meeting those of young men, seemed to ask: "Why aren't you with us at a time like this, doesn't the war concern you as well?" "You just wait," one of the soldiers said jokingly with a strong Belarusian accent, "your life will become such that you will want to die. The fascists will give you such a lesson that you will learn to appreciate Soviet rule." Everyone was quiet, but felt the same heaviness of heart and asked themselves the same question: "What should we do? What will become of us?"

The Germans occupied Lwów. In the evening, we turned the radio to the Lwów wavelength and heard: "This is the radio station named after Konovalets. In a moment, we will hear the leader of the Ukrainian partisans, Bandera."[2] Then we heard: "Fellow Ukrainians, the German Army has liberated us from the Jews and the Bolsheviks. As of today, this land and everything on it belongs to you. Take over the factories and offices. Long live independent Ukraine." Afterward, the new Ukrainian anthem was played, its refrain being: "Death to the Lachs [derogatory name for Poles] and the Jews, death to the Moscow-Jewish Commune." We were somewhat relieved: this meant that there had been no pogrom, no order to kill the Jews on the spot.

We were slightly concerned about the refrain of the anthem, but after all it was just a song.

The following day, 2 July, a large meeting was called by the secretary of the Raikom [District Committee]. Comrade Yakimets, the secretary of the executive committee, appeared on the tribune and spoke about the current situation. "I am not going to hide anything; the situation is grave. The devious attack by the Germans on our country has brought them temporary victories. The Germans have occupied several cities and are approaching Buczacz. Today, the city council will begin issuing permits to those who want to leave the city together with the Red Army and thereby to avoid capture by the fascists. We will keep fighting," concluded Yakimets, "until we cleanse our homeland from the last of the invaders; we are leaving, but at the same time we swear that we will be

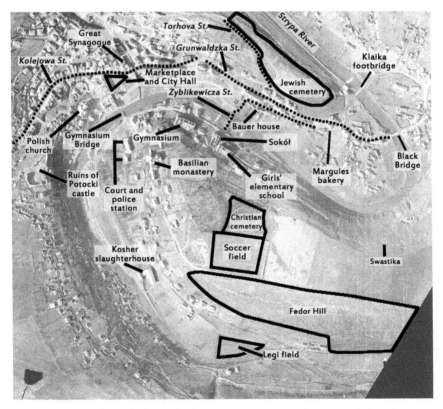

Map 3.1 Luftwaffe aerial photograph of Buczacz, April 1944, with key features indicated. Source: National Archives and Records Administration (NARA), RG 373: GX12125 SD, exps. 32, 33, 62, and 63 (combined).

back and rebuild our lives in such a way that no one will ever dare think of invading our territories again."

Immediately after the meeting, I went home. My brother and mother were already there. With the whole family together, we began deliberating what to do. My mother, who could not leave town because of her advanced age, tried to convince us that we, my brother and I, should go with the Red Army. We would not hear of it .... I said firmly that we would stay at home and share together the same fate, come what may. My younger brother did not even participate in the discussion, he left it to me. And that is how it was settled.

The following day we went out to May Third Street,[3] which led in the direction of the town's eastern outskirts. The street was filled with horse-drawn carts and people leaving town, but we were surprised that there were not more of them. Obviously, it was difficult for people to leave a place in which they had dwelled for generations, where they were born, lived through moments of joy and sadness, and where every stone, every alley was familiar. Those leaving had tears in their eyes. But all were trying to cheer each other up, saying that it was not for long, that we would see each other soon. Cars with the local firefighters, police, and higher officials of the city council, passed through the street.

Suddenly, from the eastern edge of the town, on the bridge over the Strypa River that for some unknown reason was called the "black bridge," a column of military vehicles appeared. Soldiers of the Red Army were seated in the trucks, but they appeared different somehow, happier. A soldier was playing the accordion in one of the trucks. In another, they were singing a soviet military song and, most important, they were headed towards the west, from where the barrage of heavy artillery was already clearly heard. In an instant, the mood on the street totally changed.

A wave of optimism, vibrancy, and joy swept through the hearts of the people. People were saying: "Maybe, after all"; "Did you see the machine guns, and how merry the soldiers are? Well, well, probably something on the front has changed." Our neighbor, Mrs. Filipska, stood by me. For the last two years, since the Soviets had taken over, she had been complaining to my mother about the "new order," and predicted every day that we would all be deported to Siberia. Now ... I could hear her trembling lips whisper: "God, help them save us from the German invasion." I looked at her stupefied. What could have caused the change in this woman's thinking? Or did she intuitively feel the imminent danger?

By evening, the news from Moscow shattered our hopes raised by the passing of the Red Army through the town. The speaker announced,

"After fierce battles inflicting high losses on the enemy, our army has left the city of Stanisławów and has retreated to the east."

The following day, the town was relatively quiet. But throughout the day small units of the Soviet Army passed through the town in horse-drawn carts, once more heading eastward. Tonia, a nine-year-old Jewish girl whom I knew from the orphanage, came up to me on the street and related that the previous day, during the evacuation, thirty children were left behind and now they did not know what to do. I walked with her to the "Anderman" hotel, in which the military headquarters was temporarily housed. There I met a certain colonel to whom I explained the situation in which the children had found themselves. The colonel ordered an immediate transfer of the children to the train station and it appeared that the last train was leaving in an hour. However, when the children arrived at the train station, a new obstacle came up. The only train that was still leaving the town consisted of thirty-five railcars, all crammed full with parts of factory machinery that was being evacuated. The commander of the transport, a young officer, helplessly opened his arms and said that he did not have any free space to accommodate the children, apart from the roofs of the wagons. In any case, he said, it was not in his power to leave behind the valuable machinery. In response, the colonel told him off sharply, saying that human life was more valuable than machinery at any time. For a while the young train commander tried to resist, but when the colonel, who was furious by now, threatened him with imprisonment and even court martial, he gave up and eventually the soldiers who were guarding the train began to unload the machines, or rather throw them out of the train and onto the rails. Soon, the children occupied the free railcar and the train went on its way.

It was Friday afternoon. My mother lit the Shabbat candles as usual, but suddenly another, much stronger light penetrated the room through the open windows and joined the light of the candles. We ran outside. We could see the glow of fires burning everywhere. We recognized various buildings. The train station was on fire, as was the complex of grain storage silos and the large metal factory. We heard a huge detonation, which shattered the windowpanes. That was the train tunnel being blown up by the retreating soldiers. Then came another detonation. This, we realized, was the big railroad bridge being blown up.

Sporadic gunfire went on almost until dawn. In the morning, as the first rays of light entered the room, my brother approached the window and suddenly cried out, summoning us to him. We ran to the window and saw that from the tallest building in town, the tower of the city hall, the blue-and-yellow flag of the Ukrainian Nationalists was flying, and right next to it a big red flag had been hoisted. At its center was a black swastika on a white circle. Foreboding gripped our hearts, and our throats felt dry. Alas, the Germans had finally arrived.

It was a beautiful July morning; one of those mornings that fill human hearts with sheer joy of life, when all they wish to see around them is contentment and happiness. For us it was the first day of the occupation and we fearfully awaited what would come next. The next few hours were to reveal the naked truth about our situation. We were to be confronted with what we had heard about for so many years, the embodiment of cruelty: Hitler's rule.

At 10 a.m., having deliberated this with our neighbors, we decided to send Wolcio Rudy (redhead, as he was called because of the color of his hair) out to the street to check the situation in town. After a while I saw the agile little boy making his way stealthily through the side streets towards the town center. Within fifteen minutes he was back, running in the middle of the street and shouting out loud, "You can come out, there are Germans in town but they are not doing anything, they are talking to the Jews and one of the soldiers even gave me a piece of chocolate!" He opened his hand and there really was a piece of chocolate in it. The street livened up, everybody tried to get as close to Wolcio as possible to get the most details out of him. Then I announced that I too would go. Two neighbors, Sokółecki and Sołlieb, joined me. And so, the three of us headed together toward the town center.

After crossing a few streets, we met the barber Dawid Seiler, who was returning from town. When we asked him what was happening, he answered, "Nothing much, they are like all people. They are well nourished and are sitting on the grass opposite the city hall tower. Turns out," concluded Dawid, "this was all much ado about nothing; they are not that bad." That completely calmed us down, and we quickly marched on, reaching the city hall in a few minutes. Many people were gathered in front of the city hall. Some were looking at the German motorcycles parked next to the sidewalk, others observed the motorcyclists lying on the grass, others still were chatting with each other about recent events. From time to time a motorcycle, car, or small tank drove down the street. I approached the soldiers. One of them was saying that the Germans would surely occupy Moscow that same month, that England would capitulate of its own accord, and that then the war would end.

Suddenly someone called. We all looked around and saw a German soldier and five Ukrainians, all armed with submachine guns and hand grenades, approaching from the bottom of the street. Between them were two Soviet prisoners of war. One was wearing a cap with the green a symbol of the border guards. He was wounded in the neck, as could be seen from the dirty bloodstained bandage wrapped around it. He walked silently, looking down, his head bowed. He seemed to be suffering from his injury, because he was constantly grimacing with pain. Conversely, the other prisoner kept nervously gesticulating to the Ukrainians surrounding him as he walked. Coming a little closer I could hear him explaining that he was also Ukrainian, that he had been conscripted against his will and that he had long sought an opportunity to join the Germans.

The convoy stopped in front of the city hall and the prisoners were allowed to sit on the ground. One of the guards gave a cigarette to the Ukrainian captive. He took it eagerly and lit it. After smoking the better half of it he offered the remainder to the wounded soldier. But the latter turned away in disgust with a single word, "scum" [in Russian]. The soldiers guarding them responded with kicks and beating. One of them said that from the moment they had surrounded him he had not stopped shooting at them until he ran out of bullets. After sustaining his neck wound, he had put up his arms shouting that he wanted to surrender. However, when the Germans approached him, he threw a grenade at them that he had held in his clenched fist, but it did not explode. Then they took him alive. A tall, red-haired German officer walked up to the prisoners and began interrogating them in Russian. The wounded soldier was silent, not responding in any way to the German's questions, while his colleague answered eagerly and attempted to convince the German of his hatred for the Bolsheviks and his sympathy for the Germans. At some point the Ukrainian whispered something in a hushed voice in the German's ear as his gaze turned to the wounded soldier. The German's face lit up. He approached the latter and ordered him to get up and follow him inside the city hall. After a few minutes he appeared at the door pushing the prisoner in front of him and shouting loudly: "Ja, das ist ein Jude" [Yes, it's a Jew]. As he announced this, he kept pushing the back of the soldier with a drawn pistol and ordered him to keep walking toward the bridge. Once they mounted the first few planks of the bridge, the German raised his hand and fired a shot at the prisoner in front of him. Simultaneously he kicked him with his boot in such a manner that the body fell over the barrier of the bridge and into the water with a loud splash.

That evening, when the neighbors gathered at our home, we discussed the events of the day. Apart from what happened with the prisoners of war there had been other incidents in town. The Germans, accompanied by armed Ukrainians, broke into homes and dragged the Jews out. These Jews were then forced to clean the German soldiers' quarters and were beaten for good measure. The same night there were other incidents: German soldiers led by the Ukrainian dregs broke into Jewish houses and raped young Jewish girls.

Over the next few nights the Ukrainians entered the homes of former communist activists, Komsomol members, and members of other Soviet organizations.[4] Amongst them were Jews, Poles, and even Ukrainians. They were be taken away and a few days later their bodies were found horribly mutilated, usually outside the city in some pit or swamp. In many cases their heads or other parts of their bodies had been severed. The body of one tailor, whose name I believe was Lieblich, was found with his head in a swamp outside of town, his hands and legs tied with a barbed wire. This made people fear sleeping at home, and no one knew whether he might be the next victim.

Attempts to intervene with members of the Ukrainian intelligentsia came to naught. The well-known Ukrainian eye doctor [Volodymyr] Hamerskyi told a Jewish delegation headed by [the physician] Dr. Blutreich and [the attorney and former chairman of the General Zionist Party's local branch, Dr. Benjamin (Ludwik)] Engelberg[5] that the Ukrainian intelligentsia did not support the murder of the Jews, but that they themselves were helpless, because those who were ruling now were the leaders of the previously secret Ukrainian bands.[6] In the end he expressed his hope that once the Germans took over, the atmosphere in town would return to normal.

Meanwhile, the looting, rape, and murder increased. One night, the Great Synagogue was gutted, the furnishings inside destroyed, the silver candelabras plundered, and many of the holy books torn and scattered on the floor. The scrolls of the Torah were carried all the way to the bridge. There they were unbound so that one end was attached to the top of the bridge while the other dangled nearly all the way to the water. This brought a harsh protest from the Ukrainian clergy, who categorically demanded from the leader of the Ukrainian bands, [Andriy] Dankovych,[7] to stop profaning holy sites.

Dankovych responded that he had no knowledge of any of this and that it was surely a Jewish provocation. He also ordered that the Torah scrolls be removed from the bridge immediately. Several armed Ukrainians dashed into the nearest houses, dragged out a few Jews, and made them roll up the scrolls. The whole event occurred in the presence of the abbot of the Ukrainian Basilian monastery, who proposed to the Jews to bring the scrolls to the monastery for safekeeping. Following a brief consultation, the Jews agreed to this proposal and the Torah scrolls were carried to the Monastery and put in a separate room, whose key was kept by the abbot himself.

Finally, we had some form of rule. After two weeks of chaos and sleepless nights, during which we were at the mercy of Ukrainian bands, the first posters were put up with orders signed by the Ortskommandant [local commander], Lieutenant Müller: "I order under penalty of death that within forty-eight hours all weapons, radios, or any other military equipment, be handed over to the German headquarters. Anyone who appears on the street after 4 p.m. will be shot without warning. For every act of sabotage against any German military target, ten people will be executed."

We were somehow relieved. At least the bands would not be able to roam freely at night and we would get some sleep. However, the same night even more bands of German soldiers and Ukrainian nationalists roamed the city. Furthermore, we were unable to save ourselves by escaping, because any Jew found on the street at night would be shot immediately. The Ukrainian bands were transformed into police forces and the local prison filled up with arrested Jews, Poles, and even Ukrainians known for their pro-Soviet opinions.

The following day, on which the requisition of the weapons and radios was scheduled, we heard loud banging on the door at 6 a.m. My brother and I managed to escape through the back door and hide in the garden. A few minutes later, we saw our mother coming in our direction. The way she looked, and especially her white ghostlike face, made us shudder. As she told us, a moment earlier a Ukrainian policeman had been looking for us and announced that we had to appear within the hour at the police station. Otherwise, he threatened, they would come looking for us and that would be much worse. My mother began crying and pleaded with us not to go. But I tried to explain to her that not going would only make things worse. In the end, I decided that I would go on my own and my brother would hide with our neighbors. We said goodbye the way you bid farewell from someone who had died, although I think that such a moment is easier for the dead person, for at least he does not have to see the suffering of his loved ones and does not realize that he is the cause.

On the way there I was more worried by what would happen to my loved ones and how they would manage without me, than I was fearful about my own fate. And so, tormented by these forebodings, I crossed the threshold of the house from which no one had ever returned. Behind the table, in an armchair, sat a Ukrainian policeman, whose physiognomy would have frightened the life out of any of us. I told him that half an hour earlier a policeman had arrived at my house and ordered me to come to the station. He asked for my name and then called someone named Danylo. A short, stocky Ukrainian emerged from the other room and struck me on the face with all his might: "You son of a bitch, you think I am going to wait for you here? Go over there!" With a few kicks he shoved me into the other room. "Wait here," he shouted and slammed the door. I looked around. The room consisted of one table and two chairs. How many people have already passed through this room? The antechamber of death, I thought to myself: that is how people are going to name this room after the war. And in the meantime, at home, is my mother, Oh Mother.

I approached one of the windows facing the prison yard, which was level with the ground floor of the same house. A car was standing in the yard. Two people whose faces I recognized were just about done washing the mud off a car. They were two well-known Jewish lawyers from our city, Stern and Neuman. A young German stood next to them and when they finished cleaning the car, he ordered them to inflate the car's tires with a hand pump. The Jews were not used to physical labor; they got tired easily, and this infuriated the German who constantly kicked and yelled at them. Suddenly, he ordered them to stop pumping the tires. He handed each of them a stick and, I assume, ordered them to fight each other. At first, they tried to strike each other lightly, probably hoping that the German would get bored with the game. However, when they saw the German holding a pistol, the trouncing got stronger and soon blood was flowing from both heads.

Then I heard the sound of the door opening. I turned around and saw a German standing there. He came to the table, sat down and inquired about my profession. When I said I was a radio technician, he announced that at 2 p.m. a collection of radios would begin. I would be in charge of making sure that every radio was in good condition—that is, that it had not been damaged on purpose. I was also ordered to select the best radios for the members of the local German command and the Ukrainian policemen. He concluded by adding that I should make sure to be on time. Those who have had such a near-death experience, being certain that there was absolutely no way they could escape it and having even already accepted it, and who were then suddenly reprieved as if by a miracle, will understand how green the grass and the trees appear, how the chirping of the birds sounds like heavenly music, how warm the rays of the sun feel: how beautiful the world is. I was alive. And within a few moments I was embracing my mother.

The time was close to 10 a.m. One of our neighbors, the Polish lawyer Więckowski, had been a very good friend for many years. I went to his house to listen to the radio broadcast from the "other world," as he called it, for the last time. "I don't know what to do," he complained. "How will we manage without a radio? After all, it's our only contact with the outside world. Maybe if the box were smaller it might be possible to hide." I immediately had a thought. If the box were smaller... well then? For a moment we intensely looked into each other's eyes without uttering a word. Finally, I said, "Yes, but where?" "The dead are silent," said the lawyer. I understood. Next to our house there was a garden bordering the wall of a cemetery. And that was where the radio, our window to the world, should be hidden. I immediately set about taking the radio apart. I took out the whole inner apparatus including the loudspeaker and filled the empty box with various unnecessary old parts of which I had many at home. We agreed with our friend that when he brought in the radio, I would try to hide it among the others.

At 2 p.m. that day the gathering of the radios began. Two Ukrainian policemen were present along with me. The procedure went as follows: the two policemen were handed radios by the people and put them on the floor next to the wall. There I sorted them out, putting the better ones on the left side. Some brought in damaged radios, even without tubes.[8] Since I was worried about the consequences, I told the policemen about this, but they simply ignored me. No receipts were given for the radios and after a certain number had accumulated it was no longer possible to tell whose radio was which. I was of course very glad that it had turned out this way. Then my friend appeared. I could see that he was a bit nervous. I gave him a sign that everything was okay, and soon his radio was among all the others. Altogether 900 radios were handed over to me that day. The Germans took about 150 for themselves. The next 200 were taken by the "Ukrainian dignitaries," who did not even know how to operate radios until I showed them. The other 600 were dumped into a cellar, where many valuable radios were damaged. Making use of this opportunity, I hid five more radio tubes in my pockets in case the one in our radio would turn out to be damaged.

That night, the centuries-old linden trees and headstones at the cemetery must have been surprised by the late-night intruders. There were three of us: me, the lawyer, and Maniek [Marjan Świerszczak] the gravedigger, whom we had let in on our secret.[9] The old iron key jolted the ancient gate, and we could sense the dampness and cold air. Soon our precious load was put to rest next to a big metal coffin containing the remains of a local church leader who had died thirty years earlier. Then, like three ghosts, we left the place.

Today,[10] at noon, a car drove through the streets of the town. Four Germans in SS uniforms stepped out of the car in front of the prison. A few minutes later, those who had been incarcerated there were led out of the building and arranged in rows of four. Altogether there were about sixty of them.[11] We were surprised that the majority of them were without shoes and jackets and that some did not even have shirts. They walked down the streets of the town, passing next to the alcohol distillery and heading toward the forest. They were surrounded by a tight cordon of Ukrainian policemen. Along the way, the policemen beat them mercilessly wherever they could. The car with the SS men followed a short distance behind this terrifying parade.

Soon the first rows disappeared into the forest. The car with the SS men stopped, the soldiers with their submachine guns got out and followed the people. A series of gunfire bursts mixed with single shots could be heard. This went on for about fifteen minutes, followed by sporadic shots which then ceased completely. The Germans came out of the forest, got into the car and left. Soon thereafter the Ukrainian policemen also emerged and formed into rows of four, headed by the already notorious Dankovych. As they marched back, thee sang their favorite song, "Death to the Jews and the Lachs!"

Once again, posters were put up. We read:

1. As of today, the Jews have to wear a white armband, ten centimeters wide, with a blue Star of David in the middle, on their right sleeve above the elbow.
2. Jews are forbidden to walk on the main streets. On other streets they can only walk on one side.
3. Jews have to greet every German they meet by taking off their hat. Those who do not comply will be punished by death.

Within an hour, all the Jews were wearing armbands. Jewish youths walked on the streets without a headcover. This was the only way to avoid taking off their hats when encountering Germans.

In yet another blow, shortly after that announcement, the most respected members of the Jewish community were arrested: the elderly [Dr. J.] Aba Stern, Ozjasz Freudenthal,[12] Berko [Samuel] Hersas, and others. They were told that they were being held as hostages. If the Jews did not pay the ransom sum of a million rubles within forty-eight hours, they would be shot. The former activists of the Jewish community immediately started collecting the money. The money was paid, and the hostages were released.

The Germans then ordered the establishment of a Judenrat [Jewish council] and a Jewish Police, which from now on would carry out their demands. The members of the first Judenrat were Mendel Reich as the Obman [chairman], Baruch Kramer, Dr. [Bernhard] Seifer, and Berko Hersas.[13] J. [Józef] Rabinowicz became the commander of the police, the so-called Ordnungsdienst [also knows as the OD]. Now the ceaseless demands began. First, entire apartments, including furniture, kitchen appliances, bedding, and so forth, had to be organized for the Landkommissar [county commissioner], the Landwirt [agricultural manager], the local police chief, and other German and Ukrainian "dignitaries." Every one of them also had to get a few new pairs of shoes, clothes and underclothes. Additionally, if any of them left, they took everything with them, including the pianos and furniture. Their replacement then had the same demands all over again.

All Jews were obliged to work. Some worked in the quarry, others in road repair. The majority of the Jews were employed in dismantling Jewish houses. The Germans ordered the destruction of neighborhoods where houses belonging to Jews were located.[14] My brother and I worked on restoring the telephone line from Buczacz to Monasterzyska. An additional hundred Jews were employed there. We were working under the supervision of Ukrainians. Occasionally we would bring them some vodka or clothes, and they would let us have longer breaks and did not beat anyone. Hence at that point we could not complain. For a twelve-hour working day, we received no payment, but compared to other places of work where, apart from hard work, everyone was also subjected to severe beatings, our circumstances were quite enviable.

At 5 p.m. we would finish work and rush home, because after 6 p.m. no Jew was allowed on the street. [On one of those days] we saw a new announcement in town, this time in Ukrainian: "Today at 6 p.m. all Jewish men aged sixteen to sixty must be registered. The registration will take place in the building of the city hall. Those who do not comply will be punished by death." We hurried home. We wanted to have time to eat something after a day of hard work and before we went to register. On the way I stopped by the notary's house. His wife, Stanisława, one of the most decent women I have ever known, was there. When she heard that my brother and I were planning to register, she tried to dissuade me from going, saying that she had heard the Gestapo had arrived in town and that was the reason for the registration. When I returned home, I found my brother waiting impatiently and ready to leave. "Come on, we'll be late," he shouted. Right there I suddenly changed my mind. "We will hide at the cemetery," I said, and we jumped out of the back window and ran through the garden. We sat in the cemetery until late at night and then, taking great care, we returned home. Some neighbors had returned from the registration and told us what had happened.

After assembling the Jews [led there from the square next to the city hall] in front of the police building (where the prison was also located), they were all pushed into the prison yard, which was surrounded by a

wall. Of course, all this was done with the usual beatings. After everyone was in the yard, several Gestapo officials, assisted by the Ukrainian
police, began selecting the people. This was done according to their
professions. A Gestapo-man would read out the different trades and
the Jews would have to stand on one or the other side of the wall that
surrounded the prison yard. It soon became clear that the people standing on one side were craftsmen while the other group consisted mainly
of members of such professions as lawyers, teachers, merchants, and
civil servants. After the selection, the group of craftsmen was allowed
to go home, while the others, about four hundred members of the local
intelligentsia, were ordered to stay.[15]

That night, filled with worries about the fate of those people, we
went to bed late. I was awoken by my mother violently shaking my
shoulder and pointing toward the window, from which one could see
the road leading to the Fedor Hill and forest. I quickly ran to the
window and looked out. On the road I could see the people who had
been arrested the day before. They were surrounded by a tight cordon
of Ukrainian policemen. They were led barefoot, some only in their
underwear. The car with the Germans and their inseparable submachine guns was driving slowly behind. Suddenly one of the Ukrainians
raised his head and saw me in the window. A few of them rushed
towards our house. My brother had just jumped out of the rear window
when they reached us and began beating us and pushing us towards
the road. Then our neighbor, the sixty-year-old Samotowa, ran out and
offered the Ukrainians a gold watch in return for letting us go. After
discussing it between themselves they agreed and told us to go back
home, while they fetched the watch.

In the meantime, the Jews who were being chased up the road had
already reached the Fedor Forest and soon disappeared in it, surrounded
by the Ukrainians and Germans. The shooting continued for half an
hour and then the car with the Gestapo returned to town followed by
well-formed rows of Ukrainians singing the same song, "Death to the
Jews and the Lachs." Many of them were wearing parts of clothing that
belonged to the murdered Jews, so that numerous women recognized
their husbands and sons' clothes.

It was the Day of Judgement in town. Every household was mourning
someone. Soon there was news that the Gestapo chief had summoned
Mendel Reich, the Obman of the Judenrat. Reich returned shaken and
distraught. The chief of the Gestapo, [chief of the Security Police outpost
in Tarnopol Hermann] Müller, who had directed the action, had assured
Reich that the Jews had not been shot.[16] Trucks had been waiting to
take them to labor camps in Germany. Müller added that if the Jews

collected five kilograms of gold as ransom within the next twenty-four hours, he would personally return these people unharmed to town.

Many were skeptical about the Gestapo officer's words, but something unexpected happened. Once this information reached the ears of the wives and mothers of those who had been taken, they practically besieged the Judenrat's office. They began begging, entreating and even threatening, demanding the release of their loved ones. Some claimed they were sure that the Jews had not been shot, that the shots heard were only to scare them when loading them onto the trucks. The people were in a frenzy. Everyone, even those who did not believe this story, were convincing themselves that these people had not been shot. How could it happen, out of the blue, having committed no offence, without a trial? It was impossible. Under this pressure, the Obman ordered a collection of gold. People brought wedding rings, golden watches, and various valuables. And by the very same evening, the requested amount was ready.

That evening, we were discussing the events of the day in the notary's house. The young Polish surgeon Dr. R., who was known for his sincere pro-Jewish sympathies, was just visiting the notary's home, and he proposed to me that the two of us go together to the forest to solve the riddle that was tormenting us. At 11 p.m. three of us set off: Dr. R., me, and the notary's dog, a big Austrian hound named Bianka. For reasons of safety we did not take the road but went through the fields. When we reached the edge of the forest, we let the dog run ahead of us. After walking for approximately another six hundred yards the trees became less dense. We then saw a clearing in the forest, lit by the rays of the moon. Suddenly Bianka began whimpering and lay down at my feet. I grabbed her collar and tried to silence her, hiding her behind a bush. We held our breath. However, the forest clearing was totally silent; we could hear no sound. Only Bianka remained agitated and would not leave my feet. From her behavior we gathered that there was no one in the vicinity because she had the habit of barking loudly. But there was something else that filled her with mortal fear.

After some time, I could see the doctor moving silently towards the clearing. Then he summoned me to him in a low voice. Tightly holding the dog's collar, I approached the clearing, where I saw the doctor standing over something long and dark on the ground. As I got closer, I saw a stretch of freshly dug soil in the shape of a ditch, some twenty meters long and two meters wide. Not far away was another ditch of the same dimensions. The doctor silently put the tip of his cane on the surface of the ditch and began to push it into the fresh soil. The cane went in smoothly for about twenty inches and then stopped. The doctor repeated this in a few places and then just said: "Well, yes." He then turned around, gesturing to me to follow him. We quickly returned home. I was covered in cold sweat and later, as I was trying to sleep, I tossed and turned in my bed, clearly seeing what future Hitler had in store for us.

Early the next morning, I went to visit the lawyer Dr. [Ludwik] Engelberg. I told him what I had seen. Together we went to the Obman and told him about what I had witnessed. He replied that he was aware of the gravity of the situation, and that from the very beginning he had known that the people were killed. On the other hand, he said, had he not gathered the gold, he would have had to explain to the mothers and wives why it was in vain. That would have caused even more distress and chaos. Furthermore, the Germans could compel the Jews to collect the gold in any case. That was why the Obman had decided to give them the gold at the appointed time.

The same day, at 11 a.m., Obman Reich, accompanied by Judenrat members Kramer and Hersas, went to the German gendarmerie head-quarters and presented Gestapo Chief Müller with five kilograms of gold. After carefully weighing the gold, Müller took out a sheet of paper that he had prepared in advance and ordered them to sign it. Afterwards, he read out what was written on it. The document just signed by the members of the Judenrat declared that upon the request of the Judenrat the Germans had shot four hundred communists.

After returning to the impatiently waiting women, Kramer told them that the gold had been successfully delivered and that the chief of the Gestapo had promised to arrange everything. However, when they reached the privacy of their room, the Obman fainted and Hersas started crying and banging his head against the wall. Only Kramer retained his equanimity.

The period from mid-August to November 1941 was relatively quiet. Apparently, the Ukrainian police had had enough of murdering and robbing, so they relented somewhat. You could even see a Jew walking on the sidewalk or along the main street. The situation seemed bearable. The countless demands by the Germans or Ukrainians were fulfilled immediately. The Judenrat even established a special "agency" called the "Verschaffung Abteilung" [Procurement Department]. It was headed by Motio P. and the butcher Fiszel Schwarz. With the help of the Ordnungsdienst and especially its commander, the late and hated Mojżesz Albrecht, they robbed the Jews of furniture, bed linen, and clothing. Some of these items went to fulfil the Germans' demands, others disappeared into the pockets of [the members of] the Verschaffung

Abteilung and the Ordnungsdienst, who in those terrible times were able to lead a very good life and amass large sums of money. Jews who tried to hide their belongings were mercilessly beaten, especially by Albrecht and Fiszel Schwarz.[17] Forced labor was still imposed on men aged fourteen to sixty and women aged fifteen to fifty. As a reward for their work, the Jews received food rations. The monthly ration was 2.8 kilograms of bread, 20 grams of salt, and 40 grams of groats. In fact, we never actually received groats. In a good month, we got half the ration of bread.

During that time, we (the notary and myself) decided to start listening to radio broadcasts from Moscow and London and to spread the news around. We argued over how to disseminate the news. I was in favor of printing a news bulletin on a printing machine and distributing it with the help of trusted people, whereas the notary preferred disseminating the news by word of mouth, claiming that a bulletin could easily fall into the hands of the Germans and that they had their methods of finding out who was behind it. He preferred to let a circle of trusted people into the secret and have them distribute the news further. After thinking it over I agreed with him.

The first session of listening to the radio was held in utmost secrecy at the notary's house. Only the notary, his wife and daughter, Dr. R. and his wife, and I were present. My brother and Bianka guarded the yard to warn us in case anyone approached. We listened to the news from Moscow and London. We were moved. It was a voice from another world, where the forces of evil had not yet taken over, where people did not have to wear an armband [with a Star of David] or walk in the drainage ditches. Oh, all those years we had lived without appreciating freedom. Only now do we fully understand its meaning. We jotted down the most important information on pieces of paper. The radio returned to its hiding place, Bianka to the kennel, and my brother and I went home.

The following day, we circulated the first information about the Allied Forces since the German invasion. I passed on the information to Dr. Engelberg who, under pressure from the Jews following the unforgettable "registration," had agreed to become the Obman.[18] Apart from the Obman, I also told the Judenrat physician, Dr. Seifer, Ozjasz Freudenthal, and the baker Yaakov Margulies, a highly respected member of the community, about our secret. All of them approved of my actions and promised me full support and as much help as possible. From that point on the most recent news from London and Moscow radio was disseminated to the Jewish masses.

This way of disseminating the news had good results. As [news of] the occasional minor successes of the Allies passed from mouth to mouth, they became ever greater and took on the aspect of great victories. For instance, if one morning I passed a message from Radio Moscow announcing that a thousand German soldiers were taken prisoner on the Dnieper, that same evening I heard a neighbor telling my mother that the Russians had crossed the Dnieper and taken a million Germans captive and that if they continued advancing, they'd be in town in a week. She added that she had that news from a reliable source, because someone in the Judenrat was listening to the radio.

This last part worried me somewhat because I wanted to hide the fact that the Judenrat was spreading the radio news of the Allies. Consequently, I decided to recruit some more boys and girls not connected to the Judenrat, in order to help disseminate the news. The first I found was a young boy called Milo Rozen [Shmuel Rosen].[19] I got to know him and within a few days I was sure that he would be able to accomplish this. Apart from him, I also recruited Tina Kirschner, the engineer Cyres, and Dr. Żelaźnik. They were all told to infer that they had received the news from a Ukrainian acquaintance.

In this way, time passed until mid-November. Suddenly, a new announcement shocked the town. The German chief of the Arbeitsamt [Labor Department] summoned the representatives of the Judenrat and told them he had to deliver 150 Jews to the new labor camp in Borki [Wielkie], 45 [actually 75] kilometers from Buczacz.

Nobody knew much about this camp, and people suspected that it was another German trick and these Jews would be executed. After talking it over, Obman Engelberg announced that he would not take part in selecting the people under any circumstances. He also arranged to immediately dispatch a number of trusted Poles who, for a large sum of money, agreed to go to Borki and check if it was really a labor camp. In view of the Judenrat's procrastination, the Arbeitsamt ordered it to provide a list of all Jewish men and threatened to punish the families of those who did not abide. A few days later the Poles sent to Borki returned, confirming the existence of a labor camp there. They added that they had seen teams of Jews from that camp working on the construction of a new railroad.[20] This calmed people down a little and they awaited the selection of the names with less anxiety.

At last the list appeared. Next to the names of the poorer members of the community there were also names of some of the richer Jews in town. The latter immediately sought some way out through the Judenrat and offered large sums of money in exchange. Obman Engelberg categorically opposed this, but Dr. Seifer and Baruch Kramer went to the chief of the Arbeitsamt and proposed to exchange those who were unable to work with healthy and young workers. They backed up their proposal with presents consisting of a leather coat and two pieces of cloth for a suit (if I am not mistaken). The gifts must have impressed the chief of the Arbeitsamt and his deputy, the Ukrainian Davybida, and they agreed. In reality the names that were taken off the list were of those who could pay most rather than of those who were unable to work. Both Seifer and Kramer naturally made plenty of money in this manner and did not turn down jewelry either.

When I asked him [Seifer?] about this in a private conversation, he retorted with a question: "If they take all the rich Jews, how are we going to have money to pay for the growing demands of the Germans?" But when I remarked that what he was doing was immoral, he said: "When the Russians come you can hang me, but before that happens both of us will be lying on the Fedor" [i.e., in a mass grave on that nearby hill].

Two days later, 150 men left the town on foot under the guard of the Ukrainian police and the Germans in the direction of Borki. The Poles sent after them [by the Judenrat] returned the next day and reported that they had followed the men until they disappeared behind the barbed wire fences of the camp. A few weeks later, thanks to the endeavors of Obman Engelberg and Beirish Kanner and supported by a few gifts, we were allowed by the Landkommissar to send some food packages to the camp. The packages were sent in a horse-drawn carriage. Kanner and "OD" [Ordnungsdienst] Albrecht accompanied the cargo.

When they returned, they brought a letter from the people imprisoned there saying that they were working in terrible conditions and that if they stay, they would soon die as a result of hard work, hunger, and exhaustion. Additionally, there was an incident in which one of the Jews escaped. As penalty, the Germans executed ten Jews, including a boy from Buczacz called Bunio Jurman. His mother and sister were overcome with grief. Soon thereafter, another Jew escaped. This time it was the cabby Moshe Chusyd from Buczacz. But he was soon caught and hanged on a gallows specially erected in the center of the camp for everyone to see. He was left hanging there for three days.

Having received such terrifying news, and after some deliberation, the Judenrat decided to send a new batch of people to the camp so as to save those of the first transport from dying. Since there were no volunteers, the OD organized a veritable campaign against the poorer Jews, while only taking money or jewelry from the richer ones. Just before Christmas, another German organization arrived in town: this was the Kripo, the Criminal Police [Kriminalpolizei]. It consisted of three Polish ethnic Germans. While two of them were content to be provided with clothes and shoes by the Jews, the third one, who was called Szydłowski, constantly made new demands, first terrorizing the Judenrat and later also individual inhabitants of the town. Within a short period of time he became the scourge of Buczacz.

Then came the Christmas holidays, which cost the Jews about half a million złoty. Three Jewish bakeries were busy baking bread and cakes for the Germans. The best and most expensive wines were bought. Specially ordered cakes and alcoholic drinks arrived from the Gestapo in Czortków. Two weeks later, the same had to be prepared for the Ukrainian police.[21] And all this was happening at a time when the Jews were exchanging their last pieces of clothing and bedclothes for some flour or potatoes.

After New Year's an order was issued that every Jew had to carry a "Kennkarte" [ID card] issued by [Georg] Barg, chief of the [local] gendarmerie.[22] Every day, sometimes twice or three times a day, a roll call was held, at a time when the temperature was 30 degrees Celsius below freezing point. All men between sixteen and sixty-five had to attend. My brother and I did not participate in these roll calls, despite Barg's quip, made once when he was drunk, that "A Jew must either hide well or pay well in order to survive the war." These roll calls went on until May, by which time most of the "Kennkarten" had been issued. In the meantime, we continued receiving and spreading the news from the radio.

For some time, I had noticed a strange change in attitude toward me among people. When I walked into the Judenrat I would be given right of way. Many people on the street whom I had not known before began greeting me. When I approached the bakery where a hundred people were lining up for bread, I would be invited inside, and nobody protested. This mute act of appreciation by people who despite our precautions must have learned who was responsible for the radio transmissions, made me very happy, but on the other hand I was afraid that it could also reach the ears of the Germans, and then what I would say? Any way you looked at it I would end up on the Fedor [killing site].

In the evenings we usually gathered at Tina Kirshner's house. Ziuta Gefner, Zuza Kriegel, Fanka Steinberg, Munio Freund, and others participated. Fanka usually sang Yiddish and Hebrew songs, and no matter what we talked about, we always ended up on the topic of Palestine. I recalled my brother and sister, Tina and Lolek, who left just before the outbreak of the war. We mentioned Łonek Miedwiński, Nunia Bauer, and many others. Sala Rinder talked about her husband. Even her young son, Dolus, sitting on my lap, said: "If we survive the war and father comes back, he won't recognize me." Munio Freund, rubbing his hands because of the cold, said to me: "What do you think? You are never there for the roll calls, you don't have a 'Kennkarte,' you listen to the radio. You should have been executed ten times already. And at the end, you see," he said to the others, "he will survive us all." Janek Blaukopf, who did not have a "Kennkarte" either, pointed to two 500 złoty bills and said, "I have two such 'Kennkarten': If the police stop me, I show one. If it doesn't work, the second one always does." These moments had so much good humor in them, and we felt so lighthearted, that we would often forget about the dark reality outside and felt almost happy.

One day, as I was sitting on the porch, I saw Milo Rozen running toward me. From his appearance I could tell that something terrible must have happened. And indeed, in a moment he was standing in front of me, calling out that the gendarmerie chief had stopped my brother and demanded his "Kennkarte." Since my brother did not possess one, he was arrested and put in prison with other Jews charged with the same crime. They could either be shot or at best be sent to Borki. I went to the kitchen and gently informed my mother. I said that I would go to town to see what I could do. In town I walked past the prison and from one of the cell windows I could see my brother's face. When he saw me, he tried to smile, while also gesturing me to go away. I shouted to him not to give up, that I would do everything to release him.

I quickly went to the Judenrat where I asked Kramer to do something for those who had been arrested. Kramer replied that he had already intervened and that they were not going to execute the prisoners, just send them to the camp in Borki. As far as my brother was concerned, the only way to release him was to replace him with someone else. At that moment, one of the OD-men walked into the room and said that the gendarmerie chief had agreed to deliver food to the prisoners. I asked to be the one who would to do this disguised as an OD-man and planned to exchange the uniform with my brother and stay there instead of him. Shortly thereafter I and two other OD-men, who were carrying food for the prisoners, proceeded towards the prison.

When I got to the cell, my brother initially refused to let me stay there instead of him. But I assured him that by I'd be back home by evening. In the end, getting increasingly nervous, I struck him. There was no time to lose. Any moment a Ukrainian policeman could walk in. At last we were ready. My brother left disguised as an OD-man, and I rushed to the window to make sure that he had reached the street. Suddenly I heard a noise, someone's footsteps, shouting, and the sound of a beating outside the door. The door of the cell opened, and my brother was shoved in with a brutal kick. I just managed to see that his nose was bleeding when the chief himself burst into the cell and began beating and kicking me, shouting: "Du verfluchter jüdischer Hund" [You damned Jewish dog]. "These two," he said, pointing to my brother and me, "are not to be sent to Borki. I will deal with them myself." He left the cell with a bang.

I looked around the cell. There were a few other people there apart from us: Janek Werner, Kuba Weiser, and some others. Among them were two Jews who were considered to be the richest in town. I approached the window where my good friend, Kuba Weiser the locksmith, was standing. "If I had some acid and a small saw, I'd be able to deal with the bars in the window in half an hour," he whispered. A saw and some acid. "But how can we get hold of that in this cell?" I said. "At home I would get hold of them in no time, but here!!!" We stood pondering this for a few minutes, when suddenly my friend Rózia Szarf appeared on the street. I called her by name. Eventually she heard, turned around, and not seeing anyone behind her, ran to the window. Kuba explained in detail where he had hidden the materials at home. Promising to arrange everything she quickly left. After an hour, as we were already losing hope, we saw Rózia on the street. Choosing the right moment, she approached the window and pushed in a small package. I didn't have time to thank her when she threw us a kiss with her hand and disappeared.

We decided not to tell the others about our plan until evening. Only later at night did we reveal that we were going to try to cut the grille and escape. Everyone greeted our plan with great joy. The hope that they might soon be free energized those people who had become apathetic. Kuba was already preparing for the job, when suddenly the two "bourgeois" began to protest and tried to dissuade us from the plan, claiming that we would anger the Germans, who would catch us anyway and then take revenge on us and our families. It became clear to us they were certain that thanks to their money they would be able to avoid execution or deportation to Borki. When one of them approached the door with the intention of calling the guards, my brother punched him in the jaw, and the rest of us meantime tried to calm down the other one.

Cutting the bars took two hours, and at 1 a.m. the way out was open. The two "rich ones" said they were staying in the cell because they were sure the Germans would let them out the next day, while we would surely be punished. Listening carefully and trying not to make any noise, we climbed out through the window one by one. Within a few minutes we were on our way to the cemetery. My brother and I went into our house for a moment to calm down our mother. She was frantic with worry. We put her mind at ease and soon settled down to sleep in one of the tombs.

When the gendarmerie chief discovered our escape, he was furious. First, he shot the two loyal prisoners. Then he threatened repression and announced ultimatums by which time the Judenrat was to hand us over to the police. The following day he was partly appeased by a few bottles of brandy provided by the Judenrat .... Within a couple of days, after receiving another set of bottles, this representative of the "Herrenvolk" [master race] in the town was sufficiently pacified and we were able to leave the tomb and return home.

Hunger: when you are so hungry that nothing else matters. Even the imminent threat of death seems to lose its importance. Everything is concentrated on one goal: to eat, to eat, to eat. Does hunger hurt? If someone had asked me, I would say yes, it does. I felt physical pain. But even more so, the pain that made me lose my mind was caused by seeing my mother's suffering. Only those who have known this pain can understand these words. And I'm writing this for those who have.

It began in this manner. In May 1942 special squads of the "Sonderdienst" arrived in Buczacz.[23] The men systematically plundered the villages, taking wheat, farm animals, and poultry. The roads were full of German and Ukrainian police patrols that were robbing the peasants of all the food products they were trying to smuggle into the towns. The towns were hungry. The first to feel it were of course the Jews, who no longer received any food rations. Those peasants who managed to smuggle some potatoes or wheat to the towns sold them for exorbitant prices ....

Everybody tried to get hold of something called "żarna" [hand mill] which consisted of two round stones. The wheat would be poured in between them, and by rubbing them one against the other it would be turned into flour. My brother also made such a contraption, and whenever we were able to buy a kilogram of wheat ... we would immediately ground it, trying to ensure that not one of the valuable grains was lost. One can imagine the taste of this flour, mixed together with stone dust, that made a terrible grinding sound between our teeth .... But the worst was to see our mother's torment, as she silently and courageously suffered the pangs of hunger without complaint. Only in her sad eyes could I see how she was suffering from knowing that we too were hungry. I will not forget these eyes as long as I live.

Some Jews tried to sneak out to the neighboring villages and obtain some food by bartering clothes and jewelry. Many paid for this with their lives when they fell into the hands of the German or Ukrainian police.

People began dying of hunger. Every day scores of people died; their bodies were collected from the streets early in the morning, when there were few people around, and quickly taken through the back alleys to the Jewish cemetery. On the streets inhabited by the Jews, you could see people with terribly swollen feet and distended stomachs wandering around, more dead than alive. During that time there were feasts in the Landkommissar's offices: geese, bread, sausages, wine, vodka, brandy. All of this provided for from the inexhaustible pocket of the Judenrat.

On one of those hungry afternoons I was lying on the couch. I was often resting like this at the time. I frequently felt dizzy, my whole body overcome with weakness, even my feet refused to obey me. I was asking myself, is this the beginning of the end? Suddenly I heard steps in the hallway and Dr. Seifer and engineer Cyres popped into the room. I did not have time to raise myself to greet them when they began hugging me, laughing and crying. From their incoherent speaking I managed to discern two words that made me insanely happy: "A second front, a second front!" The English had landed in France. Everything vanished. Everything was forgotten. The Germans, the hunger, the Ukrainians, the Gestapo. What is all that compared to a second front? At last. At last. In broad daylight I rushed to the cemetery to get my radio. I did not even check if anyone could see me. Now I was not afraid of anyone. A second front, the surrounding trees whispered. A second front—the dean's coffin in the tomb greeted me. A second front, the wind hummed as I ran back home.

In an instant, I turned on the radio. My mother and Mrs. Samet were crying tears of joy and praying out loud. The notary, informed by my brother, ran in. And we listened... By 3 p.m. not one English soldier, apart from those captured, was left on the French beach in the area of Dieppe, where the British had tried to establish a second front.[24] Cry Mother, cry, it seems we will not be given the chance to meet the Messiah.

Hunger again. Terrible, tormenting hunger. Today, my brother and I were summoned to work. We were supposed to arrange the electrical installations in the school building, which had been turned into a storehouse for wheat. Here the Germans kept the wheat confiscated from the villages. We waded through floors covered with layers upon layers of wheat. In some places we were up to our knees in the golden grains. We gathered the life-giving golden grains by the handfuls and, what is most important, we ate and ate and ate. If we had only been able to hide and bring some of this home. But the officer in charge had given the soldier guarding the building strict orders to examine us carefully when we leave. We had to work there for two weeks and we were very happy about that. After all, nobody was guarding us inside and we ate as much as we could. We didn't care that later we had stomach spasms and were in terrible pain. The most important thing was that we ate.

The gymnasium building was not on the main street but on a small hill adjacent to it. On one side the windows looked out to Fedor Hill, on top of which was the cemetery, whose perimeter reached the edge of our garden. Coming there every day, we noticed that the soldiers on guard changed every six hours and that only one soldier was guarding the building. The change of guard occurred at 6 and 12 both during the day and at night. At some point I discussed the matter with Maniek the undertaker and we tried to figure out how we could take some wheat out of there.

Two days later Maniek and two of his friends, Andrej and Józek, showed up. After long deliberations, the four of us decided how we would proceed. I was to make an imprint of the main door's lock. Once the key was ready, we would decide on which evening to sneak in, render the German guard harmless, and get as much wheat as we could. One evening after the key was ready, a few minutes after 6 p.m., the German who was to be on duty until midnight arrived. As I was leaving the building, I held a bottle of vodka in my hand. Responding to the German's question, I said that I had found the bottle in one of the halls where we had been working that day. He grabbed the bottle and shouted that we could leave.

At 9 p.m., when it was already totally dark, the four of us left the house. I, Manko, Andrej, and Józek. I told my mother that I would spend the night at a friend's house in town. After crossing the cemetery, we started slowly descending the hill. It was covered by dwarf pine trees nearly all the way to the school building. Stepping carefully, we nearly reached the first row of the trees. No more than twenty paces separated us from the German. From here we could observe every movement he made. He was walking in front of the building with measured steps. After a while, he approached a bench placed next to the building and took a drink from the bottle he had confiscated from me. Then he lit a cigarette. Within an hour, he had drunk a few more times from the bottle and finally sat on the bench and lowered his head.

We waited for another half hour. Then I threw a pebble at his feet. After a while I threw another pebble. When once more the German did not show any sign of life, I approached him, holding an iron hammer in my hand, and hit him on the head with all my might. The German fell down without a sound. At the same moment Andrej stabbed him twice in the heart with a knife. Thereupon Maniek and I unlocked the door and began to fill our sacks with wheat, while Józek took the full sacks out. Andrej was standing guard, listening in case the other guard approached. Filling the sacks took about fifteen minutes, after which we carried them over the hill in the direction of the cemetery. We hid the sacks in one of the tombs. I couldn't resist and filled my pockets with grains. As soon as we came home, we ground them, and at 1 am we were eating our hot porridge. Tomorrow they can torture me, shoot me, but they will not be able to take the hot porridge away from me.

The following day, when we tried to go to work as usual, the streets next to the gymnasium were surrounded by the army and no one could get through. Initially, the Germans carried out their investigations by arresting a few Ukrainians whom they had recently come to trust less. After that, they suspected the village of Trybuchowce, where they had confiscated a large amount of wheat a few days earlier. Eventually, everything calmed down. But we could grind more with our żarna at night and the porridge was much thicker. One kilogram at a time.

A few weeks before Rosh Hashanah [Jewish New Year], various incidents occurred which clearly indicated that the Jews were about to be systematically and totally annihilated. It began in Czortków, a city located 35 kilometers from Buczacz. The Germans set up electric searchlights on the streets. Machine guns were placed at every street corner. Officially they proclaimed that these preparations were connected to the anti-aircraft defense. Previously, an order was issued that all houses inhabited by Jews had to be marked with a big blue Star of David. One night the town was shaken by the thunder of heavy shooting and explosions of hand grenades. The Germans and the Ukrainians had broken into houses inhabited by Jews, shooting everyone they encountered. Hand grenades were thrown at people trying to hide in the cellars. At night the searchlights on the streets did not allow anyone to escape the hellish cauldron. The massacre went on for twenty-four hours. Altogether, over two thousand people were killed.[25] The surviving Jews were ordered to remove and bury the corpses. This action was carried out by the so-called "Toten-Kommando," a unit established especially for this purpose. This unit, led by Gestapo-man Rux, consisted of SS-men, German gendarmes, and Ukrainian police.[26]

Immediately after this event, orders were issued to also mark the [Jewish] houses in Buczacz with a Star of David. Having learned the sad lesson of Czortków, we knew what this meant. Everybody was trying somehow to protect themselves and their family from the imminent action[27] (as these bloody massacres were called), by preparing bunkers[28] [hideouts] in which their families could hide during such events. We too were preoccupied with preparing a bunker for ourselves and some of our neighbors. The site we chose for this purpose was a brick chapel in the cemetery. Several generations of Count Potocki's clan were buried in the crypt of this chapel.[29]

Above the oval stone ceiling, a triangular wooden roof had been built, forming a kind of in-between attic. There was no entrance into this attic. We therefore pulled out a few boards from the roof and made a sort of improvised door that could be locked from the inside. From the outside it seemed that there was no entrance, and anyone trying to enter without knowing of the existence of this contraption would have had to demolish the entire roof. One night we brought to it hay, which we had stuffed into in sacks so as not to leave any traces and covered the floor of the attic with it. We also prepared pails with water and several blankets.

Meanwhile in town, Obman Engelberg was able to enlist a Polish telephone operator in the Buczacz post office who, in turn, contacted a telephone operator in Czortków. Other Jewish councils under the authority of the Czortków Toten-Kommando organized the same sort of network. Thus, when vehicles with members of the Toten-Kommando would leave Czortków in the direction of another town, the Jewish councils in those towns were immediately informed by these trusted telephone operators. In this manner, living in constant anticipation, trembling with fear during the night at the sound of car horns or of shots, the High Holidays of Rosh Hashanah arrived ....

On 7 October, the city was shocked by a new blow. The Germans announced that anyone helping to hide a Jew during an action would be shot .... That same afternoon Obman Engelberg announced that we should expect a roundup the following day. At the same time, OD Commander Albrecht ordered an assembly of all OD-men who, according to the previous instructions by the Gestapo chief, were to assist in the course of the entire roundup, helping to find hidden bunkers, and escorting the Jews to the sites of execution. At 9 p.m., just as we were about to go and hide in the bunker, the Freund and Kirshner families came running in. Altogether, instead of the expected fifteen people, there were thirty-five of us that evening. Bringing everyone into the shelter, while keeping all the safety measures, took us nearly three hours. At 1 a.m. we were all lying in the shelter. The entrance was covered, and we could hear the howling autumn wind blowing through the trees.

Slowly, dawn began seeping through the slits in the roof. At 5 a.m. we heard the first shots and our hearts beat with fear. It had begun. There were more and more shots. The little six-year-old Dolus was lying next to me and staring ahead with his blue eyes. This child understood everything already. In recent days, I had been teaching him how not to make a sound while coughing or sneezing. I raised my head and looked around. Everyone was lying silently. All were trying to avoid any unnecessary movement. What does a person think about at a moment like this? I don't know what the others were thinking about, but I was contemplating that we were living in the year of 1942, in the era of electricity and radio. There were courtrooms, churches, and shelters for the homeless. There were associations for the protection of animals. And yet people were being murdered, women, the elderly, children, in broad daylight. No, no. Perhaps this was just a nightmare. Maybe I would wake up in a moment, covered in cold sweat, surprised that I could have dreamt something as terrible as this. I closed my eyes. Shots were heard. I opened them. Shots again. No, it was not a dream. Again, my eyes met Dolus's. I caressed his head and whispered in his ear about his father who at the moment was far away and did not even know what was happening to him. Dolus put his finger to his lips and with an expressive gesture warned me to be quiet.

Evening came. A strong wind began to blow. We waited for another hour. It was 9 p.m. I decided that someone had to come out and check what was going on in town. Munio, Freund, and I went. We were holding hands, so that we would not lose each other in the dark. We walked, step by step in the wind and the rustle of the trees. The contours of a house emerged in the dark. I saw an open door and shattered windows. We turned and came up to the window of a neighbor. I listened for some time and then quietly knocked on the window. I heard someone approaching and one of our neighbors appeared. When he saw us, he jumped back as if he had seen a ghost. "Run away, run away from here!" he shouted. "They will also kill me because of you. They've been shooting all day. So many dead. And so many were loaded onto railcars and taken somewhere. Escape!!!" And he shut the door. We returned to the shelter in the cemetery. All the way I kept thinking, what would I tell the people there? After a while, we were back in the attic. We were showered with questions. I answered that we had to stay put for another day. Tomorrow evening, I would go out again and we would see.

We lay there. Some fell asleep. I told my brother how we were received by our neighbor. Suddenly, I heard a noise from the outside. Someone's steps. Oh, my God, if someone were to cough or sigh in their sleep we'd be lost. I then heard someone from the outside calling me by name. I recognized the voice of Ozjasz Friedlender.[30] In a flash I was next to him, and right behind me was the inseparable Munio Freund. We learned that the first roundup was over and he, worried about our absence, came to find out what had happened to us. I gave the signal to leave the shelter. One by one, very carefully, we all left. We walked toward our house. We quickly repaired the door. We replaced the [broken] windowpanes with cardboard. Soon there was a fire in the kitchen [stove] and we were drinking tea. Some of us even started to joke. Apparently, this could also be called life. One could get used to it.

The following day, we went into town. The Jewish streets looked as if a terrifying hurricane has swept through them. All the doors were wide open, the windows shattered. Parts of clothing were scattered on the muddy streets along with shards of glass and corpses. And more corpses. Wherever you looked, there were corpses. They were lying face down. They were lying with their eyes wide open, staring into the sky. Their bodies were shrunken. Their bodies were spread out. Some faces were frozen in an expression of insane fear. Others were smiling. There were youngsters and old people, women and children. There were babies. The latter had not been shot. That would have been a waste of bullets. Their heads were simply swung against the wall of a house. A Jewish house. A solid house. A house made of hard stone.

In total, the number of the first roundup's victims totaled fifteen hundred Jews.[31] Four hundred were shot in town while trying to escape or resist. The rest were loaded onto train cars and taken away. Where, nobody knew. After some time, we learned that the men had been taken to Lwów, where there was a concentration camp for Jews in Janowska. Women, children, and the old were directed to Bełżec, where the smoking chimneys of the crematorium were waiting for them.[32]

One evening in November, we heard on the news about the landing of the Allied Forces under General [Dwight D.] Eisenhauer in North Africa.[33] Again, in that moment of joy we forgot about everything that was happening around us. But, after a while doubts arose. I impatiently tried to catch the sounds coming out of the loudspeaker. Bum, bum, bum, then at last: "This is London... Hurrah for [French Admiral François] Darlan and the Allies. Casablanca is in the hands of the Allies. The Eighth Army is on the move." We decided to wait for more details before spreading this news. What if it all ended like Dieppe?

We discussed the day's events in the Judenrat. There was tremendous joy. First of all, we had reached the day in which the Germans were beginning to lose. Second, Palestine. How we feared for its fate. So many moments of terror. The Germans had occupied Tobruk, Sollum, Mersa Matruh. They next advanced to El Alamein. So many sleepless nights. Would the Germans reach there [Palestine] too? And then ... we were afraid to consider that, but the thought kept returning. As of this day, it belonged to the past. The Hebrew teacher [Israel] Fernhof stood up. Who in Buczacz did not know Fernhof?[34] An elderly man, one of the first Zionists in our city. A fanatical lover of Palestine.

He said: "Next to the feeling of joy that our enemies have begun to lose, my heart is filled with an even greater joy. Our fate is sealed. I do not believe in a miracle that will change the course of our future. But, in Eretz Israel, where blood is born from our blood, bones from our bones, a new young generation is growing. Until today I was living in terrible fear for the future of this generation. But today I believe it is God's will that a generation of avengers will be born from them and they will avenge us. Now I can die in peace. But first let us thank God and beg him to support our allies' forces. And perhaps one of us will find mercy in the eyes of God and live until the moment of salvation."

I saw tears in many eyes. Those who did not have a hat covered their heads with a handkerchief. Soon we heard the prayer. I did not understand the words, but I understood the content: "Thank you, God, for letting us live in this moment, when justice and righteousness are vanquishing injustice and evil. We beseech you, God, help our allies. Give strength to the Eighth British Army, which is chasing the enemy away from the Holy Land. Keep General Eisenhauer and his soldiers in good health, they who have come from far away and are sacrificing their lives on the altar of freedom and justice. Let us, God, live to see the moment when the forces of evil are destroyed, when we are as free as other free men, and we will praise your name and bless it. Amen."

It was getting colder and colder. The slushy mud turned into hard soil. The cold and white frost covering the ground foreshadowed the coming of winter and with it snow. It filled me with fear. What would we do now with our shelter in the chapel? We could perhaps cope with the cold, but our footprints in the snow would reveal our hideout to everyone. My brother and I decided to look for another shelter that we could use in winter in the event of further roundups. In order to reach the orchard from our house, one had to climb several stone stairs to a road that led to the gate of the orchard. Those stairs were placed on a stone wall that was part of a cellar buried under rubble long ago. We decided to dig out the cellar, and for an entrance to leave only a small opening near the ground level, placing the dog's kennel in front of it. In that way, we would avoid leaving footsteps in the snow, while the dog would warn us by barking if anybody approached.

There was another obstacle: we had to conceal our intention of building the shelter and its whereabouts at any cost even from our closest Ukrainian and Polish neighbors. Only the notary knew about this. We started our work on a wet evening. The notary and the dog were standing guard, while I, my brother, and some other Jewish neighbors, who in the event would also find shelter there, began working. We would gather the rubble we dug out into specially prepared sacks and carry them to the cemetery, where they were emptied. By morning, the cellar was clean. We camouflaged the entrance with some dry branches and postponed the rest of the work to the next evening. During the entire following day one of us alternated in observing our work from afar to make sure no one uncalled for had noticed it. Over the next few nights we completed the construction of the shelter. We even prepared hay, water, and crusts of bread in the event the roundup would take longer.

In the early hours of 25 November, I went to the Judenrat. Upon arriving, I noticed some unusual activity. People were walking around hurriedly with anxious expressions on their faces. I did not have to ask. I knew. A roundup would occur tomorrow. Soon Kramer confirmed it. "We are expecting an action tomorrow," he said. I went home. It had begun snowing, the first snow of this winter. At home, I found more people than the shelter could hold. It became clear that there were five people too many and there was no way we could all fit in. Nor could we use our old shelter in the cemetery, since the ground was covered with white snow like a shroud.

Dwojra, one of the women, said that in the village Trybuchowce, three kilometers from Buczacz [actually 7 km southeast of Buczacz], she knew a peasant who had promised to give her shelter in the event of a roundup. I therefore arranged for only the women and children to hide in our shelter. The men, four of us including myself, would go to the peasant along with Dwojra. At 9 p.m. the others started entering the shelter. I helped my mother, who was beside herself with grief that we would not be together. I helped Dolus, his mother, and others. I charged Tina, whom I considered the most energetic among them, with keeping order in the shelter.

We were soon on our way towards the forest. The village we wanted to reach lay beyond. A snowstorm began. The wind was blowing furiously, blowing clouds of snow that greatly restricted visibility. We had much difficulty keeping to the road until we reached the forest, where things were calmer. From there we could see the lights in the windows of the village to which we were heading. We carefully approached the first houses and there Dwojra whispered to us to wait and disappeared among the houses. After several minutes she was back. As she came closer, we could discern from her voice that something was wrong. It became clear that the frightened peasant did not even want to hear of sheltering a few people and had even threatened to call the police. It was 1 a.m. and not knowing what to do, we began walking back in the direction of home. On the way, we were thinking where we might be able to hide, since we knew it would be impossible to get into the overcrowded bunker.

After some deliberation we decided to hide in the shelter in the cemetery chapel, counting on the fact that the unrelenting snowstorm would cover up our footsteps by morning. On the way, Dwojra became weak and we had to drag her so as not to leave her behind. We were totally exhausted by the time we reached the cemetery, always trying to step in the footsteps of the person in front of us. We entered the chapel. My brother continued walking a few more steps to hide the fact that our footsteps were leading to the entrance of the chapel. At last we were in the attic and lying on the hay that had already been flattened by our bodies from the previous time. I was worried about the snow I had to remove from the roof to clear the entrance. Will the falling snow cover it up until daybreak? Disturbed by thoughts of this kind, I snuggled up closer to my brother and in vain tried to fall asleep. The intense cold was hard to bear. Dwojra took out a bottle of vodka from her bag and that helped us warm up a little.

Daylight finally came. We heard the first shots, and later listened to them all day long. At around 3 p.m. I heard voices not far from us. Carefully peeking through one of the slits in the roof I saw two Germans carrying submachine guns coming down the road. Next to them was Walter, the son of an ethnic German woman, who lived on our street. They were heading directly toward us. It seemed impossible that they would not notice the snow we had cleared off the roof. I turned around, held my brother's hand, and whispered in his ear: "We are lost. They're coming straight toward us." We remained silent and motionless. We waited for a shot, or yells. Nothing. Silence. Maybe they were deliberating what to do? I waited another few moments. Then I slowly relaxed. I looked through the crack again. No one. Soon it got dark. I could not take it anymore. We left, all together. We lowered ourselves down from the roof. Munio Freund and I acted as scouts. We approached the house and saw that the kennel had been moved aside, the dog was gone, one wall has been demolished and, my God ... my knees buckled. Freund came up and hugged me, trying to comfort me, but I didn't care anymore.

I ran back to the cemetery where the others were waiting and shouted to my brother: "Mama is not there!" He stared at me in shock. He seemed not to understand yet. I grasped his hand and we ran, followed by the others. We reached the garden, went up the stairs, and looked at the place where we had seen our mother for the last time. Mother. Why did I not stay with you, Mother!!! Mom. I heard my brother's scream, as he fell to the ground, next to the sinister hole in the ground. I hugged him and tried to calm him down. "Brother, dear brother, we have to live. We have to tell Etka and Saul in Palestine about this one day. We have to avenge our mother. Calm down, I beg you." His body was shaking. He was sobbing loudly. I led him [back to the house and] into the room, we sat on the ruffled bed and hugged each other; we stayed like this without moving, half expecting our mother to walk in and tell us that it was already late, that we should go to sleep. But only the wind blew into the room, banging the open windows and tearing down the picture hanging on the wall, then leaving through the open door. My brother's body was shaking. I felt his hot tears on my hands. Oh, if only I could cry, just once.

The next day we learned that the number of the Toten-Kommando's victims that day reached more than a thousand. Judenrat member Jankiel [Jakob] Ebenstein had died the death of a hero.[35] He was ordered to help one of the groups of the Toten-Kommando, who were looking for hidden bunkers. As they were demolishing one of them, he tried to convince the Gestapo chief that no Jews were hiding in that house. He said that he was ready to guarantee with his own head that searching there was useless. But when, after demolishing the wall, they began pulling Jews out of there, Ebenstein figured that the end had come, grabbed a hatchet, and tried to strike the Gestapo-man. At the same moment another soldier shot him. That is how a man, who during his few months as member of the Judenrat came to be hated by everyone and was called an agent of the Gestapo, died a hero's death. That day he was forgiven everything.

It seemed that some of those who were deported to Bełżec that day had managed to break out of the train cars. Jumping from a speeding train was usually met by death because the Germans, who were placed in specially built platforms between the cars, shot at anyone who tried to escape. Nevertheless, some survived jumping and returned to town through sideroads and fields. Among them was Dolus's mother, Sala Rinder, who had hidden in our shelter, and she came to us right away. She was covered in blood because when she jumped her face was badly scraped. She said that her sister Tina and Dolus had also jumped and begged us to try to save them.

Soon thereafter we learned that the Landkommissar had instructed the Judenrat to immediately dispatch a group of Jews on horse-drawn snow sledges to gather the corpses scattered along the rails. I was on the first sledge, and we were heading down the field next to the train rails. Already on the third kilometer I noticed something dark on the snow. It was the body of a man. As we continued, there were more and more corpses, rigid and stiff. I recognized the body of a girl, Maniusia Gotlieb, and further on the body of Sala Berlin lying next to her mother's body. We kept going. Then I recognized Tina's blond hair. Even in death, she was still holding Dolus's already frozen body in her arms. Our sleigh was full, and we decided to return. Before we rode into town, I wanted to cover the bodies with a blanket, but Schmetterling, who was riding with me, yelled: "Don't do it! We will drive them like this through the town. Let everyone see, so that later they won't be able to say they did not know."

After the second action, many Jews started streaming into Buczacz.[36] They were deported from smaller towns like Monasterzyska, Potok Złoty, Barysz, Koropiec, and others. The number of the Jews expelled from the neighboring villages, together with those still in Buczacz after the two actions, amounted to ten thousand. The resettlement was carried out with horse-drawn carriages loaned from the peasants for large sums of money. The caravans of horse carts heading in the direction of Buczacz and carrying the remaining property of the Jews were often attacked and looted by the peasants who not only took everything, but also sometimes tore the clothes off the Jews. In response to the pleading and tears of the Jewish women they would say: "You don't need them; they are going to kill you anyway."

The Jews resettled in Buczacz were mostly housed on Podhajecka Street, next to the so-called "Baszty" [the hill of the Jewish cemetery], where a kind of ghetto was established. Each room accommodated up to fifteen people, and when that did not suffice, they began placing people in synagogues, bathhouses, and attics. Such overpopulation at a time when the price of soap was exorbitant and when hundreds of people were dying every day from hunger, inevitably led to a typhoid epidemic. The epidemic broke out on Sunday. The only Jewish hospital was incapable of hospitalizing even a fraction of the sick. And those who did find shelter in the hospital had to be placed on the floors and in the hallways because of the shortage of beds. The hospital was directed by Dr. Seifer, who managed, even under the most difficult circumstances, to gather very professional personnel and to acquire medications literally from nowhere. In addition to Dr. Seifer, other people distinguished themselves in their sacrifice for others, such as the controller of the post office, Mr. Weiss, Mr. Ebenstein,[37] and Pusia Polak, who was a real angel of love and sacrifice for the unfortunate ill.

During that time, my brother and I were living in our old apartment near the cemetery. Our old friends Ozjasz Bardach and Rózia Scharf were living with us. Rózia was in charge of the housekeeping. Walking through the town's streets, you could see posters plastered to the walls of the houses with such announcement as: "Jews spread typhoid. If you shake hands with a Jew, you might get infected." On the entrances to houses, shops, and restaurants, you could see signs stating: "Jews and dogs not allowed." At the same time, even as the Germans were afraid of the non-Jewish population becoming contaminated with "Jewish diseases," they also demanded ever more items from the Judenrat. In this case they were not afraid of using Jewish cloth for suits, leather for shoes, coats and other belongings. Nor did they have any qualms about eating bread baked especially for them by Jewish bakers.

"When power is born, God is filled with fear."[38]

That is what we might have said about Christmas that year. The God-fearing Germans had decided in 1942 to avenge themselves on the Jews for crucifying of Christ centuries ago.[39] This is how it started. One evening, before the holidays, armed German gendarmes, assisted by Ukrainians, suddenly filled the Jewish quarter and snatched thirty men and women from the streets. Those trying to escape were shot on the spot. Terrible panic followed. Everybody thought this was the beginning of a third roundup and hid in their bunkers. In the morning it became clear that there was not going to be a roundup. The Germans contented themselves with the thirty Jews they caught.

The next day these captives were taken under escort of the Ukrainian police to the prison in Czortków .... Those imprisoned were locked up in a large prison cell. Severely beaten, they were all forced to undress totally. On command, everyone had to turn with their faces towards the wall. One of the Gestapo-men read out the verdict, according to which they had been sentenced to death as punishment for the Crucifixion of Christ. The verdict had been issued by the International Union of the Avengers of Christ and had supposedly been approved by the Pope. After it was read out, the naked men and women were chased back into the cell.

The following evening ... the group from Czortków was sent out into the hall. Five young women and one man were chosen. They were taken away by the Gestapo. After a while, those who remained in the cell heard voices from the large prison yard. Through the grate on the window they could see that something unusual was about to happen. A large fire had been built in the middle of the yard. Not far away a large wooden cross was lying on the ground. Those looking from the cell noticed the five young girls and the man walking totally naked through the yard. A few steps behind them, the well-known sadist, Gestapo-man [Artur] Rosenow[40] followed, holding two big dogs on a leash. Many people gathered in the yard, especially Gestapo-men and their wives. At some point, two of the girls were separated from the rest and forced to dance around the fire. One of the Germans played the harmonica while the other used a whip to drive on the half-dead girls. On a signal the other soldier released the dogs. The dogs attacked the girls, biting their throats. The last cries of the girls were drowned by the clapping and laughter of the gathered SS-men and their wives. The other three girls were killed in the same manner. The man, on the other hand, was crucified and left hanging there, and his groans could be heard by the inhabitants of the cells late into the night, giving them an inkling of what awaited them the following day.

The next day was quiet. In the evening the cell was unlocked, and some SS officers appeared. This time it was the turn of the Buczacz group. They were chased to the yard where a truck covered with canvas was already waiting. Completely naked, driven by whip lashes, they were forced onto the truck. After a half-hour ride, the truck stopped. The people were taken out to the snow. One of the SS-men handed them shovels and ordered them to dig a hole. Urged on with yells and blows by the Germans, the Jews started digging, but the frozen ground was very hard and even after an hour of digging there was no sign of it yielding. Seeing the futility of this work, the Germans loaded the Jews back on the truck. Late at night, as they sat in the cell, these Jews talked with the other inmates about what they had experienced. All of them said they had not even felt the cold. One of them expressed the following wish: "May things end as quickly as possible. In that way we will at least know whether there is an afterworld."

Again, the following day no one bothered them. It was Christmas Eve. At around 10 p.m. the door opened and Chief Rux himself entered the cell. He was holding a piece of paper in his hand and read out from it: "Despite the intrigues of International Jewry, the son of God has been born. As a consequence, I order to free the rest of the Jews, according to the will of the Pope." There was some illegible signature. Everyone listened suspiciously, certain that this was another devilish trick by the Germans, but soon their clothes were thrown into the cell and a large pot of soup was also brought in. The following day they were all taken out of the cell. One of the women was dying and wanted to be left there, but the SS refused. Half-dead, she had to be carried out of the building, where the sleighs were already waiting. The same day they were all back at home.

The most interesting thing is that the people were convinced their liberation was a result of intercession by the Pope. No amount of persuasion would sway them. They were adamant that it could only have been the Pope. Perhaps Gestapo member [Paul] Thomanek, recently arrested in Poland, who was also involved in this matter, may shed some light on this riddle.[41]

One evening Bardach came home complaining of a headache. We checked his temperature and it was very high …. The next day his condition worsened. Dr. R. arrived and diagnosed typhoid. We were devastated. In the event of a roundup we had planned to escape, but now his condition kept deteriorating every day. He did not recognize anyone, was hallucinating, and would suddenly leap out of bed. It was difficult to tuck him back in. My brother stayed up all night, trying to give him medicine. It was all in vain. Within ten days he was dead. We buried him today. The lucky one. He died a natural death. We covered him in a white sheet, made a coffin out of a broken cupboard. We said "El Maleh Rahamim" ["God full of mercy": a Jewish prayer for the dead] over his grave. I said Kaddish [another prayer for the dead usually pronounced by the closest male relative]. We were all envious. All of us wished for this kind of death.

My brother and I were the only ones left at home. Rózia had to leave to take care of her sick aunt. Meanwhile, the terror in the city continued to spread. The OD were robbing, killing, worse than the Germans. Albrecht would walk down the streets in an OD uniform. Like the Germans, he was holding a whip in his hand and woe to whoever stood in his way. One day, my brother and I were standing on the sidewalk next to the synagogue where the resettled Jews were living. Albrecht passed and something about me must have irritated him, because I suddenly felt the blow of his whip on the back of my head. I turned around and saw Albrecht. Of course, I did not just stand there. Soon, a few other OD-men came running. A genuine battle broke out. As a result of it, I and my brother were seriously bruised and found ourselves arrested by the Ordnungsdienst.

We could hear through the door, how Albrecht was threatening to hand us over to the Gestapo or to send us to the camp in Borki. At the same time Friedenthal and Obman Engelberg came in. After a sharp exchange of words with Albrecht they let us go. The same day, some of our friends came to our house and during the conversation, one of them commented that we should get rid of Albrecht. I said that I would think about it. A few days later Albrecht got sick with typhoid and died within a week. That same week we had another unpleasant incident with the OD. As my brother was walking down the street, he saw several OD-men, who had been seizing people on the streets for the last few days, dragging our friend Ozjasz Friedlender. He was giving them quite a struggle. Without thinking, my brother ran up and tried to save Friedlender. Quite a battle developed. My brother returned home beaten up but smiling. It turned out that as a result of the fight Friedlender had managed to escape. I should mention that this group of OD-men was commanded by Fiszel Szwarc, who is apparently still alive.[42]

One night, my brother returned home complaining that he felt very cold. I suggested that he take off his shoes and try to warm his feet next to the fire. Soon he started to complain of a headache. I became numb. Is it typhus? I checked his temperature. 39 degrees Celsius. I tucked him into bed and prepared some tea. At night the fever rose to 40. Milo Rozen arrived. I sent for Dr. R., who arrived very quickly. He prescribed some medicine, promised he would bring some injections and said that what we needed most was experienced female help. Our cousin Pepa arrived in the afternoon. Having heard of my brother's illness, she declared that she would stay with us and take care of him. I mentioned to her that we did not have a bunker and that in the event of a roundup we had no chance of surviving. But she was not deterred by that and lightheartedly said, "You live only once. In any case we'll end up on the Fedor." She immediately began the housekeeping and soon the house looked very different. Seven days passed. Seven days of fear of the impending action. My brother's disease took its normal course. The doctor said that if everything would only remain calm, he would recover.

On the eighth day Milo came and reported that the Ukrainians had started digging huge pits on the Fedor and that we were on the eve of the third big roundup. For me this news was a terrible shock. This time, our turn had definitely come. I informed Pepa and suggested that she immediately return home. "And what about you?" she asks. "I ...," my voice quivered. "Well I, I cannot conceal it anymore, I am going to light the stove and cover the chimney. They say that this kind of death is easy, even pleasant. And what's even more important, we will at last learn if the 'next' world exists. We have so many friends there." Pepa was beside herself and yelled at me, calling me a coward. I shouted back, having become very anxious by now: "You don't want me to wait for someone to come and shoot him in the head and drag me away!" "We have to get a sleigh at any cost," Pepa said, "and in the event of an action we will take him to the forest." I tried to tell her that she was talking nonsense. He would not survive the cold. "Look how hot he is, he doesn't recognize us and continues to rave." But Pepa was stubborn. "I am going home today, and tomorrow I'll come with a sleigh. And that's the end of it." Then she left.

It was getting dark. I turned on the light and gave my brother his medicine. I sat next to him on the bed. He was looking at me with feverish eyes and continued to rave: "Take away those glass tubes, they are hurting me." Brother, dear brother. You don't recognize me. I touched his forehead with my lips. Mama, oh mama, his parched lips uttered. Dear brother, shall we go to see mama? Mama. My thoughts wandered desperately. Maybe the oven after all? But there in Palestine was our sister. If we died, no one would tell her. It was getting late. Outside the window someone's shoes were squeaking in the snow. I listened. Someone knocked on the window. "Open up!" I recognized Ziuta's voice. She stood at the door. I opened up and even before I heard her say it, I already knew. A roundup would occur tomorrow.

I returned to the room as if struck by lightning. What should I do, what should I do? Maybe the oven. But no. We didn't have time for the oven. So, what then? First, we had to dress him. I grabbed some clothes and began dressing him. I spoke as softly as I could. But he only went on raving about Mama and the glass tubes. Eventually, I put on him all the clothes I had. Then I put two quilts, a pillow and a blanket in a sack and rushed with them to the cemetery. Footprints! But we couldn't help that. The chapel? I would not be able to carry him up on my own. I chose a place between two graves, the third side being the cemetery wall. I pressed down the snow and put the quilt on top, then the pillow, and then the other quilt.

I rushed back home and packed some bread and a bottle of tea in a bag. I covered my brother up with another quilt, put him on my shoulder, and stepped out. The storm nearly swept me off my feet. I tried to walk, but I couldn't. I would not have the strength. But he who has death behind him and possibly life ahead, cannot give up. Forward. I walked on. I stepped with wide steps so as not to fall with my precious load. I often sank deep into the snow drifts, but I dragged myself out again. Here was the entrance to the cemetery and our hiding place between the graves. Totally exhausted, at the end of my strength, I put my brother down, covered him with the quilts, and fell next to him. Now it was my turn to sigh, Mama. Mama.

Dawn broke. We could hear the gunfire. They were shooting and shooting. There was so much shooting that day. My brother was lying calmly, but still unconscious. He had swallowed some tea but was still staring blankly. He was not even surprised that instead of the walls of the room he was surrounded by trees and graves. By the afternoon I began impatiently waiting for evening, when we would be able to return home. Suddenly we heard the sound of approaching shots and yells. The voices came from the direction of the road that passes by the cemetery wall. I raised my head and peeked through a hole in the cemetery wall. I saw women, children, and men being led along the road surrounded by a tight cordon of guards. Young and old. Mothers carrying babies, leading their young children by the hand.

They walked silently. There were no cries; only the yells of the Germans who were beating the people with the butts of their guns. There were sporadic shots. Those whose legs were paralyzed by fear of imminent death and could not walk were shot. They got closer. I heard no crying, but something akin to a collective moan coming from the mass of people. Or perhaps it was a deep sigh by the mothers who knew what was awaiting their children at the end of the road .... They came so close that I could recognize their faces. I saw the three sisters of the Stachlów family. They were calm, holding each other as they walked. Next came Salka Knobler, followed by so many others. They passed by and disappeared and were not there anymore. And after a while a terrible symphony of shots broke out, continuing until the last of those who had passed fell into the pits filled with bodies and died in terrible convulsions.

Evening arrived. I tucked my brother in again and left to investigate. I learned that the roundup would continue tomorrow as well. I managed to get some hot tea and made my brother drink it. I made sure again that he was well covered and lay down next to him. And then it was day again and the shooting resumed. And once more, people were escorted along the road by the cemetery.

Suddenly my brother regained consciousness. His fever appeared to have dropped. First, he wondered how he had come there. And when I explained, he said: "Brother, if they come, don't leave. Let us be shot together. Let's die together. It will be easier to find our mother." I kissed him and tried to calm him down. I could again hear shots. They were coming closer. I told my brother to keep quiet and peeped through the hole. Several scores of girls were being escorted. An empty truck arrived behind them. The Germans stopped it and tried to get the girls to climb into it. The two Elias sisters resisted; one of them tore her dress and yelled, "Shoot us here, you dogs, we are dying, but your time will come!" The other shouted, "I heard the news yesterday. In Stalingrad they are choking you like rats!" Two shots rang out and both of them fell down. The truck drove away. Again, we heard shots, and another group of people surrounded by Germans approached. This time they were led by local gendarmes. I recognized one of them— Szydłowski. (In 1944 Rozen and I found him in the town of Suma in Ukraine. He was sentenced to death by a field court-martial). He pulled out his pistol and the old Jew Cukierman fell down. After a while this group, too, disappeared.

The following evening, my brother was in bed, the stove was hot, and I was about to serve him piping hot tea. His fever had dropped, he was conscious and feeling much better. The next morning, almost simultaneously, Pepa and Dr. R. arrived. He said that the danger had passed and that in a few days my brother would recover.

The third roundup in Buczacz was named the "bloody action." Two thousand Jews were killed.[43] Nobody was taken away. People were simply escorted in groups to the Fedor, where large pits had already been prepared. They were forced by beatings to undress and then they were shot. The victims' clothes were taken to town, where they were stored in a special warehouse. Later they were sorted, packed in wooden crates, and taken by train to Germany. The pits in which the victims were buried were only covered with a thin layer of earth. That is why it was common to find body parts in the fields, probably dragged there by dogs or wolves. One peasant in the area of Podlesie [4 km east of Buczacz] found a human hand in his dog's kennel.

In the town's streets the bloody marks left on the white snow did not allow the town to forget what had happened there just a few days earlier. Parts of bloody human brains were scattered around, telltale signs of the "encounters" with babies. It was snowing, but the marks did not disappear. They appeared again and again through the fluffy surface as if they were determined to stay forever as living proof of what had happened. The non-Jews who passed by carefully avoided these sites. Peasant women crossed themselves. The wife of the Landkommissar, Frau Lissberg, said: "I didn't know that winter here could be so beautiful. Look, red snow." Hence later they could not say that they did not know anything.[44]

Another turning point in our lives came at the end of February: Stalingrad. A symbol of life. It was like a blood infusion for someone dying from loss of blood. Like a rainbow in a storm: Stalingrad. For the first time we saw the Germans confused, scared, seemingly panicking. [They announced] three days of mourning. For us, these were three days of wonderful joy. Three days when all the cinemas, theatres, and restaurant were closed. Three days when we could breathe freely. We knew. No one could tell where this certainty came from, but we knew. There would not be a roundup in the next three days. The gendarmerie chief walked past me on the street without noticing that I had not taken my hat off. I looked up. His head was lowered. At night we walked over to the town center: me, Janek Werner, and Kuba Weiser. We wrote with charcoal on the walls the houses: "The hour of revenge has come. Stalingrad, you murderers, Stalingrad."

The following day we realized that somebody else had been writing on the walls. Wherever you looked, you saw the word "Stalingrad." Strong police and gendarmerie patrols appeared on the streets, wearing helmets. Good. Let them read. Let them see how hated they are. The signs "Jews and dogs are forbidden" disappeared from many shops and restaurants. The farseeing owners had removed them. Who knows? Perhaps [the Soviets would return]? Vigorous debates resumed in the Judenrat offices. Things were certain to change now. Just think: one-hundred-thousand prisoners of war and [Commander of the German 6 Army Field Marshal Friedrich] Paulus himself in captivity. The British took many German prisoners of war. Surely, they would try to pressure the Germans on their treatment of the Jews. And even if Hitler did not agree, there might be a revolution. After all, German wives and mothers would fear that their loved ones might be treated as we were.

Hurrah, to the heroes of Stalingrad. Thank you for those moments of joy and hope. We believe in you and it will be easier to die knowing that the fate of the murderers has been determined with your victory in Stalingrad. When you reach the city of Buczacz, you will find us in the pits of the Fedor. Perhaps our bodies will have already been eaten by worms. Our lips will be silent. But if by chance you see the word Stalingrad on the walls of houses, you will understand how the Jews of Buczacz greeted your victory there.

The Germans slowly recovered from the depression caused by the Stalingrad defeat. The first sign was a new order. All the Jews must be concentrated on Podhajecka street and the adjacent "Baszty." We too had to leave our house, orchard, and cemetery. Saying goodbye to the house in which we were born and raised was very difficult. I wandered around the yard and garden for a long time. Every corner, every detail had its own history. The roof of the basement on which we used to climb barefoot as children. The cherry tree, on which I had first learned to climb. I sat on the swing, rocking myself and thinking, perhaps this is the last time. I heard my brother's voice calling me. The horse cart had arrived. We loaded the most essential items, the bed, the sofa, the table, some chairs, and then: farewell house—our small sanctuary of happiness. Farewell garden—the shrine of contemplation. Then we couldn't see them anymore, they were not there, they had disappeared behind the corner.

Thus, we began living in a large house. Fifteen families lived here, altogether sixty people. We already had a bunker prepared in the event of a roundup. Ziuta and her mother lived together with us in the same room. Another matter was constantly on my mind—the radio. I couldn't visit the notary as often now, and this was exactly the time when so many things that concerned us were happening in the world. I talked about this with Dr. Seifer, and he said that we could hide the radio in one of the hospital basements and listen to the broadcasts there. The only thing we had to do was to carry the radio to the hospital. I carried it piece by piece. First, the tubes in my pockets. Next, the speaker, and then the rest. Finally, we could hear every day, "This is London," and "Ot sovietskogo Informbyuro" [Russian: "From the Soviet Information Bureau"]. The only members of the hospital personnel we told about it were Dr. Seifer, Weiss, and Ebenstein. I think Pusia suspected something.

Today my brother moved out from our apartment. I managed to find him a position as an electrician in the reconstruction of the train tunnel that was destroyed by the retreating Soviet army in 1941. At that point, I didn't have to worry about him, because the Jewish workers employed there were safe in the event of a roundup. They wore on their chests rectangular signs inscribed with the letter "W" and stamped by the Gestapo. That distinguished them from everyone else, and they were safe for now.[45] On the other hand, they had to live in a special house next to their workplace. The house and yard were surrounded by barbed wire. After work, the workers were relatively free, so that my brother often came to visit me, especially to listen to the news on the radio. Recently, there had been more and more news. The Anglo-American armies were increasingly successful in Africa. The Red Army was chasing the Germans from the Caucuses and approaching Kharkov. Now, we wanted to live. Oh, how I wanted to live and see the liberation!

It was the week before Passover. I returned home in the evening. For dinner we had fish, my favorite. Ziuta knew that and didn't tell me until we sat down to the table. The behavior of these people just before death was quite amazing. They swept the floors every day, they cleaned the windows, they were angry if I didn't wipe my shoes or if I stained the tablecloth. They were quite capable of making a scene [over such matters]. I was a bit annoyed; how can you act this way in such times? But on the other hand, this very atmosphere of a home made me forget the harsh reality, if only for a moment.

The fish, which was always so tasty, did not taste as well today. I felt a strange anxiety taking hold of me. The others discerned the change in me and were worried. I explained that I was tired and soon went to sleep. My body was shaken by fever. Could it be typhus, I asked myself? Again, I fell into a feverish sleep. I felt someone tugging at my sleeve, and I heard my mother's voice. I got up. I didn't turn on the light. I lay down and tried to figure out this strange apparition. Suddenly I heard shots. One, two, then more and more. Under the window on the street I heard an injured person moaning. We dashed out. Yes, now we knew. Everything was clear. I had had a premonition. It's a roundup. Everybody dressed hurriedly. The whole house was on its feet. We dashed to the hideout. The people went down the ladder one by one into the bunker. Faster, faster. The bunker filled up. It was a little too small for everyone and there were still more people upstairs. Everybody had to fit in. Here was Sabina with her two-year-old son Dziunek. After a while, I too disappeared in the dark.

It was very crowded; you could only sit with your knees close to the chest. After an hour, it grew very hot and we suffered from lack of air. We could clearly hear the sound of shots and the cries of the wounded on the street. Then we heard banging on our house. Soon, there was the sound of boots running about and of furniture being moved. We heard steps and noise directly above our heads… They must have overturned the closet. We tried to be as quiet as possible, not to breathe. Suddenly, someone coughed. Oh, my God, we are lost. It was little Dziunek. Someone must have covered his mouth, because we could hear him choking. For a second, a split second, he cried out, and then it was quiet again.[46] Such things occurred often in those days. Children were sacrificed to save the whole bunker ….

Again, there was silence. But only for a moment, because soon we heard the banging again. At first muffled, then becoming louder and louder. Beyond doubt, they were destroying the wall of our shelter. Parts of the wall were already falling on our heads. The whole shelter was shaking from the violent blows. People were silent. Nobody moved. There was still a shred of hope. Perhaps the walls would not yield, perhaps the Germans would get tired. Or maybe God, satiated with the blood and suffering of the Chosen People, would rain fire from heaven, a fire that would engulf the people together with their murderers.

The banging became stronger. We could already see the crack in the wall through which the first rays of light entered the room. Nobody moved. Maybe, after all… But the banging continued. One last blow, and with a loud noise the bricks fell. There was a big hole in the wall through which the light entered, coming to rest on the Jews, motionless, as if in a prayer.

The face of a German appeared in the hole. Then the triumphant cry: "Juden sind da!" [There are Jews here]. The children started crying. Cry children. Now at last you can. Nobody is going to cover your mouths with their hands. Sabina, Dziunio's mother, looked at her strangulated child and turned to her neighbors reproachfully: "Why did you do it? It did not help anyway." The Jewish OD and the Germans burst into the bunker. They beat the people wherever they could and chased them out to the street. I was the third to go out. As I left, I was hit in the side with the butt of a rifle, but at that moment I didn't even feel the pain.

On the street we had to sit on the sidewalk with our hands on our heads. They tore off watches, rings and earrings from the women. Whenever the latch did not open quickly enough, a little jerk and a bloodied ear. Two local boys, the dog catchers Nahajowski and Kowalski, who had been helping the Germans search for bunkers, pulled boots from the feet of those sitting.[47] Six-year-old Julek, a beautiful boy, our mascot, emerged from the bunker. Seeing the Germans, he took off his hat and bowed. One of the Gestapo-men yelled at him, "Du bist auch ein Jude!" [You too are a Jew!] "Ja" replied Julek, smiling. To the day I die I will never forget the confused smile of this child, with his pale, frightened face.

After everyone had come out of the bunker, they escorted us, surrounded by Gestapo and OD-men, towards the prison. We passed by the city hall and across the market square to the river. The non-Jews we encountered on the streets stopped, looked, and recognized some of us, because they pointed at some people. On one of the streets, Frydźka Brecher suddenly jumped out of the group and dashed blindly forward. A Ukrainian policeman nearby caught up with her and hit her on the head with the butt of his rifle. After she fell, he finished her off with a shot.

We entered the prison yard. A few Germans equipped with wooden poles were standing at the entrance and everyone who walked through first received a few blows. We were put in a cell. A cell constructed for four people now had to accommodate a hundred. Incredible, but true. We were standing one against the other .... I saw Hena Müller, a young girl, standing by the wall. She was struggling to pull her hand out of her pocket. Finally, she succeeded and wrote in Russian on the wall: "Hena Müller, cursing her murderers, is dying here." And below that she wrote: "Farewell hopes and dreams. Farewell Eretz Israel. Avenge us!" Zelig Heiss,[48] who was also crammed in there along with his son, tried some humor. He ensured everyone that "it" [death] takes only a split second and does not hurt. Someone interrupted, saying he was told that a person being shot doesn't hear the bullet because it kills him before he can hear the blast.

Suddenly, the door opened and the Gestapo-man Thomanek[49] walked in and yelled: "Those carrying a sign with the letter 'W' step out!" Two people in our cell had them. Suddenly—to this today I do not understand how I did it—propelled by some internal urge, I rushed toward the door and screamed: "I have one!" Responding to the questioning expression on the soldier's face, I added that I was employed in the tunnel, and had only spent the night in the Jewish quarter by chance and was thus caught during the action. "Step out," the soldier growled, and soon I was standing in the corridor with the other two men who had the signs. All three of us were then led by Thomanek to the Toten-Kommando chief Rux,[50] who that day was directing the action. "These two have the plaques," said Thomanek, pointing to the two others, "and this fellow felt like sleeping in town last night and did not take it with him." For a moment Rux stared at me and then he laughed and blurted out: "Today you are a lucky dog, but you won't be so lucky next time." Then he summoned the Ukrainian policeman and told him to lock us up in another cell and to let us go after the roundup was over.

That evening, of the two thousand Jews who were seized, the only survivors were a few scores who were to be sent to a concentration camp and the three of us. We were set free that same night.[51] The next morning my brother, who had been worried about me, came to the house. I was the only survivor out of the ninety[52] Jews who had previously lived there. I told him how I had managed to save myself by pretending to be him, so that he would know how to behave in case of an inquiry.

Once more we listened to the radio and were again thrilled. This time things in Africa did not end in El Agheila [in Libya, recaptured by the British in December 1942]. Names of cities that had never been mentioned before in the news were suddenly being talked about. After Tripoli, the Mareth Line, Gabès ... Tunis and Bizert [Tunis fell to the Allies in May 1943]. These names were etched in our memory as much as such names of Rostov, Kursk, Orel, and the Donets River [all on the Eastern Front].

In the meantime, new orders were issued in town, demonstrating that the Germans were trying to accelerate the extermination of the Jews. We heard: next week Buczacz would be declared "Judenfrei" [free of Jews]. The Jews who were still alive, of whom there were about four thousand, had to leave to one of the following places: Kopyczyńce, Tłuste, Podhajce, or Czortków.

And once more the roads were full of caravans of carts piled up with bundles, on top of which the Jews were sitting. And again, along the roads, peasants armed with hatchets, pitchforks, and scythes, were calling: "Give us everything, they will kill you anyway." Meanwhile the Germans had set up a camp in town. Part of Podhajecka street was closed off with barbed wire, making it into a camp. The "camp" commandant was Zalmen Sternberg. The chief of the camp's OD was Leon Kanner. The young Jewish survivors were flocking to the camp, all the more so when it became clear that the situation in the cities to which the others had been deported was terrible. For instance, the Jews who had just been resettled in Tłuste were greeted by a roundup, whose first victims were obviously those arriving from Buczacz. The same news arrived from Kopyczyńce and Czortków.[53]

As a result of this terrifying news a real panic spread among the Jews of Buczacz. Those who could, entered the camp. Some escaped to the forest, just like that and without any plan, not thinking about how they would feed themselves or survive. Some tried to find shelter in nearby villages, in the houses of peasants they knew or those who promised to hide them in exchange for large sums of money. More often than not, those peasants first robbed the Jews of everything they had and then killed them.

Nearly every day corpses of Jews were found on the fields, in the forests, on dung heaps, and in back roads. They were terribly mutilated, their eyes gouged, their tongues cut out, without ears, noses, sometimes missing legs or hands. I remember that one afternoon a woman—who did not resemble a woman—was brought back in a cart. She looked more like some sort of horrifying monster. Her hair had turned into a terrible sticky mess. She had two bloody holes instead of eyes. Her face and body were all blue and swollen. She was still alive. The Germans did not want to finish her off. She lay like that for three days. Rattling sounds came from her throat, her body was shaking with palpitations. She died on the third day, in the evening. Her name was Kahane and she used to have a shop on Kolejowa [Railroad] street.

I no longer slept at home. I did not trust the camp in town either. I joined up with the two Sokółecki brothers and we spent the nights wherever we could. Sometimes in the cemetery, sometimes in the quarry on the Fedor, and sometimes in a half-destroyed house. From time to time, however, we were forced to sleep in town, especially in order to wash and change our clothes. On those occasions, we slept at the home of the Sokółecki brothers' sister. One morning, after spending the night in town, we heard shots on the street while we were still in bed. We rushed to the window and saw the whole street filled with Germans and Ukrainians. We got dressed in a flash and dashed through the back door to the Jewish hospital, where I knew there was a shelter. We reached the entrance of the hospital without problems, but when we started banging on the door those inside thought we were the Germans and panicked. Luckily, however, one of them recognized my voice and the door was opened. We ran with the others into the shelter.

We spent all day listening to the sound of shots outside. By 5 p.m. we thought that the searches for hidden shelters must have surely ended.

Seifer proposed that we listen to the radio. I turned the dial to London. That day the British army had entered Tunis, almost at the same time as the American Army occupied Bizerte. They captured thousands of prisoners of war and [much] military equipment. The Germans were retreating to Cap Bon. "Liberation is right ahead of us, we can almost touch it, and yet here death is grasping us by the throat," Seifer laughed bitterly. Evening arrived. We carefully opened the door. I walked out with Ebenstein. In the camp opposite us we saw lights. It meant they were still alive there. "Maybe it's the Germans," Ebenstein whispered. We decided to return to the shelter and stay there till morning. In the morning we learned that the Germans had left the camp alone; nobody was taken from there. We were also told that during the roundup shots had been fired from one of the houses at the Ukrainians and as a result one soldier was killed and the others ran away in disarray. The person who fired the shots was A. Anderman; he took advantage of the confusion and ran away and to hide in another bunker.[54]

My brother arrived from the tunnel and we greeted each other as if we had been apart for a long time. That same day we found out that the camp in Buczacz would be liquidated and the inmates transferred to the camp in Czortków. Only a few Jews were left in town: twenty-five working in the tunnel, fifteen sorting the clothes of the dead, and two at the electric power plant. These two were Janek Werner and me.

Today, people were leaving the camp. They were going with a heavy heart, knowing that they were prolonging their lives only by a few minutes or hours. Janek and I waved goodbye. "See you after the war!" I shouted. "In the next world," they replied. We were left on our own. Working at the power plant, we were supposed to sleep in the same house with the Jews employed in sorting the clothing. But we never spent the night there. We often just hid in some kind of "warren" in the plant and slept there. We were also charged with another task. There were still many Jews hiding in bunkers. They had prepared food to last for a longer period of time, but the lack of water was very hard. Every evening Janek and I tried to secretly supply them with water. Some people were also hiding in the bunker at the hospital. They included Sala Rinder, Fanka Steinberg, Mendel Reich with his wife, and others. Here they didn't even have food and we tried to supply them with some bread every day. Conversely, they did have enough water, because in the bunker there was a faucet with running water.

Today, my brother brought an F.N. 6.35 caliber pistol.[55] He purchased it from an Italian worker who was also employed in the tunnel. It had only three cartridges. The two of us, along with Janek, deliberated whether it was time to escape to the forest. But Janek said that we must have more ammunition before we go, because with only three cartridges, we would not be able to defend ourselves against the Ukrainians and Germans.

We listened to the radio again. Pantelleria and Lampedusa [Mediterranean islands invaded by the Allies in June 1943]. In the area of Orel and Kursk in the East something was happening.

We acquired a second F.N. 7.65 pistol and five cartridges. It was found by one of the Jewish workers selecting the clothing. He wanted to get rid of it and throw it down the toilet, but luckily, I saw it and took it away from him. Now I was carrying it on me at all times and I felt much calmer and sure of myself. I knew I would not be taken alive. At the last moment, I would shoot myself in the head. And maybe—I thought to myself—just before doing so I would get a chance to take a swing at one of the Gestapo-men.

On Thursday, 23 June 1943, having just brought some bread to the hospital, I sat and talked with the people there. Sara Rinder sat next to me. She was terribly distraught. "What can I do? What can I do?" she kept saying. "Look," she said. "I've lost everything. My parents, my sister, my only son Dolus. In fact, life does not mean anything to me anymore. My brother lives somewhere in Palestine. My husband is far away in Russia. If only I could be sure that someone would someday tell them about all this," she burst out crying. Cry Sala, cry, nothing helps the hurting soul more than tears. But cry softly. No one should hear this sound outside and understand that there are still a few glimmers of life here. If this can be called life.

My brother walked in, saying that he found where one of the Germans working in the tunnel kept his rifle. "Between the bed and the wall," he said. "We only have to go into his room one evening when he is not there, snatch the gun, and run." At that moment Janek Werner entered and said that four Gestapo-men had arrived in town. Tomorrow, they would start searching for people in hidden bunkers. We hastily bid farewell and announced that from now on we would visit the hideout only at night. My brother quickly returned to the tunnel and I went with Janek to the power plant. There we climb up to the attic and went to sleep.

We were awoken in the morning by shots. We were surprised. After all, they would not start searching for bunkers so early, nor could this be a roundup, since officially there were no more Jews in town. The shots continued intermittently until 10 a.m. Then we heard someone climbing up the ladder to the attic. It was Dolinowski, one of the Poles employed in the power plant. He told us that the Germans had executed all the Jews, both those who were working in the tunnel and those who were sorting the clothes. "And my brother?" I interrupted in shock. "Two have managed to escape," he said. One of them was a tall electrician, which is what my brother was called. "There was a shootout," he continued, "and two Germans were killed." Yes, I thought to myself, only he had a pistol. The Germans plastered posters announcing that as of 24 June 1943, the city was "Judenfrei." Anybody helping catch a Jew would receive a bottle of vodka and 500 złoty. Just before leaving, Dolinowski told us to leave the plant in the evening, because the Poles working there feared they would be punished if the Germans found out that Jews were hiding there.

Evening drew close. We were trying to decide what to do. Janek wanted to escape to the forest where his friend the forester might give us temporary shelter. But I wouldn't go anywhere before finding out what happened to my brother. We decided that I would go to the cemetery, and the following day would try to discover what happened to my brother. Janek would go to the forester to inquire whether we could find shelter there. We arranged to meet the following night day at 1 a.m. on the footbridge next to the plant. Janek asked me for the pistol, in case he encountered Germans or foresters on the way and would not be able to defend himself. I agreed and we parted.

I spent the night in the cemetery wandering among the crosses and unable to find a place for myself. Terribly anxious about my brother, I barely survived till dawn. From afar, I saw the undertaker with his cow. He was grazing it at the cemetery. When he came closer, I emerged from behind the bushes and signaled him with my hand. He came up to me, but I could see that he was very frightened. I asked him if he knew anything about my brother. No, he knew nothing. He had heard that someone had escaped from the tunnel, but if it were my brother he would surely have hidden in the cemetery. Clearly this meant that my brother was not alive. The undertaker left and I saw him walking behind his cow towards his home. I stayed. So, he too was afraid? What should I do now? I decided to wait until nightfall for the meeting with Janek.

Evening arrived. The sky had become overcast. The clock on the faraway Orthodox Church struck 10 p.m., then 11, then midnight. I began heading to the appointed meeting spot. I crossed the cemetery and carefully descended from Fedor Hill. I stopped and listened. Everything was silent. A faraway shot rang out, its echo piercing the stillness of the night. I continued, almost reaching the town. I stopped again. Now I had to quickly cross the road and then two hundred meters ahead of me would be the footbridge. It started raining and the clock struck one. I dashed, quickly crossed the road, jumped over the ditch, and ran through the gardens. I reached the bridge and stepped carefully. I was on the first step when suddenly I felt my foot stepping on something soft. I wandered, is it a sack? Who would have put a sack here at this time of day? More surprised than frightened I pulled a torch out of my pocket. One flash of light… It was Janek's body. Instead of an eye there was a bloody wound. The fresh blood was still running down his face, forming a red puddle on the ground. I jumped away from him, suddenly overcome with terrible fear. I ran across the road and the gardens, headed up the hill and fell breathlessly in the cemetery.

I lay there breathing heavily. Slowly, my thoughts returned. One thought would not leave me. What to do next? I got up slowly and walked to our orchard. I wanted to say a last farewell to the sites that were so close to my heart. The pear tree stood on my left, and I leaned my feverish face on its cool bark. I could already see small fruits on its branches. I picked one in the dark. Die together with me, I whispered. Mother never allowed me to eat unripe fruits, she was afraid they would make me sick. But today, even Mama would not have forbidden it. Here was the plum tree, its fruits still green. They would not make me sick. I bit into one. They were always so sour, yet this time the plum tasted sweeter than honey. They were dying before me and for me. Here was the swing. I sat on it; I should not swing it strongly. The hinges, unlubricated for a long time, might creak and someone could hear. A flash of lightning cut across the sky and thunder roared above. I approached the large nut tree. I asked myself, who would gather its nuts this year? I hugged the tree trunk. It held so many sweet reminiscences for me. This is where I declared my first love. Our initials were probably still carved somewhere high up on the tree.

The lightning intensified. The thunder was deafening. Had God woken up from His lethargy and decided to destroy the world together with the last Jew wandering in the cemetery? Five hundred złoty and a bottle of vodka. I walked over to where I had hidden with my brother during the third roundup. Somewhere nearby the lightning struck. Terrified Germans and Ukrainians were surely praying, "God, absolve us from our sins." And the good Lord absolved them and forgave them the deaths of my mother, my brother, Dolus, Sala, Janek, and so many, many others. The storm was passing. There was no more lightning and thunder. Soon, day would arrive and the first one to see me would receive a bottle of vodka and 500 złoty. I fell in the spot where I had hidden during the last roundup with my brother. Goodbye you cursed world. I will lie here until I die. And nobody will get 500 złoty and a bottle of vodka for finding me.

Part II

I remained lying in the same position, face down, not paying attention to anything, until the surrounding cold, penetrating through my wet clothes, reached my consciousness. Yet at some point I noticed that one part of my body was not as cold, as I felt a pleasant sensation of warmth just above my right hip. It was not enough to warm my entire body, but it was sufficient for me to notice it. After this first instance of consciousness, others followed. First, I was alive. I was alive, but why was I surprised that I was alive. Yes, I had wished to die. To die, just like that, a humble demand for our times. Before being led in a formation to my own funeral. Without having to undress in front of the grave and an instant before death—looking down into a pit full of writhing bodies. That must be the worst of all. That view and the knowledge that in an instant you too would be one of those bleeding bodies. It's interesting. When does a human being lose his consciousness of being? Is it at the moment of the shot, the fall, and the contact with a body shot just before, that one understands what is happening, or is it true that even the sound of the shot does not reach the awareness of its target?

I slowly stretched out my hand to check the source of the warmth, when suddenly my hand met something fluffy, something that began licking my hand and quietly whining. This completely wrenched me out of the strange state of apathy that had overtaken me, unaware of the passing time. I jumped up and initially, blinded by the light of day, could see nothing. I started to rub my eyes. The first thing I saw after getting used to the light was the sky. The June sky was as beautifully clear as a vast emerald. Next, my eyes turned to the surrounding trees, whose leaves were still shimmering from the drops left by the night rain. Then I saw the stone crosses of the graves. Suddenly, I felt the bitterness in my heart, my choking throat, and I was seized by what people usually call panic. I now clearly remembered what had happened the previous day. And the day before yesterday, that saw the total liquidation of the Jews in town. Buczacz had become "Judenfrei." For catching a Jew, a reward of a bottle of vodka and 500 złoty was announced. My brother was dead. In the appointed meeting spot, I found only Janek's body. And now I was lying in the cemetery and the first person to spot me would receive the reward.

Once again I felt something damp and warm licking my hand. I looked down and saw Kubus, a stray dog who had appeared on our street long ago, nobody knew from where. Without a number, without a collar, the dog was also an outlaw and at times escaped death from the Germans—who were hunting him down just like the Jews—only by chance. He usually wandered around our street where everyone fed him whatever they could. That is also why the name "Jewish dog" stuck to him, which was how the Jews on our street called him. And now, I don't know how, he had found me here and was sitting next to me, licking my hand and merrily wagging his tail. Yes, yes, Kubus. There is no big difference between us today. I would even say that your chances of surviving this war are better than mine. Had I been able to transform myself into a dog, I would do it right away. I would have at least run far away and guarded a farm at night and lived quietly in some village where there were no Germans. But meanwhile, look Kubus, I have not eaten anything in the last twenty-four hours. And now doggie—leave and don't return. You might lead someone to my hiding spot. I don't want anyone to become drunk tonight on the prize for the life of a Jew. Saying that, I tried to get Kubus to leave. At first, he did not want to, but eventually, after I lightly hit him, he understood and disappeared behind the bushes.

I began thinking. What should I do? There must be a way out of this hellish situation. After all, it is impossible that the only way out is a bullet in the head from a German or a Ukrainian. How would somebody else behave in the same situation? What would my older brother, who lives somewhere in Palestine, do? I was sure he would either be already dead or sitting helplessly like me. Because, what else could anyone in my situation do? Theoretically I was dead, I did not exist. Since yesterday, the town has been declared "Judenfrei."

At that same moment, as often happens to human beings, from the depth of despair an urge to revolt and a rejection of these circumstance is born. The fear of death and hopelessness disappears, and other thoughts fill the mind. After all, you are dead anyway. You have nothing to lose. Every hour, every minute of your life is a battle won against the Germans. Every day we survive brings us closer to liberation. The victory will be ours. I felt it with all my heart and with every fiber of my exhausted soul. I must only hold out and endure.

Again, I felt hunger. My good old friend. First, I felt it in my stomach, then I felt a weakness in my heart and finally I was expecting a headache. The symptoms of hunger were very familiar. I also knew that the headache would disappear after a few hours, as would the feeling of hunger. And what then? That I did not know. I had often been hungry, but never longer than forty-eight hours. I remembered hearing once that it took human beings nine days to die from hunger. A long time. And to think that not far from here in some kitchen, dinner was being prepared. If only I had an ampoule of cyanide; I heard it brings death within two seconds. Two seconds, and I would know what the world had been trying to find out for ages. Was there life after death? Did the wandering of the souls occur?[56] I wished that were true. In that case, I would have wanted to be born a real person. A real Aryan. Or perhaps it would be better not to be human at all. If, for example, I could be born again as the Landkommissar's dog—but surely not as some dog like Kubus, whose life did not really differ from mine. Nobody shot at the Landkommissar's dog. He must be sleeping on a soft rug and in two hours would definitely be served his meal.

My ruminations on this subject were interrupted by the light rustle of branches being parted and then the face of the undertaker's wife Marynka appeared.[57] I could tell she was very agitated. "Manko is ill and cannot come," she said, "and in any case it's very dangerous to be in the cemetery. The Germans might come to look here any day now and if they find you, we might also get punished. It's best for you to escape into the forest, or wherever you want. Just don't stay here."[58] In response to my question, she said that many of the Jews still hiding in town were leaving their hideouts because of lack of water. They were giving themselves up to the Germans. "So, what are you saying, Marynka, "I asked her. "Should I also go to the Germans and tell them to kill me?" "Of course," she answered, "why should you suffer? Sooner or later they are going to find you anyway. Do what you want, but you have to escape from the cemetery and to do it today." Having said that, she disappeared.

I remained alone again, but now I no longer wanted to die. I wanted to live, live on purpose so as to spite the Germans, to spite Marynka and all the others who are having such fun over this. I knew I couldn't win. I knew I didn't have any chances of holding out; in the end they would catch and kill me. But I would fight for every hour, every minute, every instant. I wanted to live not because I was afraid of death. I had accepted death long ago in my soul. But I wished to God to let me live long enough to see the hour of judgment of my nation's murderers. And then to allow me to reach the Holy Land, not in order to live—let your hand strike me down on its shores—but so that first I could tell them, if I could only express it in words, about everything that had happened here.

The sun was setting. Evening was coming, the bushes rustled again, and Kubus emerged from them, holding a large bone in his teeth. He dropped it on my knees and begged me to pat him. I was touched to tears by the intuition of this dog, my only friend. I hugged him and kissed him, the friend that hadn't left me in my most difficult hour.

It was getting darker. I tried to decide what to do. I couldn't stay in the cemetery because the frightened Marynka might reveal my hideout to the Germans. I decided to leave at night. I would walk through the forest and try to reach the village of Rzepińce, about 18 kilometers from Buczacz [actually 10 km]. During the day, I would hide in the forest and at night try to obtain some food from the peasants. And then we'd see. After all, at the end of every life, there is death, and what is the difference if it happened now or a few years later, if happen it must.

By night I had made my mind up to go to Rzepińce. I knew some peasants there, the village was far from the main road, and the Germans would surely not venture there often. Again, I checked the contents of my pockets. I kept only the electric torch, a photograph of my brother in Palestine, wearing a uniform and a fur cap, and a letter from my sister, also in Palestine. The letter was from early 1939. My sister wrote she hoped to soon acquire a certificate [of immigration to Palestine] for me and that we would surely spend Purim together. Yes, I thought bitterly. Now it's 1943, and they have probably received the certificate for me, but after the war there won't be anyone to make use of it.

At last, I set out. I left my hideout and took the path near the entrance of the cemetery, went past it and reached the sports grounds. I walked next to the football field, past the shooting gallery and reached the road leading to the forest. I looked back at the town. I could see brightly lit houses. Damn them. They were not even afraid of an air raid, they felt as safe as if they were at home. That wasn't surprising. The front was still very far.

I reached the forest. Just before it there was a house with farm buildings. It used to belong to the rich Jew Fried. Now it was inhabited by a Ukrainian named Buhay. I wondered whether I should approach the house and ask for some food. I felt that sensation of hunger taking over again, my legs were becoming weak from hunger. I carefully approach the yard that was surrounded by a fence. I was already at the gate leading inside when I was stopped by the loud barks of a dog. I could see a tall figure, holding a torch coming out of the house. I recognized the figure of Buhay. I called out to him, wanting him to recognize me, and asked for a piece of bread, saying I was dying of hunger. "Go away!" I heard in response, "the last thing I need is to feed Jews. Ivan!" he called out to someone inside the room. "Bring me the hatchet and let the dog loose!" I turned around and escaped to the forest.

I walked through the forest and told myself, this is how things would be everywhere. Nobody would give you anything. In the best case, if they didn't catch you and handed you over to the Germans, you would just be thrown out and the dogs would be set on you. The trees were thinning out, and I came out to a road on which I had to walk for another few kilometers. I felt terribly thirsty. It was even worse than the hunger. I could make out some farm buildings in front of me. It must be a tiny village. This time, I would not approach the houses. I would sneak into one of the gardens and try to fill myself with some fruits or vegetables. I left the road and walked into the first garden, blindly wading through the vegetable bed. The dogs had not smelt me yet, which was good. I felt a row of young onions, grasped a handful and swallowed them without even bothering to clean them from the soil that clung to them. I could see some bushes behind me. I reached out to them: they were red currants. I tore at them and ate and ate. Before leaving, I stuffed my pockets with green tomatoes and was soon on the road again. It felt good being full. Life, even under such terrible conditions, seemed more bearable when one was not hungry. If only there was water, but that was too much to ask.

I passed by a village and was accompanied by barking dogs. But now I didn't even think about it, I felt much stronger and kept feeling the tomatoes in my pockets. Beyond the last house, I came to a bridge over a small stream. The flow of running water reminded me of the thirst that had been tormenting me throughout the day. I decided to go down to the bank and try to get a drink. I carefully went down the slope, knelt down, scooped water with my hands, and drank. No drink in my life had ever tasted better than the water from this dirty stream. No, I would never satisfy my thirst in this manner. I pulled the cap off my head and scooped up the water. Now I could drink my fill and put out the fire that was burning inside me. I bent my head again to get more of that sweet nectar.

Suddenly I was struck powerfully on the head. I was thrown on the ground, heard voices, and felt someone stepping on my feet with hard boots. I tried to get up but was held in an iron grip. I heard someone ordering in Ukrainian to tie my hands. They tied them behind my back. My eyes were half closed. If they would only hurry up and hit me. Now I knew. I was in the hands of one of the Ukrainian bands, the Banderites, and they were never satisfied with just killing Jews.[59] I remembered that not long before the liquidation of the Jews in Buczacz, terribly mutilated corpses would be found, their eyes gouged, without noses, tongues, not looking like human corpses. This had been the doing of these bands.

One of them went through my pockets. He took out the electric torch, the letter and my brother's photograph. This photograph made a great impression on them because of the uniform and especially the high hat, which resembled hats worn by the Ukrainian Army in 1918.[60] Pointing the light of the torch at me, one of them kicked me and ordered me to get up. When I did so, he asked me who was the Ukrainian officer whose photograph they had found on me. I had an idea. I replied that it was the photograph of my father, who had been an officer in [Symon] Petliura's Ukrainian army and was killed in 1919 during the fighting in Lwów.[61] After a brief deliberation they decided to take me to the village, keep me there until morning, and leave the decision to the head of the village. The whole way, they interrogated me about the photograph of my "father," and this is probably what kept them from killing me or exchanging me for vodka. We reached a building that turned out to be the village jail. After a moment, I found myself inside a dark room and lay on the floor, exhausted.

I felt no fear. On the contrary, I was happy that it was over. After all, this was unavoidable. I might have survived another day or two but in the end, this was bound to happen. Tomorrow at the same time you will not be hungry anymore, I told myself. But neither will you see the sun, the green of the trees and fields, something whispered in my soul. Maybe tomorrow, at the same time, you will meet your mother and brother. And they, when dying, believed that in you they were leaving an avenger. On the other hand, something whispered in my ear, how can you be sure that your brother is not alive, perhaps he too is wandering around at night and needs your help? Go away thoughts! Why are you so set against me, tormenting me in my hour of death? Why do I have to think now about green trees, the scent of flowers, the chirping birds. Was the summer last year not as beautiful, and yet I never thought about it. Ah, you are proving yourself to be a romantic, but it's too late. Or perhaps the world shows off its most beautiful colors at the time of death, as if to elicit regret in the hearts of the departed. But this will not work with me. The world is not that beautiful, and I will leave it without regret. What are you saying, something whispered, the world is not beautiful? Get up and go to the window. Look out and see what the sunrise looks like in June 1943.

The dawn of your sunset.

I raised my head. The sun was rising. Through the cracks in the planks blocking the window the first rays were filtering in. I got up and approached the window. A regular window, as in every peasant hut, only instead of a pane of glass it was covered with planks. Far in the east, the sky was painted shades of violet-gold. The last dying stars of the night were twinkling in the dark blue sky. One more beautiful morning of the kind that you can see only in Ukraine at this time of year was beginning. It was getting brighter. In the distance one could see the dark line of the forest emerging from the shadows. One could already see this year's tall wheat waving in the open fields. The refreshing smell of wildflowers reached my nostrils. I heard the twitter of the sparrows and the singing of the skylarks. And this was the day in which I was supposed to die. No, not yet. I did not want to. I wanted to live through another day like this one. One more day of sunshine, liberty, nature. Perhaps if it rained tomorrow, if clouds covered the blue sky and the birds were silent, then it would be easier to die. But on this day, I wanted to live.

As if in a fit of madness, I grabbed one of the planks with both hands and pulled it. It was shut tightly, but my rage made me stronger and eventually I succeeded. With the help of the first plank I took out the other and, in an instant, I was out of the window and running through the yard, over the fence and toward the forest. I saw a peasant girl in front of me taking the cows out to pasture. I saw a bundle in her hand. Probably bread, I thought. I rushed to her, snatched the bundle from the frightened child and ran on. Once I reached the forest I kept going ever deeper into the thicket. At last, I fell on the thick bushes and tried to catch my breath. I could see the first rays of the sun through the tall trees, gently massaging my lips and eyes. Somewhere far away a cuckoo was singing. Cuckoo, how many more days will I live? The bird kept singing, on and on. I smiled sadly. Lies, just lies.

I unwrapped the bundle and found a slice of bread and some coffee. I satisfied my hunger while thinking how the poor child must have been frightened by the sight of someone so wild. I touched the beard that has not been trimmed for a week. It had grown very long. But at a moment like this I should not be thinking about such trivial matters. The most important thing was that I was free.

Evening came. I decided to go to the village of Nagórzanka after it got dark. Many peasant friends of mine, mostly Poles, lived there. Andrej, who had taken part together with me in the attack on the German wheat storehouse, also lived there. Maybe they would not chase me away with dogs. I got up and cautiously walked through the forest, listening carefully. When I reached the edge of the forest it was already dark. Since it was another 8 kilometers to the village, I decided to start out immediately. This time I did not use the road at all. I walked only through the woods and fields. I often had to cross through ditches and isolated houses. I reached the village at 1 a.m. First, I went to Maniek the undertaker's house and knocked again and again on the window of his shack. I could hear some noise inside the room and then I saw Maniek's wife Marynka. When she opened the window, I asked her for some bread and water, but she yelled at me to run away because the

Germans were wandering around the village. I told her I wanted to see Maniek, but she shouted again that I should run away and not return, otherwise she herself would call the Germans. And so, I left.

Andrej's house was not far away from there and that was where I went next. When I reached the house, I noticed a light in one of the windows, and soon the dog started barking. I saw Andrej as he crossed the yard and approached the gate where I was standing. When he saw me, he put the dog back in the kennel and invited me into the house. Soon, I was sitting in the small room of this wretched hut, lit by a kerosene lamp. I was eating bread and drinking milk given me by Andrej's wife. When I satisfied my first pangs of hunger, I told Andrej what I had been through in the last few days, without concealing how I had been greeted by Maniek's wife.

Then we discussed what to do with me. Andrej decided to invite his neighbor Jasiek [diminutive of Jan], another friend of mine, to join us. He arrived quite sleepy, having been called there by one of Andrej's sons. Jaśko [Jasiek] thought it would be best for me to stay hidden in the wheat fields behind the village during the day. We planned that every evening I would come up to the barn behind the house where they would bring me something to eat. Andrej reminded me not to raise my head so that I would not give away my hideout. They also instructed me how to walk through a wheat field without leaving traces behind. There was no more bread—they too had very little—so I left Andrej's house provided with a bottle of water and some boiled potatoes.

It was nearly dawn and I managed to reach the fields by following the bales of hay. The wheat was very tall this year. In some places it reached my chin and in others it was over my head. Carefully parting the wheat stalks, still wet with dew, I reached the middle of the field. Here, I lay on the ground. It was also wet and the cold seeped through my clothes. I was terribly cold. The clock on the church tower in the village struck 2 a.m. What I had been through in the last few days had totally exhausted me. My fatigue was stronger than the cold and I fell asleep, an anxious sleep filled with terrible dreams and visions.

I was awoken by a sensation of terrible heat and lack of air. The sun was already high up in the sky and the heat felt like an open furnace. I was thirsty but the bottle of water, which had become warm, barely satisfied my thirst. From the nearby village I could hear dogs barking, roosters crowing, the creaking of winches [pulling buckets of water from wells], and human voices. Nearby I could hear cows mooing and the calls of shepherds from the fields. Meanwhile, the sun had reached its zenith and there it stayed for a few hours. It scorched without pity. Since I did not have any shelter and was unable to move, I suffered terribly, roasting under the blazing rays. Slowly, the fireball moved west, but I had to wait several more hours until sunset.

At last it was night again. I got up and walked to Andrej's hut. Andrej was already waiting for me in front of the barn. He took me inside, and his wife brought in a big bowl of noodles. Soon, Jasiek's wife came with some corn rolls. She told me that at night I could stay in the barn, but that in the morning I'd have to leave to hide in the wheat field because the Germans often searched the village for hidden Jews. I thanked her and lay down on the good smelling hay. I could hear the clock on the church spire. Eleven, midnight, one, two. Soon it would be day. I got up, walked through the yard and headed to the field. This time I tried another part of the field, remembering that Andrej had warned me that however carefully one walks into a wheat field, some marks are always left behind. I was again in the wheat. This time I couldn't sleep. I took out the corn buns and ate. Earlier I had decided to keep them until noon, but I felt hungry and eating warmed me up a little, since once more the bitter cold was making my entire body shiver.

I could see the red ball of the sun on the horizon. It was still cold, but I knew that soon the sun would rise, and its rays would reach me and everything around me. First it would dry my clothes and warm me up with its wonderful heat. But later it would become hotter and hotter and again start burning everything in sight with its heat. I already felt those hot rays although I knew it would be long before the heat reached its peak.

If only I knew whether there were any other Jews still alive. If only there were at least someone else here with me now. If only I could exchange a few words with another person. But I had to bear sixteen hours of this terrible heat without moving, without a single cough or even a sigh. Oh, who could ever threaten me with hell again? How could a hell somewhere beyond our world compare to the one here on earth? Human beings have not only made themselves equal to God. They have surpassed Him. For He would have never been able to invent such a hell. As for you there in Palestine, my dear sister, if you could see me now, even for a moment. Did you, living there, have any inkling of what was happening to us here? Or perhaps you had already given up any hope for us and reconciled yourselves with the thought that we were no longer alive? Had I been able to appear in front of you, just for an instant, precisely as I was at that moment, filthy, with an overgrown beard, I would have needed no words. You would have grasped everything by yourself just from the way I looked. But, had I stood in front of you clean and well dressed, you would have never believed it. Because what happened there was beyond human imagination.

Somewhere near me a fly was buzzing. I observed it with affection. My only guest today and one that would surely not betray me. It sat on my leg for some time. I tried not to move my leg so as not to frighten the nice guest. But then it flew away again, pleasantly buzzing and performing a few elegant turns in the air. The sun reached its zenith. I was very thirsty, but the bottle was already empty. What should I do? How could I make the long hours of waiting pass more quickly? I tore off the ears the wheat, rubbed them between my fingers, and tried to quench my terrible thirst with the green seeds …. If only I could see myself in the mirror now. I touched my wild beard and moustache. They had really grown. I tried to see my reflection in the bottle, but I couldn't make out much. I was so completely cut off from everything that was going on in the world. The last news I heard was the occupation of Pantelleria.[62] Surely, next they would land in Sicily. May they be successful. May it not end up as in Dieppe ….

The sun set slowly, and a gentle breeze began blowing, creating waves in the wheat. The wheat was murmuring as if it were quietly praying. It was not so hot anymore. The refreshing breeze touched my face and dried it, caressed my eyes, half-blinded by the heat, and ruffled my hair. God Himself must have given life to this wind. The golden ball disappeared in the west, but the sky was still red. Slowly the sky grew darker and darker; the first stars appeared …. I could hear the bells on the church tower. I counted nine, rose slowly, stretched, and walked toward Andrej's house. I felt an emptiness in my heart that, in turn, evoked a sense of the utter hopelessness of my situation.

I was lying down again, this time in yet another field. Again, the terrible heat. I tried to calculate how many days I had been like this. Perhaps it was the eighth day. It must have been about 7 July. Sometimes I would meet Andrej or Janek in the stable in the evenings, and our scraps of conversation had to last me for the entire day. They didn't have much information about the war. Somewhere in Italy the British and Americans were beating the Germans. But, as Jaśko said, Italy was about a hundred years away from Buczacz. Nothing was happening on the eastern front either, but everyone said that soon there would be movement and then, claimed Jaśko, they would eventually get here.

I took out a piece of cake wrapped in newspaper. I eagerly unfolded the sheet of newspaper and read: "Our army is inflicting heavy losses on the enemy; they have retreated into the interior of Sicily." I muffled a cry of joy. They were in Sicily! I tore off a button from my jacket and used it to draw a map of Europe from memory on the ground. Sicily, Sardinia, Corsica. Surely Italy would be next. At the same time the British would land in France and the Red Army would begin its offensive in the east…

Perhaps that offensive could still come here before the harvest, after which the fields would no longer provide me any cover. And if it took a little longer, I would hide in the corn fields, which are not cut down until September. My God, was it possible that I would live?

The blood pulsated in my temples. My heart was beating wildly. My eyes, blinded by the sun, were seeing strange visions. This must have been the mirage I had read about. I saw huge tanks passing by. They trampled over the Germans. Soldiers wearing black caps on their heads jumped out of the tanks. They ran up to me, picked me up, and asked me questions in Russian, a language I knew so well. I answered. I reproached them for not coming earlier. I told them about the Fedor, the pits, the people undressing before their death, the children whose skulls were crushed. Everybody was silent. They were so serious. Why are you silent? Why are you quiet? ... I got up. The sun was covered with heavy clouds. Surely it would soon rain. And only my heart and head were throbbing... Stupid heart. Sleep on. After a moment of high emotions and elation, despair and doubt would surely follow. I ordered my heart to stop and put out the fire of the mirage. Sleep on. And the heart obediently extinguished the flame with the first drops of rain and fell asleep.

It rained for two whole days. It was coming down in buckets. The tops of the wheat stalks bowed low to the ground, filled and heavy with grains. I also tried to stay as close as I could to the ground. Now, I couldn't even sit up because the wheat provided no shelter. My face, hands, and clothes were saturated with water and sticky with black mud. I looked like some kind of monster. It was very cold. My whole body was trembling [... and] nearly sucked into the soft mud. Finally, night arrived. The whole day I couldn't tell what time it was, because the sound of the clock in the village did not reach this spot and the sun was covered with thick clouds. I slowly rose up and walked towards the barn.

Jaśko's wife was already awaiting me there with a bowl of hot borsht. I could see in her eyes how sorry she felt for me. She told me to enter the hut and dry myself by the fire. I went into this tiny room lit with a kerosene lamp. I was truly touched. Oh, it had been so long since I had stayed in a room with windows, walls, and a roof. I sat next to the big stove, in which a fire was burning. The pleasant warmth, so different from the terrible heat of the sun in the field, seeped into me. Jaśko sat down next to me and told me that while working in a field near Gaje Buczackie [7 km southwest of Buczacz], he had occasionally encountered Jews wandering about. Some of them even approached him and asked for something to eat. I was really moved by this information, because I had believed that apart from me no other Jews were still living in our area. Yet now I heard that they not only existed but they even walked around the fields in broad daylight. I told Jaśek that I had to meet some of these Jews at any cost. All the more so, as the distance to Głęboka Dolina, next to Gaje Buczackie where he met the Jews, was not more than seven kilometers.

Then Andrej and his wife walked in. Andrej's wife told me that Marynka, the undertaker's wife, knew that I visited them at night and had threatened to tell the Germans. In a word, concluded Andrej, she does not have a clear conscience about you and is afraid that you might live until the Russians arrive and then take revenge on her. This strengthened my resolution to go to Głęboka Dolina. I asked Jaśko for directions and decided to start out at dawn. Jaśko promised that when he gets to the fields around noon, he would bring me some food.

It was already late at night and just a few hours before dawn when I went to the barn and lay down on the soft hay. I tried to get some sleep before the next day's journey. But in vain. I listened to the chimes of the clock. It chimed 2 a.m., then 2:30 a.m. I got up, put on the old torn coat Jaśko's wife had given gave me the day before and left the barn, heading toward the fields. I walked past fields of wheat, but this time I did not stop to look for a hiding place for the day. I kept going until I reached the road. There, I turned right. Now I had to walk on the road for about five hundred meters until I reached a stone cross. I walked onto the stone road. I wasn't used to walking on a hard surface anymore. The wind was whistling in the power lines, and its sound made me uneasy. I nearly panicked, walked faster, almost running. At last, I saw the black cross in front of me.

Leaving the road, I took the path in the field. I still had to cross the rail lines before reaching the fields leading to Głęboka Dolina. In the meantime, day has arrived. I tried to hurry as much as I could and get as far from the road as possible. The danger was that German cars could appear at any moment. I felt worse and worse. My shirt, wet from sweat, stuck to my body. I again saw telephone poles in front of me. This was surely where the train passed. I walked faster and could see the elevated ground on which the railroad was built. I started running again and soon crossed the tracks. The terrain now descended into a valley. I could see a row of willows. That was where Głęboka Dolina was situated. Totally out of breath, I reached the row of willows, ran into the thicket and fell half-dead on the ground.

I stayed there for nearly an hour. I already finished the contents of the bottle I have taken with me. I felt hungry. The wet shirt made me tremble. The sky was overcast, and it began raining. A horse cart carrying manure was heading down the path in the field. I wondered whether I should stop it and ask the peasant for some food. But I decided not to. Jaśko had promised to bring me something. Looking around the area, all I saw was fields. Far away on the horizon, I could see the slightly elevated ground on which the train tracks passed. It was the same railway I had passed on my way earlier. I looked in the other direction. Behind the bushes there was another field of wheat, and beyond it a pasture. Only now did I notice that some cows were grazing there, watched over by a little girl. I decided to approach her and ask about the Jews who were apparently wandering about in this area. I tried to reach her as quietly as possible, thinking that if she suddenly saw me, she might get frightened and run away. I managed to get to her without making any noise thanks to the soft grass. Sensing my proximity, she turned her face toward me and seeing me covered her face with her hands and started screaming at the top of her voice.

I rushed up to her and covered her mouth with my hand to muffle her screams while at the same time tried to reassure her that I meant no harm. I was only hungry and perhaps she had something to eat. Gradually she calmed down and removed her hands from her face, but I could still see the terrible fear on the poor child's face. "You look so terrible, Sir," she whispered, "I thought you were a ghost." I touched my beard which has grown even more; my face was smeared all over with mud. Clearly, I did not look like a human being. I told the child that I was a Jew and asked if she knew of other Jews in the area. "I don't know where they are," she answered, "but they pass here every day. My mother always gives me more bread in case someone hungry walks by," she added. Saying that, she untied her bundle and gave me a large chunk of bread. "Unfortunately, I don't have more coffee," she said, "but if you wait, I will milk one of the cows and give you some milk in a jug." I readily agree, but I also suggested that it would probably be better for me to hide in the willows. "Don't worry," she said. "The Germans never come here."

At that same moment, two figures appeared from beyond the grass and walked toward us. I got up in fear, not knowing what to do, but then I heard the girl's voice: "It must be the Jews. They always come this way." I stood looking anxiously at the figures. When they were close, they also stopped. I waved to them and shouted something in Yiddish. I soon recognized them. They were Nacio Fritz and Benio Selzer. At first, they did not recognize me, but when Nacio looked closer he laughed and shouted: "Look at yourself! Here," he held a mirror in front of my face. I was terrified by my own appearance. The beard and moustache totally changed my face. My hair was caked with mud, forming a solid lump on my head. All in all, I looked like something out of this world. The girl handed me a jug filled with milk. I drank a little bit and gave it to the others. Now I did not feel so lonely anymore. At least there would be someone to talk to; together it would be easier to cope with our mutual fate. "Now come and wash yourself a little," Nacio said. I said goodbye to the girl, thanking her for everything and promising her that if I survived the war I would come and visit her.

Then the boys and I headed in the direction of the willows where a small spring I hadn't seen before was flowing. After washing, we walked in the other direction, to where Nacio and Benio had come from. On the way they told me that others were hiding in the wheat field: Nacio's mother, sister, and brother. Benio's father was also there. Apart from them, the Waserfal family was also hiding somewhere in the fields of Głęboka Dolina, as were the two teenagers Hesio and Salo Silberstein. During the day they usually lay hidden in the wheat and at night they would walk up to individual huts in the nearby forests and ask for food. Some gave them food out of pity, others for money, still others would chase them away with their dogs and threaten to hand them over to the Germans. Sometimes, peasants coming out to the fields would bring them some food. Thanks to the spring in the willows they had enough water. No Germans or Ukrainians had appeared yet in the fields of Głęboka Dolina. The area, which was far away from the road and bigger towns and was inhabited mainly by peasants in scattered huts located at some distance from each other, seemed an ideal hiding place for us, at least until the end of summer. And after that, laughed Nacio, it would be either the end of the war or the end of us.

As we kept walking, we passed different fields of wheat, corn, potatoes, and millet. At that point we kept low because we were near the hideout. Next to a large field of wheat we went down on all fours, along a well-trodden path in the wheat, until we reached a small opening where several people were partly lying down, partly sitting. We started telling each other what we had been through in the last few days. Later, Nacio's brother Janek acquainted me with the surroundings.

I learned that the first wooded area with two huts was inhabited by the old Kutnowski couple and their son Antoszek. Their daughter Elżbieta lived in the second hut with her husband and two children. It was enough to approach the shrubbery for the old woman, whom they called "babcia" (grandmother), to appear on the threshold. She was alerted by the barks of the dogs. She would call them names and lament that because of the Jews her house would be burned down and all of them would be killed. Nevertheless, she would soon bring out a big bowl of potato soup or wheat doughnuts and order them to eat. Her daughter Elżbieta and granddaughter Stasia would appear behind her with some bread and a jug of milk. In the second grove, about two hundred meters from the Kutnowskis, was the household of the peasant Skrabka, who lived there with his wife and two grown sons. Nobody knew much about him. Only from time to time, the tall elderly man could be seen working in the fields together with his sons. Behind them was the household of Jaśko Korkosz, who lived there with his wife and five young children. And further on was the house of the Boczar family.

"Now look there," Janek pointed to some houses that could be seen beyond. "That place is off limits for us. That big house belongs to the ethnic German Nowak. Not knowing this, Salo went to their house one morning and they chased him away with dogs. Two of Nowak's sons tore off his coat and boots, and warned that if they ever saw him again, they would tie him up and hand him over to the Germans." Before evening, I also learned that behind the Boczars' place were the houses of the Ukrainian Durda family. No one knew much about them either. That day passed very quickly and before I knew it, it was evening, and Benek declared that it was time to get food.

The three of us left together. Nacio, Benek, and me. We were walking openly, because the area seemed safe. First, we decided to visit "babcia" …. When we got near the house the dog started barking his head off and soon an old woman with a scarf on her head appeared. "Good Evening, grandmother!" Nacio shouted. "Again, the devil has brought you," she retorted in anger. "Go away, I will soon call the dogs on you." Having said that, she slammed the door behind her and disappeared inside the hut. I thought this was it and I could not understand why we did not leave immediately. Suddenly the grandmother appeared on the threshold carrying a large bowl filled with something. She came up to us, handed Nacio the bowl with two spoons and only then she noticed me. "Tfu," she spat. "Is this some kind of demon or what? Look at this hairy devil, what brought it here?" Saying this, she turned towards the other hut and called out loudly: "Elżbieta! Bring another spoon with you because another devil has appeared from nowhere!"

We ate in silence, and while Elżbieta observed us with curiosity, the grandmother would not stop whining: "Look what falls into the lap of poor people. They won't go and bother the rich. Those who have fifty acres of land will not share a piece of bread with a poor person. And God is watching this and does not punish them. It is a real Sodom and Gomora." They were mostly looking at me, probably because I was new. When we had finished eating and were preparing to leave, the grandmother came up to me and asked: "Where did you appear from today?" I told her briefly what had happened to me in the few days before my arrival in Głęboka Dolina. For a while they both looked at me and then the grandmother walked out in front of us and yelled: "Come into the hut." Elżbieta held the dog and soon we found ourselves in a poor peasant hut with a low roof, barely lit with a kerosene lamp. In the hut, we saw an old man sitting on a bench. He turned out to be grandmother's husband. Antoszko, the son, a well-built twenty-year-old, was also there. Soon, a young girl, Staszka, and her brother Ilonko, Elżbieta's children about whom I had heard before from Janek, also came in.

We started talking. Staszka handed me a three-day-old German newspaper and asked me to read it and see if there was anything new about the war. I greedily grabbed the paper. It was the official German "Lemberger Zeitung," dated 8 July 1943. On the front page, the Germans announced in large letters that all the Bolshevik attacks on the region of Orel and Kursk had been successfully repulsed.[63] Next, Goebbels gave assurances that the eastern territories would not be surrendered without fighting to the end. Finally, the paper threatened that even if the Germans were forced to leave some of these territories for a brief period, they would leave them in such a state that not even birds would ever find any food there.

I wondered about the content of these articles. I had never come across anything like this in the German press. After all, this was open acknowledgement of defeat. I began to explain the meaning of what was written to the others and soon we started talking about more realistic matters. Grandmother, now without any reference to devils, assured me that she really felt pity for us and would gladly help us more, but that the Germans had requisitioned all their wheat and potatoes so that they themselves were on the verge of starvation. She advised us to try and go to the house of Szkrabka, who was richer than she was. Maybe they would not refuse to help people less fortunate than they were. All the more so, considering the rumors that the Soviets could still arrive this winter. She warned us not to go near the buildings of the ethnic Germans or the Ukrainians. Most of all we should beware of Nowak's house. His daughters were often visited by Germans, who sometimes stayed overnight.

We left the house of "babcia" late at night and headed back to our hideout in the field. The overcast sky suggested that it was going to be a rainy night. When we reached the hideout, where the others were waiting, we found a new guest, a Jew who had been hiding in one of the villages. Someone must have noticed him and alerted the Germans. Early in the morning, looking out from his hiding place in an attic filled with hay, he had noticed a cart stopping in front of the house, from which Germans jumped off .... Zanwet, as he was called, removed the hay from the rear wall of the attic facing the field ..., jumped through it and ran into the field .... He heard shots behind him [... and] felt pain in the right side of his chest. But he did not stop and kept on running like a madman. [... Eventually] He hid in the wheat and only then felt pain and noticed that he was wounded ....

Salo and Hesio found him in the field and brought him back to us. At the same time, Janek and Beniek's father arrived, bringing with them a pot of potatoes they had been given by the Boczars. The women prepared the food, while we tried to help the wounded man. He was lying on the ground moaning softly. Nacio tore off a piece of his shirt while I tried to find the wound in the dark. The bullet had gone straight through his chest. And although I felt only a small wound in his back, the hole in his chest was much bigger. I tore the cloth into two pieces and applied it to the wound. Next, I covered his body with a shawl handed to me by Janek' mother and tied everything with a string. Salo brought a bottle of water from the spring, and that was all we could do for him under the circumstances. It started raining. Janek suggested we head over to the large stacks of hay in the field for the night. Helping the wounded man, we proceeded there and soon I was lying in the soft hay that sheltered me very well from the rain and cold. A very sweet smell emanated from the hay and soon I fell sleep.

I was awakened by yells, shots, and the sound of running feet. I heard the shouts "Halt! Halt, stop!" And then again shouts, shots, and running. Instinctively, I burrowed deeper into the hay, shut my eyes, and waited for the end. Instead, the shots became ever more distant. The yells could not be heard anymore. After some time, it became quiet. I carefully poked my head out of the hay and looked around me. Since I did not see anyone around, I ran out of the haystack to the field. While running, I recognized the bodies of Zanwet and Benio's father. Once I reached the wheat, I began crawling on the wet ground so as to get as far away from the edge of the field as possible. I heard voices coming closer to the stack of hay from which I had just escaped. I recognized the voice of Binka Waserfal begging the Germans to spare her life. And then I saw them. They were walking away from me. I held my breath, my heart started beating madly and I waited as if hypnotized. I was afraid they would turn their faces toward me. But they walked past, without noticing me.

I lay like that for another hour, and then proceeded to crawl carefully toward our hideout. There I found Hesio, on his own. He told me that he had escaped the Germans at the last moment. They shot after him, but luckily did not hit him. A bit later, Janek, Nacio, and Benek crawled in. It became clear that Binka's brother Szlomo had also been killed by the Germans, so the number of that day's victims rose to four. We lay there until evening, freezing in the ceaseless rain. In the evening, we borrowed a spade from "babcia" and buried the dead. That same night we moved a couple of miles away from there, afraid that the Germans might return.

Finally, the sun rose. The warm, merciful sun. Under the life-giving rays of the sun the stalks of the wheat and barley straightened up. We undressed and nearly naked, allowed the rays of sun to reach us with their warmth. After so many days of cold and rain we stretched our arms and bodies with great pleasure. Our clothes were already dry, and we decided to walk through the fields, where surely today many people were working. Maybe we could get some new information as well as something to eat. We left two by two. I walked with Nacio. We passed people working in the corn fields. We greeted them, and they usually responded. We tried to talk to them. We asked what was new in town, if any Jews had been caught.

We learned that hardly a day went by in which the Germans did not catch a few Jews. When caught, they were forced to dig ditches for themselves. Next, compelled by beatings, they had to undress and lie face down in the ditches, tightly packed one next to the other, their legs and arms stretched out. Those who were not in the position required by the Germans were pelted with stones until the latter are satisfied. Finally, they were shot, and then another group was forced into the ditch. They too had to position themselves tightly, their faces on the heads of those who had just been murdered, and so on, they lay in layers until the pit was full. The pits were later covered with earth by people randomly caught on the streets. The person we were talking to in the field was one of those people.

One of the laborers warned us not to wander so openly in the fields, because someone might alert the Germans. I answered that if anyone did, we would return at night and burn his house. "And if the Germans do appear, we will know how to greet them," I added, touching my pocket. When we walked away a bit, I told Nacio we had to make the peasants believe we carried weapons; indeed, had we really had a weapon, how differently we would have felt. Suddenly, I heard someone calling my name. It was Jaśko. We joined him and soon were eating fried potatoes with sour milk. Additionally, Jaśko also brought us a loaf of bread and some cooked beans. There was no fresh news from the world. There were rumors that Italy had capitulated, but no one was sure. We said goodbye to Jaśko and headed in the opposite direction.

We walked by Szkrabka's cornfield, where he and his sons were working. Nacio greeted them loudly, wishing them luck in their work. At first nobody responded, but after we had already passed them, I suddenly heard a voice from behind: "Hey you!" We turned around. The old Szkrabka had stopped working and was looking at us. "Come here," he said in a Masurian dialect.[64] We approached. "Sit down so that you cannot be seen," he said. When we sat down, he asked about the Jews killed by the Germans the day before. We began telling him when he interrupted: "And how many Germans were there altogether?" "Three," I answered. "And how many of you?" "Eight," said Nacio. "And you could not handle the three of them?!" he yelled. "Shame, shame on you. These Jews have really lost their minds!" The old man was getting really mad.

I interrupted him, saying that the Germans had weapons while we were unarmed, totally vulnerable, plus they attacked us when we were asleep. "Hmmm..." he retorted, "unarmed, but had you been given weapons, at the sight of the first German you would have thrown down your weapons and hidden in the wheat." We watched him without understanding the meaning of his words and where he was heading. We only noticed that he was very serious while talking to us. And we observed one other thing: that he had trouble walking, as if his right leg had been paralyzed. "Władek," he turned to his son, "give them each a piece of bread. And now go," he said to us. "And you, the tall one," he pointed at me, "come here tonight when it gets dark and wait at the same spot." Having said that, he returned to his work, while Nacio and I went, trying to figure out what Szkrabka had meant.

That day, we could barely wait for evening, we were so curious. What did Szkrabka have in mind and what would result from my meeting with him? As soon as it got darker, I went to the designated meeting place. It must have been around 8 p.m. There was no one there. I sat on the side of the path and let my mind wander. That same day we had learned from the peasants working in the fields that the night before an armed group of people had stormed the house of the Landkommissar. Since no one was there, they only took the clothes, shoes and weapons that were found there.[65] The terrified maid, who was forced to keep silent with a pistol aimed at her head, reported the following day that the clandestine attack had been undertaken by a group of young Jews. Almost at the same time, another group, also identified as Jews, stormed the house of the notorious Nahajowski, the town's dog catcher, who was a specialist in finding the hideouts of Jews. Nahajowski tried to escape through the window, but they caught and shot him.[66]

These were events worth thinking about, since they could transform our current situation. The drift of my thoughts was interrupted by the sound of approaching steps and soon I saw Szkrabka's younger son

Władek. "Come to Father," he said quietly. I stood up and we walked
to their house. I found myself in a very clean and well-kept peasant
dwelling. Pictures of saints were hanging on the walls. A kerosene lamp
hung from the ceiling. Szkrabka, his wife, and two sons were in the
room. One of them was Władek, who had brought me there and the
other was the older son, Jaśko. I greeted them and Szkrabka told me to
sit down on the wooden sofa. Then he asked me how old I was. When
I said I was twenty-three, he laughed and called out: "With that beard
you look more than forty!" He then told his older son to shave my beard.

After half an hour, all shaven, I was sitting at the table, eating hot cabbage soup and still wondering why I had been brought there. Szkrabka's
wife cleared the table. His sons left the room and Szkrabka and I were
left alone. He sat opposite me and filled his pipe. After smoking it for
some time and carefully observing me as he did, he asked me to tell him
my whole life story. Next the conversation turned to prewar political
topics and finally to the war. At a certain point Szkrabka asked me, if
we had any hope of surviving the occupation by wandering around the
fields. I answered that what had sent us into the fields was our instinct
of self-preservation. It told us to gain as much time as possible. We were
deluding ourselves that maybe some miracle would occur and change
our fate, but in fact none of us seriously thought that we would be able
to survive the war.

Again, Szkrabka's penetrating eyes observed me and I heard the
question: "Why don't young, strong boys like you have the courage to do
something beyond hiding from the Germans and waiting for the hour
or moment of death." I told him what I had heard that night about the
armed groups and that nobody would have been happier than me if I
had the opportunity to join one of them. The room was plunged into
silence again, only the smoke from his pipe rose up and covered the
light of the lamp. The room grew darker. It appeared as if a thick fog
had enveloped it. Suddenly, Szkrabka got up and limped toward me. He
stopped just in front of me. In the light of the lamp, obscured by clouds
of smoke, he looked to me like a giant. I raised my head and saw his eyes
looking into mine with such force that I felt they were penetrating my
very soul, as if trying to uncover all my hidden thoughts.

I calmly returned his gaze, looking straight into his eyes. Then, I
heard him speaking slowly. I began to grasp the meaning of his words in
my subconscious. "What you will hear now you must keep sealed inside
and be as silent about as a tomb. One of those armed people in the forest
visited me a few days ago. I told him about you and asked him to take
care of you, because I felt sorry for your young lives. In a few days, he
will visit me again and then I will call you so that you can meet. If he

takes you on, you will not have to hide from the Germans anymore. On the contrary, you will be looking for them. You will have the chance to avenge the lives of your families. And if you die, you will die not like a defenseless herd, but in glory, as heroes, as befits those who love freedom more than their lives. But beware not to bring shame upon an old man like me, so that no one will ever say that I promoted cowards or traitors. And now go," he said, "and every night let one of you wait in the field in the same place as today so that I can call you when the time comes."

I left his house nearly drunk with all that I had been through. My head was on fire, my throat felt as if it was choking. God, is this a dream? So partisan units really exist? And what good fate brought me there?

Three days passed. Every night, one of us waited in the appointed place. Today it was Janek's turn. He left there already half an hour ago. Nacio, Benek, and I were on the ground talking. The nights were bright now, with a full moon and quite warm. I told them for the hundredth time about the evening spent with Szkrabka. We were all very eager to join in. We were just afraid something would go wrong at the last moment. Maybe they would not let us join. Now we blessed that period in the Polish Army where we learned how to shoot. Benio was worried. What happens if they test us? I tried to cheer him up. I said that I would show him how to use weapons and that he could learn in a few minutes. In the meantime, I taught him the concept and he seemed to grasp it. There was still the matter of the women [in their group]. I decided to talk it over with Szkrabka when the right moment arrived.

It was late; we got together and went to "babcia." We sat in the hut and ate potatoes with noodles. When Staszka first saw me without the beard she could not recognize me; then she said I looked like my own son. Suddenly the dog outside began barking. We ran out: it was Janek. He was out of breath from running and shouted: Go to Szkrabka, quickly! They are waiting for you. I ran like the wind and soon arrived at Szkrabkas' house. Władek was already waiting in front of the house and led me in. I was surprised that the room was totally dark. Władek led me to the sofa and told me to sit down. I sat without moving, holding my breath.

Suddenly a flashlight was pointed at my face. The light moved from my face along my whole body. At last, an unfamiliar voice asked me in detail about my life since the beginning of the occupation. I spoke about the hidden radio and the Allied broadcasts I disseminated; the time we were already in possession of weapons and the tragic death of Janek and my brother. When I spoke about the radio, the stranger interrupted me, asking whether it would be possible to keep a radio in the forest and to receive broadcasts from Moscow and London. I replied that one could reassemble parts from a big radio into a small one. Such a radio would have to be supplied with power from a battery. I was very excited by this idea.

The first ice has been broken. Soon a lamp was lit, and I saw opposite me a young man in high boots, khaki trousers and a blue shirt. He introduced himself as Marian. After a brief conversation, he said he would recommend me to one of the leaders of the armed groups of the Armia Krajowa [AK, Home Army],[67] someone by the name of Edek. He also suggested that I speak to Edek about the radio. Finally, he promised that within three days someone from Edek's people would come and take us to the forest. I then mentioned the matter of the women. The women, for the time being, had to remain in the field. They would receive food from the local Polish peasants until we found a safe shelter for them.

I returned to the field and told the boys about my conversation with Marian. We were indescribably happy. For the first time since the "liquidation" and my escape from the town, my life began to acquire a real shape, from which the hope for a better future emerged.

The following three days felt extremely long. Every evening we waited impatiently for someone to come to us and went to sleep filled with disappointment and bitterness. Only on the afternoon of the fourth day Władek came running to our hideout and told us that an hour earlier two men had come to his home and were now speaking with his father in a closed room. One of them was apparently Edek himself. Władek also told us that they were well dressed, had guns, and were smoking German cigarettes. We could hardly wait for evening. Then, Władek came running again and called us to his house. When we entered the room, we found two young men sitting at the table. One of them, a slim, blue-eyed man with blond hair rose to greet us. "So, how are you lads?" he said. Then he shook our hands and said, "from now on call me Edek. And this here is Romek," he pointed to his colleague. We sat down to supper during which we had a lively conversation.

Edek showed great interest in the issue of the radio and asked what would be necessary to be able to receive transmissions in the forest. I answered that first we would have to somehow acquire a battery-powered radio. Then I could contact my friend Dziunek Dąbrowski, another radio technician, who possessed all the necessary tools for this work. I was sure he would be glad to help us. Furthermore, he lived just on the edge of town and should be fairly easy to contact at night. During the three days in which we waited for the men in the forest, I had already succeeded in contacting Dziunek by letter delivered by Staszka. He had promised to help with anything he could. After supper, Edek suggested that we go to Dziunek and discuss on the spot the details concerning the radio. From there, we would go straight to the forest.

We bid farewell to Szkrabka, but before we left, he made the following speech: "Today you are leaving for the forest. Maybe you will get weapons tomorrow. Remember. Never use these weapons to harm the innocent. In the days ahead, don't ever forget what you have been through. Until now you have fought in order to live. From now on you live in order to fight. Let your hearts not be merciful when you see your enemies crying for pity. Let the figures of your families, fathers, and mothers appear before your eyes. When you meet your enemies do not look for material gain. Just take their lives. Be fair in your fight, because only the just can win. And now, Go with God." He shook hands with every one of us. His wife wished us luck and gave each one of us a wooden spoon and demanded that after the war we bring them back. After also saying goodbye to Władek and Jaśko we went out into the dark.

First, we went toward Nagórzanka. We proceeded along the same road I had taken only two weeks earlier without knowing what my fate would be at the end of it. We passed by the row of willows, where I had found my first shelter when I reached the valley. We turned toward the train tracks. The pistols in Edek and Romek's hands were shining. I looked at them with envy. If only I could hold such a pistol in my hand. On the way, Edek asked us about our life in the fields. We told him about the Poles to whom we owed our lives, about our fear of the Ukrainians, and how the ethnic German Nowak set the dogs on Sala. Edek was surprised that we let them do it. "We did not have a weapon," said Nacio. "But you could have gotten matches, couldn't you," laughed Romek. "Had you burned down just one ethnic-German house, you would have seen how the others change their behavior." "And rest assured," added Edek, "that if instead of four of ours, three Germans lay dead in the field, the Germans would not have dared bother you again for a while. But it's not surprising," Edek went on, "we too were like that once."

He told us that just a few months earlier he was still living with his father at home. One day, the Germans raided their house and grabbed him and his older brother. It was one of the frequent roundups [for forced labor to be sent] to Germany in those days. That same day, together with other victims, they found themselves at the train station, being loaded onto sealed railcars. On the way, they managed to break open one of the doors of the railcar and jumped out of the rapidly moving wagon. "My brother was shot with a machine gun in front of my eyes," said Edek. "I jumped next. I heard a few shots and for a while just lay stunned on the ground. Then, when I realized I was not wounded, I ran back along the train tracks until I fell down next to my brother's corpse. I did not hear when someone walked up behind me. When I regained consciousness, I felt a strong pain in my head from the blow I had received. Armed Germans from the Bahnschutz [Bahnschutzpolizei: railroad protection police] were standing over me.

They escorted me with some others they had caught to the nearest train station. There were twelve of us and only five Germans. If we had only acted at that point, we could have easily disarmed them. But—and to this day I can't understand it—they led us like sheep. In a word, we behaved just like you did not so long ago in the fields. You at least ran away. I was at the time totally unaware [of what to expect] .... From the train station we were transported, now under heavy guard, to the main Gestapo prison in Czortków. In prison we were put two in a cell. I shared mine with Bronek, whom you will meet tomorrow in the forest. Every day, they would take some one out, and none of them ever returned. We could see some of them through the cell windows, as they were mauled by big dogs kept especially for this purpose by the Gestapo. The leader and performer of the executions was usually the Gestapo-man [Albert] Brettschneider,[68] who would visit the cells the evening before and play a special tune of his own composition on his harmonica. It was called the Death Tango.

One evening, the door of our cell opened. Brettschneider was standing there, holding his harmonica. Leaving the door half open, he walked in and sat on one of the bunks. From his unsteady steps we could see that he was drunk. "Well now, you damned Poles," he exclaimed. "Tomorrow is your turn. And now I will play you something for the road," he said, and started playing. Bronek and I looked at each other and then pounced on him. I grasped his throat and started choking him, while Bronek held his feet. Once I felt that he was not struggling anymore, I pulled the dagger from his belt and stabbed him twice, with his own SS dagger.[69] We quickly pulled off his uniform and boots. While I was dressing, Bronek played the tune we already knew so well—the Death Tango. Soon both of us were in the hallway, which was fortunately empty. Bronek walked in front of me while I kept right behind, holding the pistol to his back. In this manner we reached the exit gate. It was manned by an armed SS-man. Seeing us, he blocked our way and said something in German. In response, I shot him in the head and, jumping over his body, we soon found ourselves in the town's alleys."

At this point Edek stopped his story, because we were approaching the railroad crossing. For a moment, we stood listening and then we continued towards the road. We reached the stone cross and then proceeded along the road for another half a kilometer. We were now moving forward in two groups on either side of the road. Edek handed me his pistol and pulled a hand grenade out of his pocket just in case. At last we turned off the road, and began walking through the fields again. He hid the grenade and took his pistol back. We could talk again. Now it was my turn to tell my story. I told him about my brother and Janek; how I escaped from the Ukrainian prison; how Marynka said that the only way out for me was to surrender to the Germans; about Andrej and Jaśek, to whom I owed so much, and about everything else that had happened in the last days.

In Edek's view the peasants were not bad by nature. "It is poverty, in which they have been mired for generations, that has made them greedy to the point that for them the end often justifies the means. This is especially the case when they want to help themselves and their often-numerous family members. Apart from that, they are accustomed to constant fear of and respect for people wearing uniforms with golden buttons, and are eager to avenge themselves on the weak, no matter who they are, for what the Germans have done to them. Try to come up at night to the poorest peasant and plead with him for some food. At best, he will ask for a pair of shoes from you in exchange. But if you raid his house with a pistol in your hand, fire a shot next to his ear, and beat him on the face, he will give you everything you want. And he will be pleased that you let him live. Of course, there are exceptions, but you can identify them very quickly." We were already approaching the first houses and soon I was knocking on Dziunek's window. We spend half an hour with Dziunek, who promised to take care of the matter as long as we brought him the spare parts.

It was already after midnight and we were walking back on the same road. Suddenly Edek stopped and said: "Lead me to your Marynka, we will teach her a small lesson." We walked quickly and soon approached the house near Nagórzanka I knew so well. Before we entered the yard, Edek stopped and told me to go and knock on the window and ask for something to eat. He meanwhile picked up a log of wood and stood next to the door leading to the house's anteroom. Romek took Janek with him to the back window facing the garden. Nacio and Benek were posted to guard the road and let us know if anything happened. I knocked lightly on the window. I heard a noise from the inside, and recognized Marynka. I asked her for something to eat, telling her I was dying of hunger. Marynka recognized me and started yelling: "Go way! There are Germans spending the night at the neighbor's house. I'll call them, and they'll catch you. Go away, or else …"

I heard nothing more because at that instant Edek smashed the door with the log. The door gave in. I only heard Marynka cry out one more time, "help!" and then the door leading to the next room also broke down. There were no more cries. You could only hear the dull sound of a beating. I passed through the anteroom and the kitchen and found myself in the room. I saw Edek holding a torch in his left hand, pointing the light at Marynka's prostrate body as he continued to kick her all over. I could see half of Maniek's body visible from under the bed. His whole body could not fit in. There was a shot outside, and we heard Romek's voice calling out. Apparently Maniek's closest neighbors wanted to come and help when they heard the shouting. But the shot fired by Romek and his stern warning stopped them in their tracks.

I ran out very quickly, recalling that among the neighbors were also Andrej and Jaśko, to whom I owed so much. But Romek calmed me down and I returned to the hut. Summoned by Edek, Nacio was now covering the windows with blankets. Soon the lamp was lit. Marynka was still sighing loudly on the floor. Manko had crawled out from under the bed and was sitting on it, his head down. Edek ordered Marynka to get up and to sit next to Manko. Then, he gave me a sign with his head and said: "Talk." I began my story telling how for many years I had been friends with Manko, how together we had raided the German wheat warehouse, hidden the radio in the cemetery, and how, throughout the roundups, I had always managed to escape to the cemetery with his knowledge. Then I talked about how Marynka had threatened to call the Germans on me in the cemetery. How she had suggested I give myself up to them and how she had chased me away from the window, when I was truly dying of hunger.

Throughout this time Manko was sitting on the bed with his head in his hands. When I ended my story, Marynka threw herself at my feet, weeping and begging for mercy. Manko appealed to our friendship, saying that he had only given in to his wife's fear because she was terribly afraid of the Germans. We were all silent and looking for a sign from Edek. He too remained silent for a while. The concentrated expression on his face showed that he was really contemplating the issue. The he rose to his feet and said: "I don't know what the Germans would have done to you had they learned that you helped Jews. But as for me, I would have killed you like dogs for what you did to him. Only your past behavior," he said as he turned to Maniek, "prevents me from doing it. Fear of the Germans cannot be an excuse for you. If you are afraid of repressions by the Germans for helping Jews and partisans, I want you to know that we will punish obedience to any German orders with death. Remember this and tell the others!"[70]

We went back again to the fields. The same clock that chimed the hours when I was still lying in Jaśek's barn now signaled 1 a.m. We were approaching the road when we heard the clatter of a peasant's cart and the sound of horses' hooves. Edek and Romek rushed forward and managed to stop the cart. In response to our question, the peasant answered that he was returning from town, to which he had driven the village head. "Now you will drive us," said Edek, waving to us. In an instant, we were all seated on the cart. The peasant was blindfolded. Romek took the reins and directed the horses away from the road. The cart passed through field paths taking us into the unknown, but with much hope in our hearts.

Day was already breaking when we arrived at the edge of the forest, driving through the fields and keeping off the roads. Here we jumped off the cart, took off the peasant's blindfold and let him go. We then walked deeper into the forest. A notice attached to one of the trees at the edge of the woods caught my eye. It said in German: "Unoccupied territory. Entrance to Germans and dogs forbidden." "It's been hanging here for a couple of months," Edek chuckled, "and the Germans have not dared remove it." We walked quickly through the forest. In some spots the less dense woods allowed us to look farther into the distance. In other places we plunged into thick bushes that at first sight appeared impenetrable, but in fact concealed comfortable passages that enabled us to move quite quickly. Then we reached a valley where a small stream was flowing. We paused there to refresh ourselves with clear water.

When we moved again, I dared to ask the question that had been on my mind for over an hour: "Why did we have to blindfold the peasant?" I asked Edek. "After all, when we released him at the end of our journey, he could see where he was." "First of all," Edek said, "we did not get off next to the forest where our camp is located. It's more than a two-hour walk from there. Secondly, it's very important for us to keep the roads we use secret as long as possible. Our people live alongside all the roads we use. If the Germans appear, they light a lamp in the window and leave the window uncovered." Now I understood why during our journey Romek stopped the horses a few times and peered into the darkness, although there was no sound in the quiet night. After leaving the valley, we walked for quite a long time through a sparsely wooded forest and from there we climbed a hill overgrown with trees and even more so with dense hazel shrubs. We had to walk there in a row, one behind the other, because the thicket did not allow us to move otherwise. We walked like this for over an hour and although it was quite a chilly morning, we were all bathed in sweat.

Edek stopped twice to give us a brief respite. We were nearly halfway up the hill when Edek stopped and whistled twice. Apparently, it was a signal, because in response we heard the same kind of whistle. We turned left. A few more minutes of tough climbing and soon we found ourselves facing a small clearing where we could see some people. In the middle of the clearing a young woman was preoccupied with two pails hanging over a fire. She was probably preparing a meal. Seeing us, she walked over and to greet Edek and Romek. Soon after, I met Bronek, the hero of the escape from the Czortków Gestapo, as well as Józek and Paweł. The woman by the fire was Bronek's wife.

In all, there were eight people in the clearing, and they were the core of the unit. Together with us we made fifteen. We sat down on the ground and looked around. Each member of the group was armed with a different type of weapon. I noticed a Russian ten-shot semiautomatic gun, two cavalry carbines, two sawed-off German rifles, and three Hungarian rifles. Additionally, nearly everyone possessed personal pistols, mainly the Belgian F.N. type, and Russian or German hand grenades. My observation of the clearing and its inhabitants was interrupted by Zosia, Bronek's wife, who set a bowl of steaming buckwheat porridge, well-seasoned with bacon, in front of each of us. Everyone sat in front of the bowls, including us, and for our first partisan meal we took out the only weapon we had—the partisan spoons Mrs. Szkrabka had given us.

After breakfast Edek sent us to get some rest, which we really needed after all we had been through, and even more so, since he told us to be ready for a mission in the evening. I lay down to sleep with the first rays of the rising sun on my face. The forest was filled with the song of birds. Somewhere far away I could hear a cuckoo. I smiled to myself, recalling the cuckoo I heard the night I escaped from the Ukrainians. From this day on, I said to myself as I was falling asleep, I will believe the cuckoo. This was the first time I slept peacefully since the German invasion, knowing that I was guarded by ten loaded guns.

We woke up when the sun was already descending to the west. I was summoned by Edek who told me about the evening's mission. In the nearby village of Porchowa [18 km southwest of Buczacz] the Germans had commandeered a large estate. The German estate manager had been trying to incentivize the peasants to speed up delivery of the quotas of wheat, milk, and eggs to the Germans, by handing out bonuses of vodka, kerosene, and salt to those who most eagerly delivered their produce.

Our mission that night was to take over the warehouse with the bonus goods and to distribute them to the local population. Next, we were to burn down the estate and milk factory which was operating solely for the Germans. Finally, we were to collect food for ourselves for a few days and return to the forest.

Soon thereafter, having finished our tasty meal of potatoes and pork, we prepared to leave on the mission. It took us some time to train those who did not yet know how to use weapons. I was especially interested in the semiautomatic gun and I quickly mastered it. Finally, Edek gave the signal to leave. We walked one behind the other. Edek led the way. I walked right behind him, armed with the semiautomatic gun, followed by Nacio with a rifle strapped to his back. Janek and Bronek were armed this time with pistols only. Romek, Bronek, Józek, and Tadek were at the end. The rest stayed in the forest. When we reached the edge of the forest, the sun had already set.

We stopped, and Edek gave us the last instructions. When approaching the village, we were to divide into three groups. The first, commanded by Edek, with me, Nacio, and Józek, was to reach the estate and load a cart with as much food as we could manage. Then we were to burn down the estate and wait for the others behind the village. The second group under the command of Romek, along with Janek and Tadek, was to take over the warehouse and scatter the supplies in the streets of the village. Bronek and Benek were assigned to torch the milk factory. Edek decided that each group was to act on its own and if anything went badly, they were not to count on help from the others. He said there were no Germans in the village, but we would make sure of that again before we began the action. "The two Ukrainian policemen would hide after hearing the first shot," he said. "So, act quickly, calmly, and without hesitation."

It grew dark. On the nearby road a cart loaded with hay appeared. At a signal from Edek, Józek jumped out of the forest and stopped the cart. Soon, with our help, it was emptied of the hay. We quickly jumped onto the cart, the peasant was told in which direction to go and the horses started galloping. Traveling through side roads and fields, we arrived near the village of our destination at around 10 p.m. There we got off the cart and allowed the peasant to leave while we approached the village. Józek sneaked into one of the houses on the edge of the village and soon returned, assuring us that there were no Germans in the village. We separated in silence, each group heading in the previously agreed direction.

Edek and the rest of our group walked on the road, which he apparently knew well, and soon we saw the outlines of large buildings on the hillside ahead of us …. We reached the gate that was locked from the inside. We walked a bit further along the fence [… and] jumped over it into the yard. We saw light in two windows, and as we headed in that direction, we were suddenly attacked by two dogs barking loudly. Two shots from Edek's revolver silenced them forever. At the same time, he ordered: "Nacio and Józek—to the windows!" He himself rushed to the main entrance door. I ran after him holding the gun ready to shoot. We found ourselves in a big room with two women and a man scared out of their wits. "Where is the Landwirt [agricultural manager]?" Edek yelled. One of the women explained in a fearful voice that the Landwirt was not there. He only came sometimes during the day and was always accompanied by armed gendarmes. But he never spent the night on the estate ….

Edek ordered me to take the man to the stable, harness the horse, and come around to the entrance. Józek came running and said we should first come around to the sty, in front of which a large, freshly killed pig was lying. Then we drove to the house where the women, who appeared to be maids, had been ordered by Edek to bring down a sack of flour, a box of eggs, and some tins of honey. All of this must have been prepared for the Landwirt. When everything had been loaded, Edek pointed his loaded pistol at the women and the man and asked: "Where is the kerosene?" … The man pointed to the cellar where we indeed found a barrel of kerosene. With the help of the women we poured the liquid onto the walls, floors and furniture. We let out the animals from the stable and poured kerosene there too. Finally, we poured the remaining kerosene into the hay barn and as Nacio was opening the gate, we lit the stable, barn, and the main building. As we were leaving, we saw a large fire on our right. "It must be the dairy factory," Józek said. The flames were also rising from the estate we had just left …. We left the village and proceeded to the meeting point.

Bronek and Benek were already waiting there, since they were the first to complete their mission at the dairy factory. They had brought a large jug of sour cream with them. Only Romek's group was missing. We started to get impatient and Edek even wanted to go and search for them when they appeared, carrying huge sacks full of bottles of vodka on their backs. On the way back, Romek told us how the people of the village gathered in the night to grab the scattered things. "They nearly started fighting each other over them," he laughed …. By the time dawn arrived, we were already sleeping the sleep of the just, dreaming of the next operations. Such operations were to become the essence of our lives.

Three days went by, in which we tried to restore our clothes and shoes to a modicum of respectability. We ate non-stop. For breakfast Zosia would prepare fried eggs with bacon, for tea she made blintzes with honey. The pig was hanging from the tree, expertly disemboweled by Bronek, and we ate huge amounts of meat every day. The one thing we lacked was vodka, because the day after the operation some of the boys got totally drunk and Edek smashed all the remaining bottles in rage. We were lying down, resting after a sumptuous meal, when we heard a whistle from the forest. Józek jumped up and responded with a similar whistle; soon Marian appeared from behind the bushes. It was the same Marian, whose intervention had brought us here in the first place.

Marian brought us the most recent edition of the "Biuletyn Informacyjny" [news bulletin] issued by the leadership of the AK, and the approval by the leadership to undertake the operation against the ethnic German Nowak that Edek had proposed. I grabbed the newsletter and started reading it. My attention was caught by the last developments in the war since my escape from town. I learned that there had been a change of government in Italy. [Benito] Mussolini had been replaced by [Marshal Pietro] Badoglio, and Italy was on the verge of capitulation. Additionally, on the Eastern front the Soviets had repulsed the German offensive in the area of Orel and Kursk and were now on the offensive themselves. I keenly felt the lack of a radio receiver. If only we could listen to the news from the Allies!

Edek's voice called me away from my reading. I walked over to where he was sitting with Marian and Bronek. "Prepare the boys," Edek said. "Tonight, are leaving to Gaje [Buczackie]. And tomorrow night we will take care of Nowak." Marian also instructed me to get hold of Nowak's registry of requisitions, [... since as] the Germans' right-hand man he was in charge of the requisitions, and surely would have noted down all the information.

We set out when it got dark with the first peasant cart we met on our way. We were heading toward Gaje. Near the village of Barysz [14 km southwest of Buczacz] we intentionally got off the road, released the cart and the peasant, and proceeded on foot for another five kilometers. We spent the rest of the night and the following day very comfortably in the soft hay of Korkosz's barn. After sunset at the end of that day Korkosz' son brought the cows in from the fields in the vicinity of Nowak's house. The entire day he had been observing if anyone had come there. No stranger had come to Nowak or to Gaje the whole day.

Edek briefed us on the plan of the operation. Two of us were to take up positions at a crossing about two hundred yards from Nowak's house to guard against uninvited guests. The other two were to patrol around the house during the whole time we were inside. The remaining six were to storm the house from all possible directions and assemble everyone inside into one room. In case anyone began shooting from inside the house, Edek would whistle twice. That would be the signal to first throw hand grenades into the house and only then to storm it. After taking over the house, we were instructed to read out Nowak's and his two sons' death verdict and execute them. His daughters would be spared, but we would shave off their hair with a shaving machine we prepared in advance. "Do not set fire to the house in case other houses of Poles or loyal Ukrainians catch fire too," ordered Edek.

We moved out when it was already dark. We passed by Szkrabka's house and the farms of the Boczars and Durda … and were now approaching the ethnic German's house. Janek and Romek separated from the group and went through the fields to the crossing. We scattered around the field and surrounded the farm buildings, trying to approach the house without making any noise. I approached from the side of the barn. I was holding the loaded gun, and I could see Józek not far away also going in the same direction. I looked to the left, but I couldn't see Nacio, who should have been there. We were right next to the barn. I moved alongside the wall, reached the corner, but I couldn't cross over to the yard because I was blocked by a thick hedge that extended to the next building—probably the stable.

As I tried to figure out how to get over the obstacle the silence of the night was shattered by the barking of a dog from the direction of the gate, where Edek was supposed to enter. I heard a shot and then the dog whining. I threw myself over the hedge covering my face with my free hand and managed to reach the yard at the cost of torn clothes and scraped hands and face in time for Edek's first whistle. I rushed to the only lit window on my side of the house. Here, I encountered Nacio, who appeared suddenly. We smashed the windowpanes with the butts of our guns nearly simultaneously. From inside we could hear the noise of glass being broken, together with screams and calls for help. I jumped in through the window as did Nacio. The room was lit with an oil lamp hanging from the ceiling. No one was there. We looked under the beds, inside the closets. Having found no one, we ran out into the corridor, where we found an old woman and two little girls trembling with fear. We pushed them toward the kitchen, where we could hear Edek's voice. Tadek was also there.

An old man was standing there, his face turned to the wall and his hands raised. It was Nowak himself. Soon Bronek and Józek brought in Nowak's third daughter, whom they found hiding in a pile of dirty washing in the cellar. Asked about his sons, Nowak said they were sleeping out tonight. Outside, the boys were already gathering things we could use and harnessing the horses. Edek told us to stock up on shoes and clothing. We loaded a few sacks. It was easy to see that some of the clothes had belonged to Jews. For example, I found a monogram in Hebrew letters on one of the undergarments. When Nowak was asked about it, he was first silent and then said he had indeed received the garments from Jews in exchange for food. But, after he was thrown to the ground and kicked by Nacio, he admitted that after the roundups the ethnic Germans would receive packages with clothes and furniture left behind when the Jews were murdered.

In one of the rooms I saw a radio on the table. I rushed to it and I held in my hands—it was the magnificent five-tube "Super Telefunken." I also took the anode battery and accumulator necessary to charge the radio. When everything had been properly packed and placed on the horse carriage, it was time for the essential point of our mission. We gathered in the room where the Nowak family was held under guard of Benek and Józek. At my demand, Nowak showed me where the requisition quotas registry was kept, and I immediately seized it. Edek then gave me a signal. I took out the piece of paper and read the previously prepared text of the verdict:

"In the name of Poland! The Court Martial of the AK, in considering the case of the Nowak family, finds them guilty as traitors to the Polish nation, for collaboration with the occupier, operating against the Polish population, and culpable in the murder of four Jews shot to death in Głęboka Dolina. Nowaks' daughters have shamed the good name of Polish women by having relations with Germans for personal gain .... Therefore, the Field Court ... has decided on the following verdict: Joachim Nowak and his sons will be executed. His three daughters will have their heads shaven and so be shamed and serve as a warning to others against behaving in this manner ...."

There was total silence in the room. Nowak tried to interfere to explain something a few times, but the butt of Bronek's gun stopped him. Nowak's wife was sobbing and tried to deter us by proposing large sums of money and gold. Enraged, Paweł was about to hit her, but Edek stopped him with a hand gesture. All went silent waiting for what he would say. For a while his steel gaze rested upon us as if trying to make a choice. Then, we heard his voice. It was calm and steady, measuring each word as if he were just having a friendly chat. He turned to us: "Whose father was killed in Głęboka Dolina?" he asked. "Mine," answered Benek, his voice shaking. Edek raised his hand, turned to Benek and, pointing at Nowak, said: "Shoot." His voice was so strong and had so much authority, that it was impossible to resist. Benek shot straight at Nowak's head. Then we seized the girls, who turned as pale ghosts, and Józek very expertly shaved their heads.

Soon thereafter we were back on the cart driven by Benek, the hero of the day. We stopped for a moment next to a large billboard used for German orders. I jumped off the cart and plastered our verdict in the middle. We stopped again at Szkrabka's house, where we dumped a sack of flour seized from Nowak's house. This flour was meant for Janek's mother and sister, who were still living at Szkrabka and Kutkowski's in Gaje. We reached our camp late at night. I was eager to try out the radio but feared that in the dark I might damage it and decided to wait until morning.

At daybreak I started working on the radio. At around 7:50 a.m. we could again hear the voice we had not heard for such a long time: "This is London." At 12.00 p.m. Moscow time we listened to the latest news-cast from Moscow. At the end of the newscast the speaker announced: "Let's honor the partisans fighting behind enemy lines." We were a little proud and very happy that they remembered us over there.

It had been four weeks since I joined the unit and time had been passing very quickly. I touched my beard which had really grown and decided not to shave it until the liberation. Maybe by then, it would reach down to my knees, I chuckled silently to myself, my hand on the semiautomatic, but what did it matter, all I knew now was one thing: they would never capture me alive. We unpacked the sacks filled with clothing. There was enough for everyone. I found a silk shirt whose smell evoked the forgot-ten scent of home and my mother's warm hands. It was not advisable to think about the old days in times like this. I had already been holding a weapon for four weeks and as yet had not killed a single German. On the other hand, I realized that I was alive only in order to avenge you—my dear ones. My hand would not tremble, Oh no. My thoughts were interrupted by Bronek, who brought me a pair of elegant shoes and trousers. Soon, elegantly dressed to the last button and wiping our noses with handkerchiefs, we sat down to the evening meal, taking great care not to ruin our neatly ironed pants.

In the evening Marian came to visit us. He said that the following day we would go together to Szkrabka's. We would take the radio with us and try to bring it to Dziunek. Marian also said that Edek had praised the newcomers to the unit very warmly and asked me to write a short report about the operation at Nowak's farm to be placed in the newslet-ter. We listened to the radio again in the evening. We all sat around the radio which broadcast words of encouragement and a call to persevere in the fight. The words were supposed to keep our spirits up. What future were they talking about? What could we expect? I could not imagine life as the only Jew in town: without special Sabbath clothes in the closet; without the conversations of Jews strolling down the street on Saturday afternoons; without my mother, brother, and so many friends.

The last newscast was over and now the news was in a language I did not know. Usually at moments like this I would turn off the radio; but this time, as if motivated by some external force, I mechanically turned the button. Beautiful music emanated from the radio, a long-forgotten Chopin nocturne. It penetrated my heart, seized my soul, and took it to a different world. I didn't even know if it was the future or the past. I saw myself among my old friends, most of whom were already dead. We were laughing and playing in our old school building. I heard the bell ringing. The hall became silent. The curtain rose. The sounds of Chopin's nocturne flowed from the stage. I touched my necktie, tied the way only my sister could. My sister, yes. Where was she?

My thoughts flew several years ahead. I looked at the radio with all the different stations of the world written on it .... Perhaps my sister was listening to the same Chopin nocturne whose sounds would spell only tears if written down .... The music stopped. The announcer wished his listeners good night in some unknown language. He probably also reminded them to turn off the gas and fold the antenna before retiring to bed. And we were still sitting there motionlessly, staring at the illuminated rectangle on the radio ....

Already the following evening, we set out to Szkrabka's house. Marian and Nacio came with me. We did not encounter any obstacles on the way, and we reached the house at midnight. We found Nacio's mother and sister there, where they were spending the night. Szkrabka told us that our attack on Nowak's house had made a great impression on the local peasants. The day after the attack, the Germans arrived. They interrogated the neighbors, but soon left in a hurry, taking Nowak's wife and daughters with them. We also learned that some more Jews had arrived in Głęboka Dolina and were being helped by the local Poles. Szkrabka suggested that we pay a visit to the Ukrainian Durda family and warn them that if anything bad befalls the Jews hiding in Głęboka Dolina, they would share Nowak's fate.

We immediately proceeded to the Durdas' house. We were greeted at the gate by barking dogs. Marian stayed hidden in the yard, while Nacio and I approached one of the windows; as Nacio tried to hold off the howling dogs, I knocked on the window and demanded to be let in. For a while nobody answered, but when I threatened to use force, a woman appeared in the window and with a frightened voice begged us to leave them alone because they had done nothing wrong. I answered that we had no bad intentions toward them and asked again to be let in. Having realized that opposing us would get her nowhere, the woman disappeared from the window and soon I heard the squeak of the bolt on the door being opened.

We found two women in the house. One of them was holding a small child in her arms. It had apparently been awoken from its sleep and started to cry. I went up to her, put the weapon on the table, took the child from her arms and tried to calm it down. And indeed, the child became quiet. "You see," I said to the women, "the child is smarter than you are, it knows we don't mean you any harm." The women, reassured by my behavior, asked if we wanted something to eat. I answered that we would gladly eat something, but only if one of the men of household would join us. Nacio added that they would be able to continue their lives afterwards since nothing would threaten them from our side. After a short chat between them, one of the women went out and returned together with a tall man, her husband.

I briefly explained that we were the ones who had attacked the Nowaks and that a similar fate awaited anyone who denounced Jews in hiding and collaborated with the Germans. Durda responded that he knew Jews were hiding in Głęboka Dolina and that he was willing to help them, to the extent he was able to, in their difficult situation. His wife added that she could cook something every evening for a few people. Durda also told us that the Germans had now put him in charge of the requisition quotas instead of Nowak. Additionally, he was responsible for immediately informing the Germans of any arrival of Jews in the area. "On the other hand," Durda said, "my nomination has its good side, because I will know right away if an action is planned by the Germans and will be able to warn the Jews about the danger." We left late at night, very happy about the outcome of our conversation. At least, there was no more danger from his side.

The following morning, in Szkrabka's barn, I dismantled the radio into smaller parts, which were later transported by Staszka and Włodek to Dziunek. Włodek returned in the afternoon, saying that it would take two days to convert the radio. We decided to stay at Szkrabka's and rest a bit. [… Two days later] Władek returned with the radio. It was now the size of a field telephone ….

For the last few days we had not gone out on a mission. Our only activity was getting bread, milk, and news on the movements of the Germans and the Ukrainian militia from the local villages. Tonight, we were visited by Łużny, commander of the neighboring AK unit from

Korościatyn [25 km west of Buczacz]. He liked our camp, and mostly, envied our radio receiver. We even tried to convince him that it was also a transmitter, with which we were announcing our courageous acts to the world, but he did not buy that. He himself was also a bit of a radio technician. Before the war, he had been a professional soldier and served in a communications unit. At some point he disappeared behind the bushes together with Edek and Bronek. Soon, I too was called.

When I sat down next to them, Edek let me in on their secret consultation. I gathered that Łużny's visit was more than a mere social call. He wanted to coordinate our two units in order to stage an attack on the prison in the town of Monasterzyska. Apart from those who had been imprisoned because of cheating on their requisition quotas, some members of the AK who had been caught with illegal materials or those who were known to sympathize with the partisans were also held there. The latter were to be executed soon, and the Gestapo unit in charge was expected to arrive in town any day. According to Łużny's plan, our unit was to burn down the tobacco factory in the town. That would bring all the German and Ukrainian forces to that area of town. Łużny's group would then attack the building of the police and the prison. The problem was that if the guard escaped with the keys, opening of the cells could take a long time. Edek's solution was to give Łużny twenty armor-piercing bullets that would blast the cells' doors. It was also decided that this action would be carried out during the day and not, as usual, at night. Edek insisted on that, saying that at night all the gates were closed, which would present many obstacles to reaching the prison cells or even the factory floor.

After a two-hour consultation the final plan was agreed: the following day, Thursday, there would be a market in town to which many peasants came, and Łużny's unit would take advantage of this fact, mix in with the peasants and take positions near the prison building. The weapons for the operation, hand grenades and pistols, would be hidden in their pockets. Łużny and another member of his group would arrive in a horse-drawn cart, dressed as peasants. A rifle and armor-piercing bullets would be stowed in the cart. The signal for the beginning of the attack on the prison was to be the fire at the tobacco factory and the ensuing panic.

Łużny left in the evening, and we spent the night preparing for the operation. Everyone tried to change their appearance and transform themselves into typical, peaceful, and good-natured peasants, of the kind who are inclined to tilt their hats at the mere sight of a German. The following morning as we sat down to breakfast, Edek looked at me and yelled, "the beard, man, the beard! With a beard like that you smell of the forest a mile away!" I looked at Edek and felt very sorry for myself for having to part with the beard that I had already become used to. I started stroking the hairs that were already reaching down to my stomach. I remembered how Nowak's wife fainted when she saw me—or rather my beard. I had become notorious in the area. I had heard that mothers, when they wanted to make their children behave, scared them by mentioning the "bearded demon" from the forest. And now, everything had to end. "Shave it off immediately," I heard Edek's voice. But just as I was getting up, sighing heavily, he suddenly shouted: "Wait!" He looked at me carefully for some time, then burst out laughing. "Wonderful, you will go like this. Just take off your shoes and put on some rags. You must look like a Jew who has been in hiding for a long time and was finally caught."

Not everyone understood what this was all about, but we had all learned not to ask too many questions and completely trusted Edek. At around 4 p.m. Edek ordered everyone to assemble before marching out. He himself appeared from behind the bushes and we all gasped in shock. Facing us was a completely authentic SS officer. The skull and bones on the cap, the well-polished buttons, and all the other metal parts of the uniform shining like mirrors. Even his shoes were so well polished that you could see your reflection in them. Nacio was dressed like a Ukrainian policeman and did not in the least resemble what he had been not so long ago, a broken and wretched Jewish boy awaiting his end. Only I looked exactly as when I had reached Głęboka Dolina. But not entirely so. Because Edek, looking at me again, said: "You must look scared. Listen to me, you must look terrified! How can a Jew being taken to his death have such a happy face? You have to pretend that you are not going for a Shabbat stroll, but that a Gestapo official is walking behind you, holding a pistol to your back." I desperately tried to put on a frightened expression, but it was hard, considering the pistols and hand grenades I could feel in my pockets. Ultimately, I managed to put on some kind of expression, at the sight of which Edek and the others burst out laughing. Edek came up to me, ruffled my hair a little more, and we set out.

First, we walked along the edge of the forest. The peasants working in the fields pretended not to see us. Passing by, I noticed that not even one of them looked in our direction. "You see," said Romek, "we have taught them not to look at or see what they don't have to. The ones we meet on the road take their hats off to us." Now came the turn of today's victim, the first horse cart. We turned it around and ordered the peasant to drive in the direction we indicate. Our "civilian" rifles were hidden in the hay, but we could pull them out in an instant. Only the representatives of the "authorities," Nacio and Edek, were holding rifles between their knees. We traveled quickly along the field roads and after an hour's drive reached the main road leading to our target, the town.

We still had to get through the five remaining kilometers. We stopped next to the road. Some of us got off here. The peasant driving the cart stayed on. Romek had warned him that if he made any suspicious movement he would be shot. I was sitting immediately behind the peasant, clasping my hands on the back of my neck. That was the way Jews were forced to hold their hands when caught. Behind me were Edek and Nacio. The others were walking on foot behind the wagon, trying not to stay too far. We drove on to the road, where there was more cart-traffic... There were also more pedestrians. Our boys had really adapted their clothes to the environment. Romek was walking a few steps in front of us, looking like a typical farmhand. I turned my head a bit to see the others, but then I got hit on my back and heard Edek's menacing voice: "Verfluchter Jude" [damn Jew], and his whisper "Don't look around or I'll kill you." I stopped "looking" and kept my eyes focused on the road ahead. It was getting very interesting.

I could already see the town's church steeple ahead. Soon, the houses appeared. We had only half a kilometer left. Edek halted the horses, we got off the cart, and Romek and Janek climbed on. We continued on foot. I could feel the touch of the gun's barrel on my back. Edek, who was walking right behind me, was holding it. I walked ahead with my hands raised. My heart was beating fast. Why is that, I wondered. After all, this was the plan. And yet, not so long ago, others were led the same way. They too had to hold their hands like that. Their ears must have heard the same sounds I was hearing now. "They caught a Jew. A Jew is being escorted. Mama, they've caught a Jew!" a child was calling out merrily. Yes, the Germans had shut down the theatres, the cinemas, and the schools. Children now had to entertain themselves by watching Jews being caught. Before the war, children would cry out, "the circus has arrived!" in just the same voice. Now they said, "A Jew is being escorted, a Jew has been caught."

I don't know how it happened, but in spite of myself, I felt tears flowing down my cheeks. And again, I heard, "look, the Jew is crying!" Apparently, Edek also heard their comments, because I felt the barrel of his gun in my side and heard him yell: "Ruhe, verfluchter Jude!" [Silence, damn Jew]. We reached the front of the factory. It was surrounded by an iron fence. A Ukrainian soldier armed with a rifle was standing in front of the gate. When he saw us approaching, he straightened up, saluted Edek, and let us into the yard. Edek then asked in the broken Polish typically spoke by Germans: "Where is the guardhouse?"

"Right there," the sentry answered, pointing to a small hut. "How many policemen are there?" "One," answered the Ukrainian. "And what are you doing here?" "We are guarding the factory." "Is this gun loaded?" continued Edek, and without waiting for an answer grabbed the shocked Ukrainian's shoulder, snatched his gun and handed it over to me. I loaded the rifle and pointed it at the Ukrainian, saying "Hands Up." He obeyed. "And now," said Edek, "take us to the guardhouse and remember that if you make one wrong move you and your other friend will be shot." The policeman walked in front of us, opened the guardhouse door and yelled: "Ivan, stay calm and they won't harm us!"

We walked in. Nacio noticed a rifle leaning on the wall and grabbed it. In the meantime, some of our boys had also entered through the gate and soon Romek, Janek, and Benek joined us in the guardhouse. "Well lads," Edek said to the policemen, "quickly take off your uniforms." Watching them undress, we noticed that one of them had a gold watch, while the other had diamond rings on his fingers. In an instant their boots and uniforms were rolled into a blanket and thrown by Janek onto the horse cart that had just entered the yard. Józek appeared at the door, saying that Bronek had secured some kerosene, and we prepared to go about our business of setting the factory on fire. The factory workers, thirty of them altogether, had been gathered in one room and kept under guard.

"Wait a minute," said Edek, turning to the policemen. They were sitting only in their underwear, with various valuables spread out on the table in front them. "Whose are these?" asked Edek. They both silently looked down. "Well, in which roundup did you acquire them?" Edek prompted them. They remained silent, but their eyes nervously looked around. Edek raised his head, looked at me and nodded lightly in the direction of the policemen. I raised my gun; my heart was beating madly. It felt as if my blood was about to burst from my temples. I fired a shot, forgetting to hold the butt of the gun, and the recoil hit me in the chest. The pain caused me to regain my senses. I was looking now at the two policemen, the blood oozing from their bodies to the floor. I was surprised that both were lying there, because I did not even hear the second shot, probably fired by Edek. My temples were calm, my heartbeat was regular. A breeze came through the open window. It felt like a kiss on my cheek. That is probably the way ghosts kiss, I thought to myself. For a split second, I saw a vision of my brother in front of me. Then it vanished.

At that moment Bronek appeared in the doorway, urging us to hurry up and asking why the order to burn the factory had not yet been issued. But Edek had already rushed to the door and ordered to release the workers and burn down the factory. I saw the group of workers filing through the back door. We then poured kerosene on the warehouse, where the dried tobacco leaves were stored, and it soon began to smoke. "Now forward to the prison," Edek shouted. We ran out into the street. A few shots in the air and the crowded streets emptied. Running through the streets, we reached the prison where we met Łużny's group and the already freed prisoners. There were no Germans or police. With the first shot they had disappeared. Many horse carts with no drivers were left in the street. The owners must have also hidden in the nearby houses when they heard the shooting. The first four carts served us as escape vehicles and we drove through the empty streets of the town, singing the partisan song born in the forest, "Oh forest, our forest."

Once again, we spent our time resting, playing cards, listening to the radio, and smoking cigarettes and cigars we had taken from the factory in Monasterzyska. Our unit had grown because some of the freed prisoners had joined us. We were nineteen, of whom six were Jews. Today we received a response from the AK headquarters to my proposal that we sabotage the telegraph lines alongside the railroads and roads. The headquarters not only praised the idea but appointed me commander of the group. It was to consist of five men. We were charged with paralyzing the telephone and telegraph communications in our region. What we needed were steel hooks in order to be able to climb up the poles, and Edek had promised that we would leave tonight specifically in order to acquire them. And indeed, at nightfall Edek, Nacio, Romek, and I set out from the camp.

Our plan was to reach the big village of Barysz and get the required items there. We ate supper in the nearest farm and from there we also got horses and continued for a few miles by cart. We walked the remaining four kilometers to Barysz on field paths. It was a dark night, but our eyes had grown accustomed to it and we could distinguish every detail. On the left side of the road we saw the contours of farm buildings. A solitary farm. We decided to pass it without troubling its inhabitants. Edek was just signaling with his hand to move on when we instinctively felt there was someone in front of us. We threw ourselves on the ground. Our eyes, blinking so as to see better in the dark, began hurting. And then we saw three figures moving in our direction along on the same road.

At a silent signal from Edek, Nacio and I peeled off to the left side of the road while Romek and Edek did the same on the right. The three figures kept getting closer, and I could see the barrel of a gun hanging from the shoulder of one of them. We silently prepared our weapons and heard Edek's voice in the silent night: "Stop, who is there?" The three figures stopped abruptly, and we heard a strong male voice in Russian: "And who are you?" Edek responded with the agreed upon password: "Albatross." "Who the devil is that?" we heard one of them say. Suddenly, as if through a magic spell, the three figures vanished, and we heard the voice again: "Are you Germans or police? Answer or we'll shoot." "Partisans!" Edek yelled. "And you?" "Also, partisans!" we heard in response.

The negotiations went on for a while and then we decided that Nacio would approach them unarmed and check out who these night wanderers were. Nacio got up and slowly moved alongside the road. We saw another figure rising up next to him. For a while, they talked softly and then we heard Nacio's joyful exclamation: "Hurrah, partisans!" and the sound of kisses. We rushed up to them and were soon hugging and asking each other: "Who are you?" "Poles and Jews. And you?" "Russians." "Let's go to the farm," Edek ordered, "we'll be able to see each other more clearly there." We reached the gate. Our knocks and the loud barks of the dog, whose life we spared, woke up the farm's owner. Soon we were sitting in a room lit by a solitary oil lamp and carefully studied each other. The farmer put out bread, eggs, sour cream and even a bottle of homebrewed vodka on the table to celebrate the meeting and to keep up the good mood he must have noticed when we entered.

We sat around the table, eating and telling each other what we had been through until then. We found who our new friends were—one was an Uzbek named Sahib Nazarovich, who had strikingly oriental features but was simply called Sasha by his comrades and served as a politruk [political officer] in the Red Army. Another was the powerfully built Kola, a coal miner from the Donbas [industrial region of eastern Ukraine]. The third and youngest was the thin but tall Vania, the son of a Ukrainian kolkhoz [communal farm] worker in the Kharkov region. All three were members of the famous [Sydir] Kovpak partisan formation.[71] They had taken part in the Carpathian campaign and were cut off, with several other fighters from their unit, on the way back during a battle.

As they tried to get through to the east, without knowing the area, they were often ambushed by the Germans. Only these three had survived …. Now, since they met us, they didn't care who we were; as long as we fought against the Germans and accepted them, they were willing to join us until the arrival of the Red Army …. Kola and Vania had regular rifles, but to our delight Sasha was armed with the "pe-pe-sha" [PPSh-41] submachine gun, previously unknown to us.[72] … After some reassessment, Edek decided to postpone the raid on the post office to the following day and we returned to our camp in the forest with our three new members.

The planned raid on the post office in Barysz, was transformed into an operation against the police station, cooperative, post office, and the estate managed by the Germans. Taking advantage of a dark night, we reached the police station itself .... Kola and I took positions next to the back entrance leading to the garden. We had just reached the door when we heard Edek knocking on the front entrance and calling out: "Open up, German gendarmes." Nobody answered from within, but I heard a voice say: "Hello, inform the gendarmes in Buczacz that there is a raid." I rushed to the windows, found the telephone lines, and cut them. The house was shaken by the noise of smashing doors and windows. I ran back ... and saw a figure dressed in the uniform of a policeman emerging from the door. Kola, who was closest to the door, grasped him by the throat ... and Nacio struck him with all his might on the chest with the butt of his gun. Pushing him in front of us, we entered the room. I quickly opened the doors from within and all the others came in, apart from those who were guarding the street. Nacio and Kola were just about done pulling the uniform off the half-conscious policeman.

This time, our booty was two German rifles, two typewriters and a telephone .... The Ukrainian we caught was a known collaborator. Initially, he had served in Buczacz and had participated in roundups of Jews. Now he was the representative of the authorities in Barysz. Nacio took care of him. Next, we went to the post office situated on the same street. There, I procured the special tools to climb poles, pliers for cutting wires and two field telephones. Meanwhile, Edek and the other boys carried out sacks of sugar from the cooperative building and positioned them on the street as a present to the local population and as compensation for their maltreatment by the Germans .... We proceeded to the estate, where we seized several pigs, flour, and other essential supplies ... and then burned it down .... Soon thereafter, fresh horses from the estate drove us back into the forest.

In the beginning of September [1943], the Germans began requisitioning quotas from the new harvests. Apart from the quota on wheat, a huge quota of cattle and farm animals was also ordered. Our mission was to prevent the Germans from requisitioning that quota. The first village that received the order to provide the designated quota was Werbka [35 kilometers southwest of Buczacz]. For our part, we sent a message to the village head, threatening him with death and warning that we would burn down the first farms that filled the requisitioning quotas. The village was expected to start bringing in the wheat to the storehouse in Buczacz on 7 September. The night before we set up an ambush on the section of the road through which the carts with the wheat were supposed to pass.

At around 10 a.m., Nacio and Benek, who were observing the road from the edge of the forest, informed us that twenty wagons loaded with sacks were approaching. They did not see anybody guarding the convoy. When the wagons reached us, we jumped out and stopped them. In response to Edek's question, why they were supplying the enemy, they said that they were afraid of the Germans. "And you do not fear us?" Edek yelled. On his orders, the peasants unloaded the sacks and spilled the wheat on the road. A large pile of wheat was encircled by dry wood and set on fire. The terrified peasants sped off on their horses and escaped to their homes. We took the village head with us into the forest. The terrified man begged us to have mercy on him. He explained that the Germans had threatened to send a penal SS detachment to the village if they failed to provide the quota on time. "We ourselves hate the Germans," he continued. "After all, they are taking away our livelihood, our blood. The year before, after handing in the quotas we starved. And we also remember the penal raid by the SS last year, when they ... raped the girls and destroyed our belongings. They especially enjoyed tearing apart the feather beds and cushions and letting the feathers fly around."

"And you," interrupted him Edek, "as a reward for all that, provide them with wheat. You are afraid of their rapes and that is supposed to be your excuse. We are not going to rape or tear cushions. But we will kill every single person who provides the Germans with wheat. In this period of wartime, a single law exists, a law that the Germans have imposed, and it is the rule of power. You are terrified of it; you are willing to sacrifice everything you have and do not have because of that law. And this even though you know that after ruining you, after taking everything you have, your plight may still be the same as that of the Jews. And still, you follow all their orders in the name of that law. But I want you to know that there is another law, also based on power, but on justice as well. It is the sacred law of the partisans, which forbids looting and raping, but orders that anyone who helps the enemy will be killed. And what you have done today was a clear form of helping the enemy."

The head of the village burst into tears and promised that from that day on, he would do anything we asked him. Seeing the despair of the man, Sasha suggested that we should try to make him work with us. Edek gladly accepted this idea, ordering me and Sasha to take care of reforming the man's soul. We took him to the side and asked him why the Germans had appointed him village head. It turned out that he had been in German captivity during World War I. There he had learned to speak some German and that influenced the German Landwirt to choose him. We proposed the following cooperation with us: He had to inform us ahead of time about every requisition quota designated for the Germans. Next, they should load only a quarter of the quota's amount, which we would then destroy on the road. The Germans would be informed that the whole amount had been destroyed. "You will gain from that as well," I said, "because the three quarters will remain for you." "And what if Germans accompany us?" the man asked. "Leave that to us," Sasha said. "And what am I supposed to tell the Germans now?" the village head suddenly asked. He probably had the vision of the fat Landwirt, armed with the leather whip that he liked to tap on his boots, but sometimes also employed on the backs and heads of others.

I turned to Edek with that question and he replied with a laugh, "Well, we don't have a choice, we must give him a bit of a beating, so that he will have something to show the Germans. Otherwise they might suspect that he has entered into secret dealings with us. Don't worry," he said to the scowling village head, "the beatings of the partisans don't hurt, they come from a clean heart and might even protect you from other beatings." After a while, although he was hurting, the man was also laughing as he rubbed his backside, on which there were visible bloody signs. After swallowing some alcohol from a bottle, he got up and disappeared behind the bushes in the direction of the village.

Upon returning to our camp, we decided that same night to send letters to all the village heads in the area, proposing a deal similar to the one we had made with the village head of Werbka. Tough days and nights were ahead of us. Seriously worried about our activities, the Germans brought in a special Waffen-SS unit of about 250 men, who were joined by Ukrainian police and German gendarmes. Their mission was to hunt down and destroy Edek's unit. They often set up ambushes that we avoided only thanks to Edek's quick thinking. We moved our camp sites in the forests nearly every day. Often, we would escape from the forest at night and the Germans would enter it the next day. On our part, we were not idle either. We managed to destroy a few threshing machines for wheat that the Germans had brought to the surrounding villages in order to accelerate the milling of grains. We burned down the nearby farms and torched the houses of those who participated in raids on us. We burned bridges connecting villages with the main roads, thereby paralyzing communications with the cities. We distributed flyers in Polish and Ukrainian throughout the villages, calling on the local population to rise up and fight the occupants and to try to survive till the arrival of the Red Army. Sasha was the author of these flyers.

Whenever we passed a road or train tracks, we never forgot to destroy the telephone lines.

One day, after cutting the telephone line between Buczacz and Czortków, I connected the field telephone to the Buczacz line. The telephone operator answered my call and I asked to be connected to the Landkommissar. Soon I heard the German's low voice on the phone. I gave him regards from Edek, inquired after the health of Brettschneider, and then asked him whether he could inform me about the situation of this year's requisition quota collection operation. The German kept interrupting me, calling out "Wer [ist] da?" "Wer [ist] da?" [who is that?]. Finally, I told him that I know his name, I know that he comes from Essen, and I know the address of his family there.[73] I also added that we hold him and his family responsible for all the acts of rape, looting and execution of Jews. We returned to the forest in a very merry mood for having made fun of the Germans and were joking among ourselves.

On our way back, we crossed railroad tracks. We stopped there for a moment, and just as Edek was saying how much he regretted that we did not have any explosives with us to blow up a train, we heard the whistle of a locomotive and the sound of an approaching train. From afar, by the light in the windows, we could tell that this was a passenger train. It slowed down as it came closer to us and climbed the slope. Suddenly Edek grabbed Nacio by the arm and shouted: "The first railcar behind the locomotive says 'Nur für Deutsche.' You can jump on the step and throw a hand grenade through the window!" We moved away from the tracks. Only Nacio stayed there with a grenade in his hand. Slowly and heavily the locomotive came nearer. We could see the well-lit railcar designated "Only for Germans." I could tell that the windows were open. I stood on my toes to see if there was anyone in the carriage when a dark figure blocked my view of the window for a split second. Then the light in the window returned, followed by a deafening detonation that shut out all other sounds and the railcar went dark.

We were already far away. We looked back. The train had stopped, and we could hear shouts and cries, but no shooting. Probably there was no one left to shoot at us. Nacio was walking next to me, breathing heavily, but I could feel how proud he was of himself. I couldn't resist and hugged and kissed him. Good, Nacio. How had he managed in the darkness to see the step he held on to with only one hand? He could have fallen under the wheels of the train ... "I don't know myself how it happened," he said, "I just knew that it had to succeed." His brother Janek was sure he had seen two Germans through the window. One of them was totally bald. Romek, Józek, and Tadek were huddling around Nacio and praising him.

Only Edek had not said a word since we left the vicinity of the train but was walking silently, the collar of his coat pulled up. But we knew him already. His silence said more than our words. And indeed, a few days later an announcement arrived from the AK headquarters, noting that an attack had been carried out on a "Nur für Deutsche" railcar. As a result, six German officers, including a major, were killed. Natan Fritz, a member of the AK fighting group, had received the Cross of Valor. All of us, including Edek, congratulated and hugged him. The medal had not yet arrived, and he could not pin it on, but after the war he would receive it. Yes, after the war. After the war, everything would happen. The question was: would we be there after the war?

The first blow, the first victims. Bronek and Zosia have died. Only the day before we were sitting together. The pail still contained the remains of the supper Zosia had prepared for us. How could we have known? I went through everything that had happened the previous night .... For some time, I had known that Zosia and Bronek had a child, a three-year-old girl called Marysia, who was being looked after by an aunt in the village of Zalesie [20 km southwest of Buczacz]. The aunt's hut was at the edge of the village, not far from the forest. Sometimes at night, Zosia and Bronek would secretly visit the hut and spend a few hours with their child. I remember one day, Zosia brought her to the forest: a beautiful blond girl. Every one of us wanted to hold her. She was so sweet. Last night, Zosia and Bronek went to visit her again after a few weeks' break. I can still see her, packing some sugar, lard, and soap into her bag.

Early in the morning, the forester Krestatyi, who was totally loyal to our cause, came running and told us that a unit of Banderites had surrounded the hut while Zosia and Bronek were inside. Bronek ran up to the attic and started shooting from there. But once he realized that he had no way ... he shot himself. The Germans and Banderites raided the hut. One of them ripped Marysia from her mother's arms and killed her instantly by bashing her head on the edge of the doorway. Next, they shot and killed the aunt. Zosia's clothes were torn off and the bestial wild bandits violated her naked body. One of the Germans ordered her to stand up, pick up her dead daughter's body, and walk to the big square in front of the church. The Ukrainians made a big fire and assembled all the inhabitants of the village, one of whom was Krestatyi .... The bandits began lashing Zosia with their whips, forcing her to dance around the fire .... She was silent when she heard the laughter of the

Germans and Ukrainian bandits surrounding her, perhaps also parents of daughters just like her .... One of the Ukrainian bandits pushed her, and she fell into the fire. She jumped out, trying to extinguish her daughter's burning golden hair. Then another Ukrainian grasped her and pushed her again into the fire. She did not resist anymore but kept her head high up and called out loudly: "Death to the fascists! Edek, avenge us, Edek!" She was pushed again and fell into the flames ....

It was already almost 4 p.m. when Edek ordered to cook some food. We had been unable to touch anything all day. We were lying on the ground, absorbed deep in our thoughts, shaken by Krestatyi's account .... We were all expecting to carry out a revenge action. But instead came the order to cook and to eat .... We had barely eaten a few spoonfuls and were about to get up when Edek's voice stopped us:

"Listen boys, every one of us is deeply affected by what happened to Bronek, Zosia, and Marysia .... But giving in to despair would only be playing into the hands of the enemy. That is exactly what the enemy wants to achieve .... There is one thing I want from you. Do not forget Marysia's golden hair. Remember that the tortured Zosia, ... instead of begging for mercy, hurled into the face of her murderers: 'Death to the fascists' and 'Edek avenge us.' She said Edek, ... but surely, she was referring to us all .... Don't forget this even for an instant and revenge will come of its own accord .... I will not lead you to kill women and children, even if their fathers and husbands may have been those who tortured Zosia. We will punish only those who are guilty. This is the difference between them and us .... And now we should all rest well, because difficult days are awaiting us. The Germans are calling up a Ukrainian volunteer formation, the Waffen-SS 'Galizien.'[74] We will try to fight against this with a widespread leaflet propaganda campaign, but also take more drastic steps. I have also been notified that a strong Soviet partisan unit has appeared in the area of Skalat [70 km northeast of Buczacz]. It is led by the mysterious 'Bearded Lieutenant Colonel.'[75] They apparently even have machine guns and it would be good if we were able to make contact with them."

When we went to sleep that night, we were still preoccupied with what had happened to Zosia and Bronek, but our thoughts also turned to the mysterious lieutenant colonel. Sasha suggested that his forces might be part of the Kovpak formation. But these were only rumors. We knew nothing for certain. That same night Marian visited us, bringing news from Szkrabka that a strange horse cart had been traveling on the road next to Gaje. Observing it for several days, Szkrabka noticed that it was traveling between the villages of Wierzbatyn and Soroka, both

Banderite strongholds. Worried that the two villages were plotting against the Polish population in Gaje, Szkrabka asked us to set up an ambush before that happened. For the next few days we were so busy preparing for that operation that we somewhat got over the recent shock. We were scheduled to set out at sunset, together with Sasha and Vania, who would never agree to miss an operation against the Germans or the Ukrainians ....

The road was quiet, and we reached the Masurian Polish village at midnight. We decided to stay there for the night and carefully study the details of the following day's operation. In the yard, where we were resting, young boys and girls soon surrounded us. Every one of them wanted to see with their own eyes what they believed to be the giants from the forest... I took off my shoe and began to bind my sweaty foot. Suddenly, a young girl came up to me and handed me a silk handkerchief, saying: "take this for your feet." I tried to persuade her that it would be a pity to use something so nice on my feet, but she would not listen. We started talking. Her name was Hania. Her brother was killed during the defense of Warsaw in 1939. What she really wanted to do was to go to the forest and join a fighting group. But she was not yet allowed to do that. She had already belonged to the AK for a year and often at night she guarded the village from the Banderite fighters. Our conversation was interrupted by Edek, who came and told us to go to sleep.

I was preparing to lay down on the fragrant hay, when Edek summoned me to him again. Szkrabka's son Władek had arrived. He was the one who had informed us about the mysterious horse-drawn cart that drove past Gaje nearly every day. Observing it, Władek determined that there were usually four to five armed men in it. They spoke Ukrainian. The problem was that they usually traveled on roads in open spaces where it was hard to find a spot to set up an ambush. Władek also reported that one night, when the Ukrainians were passing next to the Pole Brytkowski's isolated farm near Gaje, they went in and seized his pig, clothes, and some money; one of them said: "You don't need this anyway, soon nothing will remain of you." It was nearly morning by the time we went to sleep.

We spent the following day playing cards and lying in the sweet hay in the barn. Around noon, Hania brought us a large bowl of pierogi [dumplings]. In the afternoon, she brought her stamp collection to show us. Looking through them we found one from Palestine. We could not express in words how moved we were. Looking at that tiny piece of land, more valuable to us now because we were cut off from it by a thousand deaths, images of the past appeared before our eyes. Hebrew lessons, evenings spent in Zionist organizations. How ridiculous and distant the differences that had separated us then seemed now. Today, we felt like one family bound together by fate and purpose. I asked Hania if she could give me that stamp and she readily agreed; soon, carefully wrapped, it rested in my breast pocket next to my heart. We spent the rest of the day cleaning our weapons and preparing for the operation.

That same evening, led by Władek, we set out toward the place where the horse-drawn cart passed every night. Marching across the meadows, we reached a stone statue situated next to a narrow field path. "They always drive through here," Władek said. We figured that this would be the most appropriate spot to stage the attack. Janek and Sasha hid next to the statue. We stayed hidden about fifty paces away, along the road. We lay like that for about three hours. In mid-September the nights were already cold, and we could feel it. We could not light a cigarette, afraid that the light might give away the ambush to the enemy. It was already after midnight and we were beginning to lose hope, when from faraway we heard the sound of horses' hooves. It was coming closer us. I glanced at the stone figure. Even though it was very near, it was hard to discern that two people were hiding next to it. We could see the approaching cart. It was already right next to the statue. "Oh, my God, what is Sasha up to?" I could feel Nacio's fingers digging nervously into my arm.

The cart proceeded past the statue, and nothing happened. It had already advanced about twenty meters when suddenly the silence of the night was interrupted by a burst of submachine gun fire that could clearly be seen coming from behind the statue. At the same time, we heard a powerful detonation. That was Janek, who threw a hand grenade. We jumped up from the ground. We could still hear the whistle of the shrapnel from the grenade in the air. With all our strength, we dashed toward the dark object, from which groans of people mixed with snorts of horses could be heard. Sasha was not shooting anymore but running towards the cart. Reaching it, we finished off the wounded with our knives. Now, after Bronek's death, we wanted to play no part in humanity. Edek appeared, and was very angry, because by killing the Banderites we missed the opportunity to interrogate them. They could have given us valuable information. But it was too late. Looking through the cart we found five rifles; the boys also removed ammunition belts with grenades and bullets from the dead. There were six bodies, but only five rifles. "Where is the sixth?" It was not on the wagon.

Suddenly, I saw a long object on the ground. I ran to it and I couldn't believe my eyes. I cried out. I was holding a real Degtyaryov [DP-27] light machine gun with a magazine full of bullets.[76] All the boys gathered around me. Edek shot a burst of bullets. Just like that, for fun. It was the most joyful music I had ever heard in my life. We didn't have to be afraid of anyone anymore. We said goodbye to Władek and went to the nearest village to get horses. Edek clapped Sasha on the back. "Kharasho [Russian: good], Sasha. They didn't even have time to shoot back." I wanted to know why he opened fire so late. Sasha explained that had he opened fire earlier, the horses would have been in front of the Banderites, and they might have jumped off the cart and returned fire. And in any case, throwing a grenade too close could have endangered us. "I preferred to let them go past me and beat them on their backside," Sasha concludes jokingly. Now we sat on the cart. But we would not allow ourselves to be taken by surprise. The machine guns were ready to shoot throughout the ride, our eyes and ears straining to their greatest capacity. Let them try. We would always have time to respond ....

One morning, we walked to the village of Komarówka [28 km southwest of Buczacz]. With the help of a rifle, we forced the sleepy village head to call the gendarmerie outpost in Buczacz and notify them that Edek with his men had arrived in the village and were now sleeping like logs after a night of drinking. With great pleasure I heard their response. "They are sending a few cars immediately." The German ordered the village head to enlist some peasants and tie up Edek's boys. He also reminded the head that for every member of Edek's "band" there was a ransom of 10,000 złoty. We quickly left the village head's house. The membrane of the microphone [in the handset of the village head's telephone] was resting in my pocket [thereby disabling it]. On the way, I cut the telephone lines, thereby cutting the village off from the world. We drove very quickly on the road leading to Buczacz and within twenty minutes were in the Komarów forest.

The road passed through the forest. We jumped off and I quickly climbed up a telephone pole and connected our telephone to the line. Upon coming down, I could hear the telephone constantly ringing between the trees. I dashed to the telephone shouting to Józek to cover the lines on the ground with dry leaves. I heard a voice shouting: "Hello, hello!" I answered: "This is Komarówka." "Why haven't you answered for such a long time?" the person on the other side said angrily. "Call the village head!" I answered that he was busy, having gone with the others to tie up the bandits. "Aha," he responded, now much calmer. "Inform him that three cars have left for the village and there will be lots of vodka there tonight." I interrupted him to say that we were promised ten thousand złoty per head. "No! No!" the German shouted back. "A lot of vodka, salt and kerosene. That's what you will get." At that very moment, Janek, who was observing the road from the tall trees, shouted that several cars were approaching. An armored car in front and three hundred yards behind it, close to each other, three other vehicles. We divided into three groups, each with six members. We took our positions on one side of the road between the trees. According to Edek's orders we were to allow the armored car to pass and then attack the three cars behind it. On one side of the road stood Sasha with his submachine gun and on the other Kola with the machine gun he had acquired.

I began hearing the roar of the approaching vehicle's engine. Oh, God, why is my heart beating so fast, how many of them are there, fifty or maybe a hundred? There are only eighteen of us. The roar got louder. I was lying flat on the ground, four grenades in front of me. Next to my right hand was the semiautomatic, with ten spare magazines also within the reach of my hand. I could hear the car now very close to us. I raised my head. Through the opening in the bushes I saw the car moving. It was painted with camouflage stripes of green and yellow; for a moment we could make out the black cross on the side of the car. It quickly disappeared, and the noise of its engine grew fainter. But then a louder roar of engines approached from where it had first appeared. I stretched my hand for the first grenade, pulled the safety pin with my left hand and held it tightly with my right. Slowly, the first car passed right in front of me. I could hear loud talk and laughter and recognize the green uniforms of the Germans. I reckon there were about ten of them. The car disappeared. My nerves and muscles were straining with anticipation. The next car was ours. I could see its fenders, the wheels slowly turning, the driver's booth becoming visible … "Fire!" I heard Edek's order.

I jumped up, hurled the grenade, and grabbed hold of the semiautomatic; but before I had time to shoot the first bullet, I heard the intermittent bursts from the submachine gun and the thunderous fire of Kola's machine gun, mixed with the deafening explosions of grenades. I couldn't hear anymore. All I could see were figures in green uniforms rolling out of the vehicle in front of me. I shot into the mass of bodies, since it was impossible to choose a target. I emptied a whole magazine, bent down to pick up another, but instead hurled another grenade. I opened fire again, but apart from dead bodies strewn on the ground or hanging over the car there was no sign of life. The machine-gun fell silent and the shooting ceased. Edek was already on the road. I also ran out. Now, I could clearly see the three vehicles. The first and the third were already being checked out by the boys. Józek and I jumped onto the third and gathered the weapons. We found some automatic guns. Sasha, Vania, and Nacio … ran past. I ran toward the first car to take over the defense, since the armored car might return at any moment, alerted by the shooting. I reached out for a gun and stepped on the leg of a German. He moaned. Hearing that, Edek ordered us to shoot all the wounded.

We tried out the German machine guns. I opened the driver's door and shot another bullet into the already dead driver. I was about to do the same with the other German lying close by as if asleep, when he suddenly opened his eyes, raised his hand, and said: "Kamerad, bitte nicht schießen" [Comrade, please don't shoot]. Benek opened the door on other side of the car and yelled as he struck the German with the butt of his gun: "Well, Kamerad, get off." As we were leading him to Edek the shooting resumed, and bullets were whistling over our heads. Evidently, the armored car was trying to scare us off, but from a safe distance. Edek ordered Kola to stop the unnecessary firing and gave the command to retreat. I disconnected the telephone and hung it over my arm. In the meantime, the boys were emptying the cars' gasoline containers and then setting them on fire. The flames engulfed everything, including the Germans' bodies. We marched quickly through the forest since we still had a few hours of road ahead of us. The ammunition we took felt heavier and heavier. Edek and Sasha led the march. We were in the middle with the prisoner, while Kola with the "Degtyaryov" slung over his shoulder walked in the back.

We reached our camp at about 11 a.m. Lunch was not ready yet. We counted our trophies: sixteen automatic weapons, twenty rifles, a large amount of ammunition and about fifty grenades. We had used up thirty-two grenades and fired about three-hundred bullets. We did not lose any of our men because the unsuspecting Germans totally lost their heads and did not even have time to shoot. Our prisoner was sitting under the tree with his head lowered. I approached him, intending to commence the interrogation that could be of the utmost importance to us. The boys, curious of what was about to happen, surrounded us. I watched him silently for a while. He was young, about twenty, his reddish hair showing from under his helmet. I took off his helmet. I turned it around in my hand for a while and looked at the swastika and the SS letters painted on it in black. On the inside was his name: Otto Helmut. I looked at him again, his hair carefully combed and parted with a straight line in the middle. Instinctively, I touched my own uncombed hair and beard and smiled to myself while I continued gazing at the sitting German. Our eyes met a few times, but he immediately lowered them and stared at the ground.

I interrupted the silence: "Otto." He trembled, surely surprised that I knew his name. "Otto," I repeated, "look me straight in the eye."

He looked at me for a moment and then lowered his eyes again. Only after Nacio, who was standing behind me, kicked him, did he raise his head again. I gazed into his eyes for a long time. I was searching for the expression his eyes must have had when they were looking at the bashed heads of Jewish children, when he was aiming his weapon at an old Jew, my mother or perhaps my brother. How these eyes must have shone when they observed Zosia's whipping. Perhaps he was the one who held the whip. But instead of the expression I had been expecting, the eyes looking at me were those of any human being begging for mercy. His expression was that of a boy who knows he had done something naughty and was now expecting some punishment, but at worse just a few smacks. "Otto, tell us about that woman in Zalesie." At first, he tried to deny it: "I wasn't there," he said, he knew nothing about it. But our boys quickly convinced him that this was not a game, and he began telling the story. We had already heard it from Krestatyi. He suddenly stopped, noticing the faces surrounding him, the expressions of rage, the burning eyes. A few more blows and he continued.

Then he stopped again and yelled, "I will not say another word! Shoot me if you wish." Nacio grabbed his hair, tilted his head back, and holding a knife in front of the prisoner's eyes slowly said: "Listen you dog, any more of your jokes and I will take your eyes out and you will have to continue your story." Now I interrupted: "Otto, after all, you surely did not do the actual killing yourself. Why don't you want to tell us?" The German looked at me in disbelief, but seemed to feel more relaxed and continued talking, repeatedly asserting that he had not participated, he was only a bystander. Everything was done by the Ukrainians and the chief of the Buczacz gendarmes—[Peter] Pahl.[77]

I looked through the items we found on him. A wallet with papers in it, a silver pen, and a golden pocket watch made by the firm "Cyma." I started with the wallet. I took out his army ID card. It noted that SS-man Otto Helmut had arrived from France in 1942. He belonged to a Waffen-SS unit. He received an award for taking part in the "Wirtschafts-Versicherung"[78] and in fighting against Judeo-Bolshevik bands. When asked about this, he naturally denied everything. But we did manage to get a few details out of him. We learned that he had participated in several roundups and the liquidation of the Jews of Buczacz. God forbid, he did not shoot. He did, however, guard those who had been caught and helped escort them to the pits. When approaching the pits, he would shut his eyes since he was unable to watch those horrors. When asked about the silver pen, he mumbled that it was a present from his fiancée. And the watch—that was a present from his father. I pointed out that the initials did not match his name. He got confused, wanted to say one thing, said another, contradicted himself, and then lowered his head and started crying hysterically. Well, that was enough for the moment. I left him under the guard of four boys and went to Edek. He had already decided. In the evening, we would take him out to the road and hang him from the first telegraph pole.

In the evening we set out. We were calm because it was highly improbable that the Germans would have gotten over what had happened to them in the morning. It would surely take a few days before they could call up more forces and start an offensive against us. In spite of that, we tried to maintain all safety measures. We taped the prisoner's mouth and tied his hands behind his back with a rope, which was held by Paweł walking right behind him. Nacio and Romek walked on either side. When we reached the edge of the forest we stopped. Edek sent two boys to the road to check the situation. Soon, Józek returned saying that everything was clear. Two groups of five boys each then took positions on either side of the road where the execution was to be held. They would protect us from any unwanted guests. Now we moved as well. We crossed a tall field of corn and potatoes, walked through a stretch of wasteland and then reached the road.

We were greeted by the familiar humming of the telephone lines. I strapped on the hooks, climbed up the pole and tied a thick rope through the hook at the top of the pole. Everything was ready. The German was brought in. Speaking German, I read out the verdict of the AK field court. "SS-man Otto Helmut is guilty of killing Jews, destroying farms and villages in the surrounding areas, and actively fighting against the partisans. For that he is sentenced to death by hanging." Edek came up to him, put the pen in his pocket and hung the watch from his shirt button. The German began to struggle and tried to speak. Strong arms held him down. Edek took the gag out of his mouth. Now, I could clearly hear the German wailing: "Kamerad, I am not guilty. I am a communist, Kamerad." No. For the death of my mother, brother and so many others. No. The noose was placed on his neck. Strong arms grabbed the rope and his cry of "Hilfe!" [help] was cut short. The lines kept humming, the pole sighed, as if protesting that it has to bear the weight of a German carcass. I plastered the sheet of paper with the verdict to the pole and we disappeared into the night.

That night we did not sleep at all. We moved fifteen kilometers away to the impenetrable Koropiec forests [around Koropiec, 25 km southwest of Buczacz]. We knew that the Germans would want to avenge their losses at any cost. And indeed, a few days later, we learned that large German forces had surrounded the forest in which we had previously camped. After several hours of firing from various types of weapons, they courageously marched into the forest and reached our abandoned camp. Of course, apart from some traces of fire and old plates, they found nothing.

That was why we were so surprised to hear that the Germans were disseminating news of having successfully destroyed most of Edek's formation in the forest. To back up their claims, they brought some terribly mutilated human corpses to the village of Komarówka and told the local population that they were Edek's people. We knew the Germans well. We were aware of the fact that they were capable of any crime, and who knows what terrible massacre had befallen those people, even though they were not Edek's men. In the evening, ten of us set out to one of the nearby villages to get food. We walked the whole way. Nacio and I quickened our steps when we approached the first village and were about a hundred meters ahead of the rest of the group. It started raining. Nacio was dressed as a Ukrainian policeman and I was wearing peasant clothes. Only my head was covered with a helmet I had once taken from the police station in Barysz. Upon reaching the first houses, we heard the sound of a horse-drawn cart. We stopped the peasant driving it and he said: "Yes, the Germans were in the village during the day, but before nightfall they climbed into their cars and drove off somewhere." I ordered the peasant to turn around and drive a few steps in front of us. Nacio and I walked behind the wagon holding on to its back.

On the way, I felt something bothering me in my shoe. I threw the automatic gun onto the cart and stopped to take off my shoe. At that instant two floodlights were switched on and lit up the cart and Nacio walking behind it. "Halt! Stehenbleiben!" [Stop! Stand still!] I heard in German. A Ukrainian policeman added something also in German. I stopped not knowing what to do. The light of a flashlight pointed at me and a voice called out: "Wer ist das?" [Who is that?] Two Germans ran in my direction. I had noticed that the cart with Nacio continued moving without being stopped by the Germans. One of the Germans noticed the helmet on my head and shouted: "Ein russischer Stahlhelm!" [A Russian helmet] "No Ukrainian," I answered in bad German.

The second German observed me and seeing that I was not armed asked who I was and what I was doing there. I answered that I was the village nightguard and told him to ask the Ukrainian policeman who had just passed by next to the horse cart. At that moment I heard the sound of bushes rustling on the side of the road from which Edek and the rest of the boys were supposed to come. The Germans switched off their flashlights, one of them waved his hand to me and they started walking in exactly that direction. I ran after Nacio and saw him standing in the middle of the road next to the horse cart. Approaching him I shouted: "Shoot before they run into our boys!" I grabbed the automatic gun and my shots mixed with those further ahead, somewhere in front of us. Some bullets whistled above our heads. We ran off the road, jumped over the ditch and found ourselves in a corn field.

For some time, we lay there without moving, flat on the ground. The shots died down. Then we heard the sound of feet running on the road, again shots, and then the explosion of hand grenades and more gunfire. We began to crawl through the corn field until we reached an open space. Now we ran through the stubble in a large circle trying to reach the spot where Edek was supposed to be. Meanwhile in the village the sounds of gunfire and intermittent explosions of grenades intensified. The glow of a fire could be seen on one side of the village. We heard the sound of engines and the clatter of tank tracks somewhere on the road. At the same time the Germans started lighting up the terrain with flares. We gathered from the flares that they were surrounding the village and that we would soon be trapped with no way out. Not knowing in which direction Edek was planning to retreat from the village, we decided to find our own way out. We walked in the direction from which no flares could be seen. After less than a mile we could see the dark edge of the forest ahead of us. We turned around only after we reached the first line of trees.

The sky above the village was red. The shooting had resumed with even greater intensity than before. The flares continued to shoot out into the sky. "What the hell, was Edek ready to join battle with an opponent a hundred times stronger than himself?" On the road leading from the forest, where we were standing, to the village, tankettes [light tanks] were driving. In the light of the flares, we could identify precisely in which direction they were heading. Suddenly, a bright flash could be seen from the left side of the road, followed by a powerful explosion. One of the tankettes was on fire. Soon, the second and third tanks were also engulfed in flames. The others escaped. The sound of their engines was becoming more distant. We had no idea what was going on. Who had the strength to hunt down German tanks a thousand kilometers away from the front line? Perhaps this was German friendly fire? Meanwhile the gunfire in the village died down. We too had to leave in order to find the way to our camp in the unfamiliar terrain ....

At noon [the following day], we finally saw the familiar edge of the forest. But we still had to cross the shallow Koropiec River before entering our familiar forest. The nearer we came to our destination the slower we walked. Anxiety weighed heavy on our hearts. Who would be there? Was anyone from the group we set out with yesterday still alive?

After all, we were the ones responsible for their fate. They had relied on us. They knew we were in front. And now, what will we tell Marian and the others? We were startled, hearing a shout, but soon we lowered our rifles. Little Stefan emerged from behind the bushes where he had been keeping guard and waved to us shouting something. We walked even slower, afraid of the truth awaiting us. "Come faster," Stefan yelled, "we were already mourning you, certain that you had been captured by the Germans! Edek, Janek, they are all there. All well, safe and sound." We answered each other's questions. "They brought a pig, cigarettes, and chocolate." We no longer waited to hear the rest. We ran as fast as we could to the clearing. We were greeted by loud exclamations of joy, endless questions and answers.

Edek told us that while walking at the head of the column he heard steps approaching. At first, he thought that we were returning. In spite of that he prepared his automatic and waited. Then he recognized German being spoken from the direction where we were supposed to be. That moment a flashlight was directed at him and without hesitation he fired in that direction. He heard a quick shout and the sound of bodies falling down. The boys ran forward and, seeing the bodies of Germans, were sure that we had fallen into their hands. Continuing to run, they hoped to rescue us before the Germans took us too far. The sound of footsteps running on the road that we had heard when lying in the field was that of our boys chasing the Germans. They encountered a group of Germans and attacked them with hand grenades.

When they were already in the center of the village, Edek heard the roar of the tankettes and understood that the Germans were planning to surround the village and cut off their retreat. At that moment a truck started rolling out of the gate of one of the yards. One well aimed grenade thrown under its motor and the truck was immobilized. In the light of the explosion Edek saw a horse cart standing not far away. The boys clambered on it and soon, spurred on by rifle butts, the horses jumped over the roadside ditch, trampling the garden fences along to road, and galloped toward the forest. Looking back, the boys could see that the fire caused by the explosion was spreading to the surrounding houses. In the meantime, heavy gunfire could be heard from the village and, inexplicably, also from the direction of the small roadside gardens .... Once they had reached the forest, they realized that the cart must have belonged to the army, since it was loaded with a slaughtered pig, a few boxes of chocolate, cigarettes, and soap ....

We moved to another part of the forest. Now we were camping in a gorge not far from the river. In the afternoon it became so warm that we bathed in the river. We drank tea, ate chocolate, and smoked fat German cigars. That was how a beautiful day in the life of a partisan ended, when after the horror of being on the verge of death you were filled with the beauty of existence and the urge to live.

The following morning, we all gathered around the fire. We were trying to shelter ourselves from the bitter cold that could already be felt at dawn. The tea in the pail came to a boil and we were just about to scoop it up when Józek, who was standing guard on the edge of the forest, came running. He reported that a group of men was heading in our direction. We sprang up, forgetting about the tea, and ran behind Józek, who was leading the way. Breathing heavily, he told us that he thought they were not Germans, but members of a Banderite band. We soon reached the edge of the forest. Cautiously, so as not to reveal our presence, we peered from behind the trees. A column of about twenty people could be seen. They were coming straight at us, about two hundred paces from the forest. Suddenly our attention was diverted to something else. In the distance, we could see another group of people. Stretched in a long, seemingly unending line, they were advancing behind the first group that appeared to be their advance guard. We could see horses and wagons, but most of them were on foot.

We stood there staring at this peculiar apparition. Edek was silent; he just uttered a long whistle. Strangely, I did not have the sense of doom I usually felt when faced with a dangerous situation. Sasha was standing erect and watching intently. He then turned to Kola and said: "Is it Kovpak?" "No, it seems to be somebody else," answered Kola. The first group approached the forest. They were only a few paces away. Sasha was speaking to Edek, then put down his gun and came out of the forest. They noticed him, stopped, and instantaneously dispersed. Sasha waved his hand and shouted something in Russian. Some people from the group came up to him, and after a short conversation and they fell into each other's arms. We ran out of the forest. We didn't yet know, who were they? But we were already kissing, hugging and leading our guests to our camp in the forest clearing. We gave them chocolate, cigarettes, and whatever else we had.

The entire forest filled with armed people. They carried the same type of automatic weapons that Sasha had, several machine guns, and some kind of weapon that we had never seen before. It was called an "anti-tank rife" [the Soviet PTRD-41],[79] as the owner of this long black gun explained to us. One of the people came up to us and asked if we would allow them to locate their headquarters near our clearing in the forest. But yes, of course. Some older people approached us. The first was short, chubby, with a long well-kept beard. Nobody had to tell us, since we already knew: he was the "Bearded Lieutenant Colonel." He walked up to us and stretched out his hand: "Welcome heroes. Let me warm myself next to the fire." We hugged him and invited him to sit down on the pail we had put upside down for him. We offered him tea, but he refused, saying we should drink first, and offer what is left to the few wounded men in his unit. Romek and Nacio grabbed the pail with tea, took along some chocolate, and went to where the carts with the wounded had parked.

Then it was time for explanations. We told him that our unit consisted of Poles, Jews, and Russians. The lieutenant colonel asked whether we know about the battle with the Germans the night before. We told him there were only ten of us and that the chocolate and cigarettes were the booty taken in that battle from the Germans. He burst out laughing and wanted to hear all the details of the fight …. When I told him about the mysterious destruction of the tankettes, he called a tall, square-shouldered fellow dressed in a German uniform and introduced the vanquisher of the tankettes. Then, he continued with his story. They were moving through the forest when they heard the sound of a fire-fight. Without knowing the exact positions of the Germans or who they were fighting against, they were unable to come to our help. But seeing the tankettes passing by, he ordered to shoot at them several times ….

We spent the whole day getting to know this formation. I assessed that it consisted of about a thousand people. I met a young Jewish physician from Stanisławów, Dr. Zimer, whose large Nagan [standard Russian service] revolver holstered on his hip did not quite suit him.[80] On the whole, there seemed to be many Jews in the unit. I also met the menacing Serdink, a Kazakh from the area of Almaty. As night fell, we had still not talked our fill. The lieutenant colonel also told us that the Germans had been on their trail for the previous two weeks and that his men are very tired from the long marches and battles. "If it's possible we will rest here for a few days," he said, and we lay down to sleep.

The following day, after breakfast, we resumed our conversation with the lieutenant colonel. He was very interested in learning more about the attitude of the local population, the quota requisitions, and the activities of the Banderites. We tried to persuade him to undertake a raid against the town of Buczacz. It was a very important site, because the railroad tunnel, through which trains carrying tanks and ammunition to the front pass every day, was situated right next to the town. On principal, the lieutenant colonel agreed, but on condition that we first send our scouts to determine the number of troops and tanks stationed in the town. Edek decided to send Krestatyi who, as a forester, would not arouse suspicion. During our conversation we heard shots in the distance. The lieutenant colonel sent some scouts in that direction, including some of our boys. I also mounted a horse, and although I was not used to riding, I somehow managed to trot unsteadily behind the boys.

We left the forest and headed toward the site from which the gunfire had come. Having almost reached the first houses, one of us noticed a horse cart with several people on it leaving the village from the other end. The leader of the reconnaissance unit looked through his binoculars and exclaimed: "The police!" The horses began galloping after the cart. Still not accustomed to the art of horseback riding, I could follow at a light trot only. From a distance I could see that the cart had accelerated, but our boys were steadily closing in on it .... Two riders overtook the carriage and were far ahead of it. Several bursts of gunfire were fired from their automatic weapons and the horses pulling the cart went down. The policemen jumped off the carriage and lay down on the road. Now, we could clearly see that there were four of them. There was a short exchange of fire. Serdink crawled toward them holding a hand grenade. Getting closer he shouted: "Who are you?" "And you?" responds one of the policemen. "We are Banderites," Serdink yelled. One of the policemen stood up and called back, "Long live Ukraine! And we thought you were partisans. Why did you shoot our horses?" "We also thought you were partisans," said Serdink and got up. He then calmly slung his gun over his shoulder and approached the policemen. Wow, I thought to myself. He really has some nerve.

The others also approached, slowly dismounted and, as if on signal, attacked the policemen. "This is what you deserve," said Serdink as he tied their hands behind their backs. "Long live Ukraine; you forgot to say Soviet Ukraine. And now, start walking to the village. It seems like the only creatures you spared there were the sparrows." Having said that, he mounted his horse, the others surround the prisoners and the procession headed back to the village. We asked the first peasant we met on the road where the policemen had been shooting. He pointed to a certain house. We rode into the yard and I saw a scene that my eyes had already almost forgotten. Next to the wall of the house I saw dead bodies lying in a row. I counted six of them. I dismounted and approached them. Among the dead, I recognized Jewish families from Buczacz. Mr. Kanner, his wife, and their eight-year-old daughter, along with Mr. Berger and his wife.[81] The sixth body belonged to a woman I had not seen before.

Serdink came up to me and asked if I knew any of them. I nodded and told him who the dead were. "Which one of you shot the child?"

I asked, turning toward the policemen. They were standing in a tight group with their heads down, not answering my question. "Where did you find them?" I turned to them again. Serdink grabbed the whip and started lashing them with all his might. One of them signaled that he was willing to cooperate and show us the hideout. He led us to the stable where we could see that a square hole had been exposed by moving the trough aside. I leaned down over the hole and I smelled the terrible odor of dampness and stench. "You did not even want to allow them this sort of life," I said to the policeman. "And now talk. How did you know they were hiding here?" "Speak!" shouted Janek, pulling out his knife, "or I will gouge your eyes out." Saying that, he pushed the prisoner to the ground. "The son of the village teacher came to our commander in Koropiec yesterday and told us that Jews were hiding here. He himself lives in the neighborhood."

I spoke with Serdink and soon, with one of the policemen walking in front of us, we went to the neighboring house. In the yard we found a young boy, perhaps twenty years old. The policeman pointed at him. We took him with us and soon mounted our horses and headed back to the forest, the prisoners walking between us. Once we reached the forest, Serdink told the lieutenant colonel everything. He summoned the prisoners and interrogated them. He then calmly turned to us and asked: "Which one of you is a Jew?" All six of us responded. "Shlepnut ikh" [Russian: "give them a good whacking"] he said, and then slowly moved away. We led the prisoners into the bushes, not wanting to frighten the horses.

That same afternoon, after speaking with us, the lieutenant colonel approved the operation we proposed. We wanted to clear the area of the Ukrainian police posts, village heads, or others who were assisting the Germans in their quota requisition actions and were a real plague for the local population. After sunset we set out in ten groups, each consisting of thirty men. Every group included two members of our own unit, who were to serve as guides and seize the collaborators. The lieutenant colonel personally dispatched each group, providing instructions and warnings. I remember his words: "Be as quiet as you can. Don't let the local population know how many of you there are and what you are planning to do. On the way speak only in Ukrainian. And remember," he said to the commander of our group: "For every drunk man in your unit I will personally pull out one of your teeth. As for you boys," he turned to Edek and me, placing his hands on our shoulders, "remember, do not harm anybody who is innocent. Try to bring back the guilty alive. Shoot only when they resist or try to run away. We do not want the people to be afraid of us. We want to liberate them from the harassment of those who have sold their souls to the Germans."

We left at sunset, proceeding along tracks we knew well. The farthest post we were planning to reach was fifteen kilometers away, where there was a large estate used by the Germans. The task was to burn it down. On the way back, we were to cleanse some villages of the collaborators. We had prepared a list of their names in advance. After accomplishing this we were to return to the forest. In the first village we passed through we confiscated several horse carts. People we met on the way told us that the Germans had been there in the morning but that in the afternoon they had left in haste in the direction of Buczacz. "Apparently spending the nights in the villages does not agree with them," Edek chuckled and spurred on the horses. A few hundred meters before the target we got off the carts and allowed their owners to return home. We continued to the estate on foot. The Landwirt was unfortunately not there. Only his portrait was hanging in the large living room next to the portrait of the Führer. For now, we just shot through their painted heads.

We heard some noise coming from the other rooms and soon Pavlo, a tall and strong turner from Kharkov, carried in the fat little estate steward, holding him by his collar. In his high yellow boots and green cap, he looked just like the demon from the local folk tales. One of the maids, a young country girl, signaled to me with her eyes and left the room. I followed her, and she showed me red stripes on her back. The steward had pursued her and when she would not yield, he whipped her and threatened to send her to hard labor to Germany. I tried to calm her down. The steward would not harass anyone anymore. Outside the horses were already being harnessed. We took four horse carts, eight pigs, a few sacks of flour and, most important, a whole barrel of home brewed vodka that we found in the cellar. We no longer needed kerosene to set fire to the house. Incendiary grenades would suffice. A few of those grenades and the whole house was in flames.

The well-fed estate horses swiftly carried us away from the burning house. In the villages on the way, we managed to grab a few Ukrainian policemen and Banderite band members known to us. Now tied up, they were forced to run behind the carts, with the sweaty half-dead estate steward in the middle. We reached the forest in the morning. The captives were put under guard next to the headquarters and we lay down to sleep, quite exhausted. We were summoned to the lieutenant colonel at around nine. On my way to him, I noticed that apart from the captives we had caught, there were others who had also been caught that night. Altogether, I counted around thirty people. Some of them wore police uniforms. I recognized some from the early days of German-Ukrainian rule, when they had prowled around, murdering Jews with impunity. The lieutenant colonel announced that the traitors would be handed over to us since we represented the only authorities in this area recognized by him: "You have the full right to judge and sentence them to whatever you deem right."

We soon began. The members of the jury were Edek, Nacio, and one of the unit's politruks we had requested to join us. I was quickly appointed prosecutor. The arrested men were brought in front of us one by one. They were asked a few questions intended to extract the truth from them and then the verdict was announced. The steward was the first. After writing down his personal information, the questions followed. "How many peasant goods did the estate rob in the past year?" "Twenty-eight hundredweights from the quota of three hundred." "And the rest?" "The rest was burned by the partisans." "Did he beat the peasants who worked on the estate?" "No, never." "And that Katarzyna, on whose back I saw the red marks?" "She did not want to work; I beat her because the Landwirt ordered me to." "Did the Landwirt also order you to rape her? Or perhaps you did it together?" As for the threats that she would be sent off to Germany, he naturally said that he knew nothing at all about that. He alternated between getting red in the face, turning all white, stuttering, trying to say one thing and then contradicting himself. Finally, he broke down completely. The judges briefly consulted each other. Edek read out the verdict: "For collaboration with the occupier and tormenting the local population, you are sentenced to death." He leaped up, shouted something, his green hat fell off his head. Janek picked it up, stuck it back on his head and led him away.

The others were brought in after him. They all repeated the same line. Their murderous past was reflected in the changing color of their faces. Some of them blamed each other and in this manner, we learned new details, which added to the long string of their crimes. One was a presumably forty-year-old thug, who looked like a fine God-fearing peasant, a husband, and father of three children. Despite this, he had the lives of several Russian soldiers, who were bestially murdered in 1941, on his conscience. The Germans appointed him village head and offered him the boots of the murdered as a reward. He was still wearing one of those pairs. "We will not take them off you," we told him. "You will be buried in them." One by one, they all came forth. None could justify or explain their crimes. They all received the same sentence. For collaboration with the enemy, for causing suffering to the people, the sentence was death.

Toward the end, the lieutenant colonel was also listening. Facing us was a tall thug, his eyes shifting nervously from one side to the other, stuttering, as he assured us that he had never been an informer for the Germans and that he was not the one who had promised a Jewish family to hide them. After the liquidation, when they came to him, he had robbed them of their last possessions and then bestially murdered them. It did not help when I told him that during our raid, I found letters of denunciation with his signature in the archives of the police building in Monasterzyska. Even when one of the other policemen we had caught told him to his face what he had done, he didn't budge. He insisted that he was innocent and even pretended to be hurt by our accusations. Why did the "comrades" come to him suddenly yesterday in the middle of the night and drag him out of bed? He invited them for a drink. The commander drank vodka with him and then out of the blue, they tied his hands to the wagon.

The lieutenant colonel interrupted him: "Who drank vodka with you last night?" "The 'commander' who came with the 'comrades,'" he answered. The lieutenant colonel turned around and left. After a while, I heard him shouting: "The commander of the second group of the intelligence unit report to me!" We were also done by then. He was the last one we sentenced. From now on, not one of them was going to harm us or the local population. I approached the lieutenant colonel. At the same time, the commander of the second unit, unaware, also approached him. I looked at the lieutenant colonel and hardly recognized him. The normally good-natured eyes, long beard, and nearly ascetic face made him look more like a rabbi than a fierce commander of a partisan unit, whose thousand men were ready to go to their death or to victory on any signal from this beloved person. Now, he was pale, his eyes burning with an ominous light as he stared at the young culprit standing in front of him. "You drank vodka with a bandit yesterday?" After a moment of silence, he repeated the question. "I had one drink, I wanted to warm myself up," was the answer. The lieutenant colonel's eyes flashed like lightning. "You drink vodka with the enemy? Is this the example you are giving your soldiers? You, a member of the People's Red Army, you think it was only vodka you drank? It was the blood of your brothers murdered in 1941. He might have exchanged a bloodied army uniform for this vodka. Turn around!" he yelled, suddenly enraged, pulling out his pistol. "Comrade lieutenant colonel," the young commander burst out in tears: "Give me another chance. I will go and perform the hardest tasks. Let me die from the enemy's bullet. But not from my own. After all, I have many military merits." "Merits," the lieutenant colonel laughed bitterly.

"Which of us does not have them and who knows if they will ever be counted if they are mixed in with such deeds."

At that moment, the unit's politruk approached the lieutenant colonel. Pointing at the pale young commander, he seemed to be trying to persuade the lieutenant colonel of something. "Write the order," the lieutenant colonel instructed the politruk. "For an assignment carried out in a negligent manner, I strip the commander of the second group of his rank and make him a private. His unit will be dissolved, and the men distributed among other groups. And now, get out of my sight!" he hollered at the still standing commander. Agitated, he sat on the ground, stroked his beard with his hand, and talked to himself: "You treat them like children, then they themselves do not know what to allow themselves. Couldn't he wait with the vodka until the morning? His merits, that is what he remembers, his merits." Slowly, the sharp features of his face softened, and his eyes regained the kindly expression we had all learned to love.

In the afternoon, the forester Krestatyi returned from Buczacz and informed us that there was a large military presence there. Apart from SS units and the Ukrainian police, a new formation of Russian traitors, the "Vlasovites," had arrived.[82] In addition to that, Krestatyi had counted six heavy tanks and several tankettes in town. Other people sent by Edek also returned, reporting that all the neighboring villages were full of soldiers. The lieutenant colonel summoned Edek to him and told him that from all the information gathered it seemed that the Germans were planning to surround and destroy us in the forest. However, familiar with the tactics of the Germans, he assured us that for the remaining day and night we should not expect an attack from their side. "Our people," he continued, "are very tired from the long marches in the last few days and they urgently need a few days of rest. That is why I would prefer to find a suitable spot to defend our positions and accept the battle rather than to fight while retreating."

Consultations began. Edek suggested a certain hill in the Koropiec forest, surrounded from three sides by the Koropiec River, over which there was only one bridge. The summit of the hill was accessible from the fourth side, but the slope there was extremely steep and overgrown with thick bushes. The scouts sent to reconnoiter the site reported that the enemy had no presence there. Despite this, the lieutenant colonel decided to wait until nighttime to relocate the unit. For the rest of the day we listened to the noise of vehicles somewhere far away. Before nightfall, two German planes flew low over the forest. Apparently, the Germans did not yet know exactly where we were camped. This was something totally new for us. We had become used to moving away as far as possible after every mission or encounter. This had been the key to our successes in the fight against the Germans. This time, even as they recognized that that the Germans knew the approximate site of their encampment, a thousand men were calmly eating their supper and going to sleep ....

The men were woken up at 1 a.m. They got ready so quietly that you could not hear even the slightest noise, cough, or sneeze. The lieutenant colonel sent out a reconnaissance team, which Edek and I joined. It took us an hour to get to the hill designated for the formation's relocation. We kept as quiet as possible on the way and reached the steep hillside without any problem. We began climbing and about halfway up the hill we came upon a line of old trenches, probably from World War I. After some more hard climbing we reached the summit. Edek and a few other men turned back to lead part of the unit—the horses and carts—toward the bridge, where the terrain was not as steep. At dawn, we were all in the new location. We found an old, half-destroyed bunker just on the top of the hill and established our headquarters there. The runners approached the lieutenant colonel from different directions, informing him about the positions each unit had occupied. The lieutenant colonel rubbed his hands together and seemed very content. A short briefing with the units' commanders took place. The lieutenant colonel said: "Your positions are to be envied even by a regular army. But, remember. There is nowhere to retreat. Our defense is spherical and giving in at one spot means losing everything. Repeat this to your soldiers. Let them show the Germans that the front line is not a thousand kilometers away from here, but that this whole Soviet homeland is one big frontline. And that we will give them no respite, until the last of them falls dead on this land."

Edek and I approached the lieutenant colonel and asked him to designate a position for our unit. We also wanted to participate in the battle. The lieutenant colonel smiled and said: "For the time being, yours will act as the headquarters' protection unit. And in case one of the spots needs reinforcement, you will go there with me." We established our positions next to the headquarters and had a light meal of bread with pork fat. It was near 8 a.m. on a sunny and clear day, and I was already thinking that all the preparations had been for nothing, when suddenly the runner came to report that the Germans were approaching the bridge from the side of the river. The bridge and meadow were in a clearly visible area. The forest, where our men were entrenched, lay about three hundred meters from the bridge. The lieutenant colonel ordered them to let the Germans cross the bridge and to open fire only once they reached a distance of thirty meters from the forest. After a few moments we heard the first bursts of gunfire from automatic weapons. I looked at the lieutenant colonel. He was holding a boiled egg in his hand and peeling it slowly. There were no more shots.

The runner arrived and reported that fire had been opened at the approaching Germans. Several had been shot dead, the others retreated and ran toward the bridge. At the same instant the forest was shaken by explosions. The Germans had begun their methodical shelling of our positions. We could hear the sounds of mortars exploding and Sasha, who was lying next to me, could distinguish them from tank shells by their sound. In truth, we felt a bit uneasy. We were not used to this kind of attack by mortars and tanks. The clutter of machine gun fire aimed at the edge of the forest added to the commotion. With each shot we flattened ourselves to the ground. I was mostly disturbed by the swishing sound made by the bullets when they flew through the leaves in the forest. This was not the first instance that bullets had whistled next to me, but in those situations, I was either running as fast as I could, or had fired back so that the sound of my own shots had blocked out that unpleasant hiss.

At some point, when a mortar shell exploded with a terrifying shriek nearby and I fell flat on the ground to protect myself from the shrapnel, I heard someone's laughter over my head. I turned around and saw a young girl standing just above me. She had a bag with the Red Cross insignia on her back. She was looking at me and laughing. In response to my surprised expression, she shouted: "Don't be afraid, it doesn't hit so quickly." I leaped up and assured her that I was not in the least afraid, that I was just taking a rest. "Well, well," she interrupted cheerfully. "No need to say that. Just two months ago I too was sure that every bullet was rushing towards me. You will also get used to it. Come," she shouted, "let's go to the front line. Someone may be wounded and need help." I followed her, but after a few steps there was another barrage. It was so strong that we were forced to prostate ourselves on the ground. We hid behind the trunk of a huge oak tree. Luba, as the girl was called, asked for a piece of paper; I found a scrap of newspaper in my pocket and we rolled cigarettes. To my surprise, I learned that she was Jewish and came from Skalat. Thanks to her Aryan appearance she had escaped after acquiring false documents and had been working as a servant at the house of a Ukrainian in some village. One night, partisans appeared in the village and she went to the forest with them. She had been through the Carpathian campaign and many of the wounded owed their lives to her. She had received the partisan medal, first class.[83] She had lost her entire family. Only one brother was alive in Palestine. She had heard that a Jewish Army had been formed there. "My brother is surely at the front. Oh," she suddenly sighed, "may he stay healthy and unscathed."

These words of worry sounded strange in the hellish atmosphere in which we found ourselves at that moment, surrounded by continuous explosions, rifle fire, and the rattle of machine guns. We took advantage of a moment of calm and moved forward again. Soon we reached the edge of the forest. Spread out in a long line, our men were lying between the trees. I spotted a machine gun, cleverly covered by branches. Crawling forward, we passed the first position and reached the commander. "No, there are no wounded. The Germans are already positioned on this side of the bridge in the meadow." With his hand, he pointed at small piles of branches tied together far away in the meadow. "They have not as yet stuck their noses out from behind those branches." Behind the river one could see tanks constantly firing. The mortars were probably operating from another side. Suddenly, the shots ceased. There was silence for a while, which felt even more ominous then the strongest fire. Then the branches began to move. The Germans got up, holding the branches at the height of their stomachs. Crouched, they were running straight toward us.

I grabbed my weapon and released the safety catch. I felt the hand of the commander on my shoulder and heard his voice. "Steady, young man, nobody shoots before I do. Wait for my signal." I looked around me. The men were sitting as if they had not noticed the approaching Germans. They lit cigarettes, they joked. Two boys were lying not far away from me. I recognized their accent. They were Kazakhs. "Listen, Manshuk," one of them said. "Can you see that tall German? What do you think, will his shoes fit me? Or maybe the other one, the fat guy?" Meanwhile, the Germans were getting closer. They were about fifty paces from us. They dropped the branches and with loud yells, shooting from their automatic weapons, they hurled themselves in our direction. I felt the tension rising in me to the limit, my throat was dry, I couldn't swallow at all. Only another forty paces, thirty-five, thirty. I felt that if something did not happen soon, I would lose my mind. And then I heard, "Fire at the fascists!"

Right away, the loud roar of automatic weapons mixed with the rattle of machine guns. I also pulled the trigger. Calm returned to me with the first burst and the slight tremor of the weapon in my hands. My eyes could see clearly again. I watched as the Germans fell, stopped, and finally turned around and ran away. I heard: "Komm, komm, stehenbleiben!" [come here, stand still!] But our bullets were apparently more persuasive, because after a while there were no more Germans left, apart from several bodies sprawled on the ground. Only from far away, in front of the bridge, could we discern a few crouched figures in green running away. I left the line and returned to the headquarters. I was just in the midst of reporting the firefight on this side of the bridge to the lieutenant colonel when the Germans opened another barrage of mortar and shell fire. The runners who arrived, reported that all the German attacks had been thwarted. In one section, which was being attacked by the Vlasovites, German officers shot the retreating soldiers from behind.

At some point, heavy fire could be heard from the side of the steep slope. Because of its natural shape it had been the least protected. Soon, another runner came to report that the Germans had quietly climbed that slope and attacked the old trenches in which one of our units was defending itself. Then another runner arrived, shouting that the Germans were ousting our boys from the trenches. The sound of intense gunfire and explosions of hand grenades indicated that heavy fighting was underway there. In an instant, the lieutenant colonel was on his feet and shouting as he ran: "Everyone with a weapon follow me!" "Follow me!" yelled Edek, who was running behind him. We all rushed after them. We traversed the few yards that separated us from the slope. There we encountered some of our men who had been ousted from the trenches. The Germans' blue uniforms could be seen in the thicket.[84] "Not one step back!" the lieutenant colonel yelled to the retreating men. "Fire!" we heard again. I reached the nearest tree and began shooting into the bushes where we had just seen the blue uniforms.

As I paused to change the magazine, I heard someone constantly shooting over my head. I looked and saw the lieutenant colonel. Standing erect, his feet slightly apart, he was holding a machine gun and shooting non-stop into the bushes. He had the same benevolent expression on his face that had made everyone love him. He was smiling, and his eyes were shining with a calm light. Suddenly we could hear grenades detonating very close to us and newly formed units of those who had been ousted from the trenches ran past us with a loud "hurrah!" We ran together with them and were soon sitting in the trenches. We could see the Germans retreating down the slope. Some were rolling down on the steep terrain. The lieutenant colonel ordered our unit to return to its position next to the headquarters. On the way back, he asked us if we had seen the Germans rolling down, how many bullets each one of us had fired and if no one was injured. Finally, he congratulated us on our military fitness ....

During the afternoon, the shooting stopped completely. It grew dark. The lieutenant colonel decided that we must leave this place that same night at any cost .... We cautiously walked towards the bridge and passed it .... We had spent the previous night marching without stopping, passing through villages and towns. But only now did we learn the real technique of partisan marches. We were spread out in one column, walking one behind the other. The carts were traveling in the middle and at the very end rode the mounted unit, grandly named squadron .... In the morning we reached a forest and after posting guards and establishing defense positions, we lay down to rest .... A new phase had begun in our lives. From the partisan fighting we had known before, we had progressed, as Edek jokingly put it, to the "classical partisans," whose methods we were learning from our Russian friends and their incomparable leader—the bearded lieutenant colonel .... Nobody would believe me when I say that in those days or rather nights, I slept while I was walking. But that is the truth. It was enough to have a few sleepless nights. During the days, we had minor encounters with the enemy, and then again marched all night ....

On one of those nights, after a day of rest in which we slept like logs, we set out again. This time we were rested, and in a good mood. At around 10 p.m. we passed next to Monasterzyska, where we had once burned down the tobacco factory. From far away, we could see lights in the windows of the houses. The lieutenant colonel decided to send scouts to check out the first houses. Ten of us, including Nacio and me, set out. When we approached the town, we left the road and continued through the gardens. The first man we encountered in one of the yards was a Pole. We learned from him that the Germans had settled on the other side of the town in the school building. He told us that Pahl, the chief of the Buczacz gendarmes, was also in town. "There, in that big house with lights," he pointed with his hand. The distance to the house was about two hundred meters. Suddenly, Nacio turned to the man and asked him if he would be willing to enter that house using some excuse and to make sure that Pahl was there. "I'd better send my wife. She might be able to get in with some pretext," the Pole said. We agreed. Two of our men kept the man as a hostage, while we went there together with the woman.

Recalling our adventure on the road we kept our weapons ready to fire all the time. We were merely a few steps away from the house when some figures suddenly appeared from behind the bend. We immediately recognized that they were Germans. A few bursts from our automatics and two of them were down, while the rest disappeared in the alleys. We stopped for a moment. The head of our group had already given the order to retreat, when the door of the balcony in the house where Pahl was staying opened. The short, stocky figure that every Jew in Buczacz would immediately identify among thousands of others, appeared in the lit doorway. Pahl. Nacio rushed in that direction, and I ran after him, ignoring our commander's order to retreat. We did not hear that somewhere behind us the Germans had opened fire and that our commander had ordered our group to return fire until we returned. We continued running and were very near the house on whose balcony Pahl was still standing. He was probably worried by the fire. Nacio stopped, raised his weapon and the flash of the bullets cut the air ending somewhere on the balcony. I could see Pahl stagger and fall.

At that moment, even before hearing the shots, I heard the familiar whistle of bullets next to me. We fell on the ground and I fired a few bursts toward the street corner from which the shots came. "Run!" I yelled to Nacio, then leaped up and rushed toward our men on the road. They were returning the German fire from there. After a few I steps I did not hear Nacio behind me. I turned around and realize that I had been running on my own. Nacio was still lying in the same spot. I returned and shook him by the shoulder: "Nacio." "Help me get up," he said, "I struck myself in the stomach while falling." I helped him get up, but after a few steps he staggered and fell again. I picked him up, threw him over my shoulder and ran, yelling loudly for help over the noise of the firefight. Someone was running toward me and soon they grabbed hold of Nacio. I unbuttoned his coat, and now we could carry him holding onto both sides of his coat. We passed by the last houses of the town and beyond the range of the bullets.

We heard horses' hooves, and as they came nearer, and I recognized Serdink. He was mad at us for getting into the fight, but our commander shrugged his shoulders and pointed at us. One of the horsemen galloped to inform the lieutenant colonel and to bring a horse cart for Nacio, who was lying on the ground and groaning lightly. I bend over him and could still not tell where he was wounded. He answered that he was feeling a strong pain in the area of his stomach. We picked him up and carried him again. On the way we were met by the horse cart. We lay Nacio down, I sat with him and was holding his head. I tried to pour some vodka into his mouth; he swallowed with difficulty and asked for water. We reached the formation which had meanwhile moved further ahead. The doctor climbed onto the cart and put an emergency dressing on Nacio. It was dark. We covered ourselves with a large cloth. Now with the light of a flashlight, we could clearly see the small entry hole on the right side of Nacio's stomach. The doctor silently washed the wound and put on a field dressing; we placed a piece of cloth on top of it and tied it with a piece of string.

We drove the whole night. Nacio moaned more and more loudly; his pain must have been getting increasingly worse. He threw up a few times during the ride and in the morning, when we reached the forest, he was already very weak. His brother Janek had left with the scouts and was expected to meet us in only a few days. Daybreak arrived, with the promise of a beautiful day. One of those days that make you feel alive, especially when they come at the end of the summer, as if trying to make the long winter months more bearable. Nacio was lying under a tree and I was just putting a rolled-up coat under his head as a pillow when he began to rattle. I called out for the doctor, he arrived in an instant; after taking Nacio's pulse, he motioned to me with his eyes. We stepped aside and he told me it was probably the end. Only an immediate operation might save him. But in our condition, that was impossible, he said. I returned to Nacio, sat down next to him and stroked his head. He soon opened his eyes. When he saw me, he tried to smile and then with great effort, as I could see from the expression on his face, he said: "Tell Janek not to cry. We will meet there anyway. And don't tell mother, only after the war." I wanted to interrupt him, to say no, to deny it, but my throat was dry, and something was choking me. I only managed to bend down and kiss his pale cheeks.

"Do you remember our conversations," he asked me, "our dreams and plans for after the war? Kiss the Holy Land for me. Remember, the first kiss will be from me." I felt the tears choking my throat. If only I could now look at fleeing Germans, hear the noise of battle, and feel the trembling gun in my hand, instead of gazing into his dying face. "Show me that stamp," Nacio said suddenly; I carefully took out the well-protected postal stamp from Palestine once given to me by Hania. I handed it over to Nacio. He raised it to his eyes, his face lit up with heavenly bliss. "Ten mils," he read.[85] "Is it true that with this you can buy many oranges there?" I nodded. I could not utter a sound. "And this tree, what kind of tree could it be?" He pointed at the drawing of a tree on the stamp. "Maybe a cedar," I managed to say with great effort. "And here it says Palestine, Eretz Israel." He sighed heavily. The hand holding the stamp was clenched, grasping it as if afraid that someone might want to snatch the hidden treasure. And that hand, stretching out toward the heart, stopped midway.

Goodbye, dear Nacio. Goodbye, brother. One of millions, but happier than millions of others, because you fell in battle avenging what had been done to the Jewish people. A gun salute for you is not enough. Another kind of gun salute will bid you farewell, the fire of thousands of shots from thousands of guns, directed at the hearts of the enemy, today, tomorrow, and every day until the last of the enemy is dead. Sleep softly our brother. Dream of the little stamp in your hand placed on your heart. *Yitgadal ve-yitkadash shmei raba* [Aramaic: Exalted and hallowed be God's great name].[86]

Once more we experienced turbulent days filled with firefights and detonating hand grenades. The nights were filled with marches and the roar of blown up of bridges, tunnels, and trains full of soldiers transported to the east to help the collapsing front. The lieutenant colonel was happy. Huge chunks of territory in Volhynia[87] were taken over by the partisans. In regions snatched from the hands of the Germans, life was returning to normal. We were spread out along the whole line of the Dniester River in Ukraine. Following several encounters with us, the Germans were so drained that they lost the will to fight us. They only followed us from a distance and occasionally shot at us. From time to time, they tried to get close and bite us, but they were quickly beaten back and that was all there was to it. There was no time to think about anything. Janek had returned. He was terribly shaken by the news of his brother's death. But the constant marches and fights did not leave much time to think about our dear ones.

We remained part of the intelligence unit, and as long as the lieutenant colonel's forces stayed in the area we would be fighting together. Most recently we had conducted cleansing operations against the Banderites and now they were hiding in their holes or had fled to the cities, where they could shelter under the wings of their German protectors. Such names of villages as Huta [Stara], Kowalówka, Marotówka, Dobrowody [all in the Buczacz district] are imprinted on my mind; I will never forget them as long as I live. One night, as we were moving along the main road, the lieutenant colonel ordered us all to acquire a horse, because the hilly and forested terrain ahead of us would be impassable for the carts. Travelling down the road, we looked more like ghosts than human beings. I was riding next to Serdink, who was in charge of securing the rear of the column. We could see the dark shapes of buildings on the left. Suddenly, we saw flashes of fire coming from there, easily noticed in the dark night. They were shooting in our direction. Serdink turned his horse toward the buildings and I heard his loud shout: "Follow me!" The horses left the road and trotted lightly after him.

My horse, a large white mare, was moving with the others. I heard the next order: "Squadron advance!" The horses started galloping, and my mare was speeding along with the others. I no longer had any control over her. I didn't hear the shots anymore, only the whistle of bullets in the air. I heard a loud "ooh, ooh," emanating from the chests of the riders. The intensity of the partisans' emotions, their feelings for their lost families, the burned houses and destroyed lives, were all contained in that sound, as well as their immense hatred for the enemy. My voice joined those of the others. I slowly dared let go of the reins and tried to shift my weapon from my back to my chest. At the same moment I heard a powerful blast. It somehow lifted me up in the air. I felt my weapon sliding away from me. I stretched out my hands and tried to hold on to it, but I couldn't reach it. I felt that I was sinking deeper and deeper. I didn't feel the fall, there was just total silence.

Slowly, I regained consciousness. At first, I felt a painful buzz in my ears. I tried to move my head, but it felt as heavy as if it were made of lead. I began to distinguish other sounds. I could hear the rattle of wheels driving on stones. I felt my body being rhythmically jarred and became aware of the fact that I was being transported. I began to recall various events from the night before: the gunshots on the road, then Serdink's orders, and the galloping horses. Finally, the blast and the fall, after which I could remember nothing. I opened my eyes, but had to immediately shut them again, blinded by the bright light of day. I slowly got used to the light and saw Janek's face watching me with great concern. "We will soon come to a rest," he tried to encourage me, "hang in there." I looked around and could see that we were in a forest. The tops of the trees on both sides of the cart were sliding away from my eyes. "Which part of my body has been hit?" I asked Janek. "You haven't been injured," he answered, "just stunned, and something is wrong with your foot." I tried to move my feet and I felt a terrible pain in my right ankle. On the other hand, I could freely move my left leg. I could also move my arms. There was just a strange humming in my ears.

Finally, we came to a stop. The doctor approached and asked how I was feeling. I answered that on the whole I was okay, just the pain in my foot was getting worse. Luba came up to me. She took off the sheepskin coat that was covering my legs and tried to pull the boot off my right foot. But that caused me such terrible pain that she soon gave up, looking helplessly at the doctor. The doctor checked my leg and said that it was extremely swollen up to the knee; that was why the boot could not be pulled off. In an instant, Luba cut the boot with a knife and revealed a bluish foot, extremely swollen at the ankle. When the doctor tried to touch my foot, I fainted. When I opened my eyes again, I could see the doctor's worried face. Noticing that I had regained consciousness, he turned to me. My ankle was broken. He was helpless, since he did not have a single cast bandage. After a while the boys took me off the cart and lay me down on the ground. Every movement was causing me terrible pain.

I began contemplating what would happen to me. I knew that I would not be able to drag myself behind the formation. Considering how often we had to leave the carts behind when we crossed forests and hills, I wouldn't be able to ride on a cart either. And even the doctor was at his wits' end. I remembered hearing about a seriously wounded man who shot himself because he had been unable to bear the hardships of the ride and refused to fall alive into the hands of the Germans. I called Janek and asked him to give me my automatic. He brought it to me without thinking. I felt better, more confident now that I was holding the black weapon. I had lived through the nicest period of the year, I thought to myself. Now, fall would come, and with it rain and cold. I didn't need to feel sorry for myself. But today, as if to spite me, the weather was beautiful. The sun was high up in the sky and the leaves were changing color. They were falling, landing on the soft moss with a quiet whisper. Just like a mother's caress—the thought crossed my mind. And the Red Army was storming across the Dnieper somewhere in the area of Dnepropetrovsk. Go away, go away deceitful thoughts. I grabbed the weapon and released the safety catch.

Suddenly I heard someone say: "Wait, young man." The sixty-year-old Cossack Pavlovskyi was standing in front of me. I knew him well, having often seen him before, and had especially noticed his huge moustache. "Give it to me," he took away my automatic. "Come on, old man," I said. "You know the doctor only nodded his head. Do you think I should wait until the Germans play with me before they kill me? You know there is no hope." "You wait, the old Cossack will do some magic [said in Ukrainian]. If there is no hope, I myself will put the weapon in your hand." For a while he stood there, looking at my swollen leg, and then he bent down and started to feel my ankle. "Can you grind your teeth and hold it for a few minutes?" he asked. "I will try," I answered. He left, taking my automatic with him. At the same moment Edek appeared. He had returned from a night reconnaissance mission. He came up to me and began questioning me about what had happened. In the end, he decided that it would be best for me to leave by cart at night along with Benek, and to try to reach Szkrabka's house. "They can hide you and you can stay there until you get better."

The Cossack returned with a bottle of vodka and two narrow wooden planks. Everybody looked on, baffled about what he intended to do. "Drink," he ordered, handing me the bottle. I choked from a big gulp of alcohol. "More, until it turns your head." I took another gulp, my eyes filled with tears, but my head felt fine. The old man got irritated. "Look at him," he said. "He looks like such a weakling, he can't count to three, but obviously he is used to drinking alcohol from the cradle." At last my head started spinning. I felt an acute pain but was not able to react to it and soon fell asleep. When I woke up, the sun had set. My head was heavy and hurt a little. Suddenly I remembered my leg. I looked at it. Two narrow planks tied with a piece of cloth were tightly attached to both sides of my ankle. On top they were tied with a piece of string. The doctor approached and shook his head at the sight of the bandage. "This goes against all medical practice," he murmured. "But maybe that's why it will work. I am not surprised by anything I see anymore." The Cossack approached, carrying my weapon. Noticing the doctor, he looked at him derisively. "Did you do this?" the doctor asked him. "How did you put the bone together?" "None of your business," the Cossack retorted. "When you break yours, I will tend to it too."

We prepared for the journey. On the first part of the way we would travel together with the formation and then, after Oteszow, Benek and I were to turn to the right and reach Gaje Buczackie through side roads. On the way, I said goodbye to my friends who wished me a swift return. After a few hours' drive our cart turned away from the road and we were left alone. Benek was driving and I held on to the automatic weapon, ready to fire. I was vigilantly looking into the blackness of the night. We drove mainly through side roads, trying to stay off the main tracks. Only at one spot did we have to go for a few meters on the main road. I felt very nervous when I heard the clatter of our horse's hooves on the paved road. But soon we were off the road and after a two hours' journey we reached Głęboka Dolina. Now we were driving through very familiar terrain. I recognized the big pear tree in the dark, then we saw the trees of the orchard where "babcia" lived. We drove in there and soon Elżbieta, who had woken up, boiled some milk for us. We stayed the night in the barn and in the morning Benek told Szkrabka about the whole incident.

Szkrabka decided that initially we would stay with "babcia." Right away, Elżbieta, along with Antoszek, began to prepare a shelter for me. They made a hole in a big pile of hay in the barn and inside they built a sort of nest in which I was able to lie comfortably and even move. During the daytime Staszka would often come for a chat and also bring me food and water. I learned from her that other Jews were hiding in the house. A Jewish woman from Barysz with her daughter Gizia, and another fifty-year-old Jewish woman from Buczacz called [Rosa] Hirschhorn.[88] They were hidden inside a double wall in the stable. After a few days, my loneliness became so unbearable that I demanded to be allowed to spend some time in the house.

From that day on, every evening I would be helped into the house by Antoszek and Staszka and would stay there until late at night. Sometimes Gizia and her mother would also come out and we would talk until early morning, telling each other about what we had been through. Szkrabka himself, or one of his sons, would come to visit. Even the Ukrainian Durda family, having learned by chance that I was there, came to visit, and brought delicious tidbits to eat. One day, Szkrabka appeared with an old grey-haired peasant, who turned out to be the most famous healer in the region. After inspecting my leg, he said that I would have to keep the bandage on for another three to four weeks and then he would try to remove it.

All kinds of news from Buczacz reached my ears. Nearly every day the Germans would discover and drag out Jews hiding in various shelters. One day Staszka, who had observed one of those scenes in town, told me that the Jews taken out after a few months of hiding often in humid conditions, had terribly swollen feet. Their bodies were covered with scabs and the whole spectacle was repugnant. I also learned that Pahl did not die during the raid in which Nacio had been killed. He had only been wounded, had been in a critical condition after his operation, but was now better.[89]

Once a week, a member of the family would go to Buczacz and bring newspapers published by the Germans in Polish and Ukrainian. Our spirits were raised by these newspapers, in spite of the propaganda they contained. The Germans still reported that they had sunk millions of tons of Allied supplies in the Atlantic and that they were defeating the Bolsheviks in the East, but they had to admit that they were retreating behind the Dnieper River .... Yet despite all this, most of the time I was alone and once more my old enemy, my thoughts, despair and doubt, began to torment me. I did not believe that my leg would be totally healed. I did not think that a local healer and an old Cossack could know more about the body than a real doctor. At best, I believed that even if I were able to walk, I would remain a cripple. Hundreds of times, in moments of despair, I would reach for my gun, wanting to put an end to it all. Yet every time I did that, something held me back. I was sure that if the Germans suddenly appeared, I would definitely shoot myself in the head. But until then, every time I put my finger on the trigger, either the dog would bark, or I would hear someone's voice in the yard, or Staszka would appear.

She was the one who offered me the most kindness, and it is especially thanks to her that I survived those critical moments. I remember

how she would sit in the shelter for hours and hours, patiently listening to me and answering thousands of questions that I would shower
on her, just trying to get her to stay longer. Each time she went to
town, I would ask her to walk through familiar streets and later tell
me about every detail she could see. One day, when she told me she
was going into town, I asked her to walk past our house. I explained
in detail how to identify it. I also asked her to bring back a leaf from
the big maple tree growing under my window. Its branches reached out
to the street. That day, I waited even more anxiously for her return.
When she did, I learned that ethnic Germans were now living in our
house. I embraced the big golden maple leaf she had brought back,
kissed it and inhaled the familiar smell of home with tears in my eyes.
I was totally devastated.

The days were already short and rainy; fall was beginning in earnest. I spent my days in the house. If a stranger appeared, I would hop
on one leg and hide behind the large oven until the danger passed.
There are many ways to describe someone's heroism, but I would
never have enough words to express the extent of "babcia," Staszka,
and Elżbieta's bravery during those days. Every time the dog barked,
or a person or cart appeared in the distance, their hearts filled with
terrible fear. I would immediately be taken to my hiding spot and
only after some time would Staszka come, still pale but already with
laughing eyes, and announce that someone had merely passed by.

Despite this, I never heard them utter a word of fear or complaint. I
myself had to tell them over and over again that if the Germans or the
police found me, they should explain that I had only arrived an hour
before and had threatened them with my weapon or with the revenge
of the partisans if they told anyone. But "babcia" would usually not let
me finish, saying that everything was in God's hands, and that the will
of man amounted to very little.

One evening, Szkrabka came with the local healer, who inspected
my leg and then proceeded to take off the planks. In the small room of
the peasant's hut, dimly lit with a kerosene lamp, it all looked like a
scene in a mystery film. I was lying on the table, the healer's wrinkled
face, surrounded by wisps of grey hair, bent over me, with Szkrabka
gravely and Staszka somewhat fearfully watching. Gradually my leg,
now free from the planks and rags, appeared before our eyes. Still a
little bit swollen, painful when touched, but there was something in it
that made me feel alive again. The healer inspected the leg again, tried
to bend the foot back and forth and then ordered to bathe it twice a
day in saltwater and massage the muscles. I tried to stand, but it was
too painful. I could not sleep that night or the nights that followed,

since the pain was excruciating. But within a few days I felt better. To everyone's relief, within a week I was able to take a few steps without help. I was still very clumsy, but my condition improved daily and after some time, still limping and stopping every few steps, I was able to walk over and visit Szkrabka on my own.

One night, appearing from nowhere, Benek woke me up. I could tell from his voice that he was very agitated. Janek was wounded and had arrived at Szkrabka's home. I quickly put on my shoes and slowly dragged myself after Benek to Szkrabka's. Janek was lying there. He had lost a lot of blood and was very pale. He had been shot four times. Two of the bullets were still stuck in his body. It took us until morning to tend to his wounds. One of the bullets was in his right arm above the elbow, the other in his left thigh. Apart from that, his shoulder blade had been bruised and a bullet had gone through his thigh in the groin area. In the morning we left by cart to Jasiek Korko, where Janek was expected to stay for some time. It was only on the following day, while staying in my barn shelter, that I learned how Janek had been injured.

For some time now, part of Polish society, especially the Polish ethnic Germans who, just before the final defeat of the Germans, suddenly seemed to remember that they were Poles, had become unhappy with the good relations between the Home Army and the Soviet partisans.[90] They did not care that it was only thanks to the help of the lieutenant colonel that we had managed to stop the Banderites from exterminating the local Polish population. Instead, citing the example of Katyn,[91] they argued that they had to kill two birds with one stone. That meant that one had to wait for the defeat of both Germany and the Soviet Union. They did not say who would defeat them. As Edek said to one of these Poles in a conversation: "You are waiting for the defeat of Russia, but for whose sake? I hope not for the ethnic German Buchhalt of Barysz, who is making nice with you while informing the Germans of your every move!"

One day something incredible happened. A Polish priest was attacked in one of the villages. All his belongings, including his only cow, were looted and the sacred images were desecrated. Of course, the gentlemen of the Buchhalt clan made a big deal out of it. They blamed the Poles, the Jews, and the Soviets. In the meantime, it became obvious that none of our units were even near that area at the time of the raid. In addition to that, it was impossible to even think that one of our own men, or any of the lieutenant colonel's units, would have dared do something like this. The deeply distressed Edek decided to solve the riddle right away.

That same night, he set out with fifteen of his lads, including Janek. After talking to the priest, it became clear that the attackers had spoken Russian with each other. But their Russian was so bad that it was easy to tell that they were only pretending to be Russians. According to the priest they might have been Banderites in disguise, or even... The priest could not complete his sentence because the house came under fire and bullets came flying through the window. Edek was the first to recover. He turned off the lamp, ran to the door, fired a few bursts from his automatic and jumped out of the house. At that same instant, a hand grenade exploded at his feet and tore him to shreds. Janek jumped out of the window and was immediately riddled with bullets. He lay there pretending to be dead. He heard the injured moaning and someone ordering in Polish to finish them off. He recognized the voice of the ethnic German Tadeusz Buchhalt. Standing over Edek's body he said: "You wanted Jewish-Communist rule?[92] There you have it." Janek also recognized the voice of Szydłowski, another ethnic German and an inspector in the criminal police in Buczacz.

When everything calmed down, Janek crawled cautiously through the yard to the garden and from there ran through the fields to the forest, where fell down unconscious. Upon regaining his senses, he looked for water and then contemplated his situation. The lieutenant colonel was far away in the forest. Additionally, the only person who knew this terrain well had been Edek. He then decided to go to Szkrabka's, knowing that we too were there. It took him three days and nights to reach the place. Without food, on foot, using only his instinct, and not knowing whom he could trust, he finally found us. And what was most important, he had kept his pistol and rifle.

The following day, after talking to the boys, I told Szkrabka about everything. He already seemed to know something about the incident. Szkrabka announced that first we had to regain our health and then we would decide how to act. I was feeling much better and staying together with Janek in the barn. His wounds had begun to heal although two bullets were still lodged in his body. Within two weeks, we were already going on visits to Szkrabka and "babcia." It was almost November [1943]. The Soviets had occupied Kyiv and crossed the Dnieper River for good.[93] That evening, we were drinking at Szkrabka's to celebrate the latest victory of the Red Army. We were already feeling so well that we began thinking about returning to one of the units. But Szkrabka was against this and said that if we were feeling well, we should guard the villages in the area at night. Since the lieutenant colonel had left the area, the Banderites were once again attacking Polish villages. We readily agreed and set out every night to patrol the area.

One day, after returning from town, Elżbieta told us that the night before a group of unknown, probably Jewish assailants, had shot through the window of the town dog catcher Kowalski's house. Kowalski, who had specialized in searching for Jewish hideouts, was wounded and died on the way to the hospital.[94] Naturally, such incidents intrigued us very much but despite numerous efforts, we were unable to find out who was behind them or to contact these people. A few weeks later, probably the same people raided the house of a certain woman called Dudzicka, who had denounced a Jewish child to the Germans. The woman was killed before she could call for help. This time we managed to find out that the attackers belong to Ducio [Dawid] Friedlender's group.[95] The group operated on the other side of town, the side of the village of Pyszkowce [5.5 km east of Buczacz]. We also learned that this group had bravely attacked various ethnic Germans and had used the money from those raids to provide Jews in hiding with food. One of the most successful raids was on the main cashier of the Buczacz train station, the ethnic German Müller, where they got away with about a million złoty.

One day, with Staszka's help, I sent a letter to my acquaintance, the Ukrainian Marusha Serebrovska, who was well known for helping the Jews even before the liquidation of the Ghetto. Jews often found shelter in her house during roundups. A young Jewish girl had been in hiding there from the time the Germans had entered town. In the letter, I asked her to help us make contact with Ducio's group.

We were very surprised when that same evening, Marusha appeared together with Elżbieta. As soon as she heard that we were alive, she had to see us, walking seven kilometers on a muddy path to reach us. Seeing us, she burst out crying. She brought warm clothes with her, socks, and even cutlets, my favorite food, which she used to prepare for me. She spent the whole night with us relating everything. She was the go-between that Ducio used to provide hidden Jews with food. She gave us all the details concerning Ducio's outfit. They were armed with a few pistols and three old sawed-off shotguns. Despite this, they were the ones who had attacked the Landkommissar. Berek Gross had shot Nahajowski. Ducio's brother, Ozio Friedlender, had killed Kowalski, and Ducio himself had shot Dudzicka.[96] They were living in a cave in the forest near the waterfall.[97] Access to their hiding place was very difficult. Marusha promised us that she would tell them where we were and surely someone would contact us soon. The following day, we said our goodbyes. Benek managed to bring some chickens from somewhere and she reluctantly agreed to take them after we said they were also meant for our brothers in hiding.

Christmas arrived, followed by the Polish New Year, which we spent with the Poles. For the Ukrainian New Year, we were invited to our friends, the Durda family. One night, while on guard, we saw from the distance two figures approaching on the snow-covered field. We were dressed in white sheepskins and nearly invisible in the snow. For that reason, they did not notice us until they were close. They stopped only when they heard my voice. I recognized the two boys. One was Janek Langberg and the other a boy from the vicinity of Buczacz whose name I did not know. We went together to "babcia," where we told each other what we had been through. Ducio's group consisted of fifteen boys. They had learnt about us from Marusha, whom they praised very highly. We sat up until morning and spent the following day together as well. The following evening, they departed together with Janek and Benek, who had decided to join them in the forest. I had to stay behind in Gaje. I was feeling better, but walking was still painful, and I would not have been able to walk very far.

February went by and it was the beginning of March. The Red Army was approaching the Zbrucz River [70 km east of Buczacz]. I would usually go to "babcia" in the evenings, where I would hear the various rumors circulating from one person to another. The roads were full of German and Hungarian army convoys steadily withdrawing to the West. There were no newspapers in town anymore. Various Ukrainian "dignitaries" and ethnic Germans were hurriedly leaving town along with the retreating German Army. At least once a week, one of the boys from the forest would visit me. Since the condition of my leg was improving every day, I was seriously considering joining them in the forest, not least because when the German army was on the move it often took up quarters in the villages and might arrive in Gaje at any moment. But one night, Benek appeared with sad news. The night before some of the boys were crossing the road to Potok Złoty and came across a group of Germans. There was firefight and as a result Janek and Ducio were killed. The news was all the more painful since we felt that liberation was not far away. The following day I decided to join the boys, and we left as soon as it got dark ....

It took several hours of difficult marching through fields and countless snow drifts. We had to slip across the main road virtually under the nose of the Germans. We reached the forest. One more hour of walking and we could hear the murmur of the half-frozen waterfall. We waded through the water and entered the cave. There was no snow here, but it was terribly cold. I covered myself with a few blankets and lay down on the ground, hoping that after the strenuous march I would fall asleep despite the cold. After lying like this for an hour, one of the boys slipped in through the entrance of the cave and shouted: "Come outside!" We could hear the artillery barrage. We jumped up and ran out into the snow. Above the murmur of the waterfall dull thuds could be heard from the east. It seemed as if the ground was trembling, but perhaps it was just our hearts. We stood there listening for a long time.

We returned to the cave and started debating. We did not feel the cold anymore. We tried to figure out how far from the front line we were. Probably not more than four kilometers. It meant that Tarnopol had already been liberated and that the barrage could only be coming from the whereabouts of Czortków. Tomorrow or the day after they might be here. And what else could we do? How could we bite the Germans a little more? After all, we had always dreamt that we would meet the Red Army while fighting, that we would show them the bodies of dead Germans and say, "Look, comrades, we too have not been idle." Then we would lead them to the Fedor and show them the pits. Perhaps this dream would come true after all. I recalled the vision I had, when I was hiding in the wheat field under the rays of the burning sun.

Slowly the rising sun stretched its rays into the cave. Suddenly the calm of the forest was broken by the sound of shots, sporadic at first then more intense. One of the boys ran in through the entrance and shouted: "The Army, a raid in the forest." Instinctively we ran out of the cave, but once we heard that the shots were coming from all directions, we understood that the forest had been surrounded and the Germans were forcing their way into it. It meant they knew we were there. But had they known precisely where we were, they would have silently sneaked up to the cave. There was no other choice. We returned to the cave and positioned ourselves at the entrance with our guns ready to shoot. We also possessed four hand grenades, and if a moment before the liberation we were to share the fate of millions of our brothers, they would at least not be ashamed of us. We could hear some shots very close to us. Down below, behind the cascade of the waterfall, we could see soldiers in green uniforms. It's the Hungarians. I recalled what the lieutenant colonel had once said about them. When they enter a forest, they pray not to find any partisans there. It seemed that this time, too, God has answered their prayers. As they passed by the waterfall, they didn't look under the arc of the falling water. Perhaps they didn't want to get their feet wet. Or maybe the sound of the falling water reminded them of the melody of fire from three automatic weapons. They left without discovering our shelter.

Despite this, we stayed on guard at the entrance until evening, replacing one another only so as to be able to rub our frozen feet and hands. We were planning to come out of the forest in the evening and get provisions for the next few days. We left in the dark. Before we reached the edge of the forest, we stopped and two of the boys went forward to check the situation. After a few minutes they returned, saying it was impossible to leave the forest at the moment. The Hungarians had positioned themselves not far away and were continuously illuminating the edge of the forest with flares. That night, we tried in two other spots, but the forest was surrounded from all sides. We returned to our hideout in the morning. We spent the first day without food, still not feeling hungry. The whole day we could hear the barrage from the southeast. The boys, sent out the following night to check, returned saying that the Hungarians were still surrounding the forest.

The following day seemed even colder and hunger—our old friend—had returned. Again, it was impossible to get out of the forest that night. On the third day, I cut off a piece of my shoe and began to chew it. The others followed my example. We figured out that it was 23 March; the third day of spring. If the front were to stop and the Hungarians did not abandon the forest, then after all the hell we had been through, we might die of hunger just one day before the liberation.

On the night between 23 and 24 March we walked to the edge of the forest. I was feeling dizzy. Red circles were flying in front of my eyes, their shapes transforming into the most exquisite food. It was enough to stretch out my hand and reach them. I stretched out my hand and bumped into a tree with my aching foot. The pain brought me back to reality. Beyond the edge of the forest we could see the light of the flares. So, they had not given up yet. Maybe we should try to blast our way through, reach the first house and grab some bread. Yes, somehow to get through. The ones who attack first are those who always win. This idea revived us. We returned to the cave to figure out a plan for getting out of the trap. We were inside. I could see that one of the boys has lightly punctured his skin and was sucking his own blood. It must be warm, I thought, I should also try it. In the meantime, I chewed on another piece of my shoe, some matches, and, for the tenth time, I licked the little box of Vaseline, which I used to polish my automatic.

On 24 March we decided to break out, and to do it during daylight. Exactly at noon, when the Hungarians would be busy eating lunch and less alert. After all, they were not afraid of anything during the day. Noon slowly arrived. I tried to suck on a piece of ice, but it gave me physical pain. I thought over our plan again. It was crazy, but perhaps that is exactly why it might work. We had decided to suddenly open fire at the Hungarians, run the short distance that separated us from a small pine grove, and from there reach Fedor Hill. We would hide at the cemetery until nightfall and then find some food in the nearest houses. Noon arrived. We were not tired anymore. We had new energy from the idea that we were doing something. We were going into battle, maybe the last battle of our lives.

I looked at the others. The last of a dying nation. And if within an hour we were to die, would anyone know about our last moments? Would anyone see the cut on Majer's arm and realize that he drank his own blood, while around the world thousands of Jews were sitting down to sumptuous meals? Oh, never mind, tonight we too would be eating a goose in one of the graves at the cemetery. Yes, it must be a goose. Even if it were still alive, we would tear it apart and eat it. We reached the edge of the forest. We stopped for an instant. Our weapons were ready to fire. I touched the grenades stuck in my belt. We continued slowly toward the line of trees. We saw the open field that separated us from the little grove. But what was going on? The Hungarians were not there. We could only see traces of wheels on the snow, some scattered hay, and what used to be a dugout for flare rockets. We kept walking along the edge, we had no time to think about this strange scene.

Then we ran across the open space and swiftly reached the grove. We ran through it as quickly as possible and reached the Fedor. We positioned ourselves on the top of the hill among the rocks. We could see the whole town spread out in front of our eyes. The Strypa River flowing down in the valley and beyond it the town, divided by a wide road. At that moment the road was packed with cars, carts, and marching soldiers. The black bridge, which connects the town with the suburbs, was literary jammed with people and vehicles. We could distinguish between the blue uniforms of the Germans, the green of the Hungarians, the dark blue of the Ukrainians and two Vlasovite fur hats. Suddenly, we heard and saw powerful explosions in the field next to the road. Terrible panic ensued on the bridge and the road. The yells reach even our ears. The Germans were jumping off the carts and running off in different directions in a frenzy. Again, shell fire, this time striking the road and bridge directly. This caused total chaos. The deserted carts were jamming the passage. The Germans dispersed into the field and disappeared in the town's streets. Suddenly, faraway on the horizon, from the side of the village of Podlesie, a few tanks appeared. They had been shooting at the road. Someone shouted: "Our boys! Our boys!"

I prepared my automatic. My hands were trembling. Our boys! I even forgot my hunger. Our automatic weapons were blazing, their clatter mingling with the sounds of other guns; even those with pistols were shooting. Pure hell was unleashed on the road. The Germans, surprised by our fire, were running around in a frenzy, turning in circles, falling down. Some of them waved white handkerchiefs in our direction. "No," I yelled knowing full well that they could not hear my voice. "No! It's the murdered from the Fedor who have arisen. It's the ten thousand you murdered that are shooting now. Fire, boys, fire! Today, we do not have to save our bullets. Watch how they wriggle. Take this and this. For the first roundup, the second, the third, the fourth and the fifth. Fire boys, for the hunger, the grief, and the tears. Fire for the crushed heads of the babies. Fire, for my mother, my brother, Janek, Nacio, and Ducio. Fire, for all of Israel."

The fire ceased. I pulled the trigger, once and twice, but nothing. I examined the magazine: it was empty. The others had also shot out all their bullets. Some last German soldiers were still moving along on the road. But soon, the Red Army tanks that we had seen from the distance came closer. They opened fire. Presently, apart from the corpses of men and horses, nothing could be seen on the road. The first tank drove onto the bridge. Its massive body pushed its way through the remnants of trucks and wagons. We could clearly see the red star on its side. We jumped up and started running, slipping and tumbling down the ice-covered slope. The little hatch on top of the tank opened and a face covered with a black headgear appeared, looking curiously in our direction. "Comrades, comrades!" someone shouted to us. The tankman, lieutenant Podgarlitsky, leaped out of the tank and ran to us. Behind him came more men from the other tanks. "Hail the eagles!" I heard the first one call. I couldn't utter a word. Tears ran down my cheeks and my throat was choking. Just like the day I had dreamed of, I thought. I kept going, hopping on one leg, stumbling, falling, rising and running again, through a thousand deaths, until I fell into life's open arms.

Buczacz, 24 March, 1944, at 2 p.m.[98]

The End.

Notes

Text courtesy of Yad Vashem Archives 03/3788. Translated from Polish by Eva Lutkiewicz. Additional translation and editing by Omer Bartov.

1. Vershigora (1905–63), known also by his Ukrainian name Petro Vershyhora, was born in Transnistria, graduated the Odessa Fine Arts Academy and worked as an actor and stage manager before the war, during which he gained fame as legendary partisan leader Sydir Kovpak's right-hand man as well as for his independent actions.
2. Yevhen Konovalets (1891–1938) was leader of the Organization of Ukrainian Nationalists (OUN) in 1929–38, apparently assassinated by the NKVD (Soviet secret police). Stepan Bandera (1909–59) was leader of the OUN-B, the radical faction that split from the OUN in 1940. Arrested by the Germans after declaring Ukrainian independence in 1941, he remained an influential nationalist leader during the war and later in exile until his assassination by the KGB; he is still revered by Ukrainian nationalists especially in western Ukraine. The more moderate OUN-M was led by Andrii Melnyk (1890–1964), who also played an important role in promoting Ukrainian nationalism in exile after the war.
3. Named after 3 May 1791, on which the Polish-Lithuanian Commonwealth adopted a constitution meant to strengthen and liberalize the kingdom, shortly before the Second and Third Partitions of 1793 and 1795 wiped Poland off the map as an independent political entity until the aftermath of World War I.
4. The Komsomol was the communist youth movement of the Soviet Union.
5. Wizinger mistakenly calls him Eldenberg.
6. Meaning the OUN. See note 2, this chapter.
7. For more on Dankovych see Bartov, *Anatomy of a Genocide*, 160, 169, 348–49 n. 29.
8. Traditional radios relied on vacuum tubes, also known as electron tubes or valves.
9. For more on the gravedigger Świerszczak, see later in Wizinger's diary as well Bartov, *Anatomy of a Genocide*, 245, 361 n. 23.
10. The event described occurred in early August 1941. For more, see Bartov, *Anatomy of a Genocide*, 163–67. Wizinger often does not provide specific dates. Since he wrote his account in 1947, based on notes written at the time, the word "today" is more of a literary device. The account often switches between past and present tense. To avoid confusion and for the sake of consistency, I have generally employed only past tense in the translation.
11. Other accounts speak of thirty-three. See ibid.
12. Wizinger mistakenly writes Freblental.
13. Reich was president of the Talmud Torah School and an activist in the Mizrahi party in 1930s Buczacz; Baruch Kramer was an Orthodox Jew, an industrialist, and a donor to the Zionist Federation since at least 1935; Seifer was a prominent prewar physician and one of the only survivors of the community, along with Judenrat member Hersas. See more on these individuals in Bartov, *Anatomy of a Genocide*, 26, 87, 99–100, 171–74, 201, 216, 221, 253, 257, 346 n. 20.
14. See more on this in Petrykevych's diary, this volume.
15. It appears that approximately 450 people were murdered in this first roundup, known as the "registration action." See further in Bartov, *Anatomy of a Genocide*, 179–82.
16. For more on Müller, see ibid., 181–82, 215, 220–21.
17. For more on Albrecht and Schwarz (also spelled Szwarc), see ibid., 170–71, 175–76.

18. Engelberg was president of the Zionist Federation's Buczacz branch in the 1930s; he is said to have escaped from Buczacz following a stint as Obman, having been warned by the Landkommissar Walter Hoffer. Ibid., 87, 345 n. 17.

19. For more on Shmuel Rosen, see ibid., 168, 171–72, 174–75, 254, 346 n. 20, 354 n. 50.

20. In fact, the workers there were building a section of Thoroughfare IV, a road planned by the Germans leading from Lemberg to the Black Sea. See Andrej Angrick, "Annihilation and Labor," in *The Shoah in Ukraine: History, Memory, Memorialization*, edited by Ray Brandon and Wendy Lower, 190–223 (Bloomington: Indiana University Press, 2008).

21. As Greek Catholics, Ukrainians celebrate Christmas on a different date according to the Julian calendar.

22. Barg (Wizinger erroneously calls him Bark), was not chief but deputy commander of the gendarmerie post in Buczacz. According to other policemen's testimonies, he was known as "Judenonkel" (Jew uncle) thanks to his contacts with the Jews; he was also described as a "swine" and a "gross person," who "drank all the time" and "pounced on Jews." For more on Barg see Bartov, *Anatomy of a Genocide*, 205, 354 n. 53.

23. The Sonderdienst (Special Service) were units made up of ethnic Germans from Poland, established by the Governor of the General Government (the part of Poland occupied but not directly annexed by Germany) Hans Frank in 1940. After the invasion of the USSR in 1941 these units also included former Soviet prisoners of war and participated in murder operations. It is not clear whether such units actually operated in the Buczacz area or were confused by Wizinger with the Ukrainian Auxiliary Police (Schutzmannschaft or Schuma) unit based in Czortków, as well as other local police forces engaged in requisitions from the local peasants. See Bartov, *Anatomy of a Genocide*, 182–84, 350 n. 34.

24. The so-called Dieppe Raid occurred on 19 August 1942. While it was never intended to open a second front, it did aim at showing resolve by the British, Canadians, and Americans. It ended up as a fiasco, with over thirty-five hundred men killed, wounded, or captured, more than 50 percent of the original landing force.

25. According to other historical accounts, most of the approximately three thousand Jewish victims of this first roundup in Czortków in August 1942, were deported by train to the Bełżec extermination camps, although hundreds were also shot on the street.

26. The term Toten-Kommando is used by Wizinger to designate the Security Police (Sicherheitspolizei, Sipo) outpost (Außenstelle) in Czortków, which consisted of about twenty members of various German police agencies. Assisted by the Ukrainian Auxiliary police, local German gendarmes and Ukrainian police, as well as the Jewish OD, this outpost was charged with murdering the Jews of the region under its control. Rux, erroneously spelled Ruks by Wizinger, was a member of the outpost. German witnesses asked about the existence of an Erschießungskommando (execution squad) commented that there were always volunteers eager to participate in the killing. See in Bartov, *Anatomy of a Genocide*, 182–85, 192–95, 197–98.

27. Wizinger uses the Polish word *akcja* (*aktsye* in Yiddish), the equivalent of the German *Aktion*, which was used to designate a roundup (either for deportation or for mass killing in situ).

28. Wizinger uses the Polish word *schron* (shelter), usually referred to in Jewish accounts in Yiddish and Hebrew as bunker, meaning hideout in this context.

29. Buczacz was owned by the powerful Potocki clan of Polish magnates from 1612 until the annexation of this region that came to be called Galicia by the Habsburg Empire in 1772. The Potockis remained a wealthy and influential presence in Buczacz until the Soviet occupation of 1939. See more in Bartov, *Anatomy of a Genocide*, 9–15.

30. Also known as Ozio or Yehoshua, he was Dawid (Ducio) Friedlender's younger brother. See more on both ibid., 152–53, 255–56, 327 n. 27, 346 n. 20, 348 n. 27.

31. On the basis of several other reports on this first roundup on 17 October 1942, it is estimated that sixteen hundred Jews were deported to the Bełżec extermination camp and several additional hundreds were killed on the streets or in their homes. See more ibid., 229.

32. In Bełżec the victims were murdered in gas chambers and buried in mass graves. There were no crematoria there; the bodies were subsequently exhumed and burned on open-air grids in an attempt to destroy evidence of this crime. The camp operated as a murder installation until December 1942.

33. The Anglo-American invasion of North Africa took place on 8–16 November 1942. It eventually facilitated the Allied invasion of Sicily in July 1943.

34. On Fernhof, see Bartov, *Anatomy of a Genocide*, 98.

35. For more on Ebenstein see ibid., 174–75, 347 n. 22.

36. The second roundup, dated by some sources as occurring on 27 November 1942, is estimated to have cost the lives of two thousand Jews; most were deported to Bełżec, and the rest were shot on the streets and in their homes. See ibid., 229.

37. Since Wizinger reports that Jankiel Ebenstein was killed in the second roundup, this is either a different person or the event in which Ebenstein was killed occurred during a later roundup, as some other testimonies suggest.

38. Wizinger writes: "Moc się rodzi, bóg truchleje." This inverts the verse from the Polish Christmas hymn, "Bóg się rodzi, moc truchleje," i.e., "When God is born, the great powers tremble,".

39. The account that follows depicts an episode described in other testimonies as the "street akcja"; it also contains some details that cannot be verified and reflect either Wizinger's imagination or stories he heard from others, especially concerning the Germans' motivation and specific cruelties such as the crucifixion of a Jew and the mauling of women by dogs. There is, however, other evidence of dogs being used by the local Sipo to attack Jews. There are also some similarities between this event and another case of a young woman's brutal murder depicted later on in this account.

40. Wizinger erroneously calls him Rozensaft. On SS-Sergeant Artur Rosenow, known for his brutality and lethal attack dog, see Bartov, *Anatomy of a Genocide*, 192, 194, 352 n. 40.

41. Wizinger erroneously refers to him as Tomaszek. On SS-Corporal Thomanek, the notoriously brutal commandant of local labor camps, who was finally arrested in 1957 by the West German police and sentenced to life imprisonment, but was released in 1979 and lived in freedom for the last nineteen years of his life, see ibid., 182, 193–96, 199, 208, 257, 350 n. 34, 352 n. 42, 353 n. 45–46.

42. See ibid., 175–76, 347 n. 23.

43. The third action occurred on 2 February 1943 and is indeed estimated to have cost the lives of two thousand Jews. See ibid., 229.

44. Which of course they did. On Henriette Lissberg see ibid., 215–24.

45. The "W" was said to have stood for Wehrmacht, Wehrdienst (military service), or Wertvoll (valuable), inter alia.

46. For another example of such instances see, e.g., Moshe Schwartz, *The Petrified Heart*, 2006, section 15, in Hebrew, retrieved 1 July 2019 from http://www.buchach. org/Buczacz/Heart.htm: "Fortunately the hideout under the cellar was ready. We were about thirty people—men, women, and children—forced to hide in the bunker …. We barely managed to reach the shelter. A few minutes later we heard terrible yells, boots stamping the floor above us and Gestapo-men running around the house. Together with us in the bunker was a little three-year-old boy who began

crying when he heard the noise above. We were all terrified, stopped breathing, and feared that the cries of the little boy would betray us to the Germans. Driven by a sudden urge and uncontrollable panic, the child's mother grabbed a pillow and put it over the child's mouth to silence it. A few minutes later the Gestapo-men realized that the apartment was empty and left it .... But the few moments during which the pillow was over the child's face sufficed to cause its death. When the young mother— her name was Mina Rosner—saw her child's blue face and realized that she had choked her only child to death, she became hysterical and screamed at the top of her voice .... She lost her mind and was never well again." But the mother's own memoir gives a different account of her child's death: Mina Rosner, *I am a Witness* (Winnipeg: Hyperion Press, 1990), 53–5.

47. On Nahajowski and Kowalski see Bartov, *Anatomy of a Genocide*, 235–36, 250.
48. On his son, Jacob Heiss see ibid., 249–50.
49. Wizinger erroneously spells his name Tomanek. See also note 41, this chapter.
50. Rux was not commander of the Sipo outpost but may well have led groups of Sipo-men and auxiliaries during such roundups.
51. The fourth action occurred on 15 April 1943 and is estimated to have cost the lives of up to three thousand Jews. See Bartov, *Anatomy of a Genocide*, 229.
52. Earlier, Wizinger mentions sixty residents. The number may have increased over time or one of these figures is inaccurate.
53. On these events see ibid., 259–62.
54. Wizinger may be referring here to Janek Anderman, who is also known from several other testimonies to have fired at the German and Ukrainian police, but to have been subsequently killed. He previously served in the OD. See ibid., 176, 253, 347 n. 25, 360 n. 20.
55. This Belgian-made Fabrique Nationale handgun was known as "Baby Browning."
56. This is a reference to "gilgul neshamot," the Kabbalistic and popular Jewish belief in the transmigration of souls.
57. On Maryna (Marynka in diminutive form) Świerszczak see Bartov, *Anatomy of a Genocide*, 254.
58. Manko is a Ukrainian variation of Marjan/Maniek.
59. The Banderites (Banderowcy in Polish and Banderivtsi in Ukrainian), were members of the more radical faction of the Organization of Ukrainian Nationalists, known as OUN-B after its leader Stepan Bandera.
60. The reference is to the so-called Mazepa wool hat worn by members of the West Ukrainian Galician Army in World War I.
61. Petliura (1879–1926) was supreme commander of the Ukrainian army and president of the Ukrainian People's Republic in 1918–21. Subsequently accused of responsibility for widespread massacres of Jews during the civil war in Ukraine, he was assassinated in Paris in 1926. Petliura is still venerated in Ukraine as a national hero.
62. A Mediterranean island between Tunisia and Sicily.
63. The last great German offensive on the eastern front, known as the Battle of Kursk, or Operation Zitadelle, was launched on 5 July 1943. The failure of the offensive, coupled with the Allied landing in Sicily on 9–10 July (which eventually led to the fall of Mussolini's regime on 25 July) and the transfer of German forces to Italy, enabled the Red Army to launch its own offensive on 12 July, culminating in the liberation of Kharkov on 23 August.
64. A dialect spoken by Polish settlers of Lesser [southeastern] Poland, also known as Lasowiacy, who originally came from Mazovia in northeastern Poland in the early modern period.

65. On this event, see also Bartov, *Anatomy of a Genocide*, 218.
66. See also ibid., 235–36.
67. The AK was the main Polish resistance organization, established in February 1942; it was loyal to the Polish government in exile and was the armed wing of the so-called Polish underground state.
68. Wizinger erroneously spells his name Bretsznajder. On Gestapo driver Brettschneider, see Bartov, *Anatomy of a Genocide*, 177, 192, 196–98, 208–9, 352–53 n. 40, 47.
69. This was either a different Gestapo official, or the story is inaccurate, since there is no record of Brettschneider having been attacked, let alone killed. He was investigated by the West German authorities in 1965 but his case was partly dismissed for lack of evidence in 1971 and terminated following his death in 1973. Brettschneider was not a member of the SS and is therefore unlikely to have worn such a dagger.
70. Świerszczak was honored by Yad Vashem in Jerusalem as one of the righteous among the nations, especially on the basis of testimonies by Shmuel Rosen and his brothers, who were saved by him. Wizinger's very different account, held in the archives of Yad Vashem, was obviously not consulted. See Bartov, *Anatomy of a Genocide*, 254, 361 n. 23.
71. Kovpak (1887–1967) was a legendary Soviet partisan leader whose formation operated deep behind German lines in Ukraine. He later held senior positions in the Soviet government.
72. One of the standard mass-produced infantry weapons of the Red Army in World War II.
73. Buczacz Landkommissar Richard Lissberg did indeed come from Essen. See Bartov, *Anatomy of a Genocide*, 213–15.
74. The 14th Waffen Grenadier Division of the SS (1st Galician), made up primarily of Ukrainian volunteers from Galicia, was formed in 1942 and destroyed in the battle of Brody in July 1944, although it was later reformed and fought in Slovakia, Yugoslavia, and Austria.
75. Namely, Pyotr Vershigora. See further in note 1, this chapter.
76. The standard Soviet infantry light machine gun in World War II.
77. Wizinger erroneously spells the name Pall. On the notorious police Sergeant Pahl, who was a member of the gendarmerie squad in Buczacz but not its commander, and who was also often posted to Monasterzyska, see Bartov, *Anatomy of a Genocide*, 200–5, 210, 215, 218–19, 225, 228–29, 347 n. 22, 25. As an SS-man, Helmut would not have been under command of a gendarmerie Sergeant. The green uniforms of the force ambushed by the partisans suggest that it belonged to the regular uniformed police (Schutzpolizei).
78. Literally "securing the economy." Wizinger may be referring here to the Volksdeutsche Mittelstelle (VoMi), an SS agency charged with the resettlement of ethnic Germans, which after 1941 engaged in collecting the property of murdered Jews. In Czortków SS Corporal Richard Pal was responsible for such collections from local sites of mass killings, including in Buczacz. See ibid., 177–78, 194–95, 350 n. 34, 352 n. 42. Possibly Helmut was attached to the police in such an SS capacity.
79. This was the standard Soviet anti-tank rifle that became obsolete with the introduction of heavier tanks in the latter part of World War II.
80. Known in Russian as "Nagan," this revolver was based on the Belgian Nagant M1895; popularly all Russian service revolvers were referred to as Nagan, irrespective of their make.
81. It is unclear which Kanner this was. The quarry owner and Judenrat member Dawid Kanner (Kaner) was shot in the "registration action" in mid-August 1941; Beirish Kanner was apparently a member of the Judenrat later on in the fall; and Leon

Kanner is mentioned as chief of the OD in the temporary labor camp created in Buczacz in spring 1943.

82. Andrey Vlasov (1901–46) was a Red Army general captured by the Germans, who formed the Russian Liberation Army under their auspices. He was tried for treason and hanged by the Soviets. The term Vlasovites ostensibly described followers of Vlasov but was popularly attributed to any former Red Army troops who fought in the Wehrmacht.

83. The medal "To a Partisan of the Patriotic War" was established in February 1943 in the Soviet Union to honor the partisans fighting behind enemy lines.

84. The reference is likely to the Wehrmacht's field-gray (Feldgrau) uniforms.

85. There were 1,000 mils in the British pound of Mandatory Palestine.

86. This is the first phrase of the Kaddish, the Jewish prayer for the dead.

87. The province just north and east of Galicia.

88. On Hirschhorn and her grandson Izidor Hecht ("Junk," later known as Viktor Gekht), who survived with her, see Bartov, *Anatomy of a Genocide*, 130, 151, 242–45, 360 n. 12.

89. Pahl was indeed wounded in a partisan action and decorated for his "bravery." After the war he returned to serve as a policeman in West Germany until his retirement in 1964. He was indicted for murder in 1970 but died the following year before judicial proceedings could be completed. See ibid., 200.

90. This refers to the specific circumstances in the region, where AK units and Soviet partisans were collaborating both against the Germans and in fighting Ukrainian paramilitaries.

91. The site of mass executions of an estimated twenty-two thousand Polish army officers by the NKVD in April–May 1940.

92. This is a reference to what Polish nationalists called the Żydokomuna—the equivalent of the Nazi term Judeo-Bolshevism. See Paul Hanebrink, *A Specter Haunting Europe: The Myth of Judeo-Bolshevism* (Cambridge, MA: Harvard University Press, 2018).

93. Kyiv was liberated on 6 November; the Red Army established a major bridgehead over the Dnieper in late October and secured the entire right bank by December 1943.

94. Interviewed in Tel Aviv in 2003 by the editor, Yitzhak Bauer, who participated in the operation, noted that his group actually killed Kowalski's father. They then tried and failed to kill the son during the funeral, following which he vanished from the area.

95. On Friedlender's group see Bartov, *Anatomy of a Genocide*, 254–56 and Bauer's interview.

96. Some of these incidents are also related in Bauer's interview.

97. Another group, headed by Natan (Nadje) Dunajer, was living in a cave near Buczacz. Both Dunajer and Ducio Friedlander were communist activists before the war. Dunajer was also killed in action. See ibid., 152–53, 177–78, 238, 255–56, 327 n. 27, 348 n. 27.

98. Buczacz was re-occupied by the Germans on 7 April, following a tactical retreat by the Soviets. Of the approximately eight hundred Jews who survived until the first liberation, fewer than one hundred were still alive when the Red Army returned on 21 July 1944. Wizinger does not describe this period and most likely joined the Soviets when they retreated in early April; he subsequently served in the Polish forces operating under Soviet command for the rest of the war.

BIBLIOGRAPHY

Amar, Tarik Cyril. *The Paradox of Ukrainian Lviv: A Borderland City Between Stalinists, Nazis, and Nationalists*. Ithaca: Cornell University Press, 2015.

Angrick, Andrej. "Annihilation and Labor." In *The Shoah in Ukraine: History, Memory, Memorialization*, edited by Ray Brandon and Wendy Lower, 190–223. Bloomington: Indiana University Press, 2008.

An-sky, S. *The Destruction of the Jews in Poland, Galicia, and Bukovina*. 4 vols. Translated into Hebrew by Samuel Leib Zitron. Tel Aviv: Shtibel, 1929.

———. *1915 Diary of S. An-Sky: A Russian Jewish Writer at the Eastern Front*. Translated and edited by Polly Zavadivker. Bloomington: Indiana University Press, 2016.

———. *The Dybbuk and the Yiddish Imagination: A Haunted Reader*. Translated and edited by Joachim Neugroschel. Syracuse: Syracuse University Press, 2000.

———. *The Enemy at His Pleasure: A Journey through the Jewish Pale of Settlement During World War I*. Translated and edited by Joachim Neugroschel. New York: Metropolitan Books, 2003.

Bartov, Omer. *Anatomy of a Genocide: The Life and Death of a Town Called Buczacz*. New York: Simon and Schuster, 2018.

———. "Eastern Europe as the Site of Genocide." *The Journal of Modern History* 80, no. 3 (September 2008): 557–93.

———. *Erased: Vanishing Traces of Jewish Galicia in Present-Day Ukraine*. Princeton: Princeton University Press, 2007.

———. "Wartime Lies and Other Testimonies: Jewish-Christian Relationships in Buczacz, 1939–44." *East European Politics and Societies* 25, no. 3 (August 2011): 486–511.

Bartov, Omer, and Eric D. Weitz. *Shatterzone of Empires: Coexistence and Violence in the German, Habsburg, Russian, and Ottoman Borderlands*. Bloomington: Indiana University Press, 2013.

Broszat, Martin, and Saul Friedländer. "A Controversy about the Historicization of National Socialism." In *Reworking the Past: Hitler, the Holocaust, and the Historians' Debate*, edited by Peter Baldwin, 77–134. Boston: Beacon Press, 1990.

Browning, Christopher R. *Ordinary Men: Reserve Police Battalion 101 and the Final Solution in Poland*. New York: HarperPerennial, 1993.

Case, Holly. *Between States: The Transylvanian Question and the European Idea during World War II*. Stanford, CA: Stanford University Press, 2009.

Frank, Alison. *Oil Empire: Visions of Prosperity in Austrian Galicia*. Cambridge, MA: Harvard University Press, 2005.

Grachova, Sofia. Interview with Bohdan Petrykevych in Ivano-Frankivsk, May 2006. In "The Diary of Viktor Petrykevych: A Gymnasium Teacher's View of the Soviet and German Occupation of Eastern Galicia (1939–1944)." Unpublished paper, Herder Institute, University of Marburg, 2007.

Gross, Jan T. *Fear: Anti-Semitism in Poland after Auschwitz. An Essay in Historical Interpretation*. New York: Random House, 2006.

———. *Revolution from Abroad: The Soviet Conquest of Poland's Western Ukraine and Western Belorussia*, expanded ed. Princeton: Princeton University Press, 2002.

Hanebrink, Paul. *A Specter Haunting Europe: The Myth of Judeo-Bolshevism*. Cambridge, MA: Harvard University Press, 2018.

Hilberg, Raul. *The Destruction of the European Jews*, 3rd ed. 3 vols. New Haven: Yale University Press, 2003.

Himka, John-Paul. *Galician Villagers and the Ukrainian National Movement in the Nineteenth Century*. New York: St. Martin's Press, 1988.

Himka, John-Paul, and Joanna Beata Michlic. *Bringing the Dark Past to Light: The Reception of the Holocaust in Postcommunist Europe*. Lincoln: University of Nebraska Press, 2013.

Hirsch, Marianne, and Leo Spitzer. *Ghosts of Home: The Afterlife of Czernowitz in Jewish Memory*. Berkeley: University of California Press, 2010.

Hoffman, Eva. *Shtetl: The Life and Death of a Small Town and the World of Polish Jews*. Boston: Houghton Mifflin, 1997.

Judson, Pieter M., and Marsha L. Rozenblit, eds. *Constructing Nationalities in East Central Europe*. New York: Berghahn Books, 2006.

Karlip, Joshua M. *The Tragedy of a Generation: The Rise and Fall of Jewish Nationalism in Eastern Europe*. Cambridge, MA: Harvard University Press, 2013.

King, Charles. *Odessa: Genius and Death in a City of Dreams*. New York: W.W. Norton, 2011.

Magocsi, Paul Robert. *The Roots of Ukrainian Nationalism: Galicia as Ukraine's Piedmont*. Toronto: University of Toronto Press, 2002.

Marples, David R. *Heroes and Villains: Creating National History in Contemporary Ukraine*. Budapest: Central European University Press, 2007.

Meir, Natan. *Kiev, Jewish Metropolis: A History, 1859–1914*. Bloomington: Indiana University Press, 2010.

Mendelsohn, Daniel. *The Lost: A Search for Six of Six Million*. New York: HarperCollins, 2006.

Mick, Christoph. *Lemberg, Lwów, L'viv, 1914–1947: Violence and Ethnicity in a Contested City*. West Lafayette: Purdue University Press, 2016.

Myzak, Nestor S. *Za tebe, sviata Ukraïno* [For You, Holy Ukraine]. Chernivtsi: Bukovyna, 2004.

Penslar, Derek J. *Jews and the Military*. Princeton: Princeton University Press, 2013.

Pohl, Dieter. "Hans Krueger and the Murder of the Jews in the Stanisławów Region (Galicia)." *Yad Vashem Studies* 26 (1998): 239–65.

Porter, Brian A. *When Nationalism Began to Hate: Imagining Modern Politics in Nineteenth Century Poland*. New York: Oxford University Press, 2000.

Prusin, Alexander Victor. *The Lands Between: Conflict in the East European Borderlands, 1870–1992*. Oxford: Oxford University Press, 2010.

Redlich, Shimon. "Metropolitan Andrei Sheptyts'kyi, Ukrainians and Jews During and After the Holocaust." *Holocaust and Genocide Studies* 5, no. 1 (1990): 39–51.

———. *Together and Apart in Brzeżany: Poles, Jews, and Ukrainians, 1919–1945.* Bloomington: Indiana University Press, 2002.

Rosner, Mina. *I am a Witness.* Winnipeg: Hyperion Press, 1990.

Rozenblit, Marsha L. *Reconstructing a National Identity: The Jews of Habsburg Austria during World War I.* New York: Oxford University Press, 2001.

Safran, Gabriella. *Wandering Soul: The Dybbuk's Creator, S. An-sky.* Cambridge, MA: Harvard University Press, 2010.

Schwartz, Moshe. *The Petrified Heart.* 2016. Retrieved 1 July 2019 from http://www.buchach.org/Buczacz/Heart.htm.

Shanes, Joshua. *Diaspora Nationalism and Jewish Identity in Habsburg Galicia.* New York: Cambridge University Press, 2012.

Snyder, Timothy. *Bloodlands: Europe Between Hitler and Stalin.* New York: Basic Books, 2010.

———. *The Reconstruction of Nations: Poland, Ukraine, Lithuania, Belarus, 1569–1999.* New Haven: Yale University Press, 2003.

———. *Sketches from a Secret War: A Polish Artist's Mission to Liberate Soviet Ukraine.* New Haven: Yale University Press, 2005.

Stauter-Halsted, Keely. *The Nation in the Village: The Genesis of Peasant National Identity in Austrian Poland, 1848–1914.* Ithaca: Cornell University Press, 2001.

Weeks, Theodore R. *Vilnius Between Nations, 1795–2000.* DeKalb: Northern Illinois University Press, 2015.

INDEX

Milton Keynes UK
Ingram Content Group UK Ltd.
UKHW051609200624
444511UK00023B/406